THE
UNIVERSE

THE
UNIVERSE

Byron Preiss, Editor
Andrew Fraknoi, Scientific Editor

A BYRON PREISS BOOK

BANTAM BOOKS
TORONTO • NEW YORK • LONDON • SYDNEY • AUCKLAND

In memory of my grandparents,
Nathan and Ethel Preiss

THE UNIVERSE
A Bantam Book / November 1987

Special thanks to Lou Aronica, Publishing
Director of the Spectra Line, for his care
and support.

Book design by Leslie Miller
Associate Editor for Science: Ruth Ashby
Associate Editor for Science Fiction: David M. Harris
Photo Editor: E. Bruce Stevenson

Library of Congress-in-Publication Data
The Universe.
(A Bantam spectra book)
1. Cosmology. I. Preiss, Byron. II. Fraknoi,
Andrew.
QB981.U55 1987   523.1   87-47572
ISBN 0-553-05227-6

Published simultaneously in the United States and Canada

PRINTED IN THE UNITED STATES OF AMERICA

DW 0 9 8 7 6 5 4 3 2 1

CONTENTS

FRONTIER

BYRON PREISS

TWO HUNDRED MILES SOUTH of Brownsville, Texas, on a Mexican beach known as Rancho Nuevo, an annual event of unquestionable ecological importance occurs. It is known as *arribada*, or arrival.

In the cover of night, with the males waiting safely in the waters of the gulf, 95 percent of the female population of the species known as *Lepidochelys kempii*, or Kemp's ridley, comes ashore. It is nesting time. Clutches of an average of 110 eggs are laid by these sea turtles, and those eggs which do not fall prey to predators and thieves hatch. The hatchlings scramble for the relative safety of the sea. There they survive in open waters filled with weeds and drift lines until they reach adolescence. Then they are ready for the coastal areas in which young turtles become adults. The rest of their natural lives is spent in feeding grounds except for that time, once a year, when nesting season occurs. Then the vast majority of Kemp's ridleys, that incredible 95 percent, returns from Cedar Key, Florida, from the Sargasso Sea, from places as far north as Cape Cod and as far east as the Azores, to the seventeen-mile-long beach at Ranch Nuevo, where, protected by the Mexican government, they complete and begin a cycle of reproduction that has survived for centuries. Despite cold waters, poachers, and the incidental capture and drowning in shrimp nets that in the last two decades has diminished their female numbers from approximately two thousand to between five and seven hundred, Kemp's ridley has survived.

How does a sea turtle cross a wide expanse of the globe aided only by the natural compasses of magnetic fields, ocean currents, tides, and the constant metamorphosis of the sky? Why do so many of these four-legged creatures travel a labyrinthian path to and from an isolated beach that is the center of their universe? What yearnings does a sea creature have for distant shores?

We might as easily ask how man, a two-legged creature who begins life more helpless than a ridley hatchling, can send a messenger to other planets.

Or ask why humanity, through countless ancient cultures long vanished from our planet, has maintained a fascination with the cosmos. For what reason do we yearn to travel to the stars? Like those ridley hatchlings struggling to make it from the beach to the water, are we scrambling to transcend our Earth-bound nest in order to reach the frontier of a universe brimming with intelligent life?

Finally, might we ask where our own Milky Way galaxy is going? For it too seems headed on a cosmic journey. According to a symposium of the American Physical Society held in April 1987, our Galaxy and its neighbors, including the Virgo cluster and the even more distant Hydra-Centaurus cluster, are all streaming toward an extraordinary confluence of galaxies three and a half times farther away from ours than the Virgo and fifteen to thirty times larger.

Yet in seeking an answer to that question, we must confront a body of knowledge that has evolved since the 1930's, showing that the motions of the galaxies in large clusters of galaxies are influenced by gravity stronger than what could be expected from the stellar matter in these clusters. As Wallace Tucker more fully explains in his lucid essay, if there is more gravity than this visible stellar matter could account for, then some source of gravity is "missing." Scientists have been struggling to find this missing or "dark" matter, for it is thought to compose roughly 90 percent of the intergalactic space between clusters of galaxies.

For a few years, the neutrino, a sub-atomic particle that interacts very weakly with ordinary matter, had been considered a potential constituent of that missing matter, but the pulse of neutrinos from the explosion of a supernova this year in our neighboring galaxy, the Large Magellanic Cloud, has yielded new information that adds to the evidence that neutrinos, of the type closely associated with electrons, have very little or no mass, and thus little or no gravity—at least not the type of gravity explained by Newton and Einstein—and as a result, cannot be considered a major component of dark matter. Nonetheless, Supernova 1987A is confirming expectations that detection of neutrinos can lead to a new and reliable form of astronomy which uses neutrino pulses the same way telescopes use radio and light waves. A fraction of neutrinos can be detected in several thousand tons of contained water by monitoring the tiny flashes of light emitted by a neutrino when it interacts with another sub-atomic particle.

Supernovas, or exploding stars, may well shed light on missing matter and other issues in astronomy. As David J. Helfand describes in his essay, supernovae are cosmic forges for the more than ninety elements on Earth. The forces of a supernova are so explosive that their shock waves compress the clouds of gas and dust between the stars of a galaxy and consolidate them into matter that eventually becomes new stars. This cycle of renewal parallels that of Kemp's ridley. As the species returns to its beach to nest, thus does the death of one star lead to the development of another.

In some ways, we know more about the movement of stars that are light-years away than we do about the movement of the Kemp's ridley turtle. We share with that turtle a natural yearning for survival; we share with those stars an inevitable cycle of life and death. Yet it is life, not inanimate matter, that remains more unfathomable to us despite our advanced technology. At a time when the life and death of a star can be monitored, plant, insect, and microbe species are vanishing from the Earth at a rate not seen since the end of the age of dinosaurs roughly 63 million years ago. Most of these extinctions result from human expansion. As we encroach upon the habitats of other living creatures, we destroy them. Without the diversity of life they represent, without the resources that spring from an abundance of life, our ability to cure disease, learn from other species, develop new ways of communicating with other forms of life, even alien life, may be severely limited. At a time when we can launch men and women into space, and send probes like Voyager II to the outer planets, millions still starve, millions still fight, and millions still dream. We are children in the cosmos.

Ridley, man, and star all share a common origin and a common element: carbon. A meteorite formed in the explosion of a star was recently found to have in its atomic composition grains of diamonds. These tiny interstellar particles are also made of carbon, probably developed in the violence of a supernova explosion. Trapped within those diamonds are the raw materials of a collapsing star. By studying them and the xenon gas trapped within them, we will be gazing at materials that predate our solar system. They may have important ramifications for our understanding of interstellar matter and may lead to new forms of synthesis of diamonds at low pressures.

These diamonds symbolize the way in which abstract scientific research brings tangible benefits to humankind. Yet as we gaze at the distant past through electron microscopes, children in Ethiopia are starving. Mothers and fathers lie wounded in Lebanese hospitals, the victims of faceless violence. South African schoolchildren are held by "their" government as hostages to apartheid, a process that judges freedom by the pigmentation of a person's skin. Soviet schoolteachers are held prisoner because they choose to identify themselves not as atheists, but as practicing Jews. In Southeast Asia, the Vietnamese use Russian rifles to kill Cambodians. In Afghanistan, American-backed rebels use captured arms to kill Russian soldiers. We can more safely visit distant galaxies than we can walk the streets in many parts of the world. For all the magical wonder of the constellations above us, in cities around the globe, many kids don't even get a chance to see that the stars exist. They have so little sky. The flare of Supernova 1987A, the brightest seen on Earth since 1604, was an event that may add much to our understanding of the universe, but its appearance was obliterated in cities by the lights of modern man.

In the wilderness and in the observatories of the world beyond those city lights, the stars display their mysteries. Astronomers study the energy of eons past to understand the future. As you will discover in *The Universe*, astronomy is an abstract art, a precise gathering of distant signals, that takes humanity to the frontier of the stars.

The astrophysicist Fang Lizhi, who has been called "China's Sakharov" and who was dismissed from his post as vice president of the University of Science and Technology in Hefei, China, for supporting academic freedom, states: "Since physicists pursue unity, harmony . . . how can they logically tolerate unreason, discordance and evil? Let us look at the postwar years. . . . It was natural scientists who were the first to become conscious of the emergence of each social crisis . . . environmental pollution . . . energy crises . . . disarmament. . . . All this is not accidental. In the first place, science and technology in our modern society occupy a very important position: many social problems are often unclear to those without a scientific background. In the second place, many natural scientists are aware that their role is not limited to technology alone, but that they should consider themselves responsible to the entire culture. . . . Physicists' methods of pursuing truth make them extremely sensitive, while their courage in seeking it enables them to accomplish something. . . . Intellectuals, who own and create information and knowledge, are the most dynamic component of productive forces. . . . People who have internalized the elements of civilization and possess knowledge . . . have hearts which are relatively noble. . . . If people with knowledge are needed only for technical progress, and if intellectuals are not expected to have original ideas and contributions to make in other fields, including social and political fields, then education will remain a master-apprentice affair. Einstein said that the aim of education is to develop people with a harmonious character, capable of engaging in independent thinking."

In this book, we gather together the scientists, the intellectuals, and the artists, to learn about and speculate upon the cosmos. The world right now desperately needs both the physicist and the dreamer. G-d has blessed us with the most magnificent world imaginable. We have barely made the first steps in seeing all the light in the darkness. Perhaps it is the dreamer who will find out the nature of dark matter; perhaps it is the scientist who will find solutions to needless hunger and mindless war. For them both, the bounty of the Earth and the cosmos is the currency of hope. Humanity must use what it has been blessed with to survive. Then, as in Paul Simon's phrase, we all might be dancing together "with diamonds on the soles of our shoes." They will be the diamonds of the stars and it will be a dance of peace.

I think I speak for all the contributors of the book when I say we share a hope for peace.

I would like to thank the talented individuals who contributed generously to *The Universe*. Lou Aronica, director of the Spectra imprint, has supported and sponsored us with unqualified enthusiasm and seasoned insight and has communicated that enthusiasm with confidence. Lucy Salvino, Production Manager/Manufacturing, and Barbara Cohen, Production Manager/Design, made sure that the highest standards of printing and design were upheld. Nina Hoffman, Vice President and Director of Subsidiary Rights, arranged for spectacular third-party involvement for the book. Associate Publisher Liz Perle and Managing Editor Donna Ruvituso provided tremendous support.

Our Associate Editors, Ruth Ashby and David Harris, worked closely with the various contributors of the book, and I am grateful for their invaluable input. Scientific Editor Andrew Fraknoi, Executive Officer of the Astronomical Society of the Pacific, has our appreciation for his unflagging and extraordinary critical attention to all of the scientific content of this book. Without his contributions, it would be substantially diminished.

To the authors, scientists, and artists in the book, we collectively express our gratitude. To the photographers, especially David Malin, who is regarded by some as the finest astronomical photographer alive, a special thanks. Our appreciation also to E. Bruce Stevenson for his splendid coordination of all the photographs in the book.

Leslie Miller, who consistently designs elegant work for her own Grenfell Press, has produced a tasteful design for *The Universe*. My thanks for her patience, time, and talent.

To those of you who are reading this book after having read *The Planets*, a special thanks for being with us again. Let me echo my introduction to *The Planets* by quoting from Harvard professor of science Edward O. Wilson: "The time has come to link ecology with economic and human development. When you have seen one ant, one bird, one tree, you have not seen them all. What is happening to the rain forests of Madagascar and Brazil will affect us all."

This book is dedicated to the diversity of the universe. Humanity, animal species, habitat, planet, and star all share a glorious existence. Through our hopes and our prayers, we must do our part for their survival.

THE UNIVERSE: AN INTRODUCTION

ANDREW FRAKNOI

> There is nothing like astronomy
> to pull the stuff out of man.
> His stupid dreams and red-rooster importance:
> let him count the star swirls.
>
> —ROBINSON JEFFERS
> from "Star Swirls"

IF WE COULD TRAVEL FAR BEYOND the protective blanket of air that shelters our planet, beyond the ancient craters of the moon, and beyond the orbits of the nine known planets, we would reach the realm of *interstellar space,* where our solar system leaves off and the rest of the universe begins. What lies in that realm has always challenged humanity's curiosity and imagination and fueled the fires of scientific inquiry as well as fictional speculation. This book is an armchair tour of the universe, with some of the best minds in both camps as your guides.

Let's begin with a brief introduction to the universe—designed to make you familiar with its "geography" and with the ways we describe its structure and contents. Equipped with these ideas, you can then confidently tour the cosmos, and see it as we understand it today—not as just a velvet backdrop for the peacefully twinkling stars, but as an active (even violent) realm, filled with objects sometimes so bizarre that it is difficult to find the vocabulary to do them justice.

Einstein once wrote (and I paraphrase him) that the most incomprehensible thing about the universe is that it is comprehensible. While no responsible scientist would claim that we *fully* understand even a small part of the cosmos, it is remarkable how far our understanding has come in the last few decades. This book is more than a mere chronicle of that understanding; it is also a tribute to the inspiration it can provide.

THE LIGHT-YEAR: THE UNIVERSE MEASURED

The Moon, our closest cosmic neighbor, is some 240,000 miles away from us, on average. The Sun is separated from us by 93 million miles of interplanetary space as we circle it in perpetual obedience to its gravitational grip. Most of our solar system and all of the rest of the universe lie much farther away than that. Clearly it is impractical to continue using units designed for Earth measurement to make our way outward from our home base. Instead, astronomers express cosmic distances in units that recognize that the universe seems to have a maximum speed built into its inner workings: the speed of light.

According to everything we understand today, nothing can travel faster than the speed of light and still be part of the universe as we know it. The fastest that information of any kind can travel from point to point is the speed with which a beam of light (or pulse of radio waves) can carry it: about 300,000 kilometers or 186,000 miles each second. A distance of one light-second, then, is the space light covers in one second: 300,000 kilometers. One light-minute is the distance light travels in one minute—18 million kilometers—and so forth, on to light-hours, light-days, or any other light travel-time units we wish to construct.

The unit most appropriate to measuring the distances to the stars is the *light-year*, a span covering about 9.5 thousand billion kilometers. A piece of string one light-year long would wrap around the equator of the Earth 236 million times; yet the nearest star beyond our Sun is more than *four* light-years away.

THE ORGANIZATION OF THE UNIVERSE

A slow process of growing up begins when a child realizes that the house in which she lives is not the only house, that her family is not the only family, and that even the community in which she lives has many counterparts elsewhere. So, too, the human process of maturation involved the gradual realization that the planets and stars were not just lights on the backdrop of the sky, but other worlds and other Suns beyond our own.

Today we know that the Earth is one of nine planets circling the star we call the Sun. Unlike stars, planets do not shine under their own power, but simply reflect the light of their star. The Sun, planets, satellites, and assorted smaller "debris"—like comets, asteroids, and meteors—make up our *solar system*, the local "neighborhood" that gave us birth. On average, light takes about five hours to get to us from the most distant planet, Pluto. (Actually, while Pluto is usually the most distant planet, its orbit is so eccentric that for about 20 years out of its 248-year swing around the Sun it actually comes inside the orbit of Neptune and becomes the eighth planet in our solar system. It crossed to this inside post in 1979 and will remain there until 1999.)

The next star system is almost seven thousand times farther than Pluto, and lies in the direction of the constellation Centaurus—a star pattern that is not visible from the continental United States, but is easily studied in the Southern Hemisphere. Between us and this system—called Alpha Centauri—lie vast gulfs of *interstellar space,* a vacuum finer than any we can produce on Earth. Yet this space is not completely empty. On average it contains *one* lonely atom in every thimbleful of space and, as you will read, there are enough thimblefuls of space out there so that the total number of loose atoms—raw material—in the cosmos is quite impressive.

Alpha Centauri is actually a triple star system, three stars moving around each other in a stately and ever-repeating dance. Our eyes show only one dot of light, but our telescopes can reveal the three distinct suns: one yellow, one orange, and one red.

The next-closest star is a dim reddish dwarf star that is visible only through telescopes and lies about six light-years away. It is called Barnard's star, after the astronomer who first called attention to it, and can be found in the constellation of Ophiuchus.

Beyond these two "neighbors" lie other stars and beyond them still others—in every direction we look. All the stars you can see with your naked eye on a starlit night lie in a vast grouping of stars we call our *Galaxy.* Since we are inside this grouping, determining its shape was no small task—akin to getting a good look at your own body from inside your pituitary gland. Still, today we know that our Galaxy is a flat disk of stars, gas, and dust, with a bulbous core from which the vast spiral arms of stars that define the disk wind outward.

The Sun is one of 200 billion to 400 billion stars that compose our Galaxy, and it is not particularly special in its size, brilliance, or location. We are not in the center of the Galaxy or even on one of the main spiral arms; rather, we find ourselves on a small local spur, some 30,000 light-years or so from the center. If some vast cosmic surveying organization were making a list of the most important or interesting places in the Galaxy, there is no guarantee that we would be included.

From our vantage point in the galactic outskirts, we see the Galaxy's disk as a band across the sky, the soft glow of the nearer stars blending their light together into a skein of light we call the Milky Way. Much older than the Sun and the Earth, much larger than the parts we can see, the Milky Way is our cosmic island or continent—an enormous pinwheel turning slowly in the dark of space.

Beyond our Galaxy lies *intergalactic space,* an emptiness so great that the average concentration of matter is only one atom every cubic meter. But throughout that space, as far as our telescopes can see, there are other islands of stars and still others beyond them. We have reached the realm of the galaxies, where our nearest neighbor is more than 150,000 light-years away. Like stars, galaxies also come in groups—some large, some small. The Milky Way is part

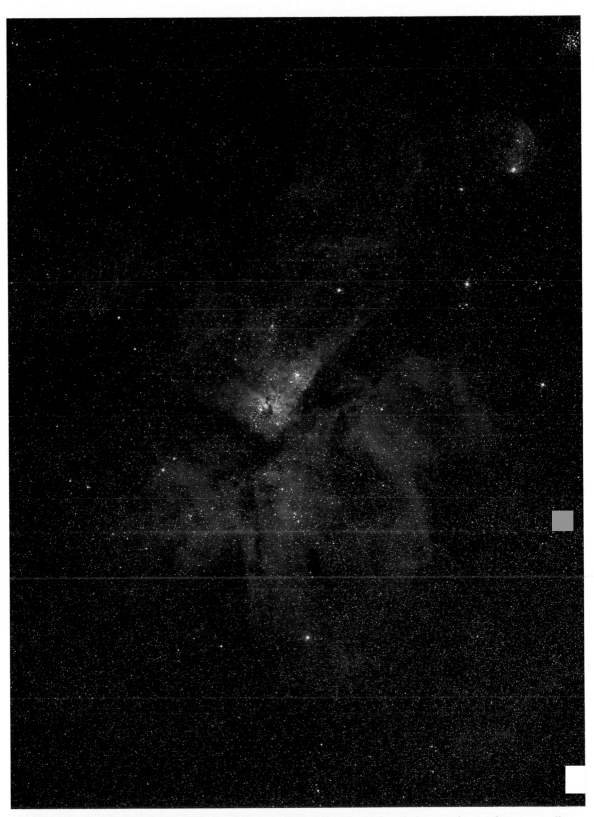

The Eta Carinae nebula (NGC 3372), sometimes also called the "keyhole nebula," in the southern constellation Carina. Photo credit: National Optical Astronomy Observatories.

of a loose grouping of about two dozen galaxies which we call the *Local Group*. Beyond its confines lie other groups and clusters, which, in turn, seem to collect into *superclusters* stretching for many millions of light-years.

Astronomers have just recently begun to look at whether the arrangement of clusters and superclusters of galaxies might not itself have some shape or structure. There is the possibility, just beginning to show on our very deepest surveys of the universe, that the chains of clusters and superclusters may form a three-dimensional set of bubbles, surrounding much emptier parts of space we call *voids*. But as this book goes to press, it is simply too early in our investigation to say much more about the largest-scale structure of the universe; we must wait until the next generation of large multiple-mirror telescopes on Earth and large orbiting instruments in space gives us a clearer glimpse of the cosmos at large.

ASTRONOMY AS ANCIENT HISTORY

One important point to keep in mind about our exploration of the universe is the special meaning these large distances give to the notion of cosmic "current events." Today on Earth, television and communications satellites have spoiled us with their virtually instantaneous ability to bring us news from any part of our globe. But all news is old news when we look out into the universe.

Light from the moon takes a little less than two seconds to reach us— explaining why there was just a bit of hesitancy about the conversations between Mission Control and the lunar explorers of the Apollo program. Two seconds had to pass while the radio waves made their way to or from the Moon at the speed of light.

If the Sun were extinguished tomorrow—a prospect for which you definitely do *not* need to add a clause to your homeowner's policy—it would take about eight and a third minutes for the news to reach us.

The light an Australian astronomer would see tonight from the Alpha Centauri star system left those stars more than four years ago and has taken all that time to make it here, even though it unwaveringly traveled at the speed of light. Light from more distant stars can take hundreds or thousands of years to get here.

The light that just left the other large galaxy in our Local Group—called the Great Galaxy in Andromeda—will not be reaching us for another 2 million years. And the light we see from more remote galaxies left them at a time so long ago that humanity was nothing but a "glimmer in nature's eye."

Some people find the delay in the arrival of cosmic information a frustrating feature of the universe. They complain that it means we can never truly learn what is going on in remote regions of the universe *now*. But astronomers are fond of pointing out there is no such thing as a *universal now*—how soon any observer in the universe learns about a particular cosmic event depends entirely on how far away from that observer it happens to be located. It is far better simply to regard "now" for events in the universe as the time when the light reaches us. If a star some six thousand light-years away explodes, the brilliant burst of light will take six thousand years to reach us. By the time we see the light, the explosion (local time at the star's location) has happened six thousand years ago. But as far as we are concerned, the explosion happens when the light arrives, and the explosion will have its first anniversary one Earth year after that.

Astronomers don't regard the delay of cosmic information as an annoyance we strive to overcome; actually, it turns out to be perhaps the greatest boon that astronomers have. One of the ultimate tasks of astronomy, after all, is to reconstruct the history of the universe and understand the events that have led to our present cosmic circumstances. If all information from distant regions of the universe arrived here instantaneously, the events of the past would be irretrievably lost to us. But this way, the light travel time from distant objects guarantees that we will always have a window to the past. As modern telescopes enable us to look farther and farther outward, we are at the same time looking further and further back in time and we can glean the clues we need to understand the development of the cosmos over billions of years.

INVISIBLE ASTRONOMY: THE UNIVERSE UNVEILED

Most of us, when we think of the universe, see it in our minds the way our eyes (as helped by telescopes) reveal it to us. And that was indeed the universe as previous centuries or generations understood it. But today we have learned that the information that our eyes perceive is only a meager portion of the total information the universe sends us. In addition to the visible-light universe, there are the *invisible* universes revealed by our instruments—invisible universes that have shown us numberless phenomena simply not accessible to our eyes.

Light is only the most familiar example of a broad range of waves that can carry information at the speed of light. Because such waves are created by the interaction of electric and magnetic forces, we call them *electromagnetic* waves. Some vibrate less frequently than light; others are more frequent vibrators. Together, the broad range of observed waves (or radiation) is called *the electromagnetic spectrum.*

For historical reasons, this spectrum is divided into six broad categories. Starting with the least-energetic radiation, we have radio waves, infrared waves, visible light, ultraviolet waves, X-rays, and gamma rays. Each must be observed with specialized instruments sensitive to its particular characteristics. Radio waves, for example, are picked up by huge metal "dishes"—round antennas that can collect and reflect faint cosmic radio signals into powerful radio receivers. Many bands of the spectrum are completely, or at least partially, blocked by the Earth's thick atmosphere and we must "rise above" the problem by putting our instruments aboard aircraft, balloons, rockets, or orbiting spacecraft. But the results have been well worth the effort and expense. Since different ranges of waves are often produced by completely different mechanisms in the universe, each kind of radiation can tell us about a different set of phenomena operating in and among the stars.

It is important to keep in mind as you read this book that it is an act of egotistical "light chauvinism" to regard the information we gather from light as superior to or more real than the information brought our way by radio waves or X-rays. The fact that we happen to see the narrow range of waves we call light is nothing more than an accident of evolution and local circum stances. To be successful in a competitive world, larger organisms have to have a way of sensing their environment. Human beings evolved to see those waves that are most abundantly available in their world. What we call *visible light* is just that set of electromagnetic waves that our Sun puts out most copiously.

Had we developed around a star that shines most brightly in infrared waves, we might well have developed infrared sensitive eyes and a view of the universe centered on infrared waves. In that case, stars like our own Sun would look much dimmer to us, while—as you will see in the science chapters of this book—young stars still being born and old stars nearing exhaustion would seem much brighter. In a way, our eyes are *filters*, keeping out the bulk of information available from the universe. Overcoming this handicap has been a central theme in the development of twentieth-century astronomy.

In fact, it is fair to say that the acceleration of our understanding about the universe has been a direct result of the acceleration of our technology. Each time a larger telescope or a telescope tuned to a new region of the spectrum has become available, we have learned about previously unsuspected or mis- understood phenomena. The discovery of such exotic objects as pulsars, quasars, black holes, and cannibal galaxies—all of them described and explained in this book—was a direct result of the application of new instruments and new tech- niques to questions that light waves alone could not help us answer.

That is not to say that there is no role left for *optical* telescopes—as the light gatherers are called. We continue to dream about and occasionally build larger telescopes to help us collect light from even more distant regions of the cosmos (and even earlier epochs). As this book is being written, astronomers are eagerly awaiting the launch (once the U.S. shuttle program resumes) of the Hubble Space Telescope, the largest and most sophisticated instrument ever put into orbit, and the completion—atop an extinct Hawaiian volcano—of the Keck Telescope, whose ten-meter-wide mirror will make it the largest optical instrument we have ever fashioned. But more and more, the light gathering goes hand in hand with radio, ultraviolet, or other invisible surveys of the sky, and a complete understanding of complex members of the "cosmic zoo" requires pooling the information from every part of the electromagnetic spectrum.

Welcome then to the universe—the largest of all subjects for a book. We don't claim to have covered or even understood all of it in this one. But we hope to show you enough of its mysteries—solved and unsolved—to whet your appetite for a lifetime of further exploration. (A listing of other interesting books follows the main chapters.) And, in particular, we hope the merging of fact and speculation in one book will inspire fans of each kind of writing to learn a little more about the other. It is, after all, at the frontier of human knowledge that the realm of the imagination and inspiration begins—and it is at that boundary of our understanding that the scientist and science fiction writer can amiably meet.

WHAT IS THE UNIVERSE?

ISAAC ASIMOV

UNIVERSE IS FROM LATIN WORDS MEANING "turning as one." The universe is everything, treated as a unit. It is all the matter and energy that exists.

We have the disadvantage of studying the universe from within. We can see those portions near us, but the farther portions become progressively dimmer, progressively more blurred. With all our instruments, much of the universe remains too distant and dim to see at all—let alone in detail.

From what we see, though, we can come to some conclusions; so suppose we imagine we are viewing the universe from outside, under such conditions that we are aware of a large part of it at once. (This is impossible, of course, since there is no such thing as "outside the universe," but let us imagine it anyway.)

To us, any large portion of the universe would look like a three-dimensional mesh of fine strands of light, with empty spaces between. There would be a great many small empty spaces, a smaller number of larger ones, and a still smaller number of still larger ones. As for the lines of light, they would here and there gather in small knots or clumps of light, with a smaller number of brighter knots, and so on.

The universe would most resemble a sponge built of light. The curving lines and sheets of light are built up of about 100 billion dots of light (some considerably brighter than others). Each of these dots is a galaxy.

The universe as we would view it would be most notable for its stillness. Nothing whatever seems to be happening to it. The reason for this is that no progressive change large enough to be noticeable under our universal view can possibly take place at faster than the speed of light. The speed of light (186,281 miles per second) may seem incredibly fast to us, but on the scale of the universe as a whole, light may be considered virtually motionless.

Suppose, for instance, that as a result of some unimaginable event, the central point of one of the galaxies of the universe ceases to emit light. It grows

DARREL ANDERSON

dark. Suppose that a wave of such darkening spreads outward from that central point in all directions at the fastest possible speed, that of light. We, watching from without, might see the galaxy (visible to us as a dot of light) begin to grow slightly dimmer, but it would take tens of thousands of years before the galaxy would blank out completely. It would take hundreds of thousands of years for the darkening to extend to other, neighboring dots. It would take some 12 *billion* years, at the very least, for the entire universe we see to darken.

If we began watching at any stage of this universal darkening, we would see absolutely no change in the course of a lifetime, and very little in the course of a hundred lifetimes. (The same would be true, by the way, if the universe were dark to begin with and began to grow light from some central point, the influence spreading outward at the speed of light.)

We ourselves are as much prisoners of our place and time as everything else is. We cannot, under any circumstances we know of, go faster than the speed of light. But even at that speed it would take us about 160,000 years to go to the far end of our own Galaxy and back; and 4.6 million years to travel to the Andromeda galaxy, our nearest large neighbor, and back.

It is not likely that we will be able to go at the speed of light, however. The greatest practical speed may prove to be no more than a fifth the speed of light, in which case it would take 800,000 years of the astronaut's time to visit the other end of the Galaxy and return, and 23 million years to visit the Andromeda galaxy and return.

It may be, then, that with the best will in the world, any person in his or her own lifetime may be able to do no more than visit the very nearest stars, and from the universal view that travel distance will be essentially zero.

Suppose, though, that as we view the universe, we overcome its motion-lessness by imagining that we speed up time a millionfold. Or, alternatively, we can imagine that some kindly superbeing has taken a detailed photograph of the universe every hundred thousand years and that now we have the opportunity to run the film through a projector at the usual sixteen frames a second.

At this speed, the galaxies undergo rapid changes. Each one spins rapidly about its center. If it is a spiral, the spiral arms may disappear and reappear. None of these changes would be visible from our universal view, of course. The dots of light would remain merely dots of light.

At this speed, also, some galaxies will be exploding in a sudden burst of light; some will develop black holes that will grow enormously and devour millions of stars in a matter of seconds. Other galaxies will collide or merge and in the process produce vast jets and incredible showers of radio waves and other radiations. None of this will be particularly visible either. Some of the dots of light in our universal view may brighten slightly and others may dim slightly, but we probably wouldn't notice these happenings without careful measurements, if then.

In that case, will even speeding up time do nothing to change the universe? Not so. There is one change that is the overwhelming fact about the universe.

As we watch the film run we will notice that the universe is visibly *expanding*. The holes in the spongy structure will slowly grow larger, and the curves and swoops of light will slowly thin out and spread apart, so that the intensity of light in any one spot will dim. In short, the universal sponge will grow larger and larger and dimmer and dimmer.

We might, just for fun, also decide to run the film backward. In that case we will see the universe visibly *contracting*. The holes in the spongy structure will slowly grow smaller, and the curves and swoops of light will slowly thicken and tighten. In short, the universal sponge will grow smaller and smaller and brighter and brighter.

If we run the film in the normal direction indefinitely, the universe may continue to expand and dim until it is too dim to see at all. If, however, we continue to run the film in the backward direction, there is a limit to the length of time we can do so, for eventually the universe must shrink to nothing.

In fact, if we start at the present and run the film backward at 100,000 years every sixteenth of a second, then in about two hours the universe will be seen to contract itself into a tiny dot that is unbearably bright (though not in visible light) and unbearably hot, and then it will blink out into nothingness.

If we start at that point of nothingness and run the film forward, the dot will appear with its unbearably bright heat and quickly expand and cool. That is the Big Bang, in which, astronomers now suspect, all the matter and energy of the universe were formed out of "nothing," in accordance with the peculiar rules of quantum theory.

The Big Bang presents astronomers with a fascinating problem. At the moment of the Big Bang, that original point of light must have been homogeneous. Everything in it must have been completely mixed. As it expanded, it should have stayed completely mixed. The whole universe today ought to be just one large, ever-expanding, ever-thinning gas, which would always be the same everywhere in the universe.

Instead, from the universal view we see a terribly uneven universe. Matter and energy have coagulated into the dots we call galaxies, and these have, in turn, collected into lines and curves of light that give the universe a spongy appearance. How can the universe have gone from a featureless dot of light to a sponge? Cosmologists are still arguing over it and trying out various theories, some of which you will read about in this book.

Another problem is this: Will the universe expand forever?

The universe is expanding against the pull of its own gravity, and as a result its rate of expansion is slowing. But is this braking effect of gravity sufficient to bring the expansion to a complete halt someday and start a contraction instead?

That depends on the quantity of matter in the universe, for matter is the source of the gravitational pull. At the moment, it seems that the amount of matter we can detect is not more than about 1 percent of the quantity needed to stop the expansion someday. Yet there are also some independent indications that the expansion *will* stop someday. If that is so, it means that there is at least a hundred times as much mass in the universe as we can detect so far.

This is called "the mystery of the missing mass," and cosmologists are arguing over this mystery heatedly.

Studying the cosmos from within, making our measurements of the faint beams of light it sends us, and arguing as we humans always do, we probe our way toward a better picture of the universe. We've still got a long way to go.

ART AND SCIENCE FICTION UNBUILT CITIES/REALIZED DREAMS

RAY BRADBURY

Is there a relationship among art history, daily and Sunday comic strips, the great illustrators, and the evolution of science fiction?

Do science fiction and its unreal mirror image, fantasy, have wild roots in the art metaphors of the nineteenth century?

Does it all influence a mob of twentieth-century film magicians?

Finally, do these celluloid geniuses reinfluence the others?

We might as well ask: Are houses haunted? Does life thrive on other worlds?

Yes.

How so?

Houses are haunted by Fuseli/Blake/Goya imaginations.

Far worlds are seeded with Frank R. Paul/Robert McCall dreams.

Here-and-now-cities sprout from old Méliès sprocket-dancing pictures, "Little Nemo" full-page Sunday architectures, and skyline images from William Cameron Menzies' art-directed *Things to Come*.

In the ricochet between night remembrance, palette and paint, printed word, and phantom cinema, a multitude of new worlds, spoken, seen, or watercolor-sketched, have come to birth.

A vast and movable feast. I will try to bite off a chunk.

Where to start?

Most of my generation, as young readers and writers of time-traveled pasts and hoped-for futures, were seized into them by two artists: N. C. Wyeth and J. Allen St. John. Wyeth piloting his great metal white whale under-the-sea

Nautilus. St. John astride his eight-legged thoths, dusting the acres, atrot along dry Martian seas.

We all knew that Wyeth's Captain Nemo never was and that St. John's Mars could never be. Yet amid all the chalkboard configurations of new physics and Viking Landers, we now know that the thoths will rove forever in the blowing Martian nights and Verne's crazed captain will always rave under the tides—and all because Wyeth and St. John did more than facts and physics can to figure out God's dreams for man. Both artists could describe the madness that is youth and the limitless territories that exist between a youngster's left ear and his right.

Carl Sagan, Arthur C. Clarke, Bruce Murray of the Jet Propulsion Lab— the list of young dreamers who did not grow old is endless. The meadowlands of Cape Canaveral are strewn with grown-up kids who swam after the grand concourse of submarines or marched behind the impossible thoths in a storm of red.

My experience differs little from theirs. Fairy tales wakened me, Wyeth and St. John sat me up, and the bright covers of *Amazing Stories* and *Wonder,* and Buck Rogers in the 1929 daily papers, exploded me into the universe.

I never came back.

Would that more teachers learned the exquisitely direct relationship between sighting a metaphor and the impossible desire to live forever.

Why want to live forever?

So as to be able to stroll in the channels of those dead Martian "seas," or stand on the rim of that Grand Martian Canyon which is as long and almost as wide as our entire continental United States.

So as to be able to stride into the front covers of the twenties' science fiction magazines and never come out. To be encompassed, devoured, assimilated by those wondrous metaphors of humanity's childhood dreams.

For that, almost completely, is what science fiction means to me. It is the history of towns and cities yet unbuilt, ghosting our imaginations and lifting us to rise up and find hammers and nails to build our dreams before they blow away.

I dare suggest some few architects, if you asked, would say the same: that a Frank R. Paul cover painting on an October issue of *Amazing Stories,* 1929, caused them to buy pens, pencils, rulers, and drawing boards to paper up a concept and create a living world.

If you bombarded an audience with three minutes' worth of covers from the old science fiction magazines, each screened for just two or three seconds, the effect would be stunning. For city after city, wall after wall, avenue after avenue, would strike the retina and stimulate the brain. How could you not, after seeing all that explosive stuff, want to stick around and be part of the fantastic years ahead?

I was reminded of this all over again just last week, when some mysterious

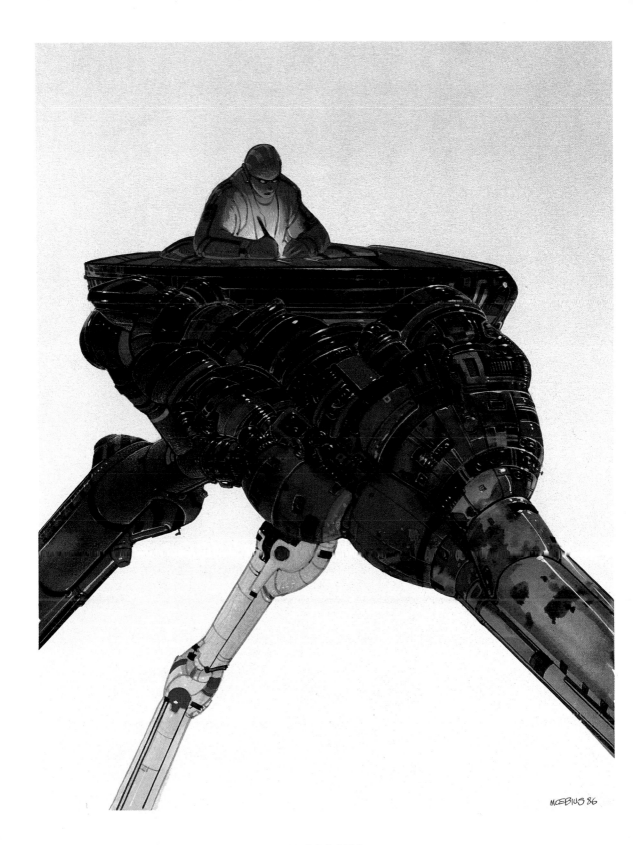

MOEBIUS

friend sent me a complete set of tearsheets from the serialization of H. G. Wells's *The Sleeper Awakes*, which appeared in *Harper's Weekly* in 1892. In vivid illustration following illustration, the concept of a man plastered against a crystal dome four hundred feet above an incredible future city, staring down in wonder at its skyports and car-streams, was enough to locomote the old engine and ventilate desire.

It was thus with all the H. G. Wells stories and the Verne tales published between 1850 and 1912. The future was actually there. You could touch it on the bright paper. You could smell it in the oils and perfumes that permeated the ink.

It was thus when Buck Rogers awakened, in October 1929. With the help of Wilma Deering, who found him wandering out of a long-wintered sleep and strapped an inertron belt on his back, a million hearts leaped to life that afternoon and never stopped leaping.

These futures, so wonderfully pursued in color and line, repeated in the Sunday full-page spreads, collided with the future actually built in the 1933 Chicago World's Fair, and again in New York in 1939. I walked through those fairs, brimming with tears of joy, glad to be inside the covers of *Amazing Stories* at last, closeted with illustrations come to life and reared to touch the sky and the soul. When the two fairs were torn down, part of my heart fell with them. The future was suddenly sunk and lost. My heart would break if it never returned.

I, like others aged twelve, built the futures out of papier-mâché in my backyard, in order to guarantee its return, and repeated the stuffs in my first stories. As I grew into my twenties I knew that if I wrote long enough and hard enough and willed the future to return, one day it would.

So the world we live in today is the direct result, I think, of the artwork, the illustrations, and the architecture of only-yesterday's artist, who influenced films and comic strips as well as young writers and budding scientists.

If you flip back through the years 1905 to 1915 you will find the incredible cities, the impossible architecture of "Little Nemo," as drawn by one of the greatest cartoonist illustrators of the century, Winsor McCay.

Simultaneously, in France, the magician-become-cinema illusionist Georges Méliès was popping rabbit films out of hats, full of Verne/Wells imagery, alive with architecture, impossible beasts, moon landscapes, and a pomegranate imagination that refused to sit still. If Méliès influenced McCay or if McCay influenced Méliès, I do not know. They are twins, racing down the same genetic track, so devastatingly full of the life force that they knock everyone head over heels before them.

The histories of cinema and comic strips parallel each other on similar rail tracks, speeding on up through our century, rushing over mile-high viaducts, racing toward our elusive tomorrows.

The combination of all these metaphorical art forms, comic strips, magazine covers, magical films of the early twentieth century, and the World's Fairs in between, have produced the architectural science fiction films of the last twenty years.

Architectural science fiction films?

I use the description because these films have knocked apart and rebuilt our concepts of the future. They are the manifestations of the words of science fiction and the architecture of our dreams.

2001 for starters. Next, the big artillery that knocked us flat out: *Close Encounters of the Third Kind, Star Wars, The Empire Strikes Back,* and the charming *Star Trek II, III,* and *IV.*

Long before them, there were *Metropolis* and *Things to Come,* echoing and presaging the wild fancies of Frank Lloyd Wright and the unrealized blueprints of Norman Bel Geddes.

The unbuilt visions of lost architectural genius have at last been raised from the graveyard sands and reared on fifty-foot-high and ninety-foot-wide screens by today's production designers and science fiction illustrators.

It was the cities we went to see.

For let us face it: In the final moments of *Close Encounters,* that is not—I repeat, not—a Mother Ship that drifts down from the universe. It is an entire country, a land put up in a massive architectural pod, so irresistible that in hearing its five Pied Piper notes played again and again, the children of the world, myself included, rushed across the tarmac in our minds to get aboard and go away forever.

Such is the pull of futures riveted together as cities that pretend to be ships.

In *The Empire Strikes Back,* more cities, more architecture. What is the Emerald City doing, suspended on its own platform in a weird skyscraper, waiting for our seekers?

And, again . . .

Why do we go back to see *2001* over and over and over? Surely not for its one-track acting and baffling finale. We return to it because the very possibility of interpretations frees us to carom off into the greatest of all architecture of the future: the universe itself.

Which finally is the subject of this marvelous new book you hold in your hands.

Who will ever forget their first cinematic trip into the unknown universe? The first sighting of that immense city-ship adrift to Strauss waltzes on the first night of viewing *2001?*

Or that first thunderous explosion of a *Star Wars* rocket blasting across the stars? The night I heard it, a thousand people gasped with shock, knocked in the pits of their stomachs. The glad cry that followed the shock was like the cry of a thousand babes slapped into life: pure joy at the sound of the future.

I am reminded of an article I wrote for a major New York magazine a few years back. The magazine hated the aesthetic concept of my article so much that they paid me off and trashed the piece. What had I said that knocked their wigs askew?

I simply pointed out that science fiction and science fiction art were revolutionizing the world of the museum, the gallery, the concert hall, the cinema, and all or most of fiction.

The cultural impact of your average science fiction film made kids wandering into art galleries wonder where all the metaphors were. They found instead drip-dry, cross-hatched, and empty canvases, bereft of any romance, poetry, image, or so much as one half of a dogeared haiku symbol. If the cinema screens could flood their minds with such vivid portraits of imagined dreams, why not the art galleries?

From the imaginative film came the inevitable bleed-over and discovery of such illustrators as Rackham, Dulac, Grandville, Doré, and the Victorian pre-Raphaelite painters. All because kids ran off to *2001* and fell off a one-thousand-story building, into the Past as well as the Future.

So the new-old clichés of the abstract and super abstract revolution were cut across at their nonexistent knees by a riot of heretofore uninformed teenaged art critics who demanded story, symbol, and the reinvention of taletelling.

What fragmented the art galleries soon knocked a few orchestra conductors off their podiums. What started as a hum-along with the Strausses through two hours of *2001* prolonged itself into science fictional symphonic evenings with Berlioz, Vivaldi, and a half-dozen others. The kids in their bright ignorance stumbled out of John Williams's score for *Star Wars* into "The Four Seasons" and "Symphonie Fantastique." One helluva way, the aesthetes protested, to be educated to the finer impulse.

What, after all, did these damn-fool kids know about art?

Almost, you might say, everything.

They knew that life without image or metaphor is empty and meaningless. Hell, they said, you can learn that from the Bible. Witness Daniel in that old lions' den. Once the cage doors slam and lions roar, you never forget that, do you? Well, then, in this age of machines that embody all the metaphors of man's dreaming in the past hundred years, how come the galleries empty of concept, vacuumed free of one lint-thread of idea, long lost from dream? You do not go to visit an elevator shaft with no elevator in it, do you? Better one bottomed out in trash, if necessary, as long as you, in the finale, are lifted.

Well, if I have beaten the dead thoth a dozen times too many, forgive. Not all of our teachers, our intellectuals, our movers and shakers, have yet discovered that this is the greatest age of metaphor, because the metaphors have peeled off the canvases, marched out of the haunted World's Fair grounds, leaped out of the comic strips, and unreeled themselves from cinema screens and computer tapes to become our whole existences, our lives, our further dreams. The artistic haiku of just the other morning has become the logarithm written to displace the astrological star houses above us.

If educators only knew, if parents only truly understood, our children today are all quasars, galaxies, black holes, laser discs, and rocket-submarines built to submerge and swim in Jupiter's soups. The architecture of the future is the substance of their dreams, fed by some of the best wishing artists, authors, and architects.

We are all kin to the Gustave Doré and John Martin landscapes that caused the roustabout sorcerer Méliès to film his secret moon, and Winsor McCay to walk his small boy Nemo upside down through inverted boulevards, and cause yet further films to be built around that grand door and wall and the huge skull on Kong's island. Ending at last with the birth of Spielberg and Lucas, who picked up the bottle marked DRINK ME—inside of which was the whole history of magazines, comics, science fiction covers, nineteenth-century painters and etchers—and drank the whole damn thing until the founts of Technicolor squirted out their ears.

The worst, you might be tempted to say, is yet to come. Yes, but the best also, I say. Why not the best? Science fiction remains the architecture of our dreams, and science fiction illustration will continue to inspire our next generation of dreamers.

OUR GALAXY

ESSAY BY

ERIC J. CHAISSON

SPECULATION BY

GREGORY BENFORD

OUR GALAXY

ERIC J. CHAISSON

M.I.T., Harvard University, and Wellesley College

The next object which I have observed is the essence or substance of the Milky Way. By the aid of a telescope one may behold this in a manner which so distinctly appeals to the senses that all the disputes which have tormented philosophers through so many ages are exploded at once by the irrefragable evidence of our eyes, and we are freed from wordy disputes upon this subject, for the Galaxy is nothing else but a mass of innumerable stars planted together in clusters. Upon whatever part of it you direct the telescope straightaway a vast crowd of stars presents itself to view; many of them are tolerably large and extremely bright, but the number of small ones is quite beyond determination.

And whereas that milky brightness, like the brightness of a white cloud, is not only to be seen in the Milky Way, but several spots of a similar color shine faintly here and there in the heavens, if you turn the telescope upon any one of them you will find a cluster of stars packed closely together. Further—and you will be more surprised by this—the stars which have been called by everyone of the astronomers up to this day nebulous, are groups of small stars set thick together in a wonderful way, and although each one of them on account of its smallness, or its immense distance from us, escapes our sight, from the commingling of their rays there arises that brightness which has hitherto been believed to be the denser part of the heavens, able to reflect the rays of the stars or the Sun.

—GALILEO GALILEI
The Sidereal Messenger
Venice, 1610

TIMES HAVE CHANGED in the nearly four centuries since Galileo first turned his inch-size ocular toward the starry heavens, thus hastening a scientific revolution of unsurpassed magnitude. Today, we are experiencing a parallel period of grand technological progress, a veritable scientific revolution in its own right, for with modern instruments contemporary astronomers are now scanning the *invisible* cosmos as Galileo's telescope once revealed the visible universe. Of particular significance, during the past two decades we have learned how to detect, measure, and analyze nonvisible radiation streaming to us from dark objects in space. And, although ours is clearly a time of learning, of groping in the blackness—more a period of exploration than of mature science—what we have found thus far would have amazed even the father of modern astronomy.

I started my career in astronomy by coming in through the "back door" of physics more than a decade ago. Since much of my training concerned microwave measurements, the first telescope that I used was not an optical device at all. It was the big 120-foot Haystack radio antenna to the north of Boston, an instrument rising some sixteen stories above the ground yet fully able to track a bird in the sky. The celestial object I monitored in those first observing sessions was a gaseous nebula having only a catalog number as a name: W49. Embedded in a completely invisible region of star formation best studied by sampling its radio emissions, W49 resides on the other side of the Galaxy, nearly 40,000 light-years from Earth. This astronomical beacon is terribly remote, far beyond anything Galileo described in his pioneering observations of January 1610. But it's not the concept of astronomical distance that astounds me as much as the concept of astronomical time.

Working the equipment in the control room, I was enthralled to realize that W49's radio signals had been traveling through the near-void of outer space for some 40,000 years. To witness its radiation today, tripping the receiver and rousing the recorder, was a sort of revelation. My thoughts drifted into the past, the truly distant past. The radio signals I was examining had begun their journey to my equipment dozens of millennia ago, well before the last ice age had broken its grip on Earth, even before humanity had crossed the Bering Strait to become the "first Americans." Early in the radiation's cruise this way, the wheel was invented by our ancestors, who were also responsible for some of the earliest prehistoric art found on cave walls in western Europe; later, the glaciers retreated, the bow and arrow were devised, agriculture was discovered; civilization, pyramids, cathedrals arose. Still, the signals raced onward at the speed of light. As W49's emissions which I was to study neared Earth, I was born, my radio telescope was built, and together we met one night in the early 1970's. My instrument had become a time machine.

Observing the cosmos creates an eerie feeling, an uncanny experience. While most citizens sleep, astronomers are one with the universe—straining to fathom, yearning to understand, mentally plugged into the grand scale of worlds far, far away. But even for us, our view of the universe is delayed. Given the finite speed at which all radiation travels, we perceive the universe as it was, not as it is.

In many ways, today's astronomy resembles archaeology. Not having lived at the time of our ancient ancestors, archaeologists sift through earthly rubble, retrieving artifacts and bony remnants from unrelated localities scattered across our planet. Their objective, of course, is to decipher how the remains can be joined together to yield an overall picture of our culture and ourselves. Likewise, astronomers observe various objects in unrelated regions of the cosmos. Finding some young objects here, some old ones there, and more than a few that boggle our minds, we try to discover how each object fits into the cosmic scheme of things. Terrestrial bones and celestial objects are like the pieces in a grand jigsaw puzzle. The picture becomes clear only when each fragment is found, identified, and fitted properly into its place among all the other pieces.

SIZE AND SCALE

Deep space harbors myriad objects looking strangely unlike stars. Photographic time-exposures, taken with even the small 6-inch telescopes astronomy hobbyists might have at home, often reveal fuzzy, lens-shaped images in the sky, resembling disks more than the bright, round points of light we call stars. The eighteenth-century German philosopher Immanuel Kant regarded these flattened objects as "island universes" far beyond the confines of our own star system. The term is a bit old-fashioned; it is difficult to imagine there being more than one universe, since the word's definition is "the totality of all things." But Kant was correct in arguing that these nonstellar patches of light reside so far away that they are imperceptible to the naked human eye—in fact, well beyond the 40,000-light-year distance of W49.

Not until about half a century ago did Edwin Hubble use the 100-inch telescope on California's Mount Wilson to resolve these blurry and distant beacons into galaxies—huge structures of matter that are now known to have formed not long after the Big Bang creation event. Spanning roughly 100,000 light-years across, galaxies might be better described as gargantuan; a single light-year, after all, equals the distance traveled by light in a full year, namely about 6 trillion miles. Unquestionably, galaxies are typical of the size and scale from which today's popular adjective *astronomical* derives.

Furthermore, with literally hundreds of billions of stars bound loosely by gravity, each galaxy houses more stars than people who have ever lived on Earth. If you could exact a tax of a penny per star, a stellar census of a single galaxy would make you a billionaire. What's more, we now know that space is strewn with enough known galaxies to make every inhabitant on Earth that rich. Astronomical indeed.

Silently and majestically, galaxies twirl in the faraway realms of the universe—huge pinwheels of energy, matter, and perhaps life—simultaneously imparting a feeling for the immensity of the universe and for the mediocrity of our position in it.

Floating proud and mute, our daytime Sun as well as all the nighttime stars share membership in one such galaxy—a vast assemblage of stars termed the Milky Way. But just what do we know about our galactic home in space? What is its structure, composition, size, and scale? And what are the problem areas in our understanding of our Galaxy that are now being addressed by late-twentieth-century researchers?

Optical (visible light) studies of star clusters long ago established the existence of a roughly spherical halo of old stars around us, stretching some 100,000 light-years across. This halo is divided into two hemispheres by a disklike layer of younger stellar objects, often noted overhead on a dark night: the Milky Way itself. Though we can't see it fully, this so-called *galactic plane* is shaped like a double sombrero clapped brim to brim and nearly a hundred times thinner than its full expanse. When we compare what we can see of our Galaxy with other galaxies, it appears that our Milky Way Galaxy resembles a spiral like many other galaxies, stoked with hundreds of billions of stars unevenly interlaced throughout chaotic swirls of interstellar gas and dust.

Half a century ago, these were only inferences. The ubiquitous galactic dust obstructed our view of all but the nearest portions of the Galaxy and kept astronomers literally guessing about its precise nature and shape. And many of these inferences were hard to swallow. After all, even well into the twentieth century, our brightly shining and oft-worshipped Sun was regarded by science and society alike as inhabiting the center of not only our Galaxy but the whole universe as well. So it was something of a shock when the American astronomer Harlow Shapley showed in the 1920's that the Sun resides neither in the middle of the halo of old stars nor in the center of the disk of young stars. Indeed, at 30,000 light-years from the hub of the Milky Way, our star and its system of planets are far removed from the core of the Galaxy. "We reside in the galactic suburbs," Shapely used to say.

Even today, when radio and infrared telescopes—which receive radiation that can penetrate dust—give us a more genuine perception of our Galaxy, it's hard to know exactly what it looks like. We live inside the Milky Way, confined near the edge of this truly expansive assemblage of stars, and we can't get outside it and look back. Frustrated by this problem one evening in my office at the Harvard Observatory, I wandered to Cambridge Common, where I perched myself on the back of a bench near the periphery of the park. Straining to fathom the locations of crosswalks, benches, and trees, I gained some insight into the problem of trying to map the Milky Way from within. Barring myself from walking, bicycling, or otherwise sauntering about, I soon discovered that mapping the park's layout is no easy task. Any resulting map would likely be subject to distortion, obscuration, and incompleteness. Especially intriguing objects—notably the grand monument near the common's center—seemed shrouded in mystery, for they resembled none of the familiar shrubs and benches near my edge of the park. And so it is with our Milky Way Galaxy. Relegated perhaps forever to the galactic boondocks, we strain to unravel the spread of stars, gas, and dust in that part of the universe housing our Sun and its planetary system. Not surprisingly, our view from the suburbs is limited.

How bad is the barrier of cosmic dust that hampers our visible-light view? Not even the world's largest optical telescopes—atop America's Mount Palomar or the Soviet Caucasus—which multiply our human vision by more than 10 million times, can see much of our Galaxy because of it. Pound for pound, the Milky Way is a relatively dirty place, and light from distant stars just can't penetrate the innumerable accumulations of interstellar dust, any more than a car's headlights can illuminate roadside objects in a dense terrestrial fog. (If we could compress a typical parcel of interstellar space to equal the density of the air on Earth, this parcel would contain enough dust to make a fog so thick we'd be lucky to see our hands held at arm's length in front of us.) But for the last two decades, radio and infrared astronomers have penetrated the fog by probing the Galaxy for long-wavelength (invisible) radiation virtually immune to scattering by the galactic debris.

The results, still being massaged, interpreted, and debated, are causing us to reevaluate our conception of much of the Milky Way. This is especially true in recent years regarding our understanding of the composition of the cosmic "raw material" sprinkled amid the stars, of a tremendously extended halo of thin, dark gas engulfing the entire spiral-arm system, and of an enigmatic "something" residing dead center in our Galaxy's heart.

THE MATERIAL OF INTERSTELLAR SPACE

The dark spaces among the stars of our nighttime sky are not empty. Interstellar clouds harboring vast quantities of gas and dust lurk throughout our Milky Way Galaxy. These nearly invisible clouds, which have cooled to a temperature of close to absolute zero (or some $-273°C$), are often associated with hot, luminous stars, whose energy outputs are so large that they were probably born only recently in the life-history of the Milky Way. Astronomers have long thought that stars must form from the material in such clouds, and recent radio and infrared observations tend to confirm this idea. So the clouds of gas and dust roaming in interstellar space are the breeding grounds of the stars described so eloquently by Galileo several centuries ago.

Interestingly enough, a combination of radio and ultraviolet observations during the 1970's proved that the abundances of many chemical elements—at least their amounts in gaseous form—are much lower in the galactic clouds than in our solar system and in stars. The most likely explanation for this unexpected discovery is that substantial quantities of familiar elements such as carbon, oxygen, silicon, magnesium, and iron have been used to form the (infamous) interstellar dust particles. This idea is supported by infrared observations sensitive to the way that iron and magnesium silicates (material we expect to be in the dust grains) absorb radiation. If our interpretation of these infrared measurements is correct, then these interstellar dust particles must account for at least a fraction of the elements missing from the interstellar gas. Even so, a complete chemical identification of interstellar dust remains an unsolved problem today.

Sprinkled throughout interstellar space among the dark clouds (and especially between the spiral arms) is a more tenuous medium of gas and dust— much more rarefied than the dark clouds themselves. In fact, at about a single atom per cubic inch, this largest volume of galactic matter is several orders of magnitude thinner than the best vacuums achievable in physics laboratories on Earth. This medium, totaling roughly enough matter to form 5 billion Suns, is slightly warmer than the dark clouds, averaging about −200°C.

Here and there, where hot stars happen to encounter it, this medium is heated to about 10,000°C, thus forming the great glowing regions known as gaseous nebulae. These are the spectacular and colorful objects, usually several light-years across, whose images often adorn all manner of advertisements, wall posters, and the centerfolds of most astronomy textbooks. Energized in this way, the interstellar gas forms a hot, charged plasma sometimes called the fourth state of matter. The W49 object that I spoke of earlier is such a nebula, though an entirely invisible one.

In addition, orbiting ultraviolet and X-ray telescopes sensitive to much hotter gas have discovered a small amount of interstellar matter in the form of vast bubbles having temperatures on the order of 500,000°C. Comprising a kind of "intercloud medium" amid some of the more conventional clouds, this thin but superheated gas extends far and wide throughout the Galaxy; it might conceivably stretch even into the unimaginably large intergalactic space among the galaxies. While the origin of this seething plasma is unknown, astronomers do suspect that the concussions and shock waves emanating from exploding stars called supernovae are capable of heating very thin gas to as much as a million degrees or so. (You can read much more about supernovae in David Helfand's chapter.)

Rounding out this short inventory of galactic matter, we have the molecular clouds—regions that contain not only dust and elemental gas, but also a surprising array of more complex molecules, chemical groupings of from two to a dozen atoms. Radio investigations have been especially helpful in revealing that such clouds reside not alone in space, but in huge complexes, some spanning as much as a hundred light-years and harboring enough loose gas to make roughly a million stars like our Sun. These complexes, of which there are now about a thousand known in the Galaxy, each contain numerous individual clouds some thirty to sixty light-years across. In turn, within these individual clouds lurk much more compressed and extremely dark regions often less than a light-year in diameter. It is in these compact "cloud cores" that star formation is observed to be occurring. (See Martin Cohen's chapter.)

Perhaps the most fascinating aspect of the molecular clouds is their composition. Now totaling more than sixty "species," the pharmaceutical array of molecules observed in our Milky Way's darkest regions include ammonia, water, and a wide variety of organic molecules such as formaldehyde (embalming fluid) and alcohol. Many of the chemicals found in space are thought to have played important roles in the prebiological processes that led to life on Earth. Unfortunately, we are currently uncertain how most interstellar molecules form, although the presence of sheltering grains of dust in the clouds seems to play an important role. The subject of astrochemistry, with its unfamiliar conditions and unearthly temperatures and densities, is only now being developed for the first time. Those books on our shelves labeled *General Chemistry* are mistitled; they should really be called *Earth Chemistry*, as we are only now beginning to deal with a truly grand or universal chemistry.

Thus, our understanding of interstellar matter has in recent years changed dramatically as a result of an improved capability to capture invisible radiation. Astronomers have rather recently come to regard the interstellar medium as composed of several quite different phases, each having widely differing temperatures and densities. And whereas we had previously considered gaseous nebulae as the largest individual entities within our Galaxy, we now realize that, despite their great extent, such glowing nebulae are mere islands of hot gas within an ocean of cool, dark atomic and molecular clouds.

THE GALAXY'S CORONA

As noted earlier, the oldest of the Milky Way's stars—found in tight-knit groups called *globular clusters*—delineate a spherical halo roughly 100,000 light-years in diameter. This much has been known for decades, as these dense clusters—which are brightly visible beacons in our Galaxy—have long been studied by optical astronomers employing conventional methods. In fact, these are among the stars used by Shapley to argue that the Sun has no special location in the larger scheme of things. These old groups of stars are also thought to outline the more spherical shape of our *proto-galaxy*, the primitive cloud from which our Galaxy originated some 12 billion years ago.

But the Galaxy outlined by the globular clusters has now turned out to be merely the "tip of the galactic iceberg." In a recent and dramatic development, radio and more indirect visible-light observations are helping us discern a much more extensive halo of thin, cold, invisible matter that seems to dwarf the inner halo of globular clusters. This extended halo, or corona, reaches well beyond the 100,000 light-year limit considered, until recently, to demarcate the typical dimension of our Galaxy. Such coronas have been inferred for several other galaxies as well, leading us to suspect that most galaxies are much larger than suggested by their optical photographs. Just how much larger is uncertain, as the observational research is still in progress. But there is some evidence that the dark matter in a galaxy stretches so far beyond its visible images that it might merge with the invisible extensions of neighboring galaxies.

These findings have caused an obvious revision of the large-scale features of our Milky Way. At face value, they demonstrate that we have underestimated the size, scale, and mass of our Galaxy. As things stand now, its size is at least

(Top) A false-color image of part of the plane of our galaxy about 120 degrees away from the center, looking toward the constellation of Cygnus. Assembled from data taken with the Infrared Astronomical Satellite (IRAS). Photo credit: JPL/Caltech/IPAC)

(Bottom) The Large Magellanic Cloud, a satellite galaxy of our own Milky Way. Because of its proximity, astronomers can study its stars and clouds in more detail and compare them with their counterparts in our galaxy. Photo credit: National Optical Astronomy Observatories.

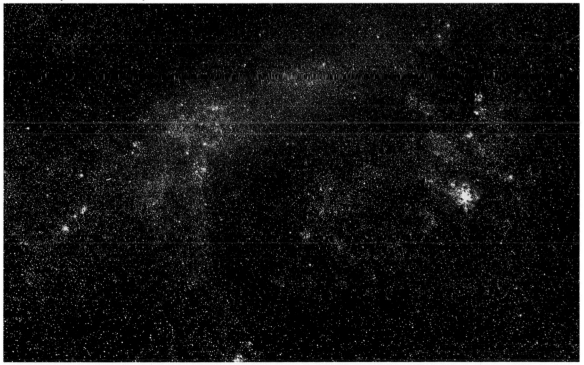

double and probably triple (and possibly even larger yet) than astronomers thought a mere decade ago. The gas in this galactic corona is exceedingly thin, though, implying that our Galaxy's mass probably need be adjusted less than its size—at most by about a factor of two. Now totaling approximately 500 billion solar masses, our Milky Way must nonetheless be elevated to the rank of a major spiral galaxy.

The corona's low density—at best that of the terribly tenuous medium among the dark clouds and between the spiral arms—probably explains why no one has ever observed a conventional star, cloud, or nebula in the corona; there's apparently not enough matter *per unit volume* to fabricate even the simplest structure, such as a flimsy cloud. Another alternative that astronomers are considering is that the coronal material could be in the form of old, burned-out stars. This could also explain why we cannot see anything in the corona from our vantage point. And there are more exotic candidates for this material as well; these will be discussed in a later chapter. In any case, because of the tremendously large total volume of such an extended halo, we now suspect that there may well be roughly as much hidden mass there as in the visible spiral-arm disk itself.

Actually, there might well be one known structure in our Galaxy's corona. The Large Magellanic Cloud can be easily seen with the naked eye from any location south of Earth's equator. Looking much like a dimly luminous atmospheric cloud, it has undoubtedly served as a source of celestial wonder to residents of the Southern Hemisphere since the dawn of civilization. Even so, this cloud and its companion, the Small Magellanic Cloud, are named for the sixteenth-century Portuguese voyager Ferdinand Magellan, whose round-the-world expedition first brought word of these giant fuzzy patches of light to the European civilizations in the Northern Hemisphere.

The Magellanic Clouds, called dwarf galaxies in all the textbooks, are gravitationally bound to the Milky Way; they not only slowly orbit our Galaxy, but also accompany it on its general trek through the cosmos. Yet, given the distance to the Large Cloud of roughly 150,000 light-years, some astronomers have begun to argue that we must reassess the status of these clouds as galaxies. A few of us feel that, since large quantities of invisible matter populate the darkness well beyond the outermost spiral arm, then perhaps these clouds are not deserving of the title *galaxy*, or even *dwarf galaxy*. Should this idea prevail, the Magellanic Clouds are merely rich clumps of galactic matter far from the Galaxy's center. Only further research, directed toward a more complete mapping of the full extent of the Milky Way's corona, will tell if these clouds are genuine galaxies or merely forlorn regions of star formation in an otherwise structureless halo.

THE HEART OF THE GALAXY

The exploration of the central regions of our Milky Way Galaxy, some 30,000 light-years from Earth, continues to be one of the most perplexing and fascinating areas of astronomical research. Although the core of our Galaxy is totally obscured by interstellar dust and thus cannot be studied with optical telescopes, radio and infrared observations of the innermost few hundred light-years have yielded spectacularly unexpected results. Data obtained during the past half-dozen years imply the presence of rapidly rotating hot gas, suggestive of a colossal whirlpool at the very heart of our Galaxy.

Much of the mystery surrounding the galactic center results largely from our inability to see it. The dark dust clouds within a few thousand light-years of our Sun effectively shroud what otherwise would be a stunning view of billions upon billions of stars tightly concentrated in and around the bulge of our Galaxy's midsection. To make matters worse, for those of us (including most professional astronomers) at mid-northerly latitudes, the constellation of Sagittarius, in which we find the nucleus of the Milky Way, rises no more than twenty degrees above Earth's horizon, granting precious little observing time for this most alluring area of our galactic home. Residents of the Southern Hemisphere, on the other hand, have long noted a dramatic richness associated with the Sagittarius region high overhead.

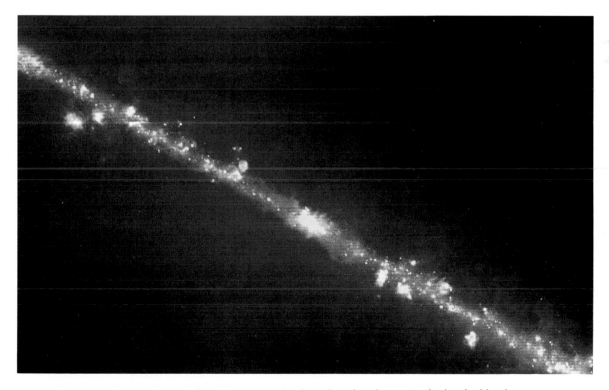

Image of the central part of the Milky Way as seen in the infrared with IRAS. The bright-blue knots are regions of hot gas and active star formation. Photo credit: JPL/Caltech/IPAC.

By capturing the infrared and radio radiation that is virtually unaffected by galactic debris, we have recently begun to explore the central regions of our Galaxy in some detail. Infrared observations indicate that the galactic-core environment harbors roughly a thousand stars per cubic light-year—a stellar density well over a million times that in our solar neighborhood. Had any planets been associated with these galactic-center stars, they would doubtless have been rapidly ripped from their orbits and obliterated, as the stars must experience frequent close encounters and even collisions. We also receive infrared radiation from what seems to be a hierarchy of warm clouds rich in dust in the central regions. By contrast, the radio emissions we receive from the center arise from relatively cool gas within interstellar clouds (50°C), as well as from hotter gas within nebulae (5,000°C) and myriad sites of loose galactic gas having lukewarm temperatures.

While the galactic center's mysteries are beginning to unravel by decoding radio and infrared observations, our understanding of this most intriguing galactic locale is still plagued by unexplained phenomena. Astronomers now have a fairly good "road map" of the innermost regions, but we have yet to understand the precise mechanisms at work there.

To help put our findings to date into a simplified perspective, imagine a series of six views, each centered on the Galaxy's core and each increasing in resolution by a power of ten: The first visualization, conceived from a considerable distance beyond the Magellanic Clouds and directly above the plane of the Milky Way, renders the full Galaxy's morphology—its spiral arms of stars, gas, and dust; its compact, bright nucleus; and its extensive, invisible halo. The scale of this initial mental image measures some 300,000 light-years across. The second view, still centered on the core but magnified by a factor of ten, spans 30,000 light-years and is highlighted by the great circular sweep of the interior spiral arm. Moving yet another order of magnitude closer, the third frame depicts a ring of matter made mostly of giant molecular clouds and gaseous nebulae, each a few light-years in average size; this entire flattened, circular feature, about a thousand light-years in diameter, rotates rapidly (with speeds around one hundred miles per second) and is also known to be expanding (at a comparable velocity) away from the center—as though it were a cosmic version of a smoke ring released from the mouth of a successful, cigar-puffing businessman.

The next frame, now some 300 light-years across, is filled by a pinkish ionized cloudiness surrounding the reddish heart of the Galaxy. (We infer the regions' colors, despite their invisibility, from their temperature and density.) The source of energy producing this vast cloud of plasma is currently unknown, as is the case for the expanding ring in the previous frame, though the two may be related. The penultimate image, spanning 30 light-years, depicts a tilted, spinning whirlpool of hot (10,000°C) gas that marks the core environment of the Galaxy. The innermost sanctum of this gigantic whirlpool dominates our final visualization (now a few light-years across), where a swiftly spinning, white-hot disk of superheated (1,000,000°C) gas nearly engulfs an enormously massive object that is, at the same time, too small in size to be pictured (even as a minute dot) on this, the finest of our six scales. We shall return to this mysterious object in a moment.

The consensus among astronomers today is that the galactic center is an explosive region—and one quite unlike anything discovered anywhere else in our Galaxy. The best evidence for the explosiveness is the ring of matter noted above to have been expelled from the center with relatively high velocity. Based on the observed expansion velocity of that ring, we can surmise that a major explosion probably occurred at or near the Galaxy's nucleus some 10 million years ago. The violence must have been considerable, since estimates for the amount of matter now in the ring average 100 million times the mass of our Sun. Other suggestive, though less well documented, observational evidence for additional rings of matter at differing distances imply that titanic explosions might be regular phenomena at the center of our Galaxy.

The problem—or the mystery—concerns the cause of the explosions. Whence might the explosive energy arise? What is the source of the violence capable of sending *100 million* solar masses hurtling outward toward the galactic suburbs? We can only speculate about the answers at this time, but a leading contender for the cause of the violence is a supermassive *black hole*, millions

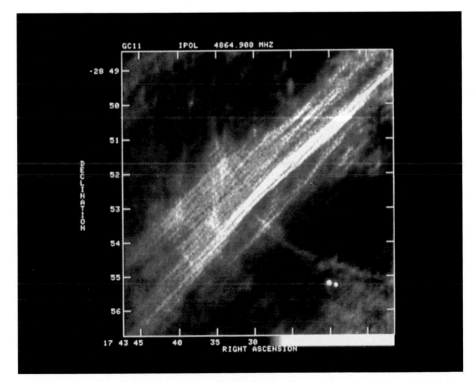

Sagittarius A, the radio source that marks the center of our galaxy, roughly 30,000 light-years away. False-color radiograph taken with the Very Large Array telescope. Observers: F. Yusef-Zadeh, M. R. Morris, D. R. Chance; photo courtesy of NRAO/AUI.

of times more massive than our Sun. Not that the hole itself need be emitting matter and energy (lest it violate the best ideas about black holes, which are explained in more detail in William Kaufmann's chapter). Instead, our ideas focus on the vast disk or doughnut of material being drawn toward the hole by its enormous gravity. The outer parts of such a region might regularly experience gravitational instabilities as in-falling matter accumulates, possibly causing periodic expulsions every 10 million years or so—a galactic quake of sorts.

A key factor in this research, drawn from both radio and infrared observations, strongly implies that the gas in the galactic center is spinning much faster than we expected when we simply extrapolated the movement of the well-studied matter in the suburbs of the Galaxy. The observations show a dramatic rise in rotational velocity toward the center. Apparently, the very heart of the Milky Way is spinning furiously; the closer we probe toward the very core, the faster the matter there swirls, much like a whirlpool of water approaching a drain.

This discovery was quite a surprise to observers and theorists alike, not least because of a simple yet perplexing problem: How does such a vast galactic whirlpool maintain its structural integrity? After all, regions of rapidly rotating matter produce strong outward (centrifugal) forces tending to push the gas away, much like those casting mud from the edge of a spinning bicycle wheel. Unless some other force pulls back on the galactic-center whirlpool, its gas should be flung into the outer parts of the Galaxy. How can such a huge vortex of matter remain intact without breaking apart and dispersing its contents? After eliminating a long shopping list of possibilities, very strong gravity seems to be the only viable way to hold together such a huge quantity of matter.

A simplified model capable of accounting for most of the bulk features of the galactic center calls for a (hundred square light-year) region of hot, thin ionized gas to surround a much smaller core of hotter, denser gas. This inner core, around which the gas we can observe swirls, is thought to contain—and this is the punch line—a tremendously compact object housing as much mass as 5 million Suns, all packed into a region hardly larger than our solar system. Why so much mass? Because this is the amount needed for gravity to keep the whirlpool of gas from dispersing. Such a model permits (in fact requires) an increase in gas velocity toward the galactic center, in reasonably good agreement with the observed data.

Though the details are understandably controversial at this time, many astronomers now agree that a supermassive, ultracompact "something" resides in the very center of the Milky Way Galaxy. And since its mass is much too large to be any sort of ordinary star or star remnant, and the observations could not easily be explained by an anomalously rich star cluster, the hub of our Galaxy would seem to be a huge black hole in space.

If our knowledge of the galactic center seems sketchy, that's because it *is* sketchy. Frankly, as noted at the outset of this chapter, astronomers are still learning to grope in the dark, literally, to sift through the clues hidden within invisible radiation. In particular, we are only beginning to appreciate the full magnitude of this entirely novel realm deep in the heart of the Milky Way. It is in this sense that our research should perhaps not yet be judged as mature science. Rather, it resembles exploration—but absolutely fascinating exploration enabling us to return from our telescopes with tales of grand monuments at the core of our galactic system.

Perhaps Robert Frost best anticipated our quandary long before the invention of the radio and infrared equipment now used to probe our Galaxy's heart:

> We dance 'round in a ring and suppose,
> But the Secret sits in the middle and knows.

Despite the apparent diversity of the topics surveyed in this chapter, our studies of the Milky Way Galaxy will continue to address a unifying theme: the varying interrelationships among the many components of galactic matter. Comprising nothing less than a "galactic ecosystem," the evolutionary balance between these components might be as complex as that of life in a tidepool or a tropical forest. And, as we have seen, only by being receptive to information from the Milky Way in all the electromagnetic wavelength bands in which it chooses to radiate can we hope to understand some of nature's unearthly phenomena within our Galaxy.

The topics I chose for discussion here are but a few of the issues that astronomers are grappling with today and that will drive Milky Way research during the next decade. Whatever progress is made, we can be virtually certain that the new instruments scientists construct to address these issues will also reveal completely unsuspected phenomena in our Galaxy. From the time of Galileo himself, surprise has been among the hallmarks—and pleasures—of astronomy.

MANDIKINI

GREGORY BENFORD

THINGS WERE GOING FINE until Hard Ella landed on a Snout.

She had jumped from the far rocky ridgeline, tumbling slowly to give her inbody scanners a look at the distant terrain.

"Nosee sunflowers," she had reported over comm, and headed down for her bounce in a long, lazy arc.

The Snout must have sensed her coming. Snouts had surface sensors and had adapted on this world to a lot of airborne traffic.

Black Sam saw her hit, her shocks smoothly compressing—and the ground broke open.

She shrieked, a thin high cry of surprise hardening into fear. Her left shock stopped its accordion fold and locked firm, throwing her sideways as the brown soil split like a vast cynical smirk.

She flailed to her right and locked that shock too. Something whipped out of the widening ground-grin and wrapped around her left foot-armor.

"Naysay! Don't loft!" Black Sam called. "You'll tear off a leg."

And die, he thought. They were too far from a Casa to get her medical help in time.

He kicked his power-pack into override and shot along the terrain, letting his downlook skate for him as fast as it could. Hard Ella's ceramic body-armor arms chopped futilely at the spindly tongues that grabbed at her legs.

Hard Ella spat out words between deep, strained gasps. "I can't—damn!—break its—"

"Hammer your shocks open," Shagfoot yelled. He was ten klicks away and no use, but Black Sam yelped agreement with his advice.

The Snout broke its granitic cover and surged free. It was angular and scarred from its perpetual burrowing after metals. Ports popped open on both sides of a rusty, tapered nose. Polished blue lenses peered at its catch with a gaze much like a real creature's.

48

The analogy with animal forms was false: The nose was a fan-drill, and smelled nothing. Its rear drum-dishes saw sonic pulses, nothing optical at all. The articulating wormlike tendrils were fashioned to intrude into the cracks of deep rockbeds, not to pluck and eat. But that did not lessen Black Sam's instant impression that Hard Ella was caught in the maw of a huge, lumbering beast of burnished hide and grasping feelers.

Black Sam knew that some of the Snout's ports were cluster-perceptors that tasted the dim infrared far better than they did bright sunlight's blare. The Snout would detect his approaching jet flame then, and turn this way.

"I'm coming in!"

Acceleration kicked him in the back. Black Sam felt a moment of reeling dizziness, the sensation that he was in fact falling straight down the side of a massive building.

The Snout coiled its nose toward him.

As the steel-ribbed thing diverted its attention, he deliberately triggered his jet exhaust into overload.

Fuel jammed. The chamber squeezed, belched.

A thick wad of incandescent crimson rage spat behind him, throwing Black Sam up into the green-streaming sky. His wake billowed into Snout-blinding brilliance.

"What the—" Shagfoot yelled.

"I'm coming in with a cut!" Black Sam called.

Hard Ella was groaning with effort, thrashing against the Snout. Black Sam turned and plunged downward. The Snout would take a few seconds to decipher the overloads he had given it—a sonic boom for its acoustics, the crimson glare for its infrareds.

He slammed onto the Snout's ribbed mainbeam. Plates buckled under his shocks, just behind its infra-eyes.

Black Sam thumbed over his cutter and carved a neat circle around Hard Ella. The Snout bucked, trying to shake him off. It had just grasped a morsel of Hard Ella's suit—high-grade alloys—and thought some other ore-sniffer was trying to snatch the prize away.

No time to convince it otherwise. Black Sam sent quick spokes of cutter-jab into the exposed circuitry near his boots. Components sizzled. The Snout bucked again, hard. It reached for him with its coiling black snakelike flex-borers.

But Hard Ella was free. Black Sam's cutter had sheared away the ore-seekers. She took a quick step off the Snout's acoustic dish, to get clear of reflected backwash, and hit her thrust bottles. Black Sam got away, too, as she shot into the sky.

He burned away from there on full bore. There was a small icy spot in the center of his back—the chill of fear. It came every time he cut away from a fight with a mech.

If the Snout unlimbered electron-beam defenses, he knew it always aimed for the spine. Snouts didn't know much about humans. They did recognize a bipedal morphology, though, with a central neural axis. Snouts would figure he was just an adapted form that hung its primary limbs and subunits from the long spine.

Which was a halfway decent description, except that it left out the fact that he was alive, not a machine. So the Snout would go for the most exposed vital part, figuring the central axis would be shielded with polycarbon but still vulnerable to a shock-impact weapon.

If it came, the bolt would be pulse-compressed, designed for max shock stress at the spine. Black Sam felt the icy circle move downward as he vectored over, pushing at high ram for the hills.

Nothing came.

Not that he would ever register it. The electron beam pulse would turn his organs to jelly before his neurons got the story.

When he cleared the ridgeline he swooped down behind the first slag mound. A shot whooshed by overhead, the air crackling in its wake.

"Missed me!" he called, though he knew no Snout bothered to understand humanspeak.

He ignored a Rooter chugging away at a glassy heap of waste nearby, seeking some alloy. He realized he had been holding his breath, and panted, searching the sky. Purple worms crawled at the edges of his eyes.

There was Hard Ella, scooting for the far mountains. She hadn't said a word, just kept on riding her amber flame toward their regroup point.

Against the flowing ivory fluorescence of the void above, she was a dark mote. The streaming gossamer river hung in the blueblack sky, the Mandikini. It seemed that she was already in its billowing currents, voyaging.

The Snout was a mere passing incident to her. She sought the great turbulent swells above, relentlessly.

Snouts were bad, but not the worst. She had been lucky.

And getting away had used up scarce suit supplies without yielding a single clue about where sunflower fields were.

Black Sam didn't want to bring it up that night, when they and the others of the family lay sprawled and sated in the Trough.

"Maybe should go back, track that Snout," he said carefully.

Hard Ella shook her head quickly, shiny black curls tumbling in the low gravity. "Nosir noway!"

"Might have some them actuators." Black Sam sucked on a chem feeder.

"Why?"

" 'Member that Snout lasyear? Ripe full of 'em."

"Heyno I say," Shagfoot interrupted. He rolled over, grunting, crimping his chem leads but not noticing. "Th' Snout was carryin' for t'others.

'Member?—actuators all in pouch. Enough actuators in 'im for hunnert Snouts.''

Black Sam rubbed his stubbly beard, tasted the cloying sweetpap he had scrounged for supper. ''You're guessin'.''

''So's you.'' Shagfoot cracked a gleeful grin.

Black Sam leaned back, tired. He didn't have much stomach for an argument. He intended to enjoy this place while he could.

After the Snout trouble, they'd found this Trough, tucked back in an old gully. It was old but still in use. The big moly-alloy doors had been crimped in by something outsized. Six of them had ventured in, scampering like mice through the rows of vats and repair modules and iron-ribbed casements. Nobody knew what half the gear did. But the place was empty, which is all they had to know right now.

The Marauder-class machines sometimes stopped in at Troughs to resupply themselves with crude chemical foods, or get their limbs lubed, or clip in components. If none came for ten thousand years—and Black Sam had seen some Troughs where that was so—the air would still reek of coarse wheat, the auto displays still offer themselves, electrical auras continue to entice vagrant machines.

Troughs were immortal. Some said they were made by the first crude machine civilizations to come to the center of the galaxy, and were a kind of fossil. Others argued that Troughs filled a function, or else would have been wiped out by natural selection.

Black Sam and Hard Ella and Shagfoot had considered none of this. They first reconned the broad pitted plain outside, baked hard by its blue sun. There were no Snouts or Trompers or Wigglies in the neighborhood. Or so Shagfoot said—he carried the 'tector gear. They made sure no machines were docked inside the Trough. There was some risk, but they were bone-tired. They decided to lay up in it for at least a night.

So they unsuited, relaxed. Hard Ella found a vat of sweet yeasting stuff, its foamy yellow head rich in protein. Wigglies usually ingested chem foods, to nourish the bioparts they had inside. Trompers used the Troughs' blue-green lichen, which grew in long strands from the high, arched ceiling. Shagfoot said Snouts had living poly-bind joints, and ate big slabs of mossy black stuff to replace their abraded tissues.

There was no reason humans couldn't get some good from the stuff, even if the milky dark yeast drink tasted like fried, salted grease.

''Crap-pap,'' Black Sam said finally, spitting out some. It stained Shagfoot's overalls tar-black.

''You break, you fix,'' Shagfoot said, too zotted on extenso-bread to care. He shucked off his grimy overalls, grinning, and tossed them to Black Sam.

''Gotta go back to a Casa,'' Black Sam said. Casas had true food, designed for humans by the Dads. But Casas were rare, ancient. ''Can't drink this slop an' hunt sunflowers all day.''

"Have to," Hard Ella said cuttingly. "We're down to maybe a kilo of Kickers."

Without Kickers as stimulants, they couldn't respond to crises, like the Snout. And the last Casa they'd been in had run out of Kickers, would take ten days to regrow a new batch.

"Better us get on sunflower, fast," one of the Brothers said lazily.

Black Sam nodded, feeling woozy from fatigue, but prickly too. Something was sending up warning flares in the back of his mind, but he couldn't tell what, yet. "Maybe we should break up, hunt in wider circles," he said carefully. "Better odds—"

"Family stay together—that Dadsay!" Hard Ella's clipped words made other Brothers and Sisters sit up, weave back from their private visions. Most were jacked into 'tainment cubes, drifting on visions a millennium old.

"Dadsay, not allsay," Black Sam put it squarely. It was one thing to follow the advice of their revered and longdead fathers, for that encoded advice had kept them alive now for years upon years. But it was another to not think for yourself. Black Sam said all this rapidly, not letting Hard Ella interrupt, and finished: "Is now time for wesay!"

"Black Sam stand for Dad?" Hard Ella asked bitingly.

"I say things flat," Black Sam answered, looking around at the Family, making eye contact to see if they were with him. "No need you walk on them."

"Call vote?" Hard Ella asked.

"Nosir!"

"Want replace Dad with Black Sam?" she persisted slyly.

"Sometimes allsay better than Dadsay. We find no sunflower, we eat in crap-pap Trough for another season."

Nobody took those words easily. They remembered the days of living in Casas, those tunneled-out places left by the Dads of days before—times stretching back centuries, to the era when men had walked large in the center of the galaxy, been lords of the streaming energies that laced the sky.

Now they were reduced to scattered tribes, the wandering Families. New breeds of self-building machines had moved from star to star near the galactic center, hopping easily among the closely orbiting worlds. The machines sought more materials to build themselves, expanding by Darwinian pressures into the energy-rich lands that once had been held by men.

Some of the Dads said that the new machines had always been in the Center, were far more ancient than men and women. The tale was that the massive Trompers and vast Lectors had been gone for a thousand years, working in close to the black hole that was the true dark source of the Center. The machines had labored there to change the disk of accreting dust and gas, to fashion it to intelligent—that is, machine—uses.

To all this, humanity was incidental, unimportant.

Black Sam could not judge the wisdom of the Dads, but he knew how hard

B.E. JOHNSON

things had been the last few years. The black hole that chewed its diet of dust only a few light-years away was waxing again, blooming blue-hot, poking a glaring hole in the sky. Streamers broke from it, gouges of orange and jet-yellow. Black Sam had watched these flame-spikes strike their world's upper atmosphere, spreading desolation.

They called their planet Berg, for reasons known only to the Dads. Once it had provided rich loam and water. Now the searing Eater in the sky baked all to dust, and the Families rummaged their own once-rich lands for food.

Humans had lived in balance with the machines for a millennium, as testified by the ancient Troughs. But now the mechs spread everywhere, devouring.

"Yousay not wise," Hard Ella said sardonically.

"Sometimes is onlysay," Black Sam said, trying to keep his voice flat and calm, because that was the way to beat her.

She was older, had been raised by Dad and Mom to lead. The Family knew that. But she wavered at the hard moments, sometimes, and they knew that too.

"We stick, we hold," Hard Ella said.

"Stick and starve," Black Sam began. "If we search wider, find—"

Then a faint tinny sound came and he knew what had alerted him. Something coming.

"Flank it!" he whispered.

The others roused instantly from their stupors, bone-tiredness swept away on an electric adrenal surge.

The inky bays of the vast old Trough held a thousand hiding places. The Family faded into them, weapons plucked from their clips.

Black Sam had kept his hydraulic boots on. He leaped for the high girders. He landed amid flakes of rust and the worn-out blue foam carcasses. He hunkered down and aimed a ramrod launcher at the main corridor.

Down the shrouded lane came something slick. It had a narrow ferret head and was folding its shiny wings as it scurried. Black Sam recognized the sectioned, tapered body: a Crafter.

No need to be careful with it. It could fight well if alerted, but here, boxed in . . .

A blue bolt struck it in the side. Black Sam fired an instant later, driving an iron bar into its hind shank.

It reared, tried to unfold its wings, spun its treads with frantic energy—and died.

They picked it clean in minutes, yanking free plates and servos, booty used to maintain their own suits.

Black Sam didn't care for the obvious; he had aimed his ramrod for a vital choke-point in the circuitry. While the others scavenged, he carefully shut down the Crafter inboard cyber-defense mechanisms, so the thing could not fry its own memory. The Crafters had long ago evolved internal circuits to protect their own expertise, from men and rival machines alike. The dead took their secrets with them.

"Read the mechsay," Hard Ella ordered.

"Have." Black Sam cut away an ebony board of chips he could use.

"Goodsay?"

"No map. Only senso-memory."

"Damn!" Hard Ella lost her careful air of leadership, smacked the Crafter's polished manifold with her palm.

"Can read, though." Black Sam smiled, eyes twinkling.

"Do."

"Have."

Suspiciously: "And . . . ?"

"Last entries show valley. Big mountain in view."

"Can you—?"

Black Sam nodded. "Recognize it from three, four year back."

"So?"

"In one frame is sunflowers."

They vectored in along five axes, to confuse any defenses. But there were no Lancers or Zappers on duty, and nothing rose to meet them.

Probably because the sunflower field was just beginning. Dutiful crawlers hauled raw materials in from distant mines. Drones ran the makeshift factories which reduced the ore. Crafters fashioned it into silicon platelets, boron circuitry, electroplated capacitors, slick Mylar sheets, orange sealant cores.

At the center of this blur of activity were spindly, wasplike mechs. They assembled the flowers: great fields of yellow rectangles, marching remorselessly to the horizon.

The Family invaded each autofactory, kicking in doors, searching for supervisors. The few they found had no defenses. The mechs froze in rigid, comic postures when Shagfoot fried them with crackling storms of microwave noise.

"Easy," Hard Ella said, her voice confident as they crossed the parched valley.

"For a while," Black Sam said. He eyed the horizon uneasily.

The intricate system of roving mechs, laboring Crafters and endlessly varied functionaries—all this was guided by an unseen hand, the overmind of the planet. Or so said the Dadspeak, when the Family tapped into it.

Black Sam doubted that the overmind still controlled all the machines. The returning robo-horde from the black hole had brought rogue breeds with special functions. They roved and worked, following their own unspoken drives.

"Somebody'll send malf-tenders to fix this field," Black Sam said.

"Not before we're fargone," she answered crisply. "Come on!"

The flowers were high-efficiency energy-storing panels. They did not trap the solar light that fell on Berg from its waxing blue-green star, as would ordinary panels. Instead, they were fashioned to harvest the electron flux of the streaming silvery river overhead.

For this was the huge project the Dads had long spoken of: to harness the great reservoir of energy that flowed a short distance farther from the sun. The overmind had known of the ripening of the Eater, and of the plasma jets that spewed out from it. Everywhere on Berg, mechs hastened to partake of it.

Hard Ella had driven the Family to try to sup some trickle of the wealth to come. They were mere humans, no match for the vast strength and knowledge of the machine armies. But once they lofted into the prickly light of the great currents above—the Mandikini, the Dads called it, an old Earther word for an ancient river of water—then there were swarming riches to plunder.

To hijack. To give them back some shred of their dignity, in a world where machines regarded humans as mere irksome vermin.

Black Sam labored with the others. It was hard grunt work, and they were afraid at every moment that a bright plume would flare in the sky, and Lancers descend to run riot.

They had to put together a ship that could carry them into high orbit around Berg. They broke some Crafter hulls down into parts, attached launcher pods from a half-built hulk nearby, and worked a hundred routine miracles—all in a passing day.

Black Sam had no clear idea of exactly how the mech ecology of Berg used the sunflowers. The Dadsay spoke of times when the Eater blossomed in the sky, and was answered by sunflowers of Berg. The sunflowers were lofted into the ivory flux of relativistic electrons—churning vortices that swept by Berg— to intercept some small fraction of that flow. Somehow the consuming energies of the Great River aloft were harnessed by the sunflowers, and their wealth conveyed down to the mechs of Berg; but the Dads knew not how, or at least left nothing in the Dadspeak to instruct their children.

"Think you of how we plunder, once we walk the sky?" Shagfoot asked Black Sam as they worked.

"A little."

"And Hard Ella?"

"What of her?" Black Sam was tired, irritable.

"She'll knownot until we get there, I guess."

"We must plan!" Black Sam slapped two cowlings together and popped the interlacings, finishing a hull seam.

"No time!" Shagfoot's face crinkled with wry mirth, as though he had seen everything before in his long life and was only amused by the torments of their rude, low existence. Black Sam wished he had some of that quality. He could not forget the glories of the time of the Dads. He hungered for it.

"We must revive Berg," he said solemnly.

"Berg is vast. Know you that it was once covered in ice?"

Black Sam frowned, scoffed. "Nonsense!"

"I saw a frame of it—ancient, venerable time." Shagfoot traced figures in the air with his gloved hands, eyes rapt. "Sheets of ice wrapped all, but for a tawny belt at our world's belly girth."

"No ice now," Black Sam said doubtfully.

Suddenly sad, Shagfoot murmured, "Yea, the Eater waxes. Our star swoops near its hungry maw. When I was a thin-legged boy, the sky blazed with myriad star-points, jewels scattered in oil. Now the Eater flares. It blares across the night sky with its forked jets. The stars are dim beside it. Our ice is spoiled vapor, longgone. Berg will be a baked stone, ere I die."

This was the longest speech Black Sam had ever heard the tough old man give. Some wellspring had spouted free after decades of running slow and silent beneath hard ground.

"If we tap the Mandikini—"

"We shall not eat Hard Ella's dreams."

"Once we're up there—"

"Mere gestures, we make." Shagfoot's voice was suddenly bitter, dry. He turned away to reprogram a small labor-robot, his face once more a weathered almond mask. The wellspring was capped.

They lifted just in time.

The Family vectored aloft in two separate launcher pods, orange flames pressing them skyward.

As they roared free, three blunt cylinders glided after them: Lancers. Swift death.

Only when Shagfoot ran their burn at the danger level did they leap ahead of the pursuers, gain the momentum to outrun the yellow nuclear fireballs that burst and licked aft of them.

The Family seared and blackened their ships' acceleration chambers. They rose from Berg and thrust toward the shimmering veil of the Mandikini.

Then came the sunflower blossoming. Their stolen labor-robots had dutifully arrayed tall stacks of the sunflowers, all hinged and stored with that endless pinpoint care that marked the machines' handiwork. Humans had long abandoned hope of matching the mechs' craft and energy, their bountiful, forgetful wealth. All they could do was snatch fragments of it.

At Hard Ella's order, the sunflowers unfolded. Great fans of them sprung from the Family's ships, yellow motes blossoming in the blackness.

The Family waited. Hard Ella spoke little, though her teeth ground behind a working, muscled jaw.

At first the winds of Mandikini blew softly, a mere brush in vacuum.

In a day more, they strummed through the Family's ships.

Inside, the air thickened with oil and sweat.

Food ran out.

The Mandikini's voice rose. Deep bass notes ran the length of the ships, like the callings of great gray beasts.

Plates and bulkheads groaned. The gauzy wires that laced the sunflowers ran bright with surges of energy. Red lightning danced along them.

Hard Ella saw the truth first.

"The sunflowers—they harness the electrical currents of the River." She laughed. "Of course! The Eater! The thickening dust-disk that orbits it—that forms a turning dynamo."

"And calls up currents?" Shagfoot disbelieved, eyes crinkling.

"The Eater loosens electrons into its Mandikini. The outward flowing child-stream steals volts and amps and all the zoo of things electrical." Hard Ella spoke rhythmically, almost like a chant.

She invoked the names of quantities the Family knew as entities, not measures. Long centuries of hardship and defeat had hammered their once-bounteous heritage of knowledge into flat, firm rules of thumb.

The Families of Berg had long since reduced the knowledge of science to a set of animated guides, pictures, projections of the human need to animate the world with understandable cause. The mechs were driven by sciences which the Family saw as spirits, unfathomable. Their understanding of the world was precise and detailed, yet did not use the impersonal landscape of the ancient quantitative lore. Electrons were tiny beasts who willed the motions of larger beasts; such was obvious.

Black Sam frowned. "So the sunflowers tap . . ."

"And would return their bounty to Berg," she said jubilantly, vindicated.

"Lucky we, who have made a craft of stealing," Shagfoot said with his worn smile.

"This is yesway, I say," Hard Ella boasted.

"We can tap this fountain from the Eater?" Black Sam asked wonderingly.

"Can! Must!" Hard Ella's eyes narrowed with stern authority.

But Shagfoot only snorted. "Berg needs ticklings of water, not the dance of electron-beasts."

Hard Ella bristled. "We take first riches first."

"May be last," Shagfoot said mildly.

"You challenge my rule?" she demanded.

"Naysay, victor." Shagfoot pointed a stubby finger at the screens, where the shadows of worlds and ships glided, their own centermost. "But glance you."

Hard Ella gasped. Black Sam nodded grimly, his suspicions confirmed.

Black blobs swelled ahead.

"The swimmers of this river draw us near," Black Sam said. "We are small enough to swallow."

And something in him relished the coming of these huge beings, these mountain-minds in the sky he had heard of from the old, weathered Dadspeaks. Something in him wanted to see such massed purpose, no matter what the cost.

The thing that swallowed them was a luminous, perfectly circular disk, cut through at the center by a spiky, bristling tower.

Its axis harvested glimmering, racing arcs which shot across the plain in phosphorescent waves. Webs of green spiraled inward to the tower, carrying something unknown, some alien product made for a machine civilization which was as incomprehensible to the Family as was a whirling helicopter to a cringing field rat.

The light-encrusted central tower jutted hundreds of kilometers above them. Huge web antennas poked at distant star-targets. And in the distance glowed the forking Mandikini flux, silent and ivory and somehow spongy, soft.

Their tiny elliptical ships seemed sucked across the plain by luminous traceries. Their walls crackled; the battered deck heaved like something roused from sleep.

"The Dadspeak sotold, once," Black Sam whispered.

They had gathered before the swell-screen, the Family mute and staring.

"I heard no hotspeak of such craft," Hard Ella said, her voice bone-bare and trembling.

Shagfoot laughed dryly. "Described, it was. But only by Dads about to go down its gullet."

"We must escape," Hard Ella said.

Black Sam studied her for a moment, for once could see behind her hard carapace of training. She had always held herself apart. He had thought she was following the primacy of command, an aloof exactness. But now he sensed the real cause.

The Dads drove her, through their ancient encrypted voices. And as well through the Aspects they could cast upon her, through the tap-in drodes which fitted into her helmet.

The Family took the presence of the Dads as a welcome legacy, a vital link to stored knowledge. But Black Sam suddenly saw that the Dads jerked strings in Hard Ella, made her dance to their musty programs. Knowledge was imperative. Her face was rigid, a wall behind which old furies raged. She held vast energies in check. With them she guided the Family, even now in its ever-dwindling numbers.

Once there had been more than two hundred in the Family. But time had whittled them down. They numbered a mere seventy-three now.

Deaths had come from a thousand sources:

Mechs who hunted organic forms.

Accidents among the tattered, gilded cities left by unknown machine societies.

Simple mind-blow, from jacking into cyberspaces which no stunted human brain could navigate.

And machine-made diseases, in water or food among the old ruins, like poison left for vagrant animals.

The Family had suffered, had withstood losses, was now a mere echo of its old self. Their sure slide had begun when they left their comfortable haunts, driven by encroaching mechs and by the whisperings of the Dadspeak.

Black Sam paced with undirected anger, jamming his fists into his jacket pockets, face raw from the cold of the cabin.

All the pain, all the loss . . . he felt it flood through him.

All to restore Berg to watery life, to bring again the moist glory of the Dadtime.

Hard Ella was talking, describing ways to slip free of the flickering forces that clasped their ships.

"These beings, they'll expect that," Black Sam said suddenly.

"So? We vex and fight them," Hard Ella barked. "Say I!"

"Would not better to zag against their zig?" Black Sam said calmly.

"Black Sam fears these river-drinkers?" Hard Ella taunted.

"Naysay," Black Sam said, gesturing at Shagfoot for confirmation. "But why struggle now? Wait until they draw us in, think us dead craft."

"I . . ." Hard Ella frowned, confused as if by inner crosstalk.

"Lie doggo," Shagfoot murmured. "Many times, I have."

Hard Ella confronted the Family. But heads turned away, pretending to study the shifting lux-screens. Black Sam saw that they were awed by the vast sparkling landscapes surrounding their puny ship, and felt in their bones the brooding strangeness outside. Hard Ella began to speak to them of their warrior legacy, of battles fought against Lancers and Divers, of great dead deeds.

But Black Sam glimpsed in the Family their true nature, after generations of being hammered down by relentless mechs and the raw wind of the splintered sky. They were things that scurried now, not zestful hunters.

They could regain the legacy—Black Sam was sure of that. Not by listening to the hard sure voice of Hard Ella, but by experience alone. The time for talk was past.

"I yeasay we doggo," he broke into Hard Ella's orders. "What says the Family?"

They hesitated, glanced guiltily at one another, gathered shreds of courage. In each face lurked the wan, scurrying bravery of the sought, the hunted.

Their halting chorus held a tinge of hope.

"Yea."

"Must."

"The Dads would nod, I knowso."

"Yea, yea, yea."

Their ships' hulls worked with fine-spun traceries of violet as the tower drew them into itself.

Low bass notes sounded. Metal rang.

Something felt for purchase on the outer skin.

Across the glimmering alien plain, Black Sam saw the crescent of Berg rise. He was shocked at this first full sight of his home world. This was not the Berg he held in his mind's eye, not the rich verdant land.

Hard Ella rasped impatiently: "Let's go out the aft lock."

Shagfoot shook his head, took a belaying torch from a young man. "They'll have wrapped them in that green soft ply. Remember how Obie died?"

Hard Ella pressed her mouth into a firm white line. "That was on Berg. Here—"

"They're smarter. Quicker. The Dads knew that." Shagfoot took the torch and began shearing through ribbed support girders.

"You'll carve up our ship?" Hard Ella demanded.

Shagfoot murmured simply, "Must."

Hard Ella opened her mouth, then closed it slowly, reluctantly. Respect for Shagfoot flickered in her face. She stood aside.

Shagfoot began. But before the white-hot glare cut full through the metal, he turned to Black Sam. "There were things that carved the air of Berg once," he said in a voice of gravel. "Like us. Organics. They waved themselves in air and flew."

"Yeasay? No! Impossible."

"Was so. No mech could do that." Shagfoot frowned, remembering. "The Dads called it *bird*. So it may be with this place. It is like a bird too."

Black Sam shook his head, seeing nothing in the words. Shagfoot shrugged and turned to make the cut.

"Once I'm outside, I'll go up," Black Sam whispered on comm. "Send five Family down, then cut around toward that V-hatch, the one we saw coming in."

The ship's hull separated raggedly, servo-bolts popping under the wrenching forces.

Black Sam slipped out and veered wildly. Something shot at him and missed, wreathing the whole hull with golden fire.

He sped around a huge cylinder. It was lined with parabolic bowls, and in the distance tiny robots labored.

Airless, silent, the metallic landscape rose against the distant hard black. Black Sam wheezed, tasting the tired suit air. He allowed himself a high-oxygen gasp, then got himself under control.

The tower was even larger than they had estimated. He could see it curve away, and under max mag of his opticals could make out ident-patches on the more distant robots. The tower was at least ten kilometers around, probably more. Ten antennas ringed the tower, each far larger than the makeshift human ships.

He flew over a team of mechs, who launched themselves at him. He threw tolo-twine and caught them mid-waist. The program tripped in upon contact, boring into them with jammer signals, burning away their surface command structures.

In an instant the mechs forgot entirely the signals they were receiving from some command nexus. They struggled, and as Black Sam flew on, they followed the embedded command the twine sent and carefully untangled themselves from it.

As he touched down beside a lock with worn gasket seals, the twine retracted, sending him a confirming yelp of victory. It sounded like a dog, a creature Black Sam had never seen but knew once accompanied the Dads and fought with them. A dog had told the story of the Farnfax War in an old Aspect history, its voice a low growl in Black Sam's mind. Black Sam had wondered if the ancient dog-form truly had walked on four legs, like a mech.

Shagfoot met him, coming in hard and landing against a conveyor complex.

"Lost two women at the ship," Shagfoot said.

"How? We—"

But Shagfoot had already swept ahead. Black Sam tumbled into the lock after Shagfoot. As it sealed he saw Family spilling from their makeshift ships.

The two men dodged through C-shafts. Killer bursts of microwave spat at them from intersecting corridors, but they had shut down their inboard receivers. A mech always thought it could kill you with mech weapons, never believing that organic forms could shut out the electromagnetic spectrum and still function.

Shagfoot set a fast pace, two centuries of experience behind each move. Hard ceramic yellow greeted them as they entered a vast bowl. Black Sam had seen a design like this, in an ancient city made by spindly walker-type mechs. He stayed away from the center, where he knew fusion pellets sometimes blossomed into momentary suns, for some unknown purpose. Mechs swarmed at the far side of the bowl but they did not recognize the men immediately. By the time they did, Shagfoot had guided them through to another tunnel. Acceleration slammed Black Sam forward.

Ahead were convoluted conduits, wiring, huge slabs of machine rep units . . . and something Black Sam recognized.

"Is that . . . ?"

"Yea. The mainmind."

It took only moments to attach the charges he carried, find the right cables, and check it over carefully. Shagfoot called quick timing signals while he worked the hard part—the override inputs that would deflect incoming help. Even so, bolts snarled around them from distant mechs. Overloads arced along the cylinders and shafts, voltages seeking vulnerable human forms.

"Yeasay?" Black Sam called.

"Cut free!"

Black Sam ram-accelerated for the outer skin.

Behind him came a high whine—

—a *crump* he felt through his suit—

—and then a sudden silence. He realized he had been in a bath of suppressor electronics signals for the entire time inside the tower, and now they had ceased.

"Shagfoot!"

"Behind you."

"There's something following."

"Yeasay."

"It's fast!"

"I think I can—"

"This way."

"Wait, I—"

Black Sam came clear of the tower as blue flames licked from the tunnel behind him. He knew nothing could oxidize in this vacuum, but the escaping gases yielded up their stored energy with a dancing, fitful radiance. They forked out behind him, ghostly arms reaching for something to scorch.

And drifting from the tunnel mouth, tumbling, came something the blue things had found.

Shagfoot had died without a parting sound. He spun in stately revolution, like a planet in a dying gyre. Black Sam approached. He saw within the carbon black that mercifully blanked the swollen, distended helmet, concealing the head which had exploded inside.

The giant clamper-arms that embraced the human ships were stilled, their jaws crimping the burnished steel.

They tapped into the racing communications of this vast plain and discovered that the mainmind was hurt, not killed. It was confused for a while. Yet the vast circle-world still roiled with collecting energies.

Black Sam landed on a scraped hull and watched waves gathering inward, enormous surges rushing with exact resonance to their concentric completion at the base of the vast tower.

He had fought now for hours, seen Family members blown to frags by pulses of energy he did not comprehend. It seemed this vast artifact was alive with sleeping resources, huge reservoirs of unfathomable wealth.

The man he had been was no more. He shook his head, still swamped with the strange things he had seen.

But he knew what it meant. Shagfoot had felt it too. Now Black Sam sensed something he could not easily put into words. Yet he knew what to do.

Hard Ella met him. Her boots clasped the hull with a ringing *clank*. "We

singsay our ceremony for Shagfoot when there is time. First we must consolidate, take—"

"The place is dead." Black Sam slowly reeled in coiling tolo-twine, his arms
heavy with fatigue.

"You've checked?"

"Yeafold, the whole tower."

"Those charges . . . "

"Shagfoot knew where to plant them, how to set. He remembered. From
the old times."

"The Dadspeak knows so much—"

"No Dadspeak!" Black Sam glowered, a slow anger building within his
seeping weariness. "Not them! *He* did it."

"Well, I know, but—"

"Nosay, you *no*say! Shagfoot walked a thousand dusty man-cities, a thousand more of the mech warrens. He learned the old mech ways and knew their
softnesses. *He.*"

"We honor him, like all Familyfolk. For now we must seize this place,
direct it to Berg."

"For what?"

"Open eyes! This station was built by alien minds, ones we nosee on Berg.
The mechs only service it."

"I know."

"These giant spokes that jut so"—she gestured at the spikes that bristled
from the tower—"they send radiations—I nosee what kind—to other mech-
worlds."

"So?"

"We can harvest them for Family! Use against Lancers, Divers—"

"None brings water."

Hard Ella said angrily, "The Dadspeak says this is first step!"

"Dadspeak dead."

The words fell between them with the weight of ages.

Hard Ella gaped. Her eyes clouded with her inner voices, ancient whispers.
"What . . .?"

Berg rose brown and rutted above the fruitful, wave-washed plain.

Black Sam stood upon a huge bulwark of speckled, time-worn polycarbon.
It was bigger than the two crude human-made ships that dangled from it on
shiny tethers, yet it was itself a mere small dab on the tower.

Black Sam had about half the Family at his back. The mechs he had com-
mandeered hovered nearby, their weapons ready.

Hard Ella shook her head. "I still cannot believe."

"We give you what we can." Black Sam said it without anger, for he was
sad but resolute.

"But you give us only these *ships*."

"And the supplies you can carry."

"We could have *Berg!* Our motherworld. See—"

Hard Ella swept her hands at the globe of Berg that brimmed beyond the plain. The Family had never seen their world save in the Dadspeak. But there it had been green, lush, with great lakes shimmering blue.

"Yeasay, *see*," Black Sam spat out bitterly. "A dried husk of a world. Not the fruit the Dadspeak said, but the pit of that fruit, now eaten. The Mandikini has baked it brown."

Hard Ella began grandly: "With energies such as this—"

"We could do battle with the Lancers, yeasay. Win Berg? I think you might. This vessel is big, powerful. But you will find no water in it. No water anywhere near the core of the galaxy, now that the Eater gnaws the sky. The Mandikini is the only river that flows in our time."

Hard Ella stood ramrod straight. She had lost the war of talk, the debate that had in the last two days persuaded the fraction of the Family behind Black Sam to remain with him. "You betray us," she said simply.

"You can always stay," Black Sam said mildly.

But he knew she had to return to Berg. The Dads spoke to her, through her. Their undying love for a lost Berg would resound forever through the Family. An old allegiance to lands and times forgot.

"I . . . I must return."

"And we must sail."

"For what?" She was all bitterness now.

"For what you seek. A planet rich and moist."

"We could have it in Berg!"

"The Eater will consume Berg in time. It will chew more stars, like the one it gobbles now. It will drive a steady storm of the biting, piercing radiations. In such a hail we cannot live."

"Surely—"

"No organic beings can. Berg will be left to the silicon-jacketed crawlers, the Crafters, the things of metal. Beings without remorse for the old wet time."

"There must be a way. . . . "

Black Sam put his hand on her shoulder and turned her gently to look at the brown disk rising. It cast a baleful light upon the iridescent wash that a billion panels made, a flood of unnamed energy. "We can use that to voyage. Direct the energies, ride the Madikini flux outward. That is what the beings who built this intended, I am sure of it. This is a starship, not a mere drone energy collector. If we can master it . . . "

He did not say the rest. Already he had learned to hold his visions to himself, to let them out in bits and pieces, lest he alarm the Family who stayed with him.

It must be possible for humans to escape the inferno of the galactic center.

Legend held that humanity had not been born here. Old tales, far back in the withered recesses of the Dadspeak, told of silvery ships that came in, riding splintered light. From where, even the Dadspeak had nosay.

Humanity could escape the Eater, *must* escape. That he knew.

As Berg's rutted face hung near, Hard Ella and her share of the Family began to enter the human ships. Hard Ella looked back once, sadly. Black Sam knew her Dadspeak was already fretting over how to use the resources they took, how to fashion such spirits for the transformation of Berg.

That was her destiny. But not his.

Black Sam looked upward. The Mandikini twisted and streamed beyond, heading outward. It was like a vast gauzy tapestry flown by the Eater, a flag, and if humanity was to endure in a galaxy given to vicious energies and implacable machines, he knew it must be their banner too.

STARS

ESSAY BY

MARTIN COHEN

SPECULATION BY

BEN BOVA

STAR BIRTH AND MATURITY

MARTIN COHEN

INTRODUCTION

To be a star is to know eternal stress. To live as a star is to walk a never-ending tightrope, knowing that there can be only one outcome—your fall. In this chapter we focus on stars, seeking to answer several critical questions. What do we mean by a "star" and where do stars come from? What is this balancing act and how does it shape stellar existence? What processes delineate the formation of a star and how did our seemingly constant Sun arise? And how did we and our solar system come about? All are readily posed, obvious questions, yet to how many of them can we only hazard an answer?

WHAT IS A STAR?

Quite simply, a star shines; that is, it is self-luminous, but not merely in the human-centered sense of radiating "light"—that tiny sliver of the entire electromagnetic spectrum to which our eyes happen to be sensitive. Any form of radiative energy output will suffice: for example, heat (or infrared) radiation. But simply giving off radiation is not enough to qualify a celestial body to be a star. Our giant planets Jupiter and Saturn generate their own energy internally, quite apart from the energy that they intercept from the Sun. Yet we do not refer to Jupiter as a star. Technically, it is a "failed star" because it will never have access to a crucial form of energy whose generation we may take as the main characteristic of a "mature" star like our Sun.

NUCLEAR FUSION

Mature stars shine by the same process of *nuclear fusion* that powers the most destructive weapons on Earth. When small nuclei fuse (or bind) together with great force, some of the substantial amount of energy that was in the form of matter can be released. In the Sun, for example, four separate nuclei of the simplest element, hydrogen, fuse together to make the nucleus of the next more complex element, helium. If we could "weigh" the resulting helium nucleus, we would find it actually weighed less than the four hydrogen nuclei with which the process began. Some of the mass has turned into energy.

Fusion is not an everyday occurrence, at least not in our lives on Earth. The reason for this is simple to see. A hydrogen nucleus is nothing more than a familiar proton, the subatomic building block with a positive charge. To bring four protons together is a significant challenge, since like charges repel—the closer the protons approach, the more they want to move apart! Only when they get extremely close will the more powerful nuclear force take over and bind them together.

It requires tremendous speed and density of material before the protons can be rammed into a helium unit—in a star such velocities are encountered only when the temperatures exceed 15 million degrees (on the absolute or Kelvin scale) or 27 million degrees Fahrenheit. Nature provides just such an inferno in the seething hot centers of stars. (It is an inferno humanity has only recently learned to duplicate—on a small scale—in our hydrogen bombs.)

How do the centers of stars become so hot? Although the Sun and other stars are balls of gas—no solid layer can be found within them—they are *vast* balls of gas. Our Sun, for example, contains enough material to make more than 300,000 Earths. The weight of such an enormous amount of mass exerts a prodigious pressure on the core of the Sun. As our star came together, this pressure from the overlying layers crushed the matter in the center together until the central temperature was hot enough for hydrogen to fuse.

Once fusion begins in the core of the star, the energy it generates can set up a counterpressure to balance the crushing force of gravity. But the star cannot permit itself even an instant of relaxation, of diminished temperature and pressure, or gravity will gain ground, squeezing the core even more fiercely

HOW LONG CAN A STAR LAST?

Hydrogen fusion in a stellar core offers a good bulwark against gravity as long as the fuel lasts—for some 10 billion years in the case of the Sun. Stars spend the bulk of their lives undergoing core hydrogen burning, thereby defining what astronomers call the *main sequence* (or *mainstream*) of typical stars. But gravity is relentless and when the central "fires" die down—as they must, since their fuel supply is always finite—gravity is there, waiting. The entire life cycle of a star is a response to gravity's fearsome and ultimately unappeasable grip. Birth, maturity, and death are all consequences of the stellar balancing act, as we shall see.

Although fusion is a relatively common and simple process, it does require that a star have a certain minimum mass before it can achieve the threshold core temperature for nuclear ignition to take place. That is why objects like

Jupiter, or even objects one hundred times as massive as Jupiter, are failed stars, since they can never get hot enough to complete the fusion of hydrogen to helium. In fact, a star needs approximately one tenth of our Sun's mass to burn hydrogen into helium. Beyond this threshold, the more the merrier.

Stars that are more massive than the Sun eventually become capable of even more exotic forms of fusion to stay the pull of gravity. This is because the cores of these stars, gravitationally compressed by even greater overlying volumes of gas, can reach far higher temperatures when their hydrogen runs out, permitting more complex nuclear alchemy. (Even so, these exotic processes do not occupy more than a small fraction of any star's life: Fusing hydrogen into helium truly represents the longest-lived process for any star.)

You might naïvely expect that a more massive star, having access to so much more nuclear fuel than a lightweight one, would have a correspondingly longer lifetime. Actually, quite the reverse is true: The bigger the star, the hotter it can get and the more spendthrift its rate of fuel consumption can become. A star ten times the mass of the Sun can look forward to only about one thousandth the span of our star's life!

Of course, even a thousandth of the Sun's life is much longer than even the longest-lived generation of astronomers. Astronomers never have the opportunity to watch any individual star evolve completely, or even through an appreciable fraction of its life. How, then, can we ever hope to describe the life cycle of any individual star?

As an analogy, imagine the problem an alien visitor to the Earth might face if it were asked to construct the history of a typical human being from observations made over the span of no more than a minute or so. Clearly, watching one individual would be fruitless. A better strategy would be to take snapshots at a variety of key places—a maternity ward, a kindergarten, a high school, a city street, a senior center, and a funeral—and then reconstruct the life sequence of a human being from these glimpses. In the same way, the astronomer hopes to order his set of different stellar snapshots to delineate all the various stages in the life of a single star. Our alien visitor would also have to avoid confusing other life forms or moving objects—gorillas, dogs, sparrows, robots, and perhaps even cars—with stages in the development of a human. So the astronomer strives to sort out different members of the "astronomical zoo" and not mix up their life stories. For example, we have found that it is important to consider high-mass stars (with their more exotic fusion processes and, as you will see in the next chapter, more violent deaths) from the stars of lower mass (and more "socially acceptable" behavior) like our Sun.

STELLAR NURSERIES AND STAR BIRTH

The fact that high-mass stars have such short lives provides a vital clue to the location of at least some places where star formation has recently occurred.

Since massive stars live such a short time (on the cosmic scale) and move through space in relatively slow motion (only about ten kilometers per second!), these luminous beacons are always located close to their birthplaces. Even right at the catastrophic ends of their existences, high-mass stars have not drifted far from their nurseries. Consequently we can use their locations to identify sites of recent (at least high-mass) star formation.

When we examine these nurseries we still find an intimate association between young stars and their "prenatal" clouds of glowing gas and obscuring dust. Star life begins in giant agglomerations of gas and dust. Within these clouds, individual centers can be identified that are steadily contracting under the action of self-gravity—the mutual pulls of one piece of cloud on another. It is in these extremely distended, very tenuous—but denser than the surrounding cloud—and slowly rotating chunks that stars have their origins.

So vast are these centers of contraction that it can take light several months to travel across one. It should, therefore, not be surprising to learn that it is not necessary to coax *all* of this rarefied volume into a tiny star core—merely the central parts. The collapse of a star is extremely centrally concentrated: The future stellar core is built up in density much more rapidly than the swirling low-density envelope around it. In fact, the rest of the collapse process preserves this central bias, and even when the star is eventually "born," it is still a tiny, high-density structure embedded in a large, slowly falling rain of cloud material.

Astronomers divide the journey of a so-called *protostar*, from cloud contraction center to star, into well-differentiated steps. First comes the *accretion* phase during which the protostar accretes, or draws inward, much of its infalling piece of cloud. Second is a critical stage in which a strong wind blows from the protostar and essentially terminates the major accretion by dispersing the dusty cocoon in which the star formed: Only a trickle of accretion then remains. During this second stage the fledgling star—which has been surrounded by a considerable amount of dust—first becomes visible in ordinary light to the outside world.

That is not to say that stars in their accretion phases cannot be studied at all. Little or no light escapes because the light and ultraviolet radiated by the heating core are trapped by the in-falling gas and can be absorbed by grains of dust within the envelope. As a result, the dust grains emit heat, or infrared radiation, at wavelengths much longer than those of visible light. This radiation can be detected with ground-based telescopes in dry, high-altitude locations and with specialized infrared telescopes in Earth orbit.

In a sense, then, the dust grains serve as our intermediaries: Although the visible light cannot escape from the layers of in-falling gas, the dust can radiate some of the energy away as infrared and signal the presence of the protostar to us.

It is this sustained leakage of energy from the incipient star that allows the star to continue to collapse and its core to become denser and denser. Once the stellar wind has cleared away the dust and we can optically recognize the star, astronomers say that it has entered its *pre-main sequence* phase. After a period of further contraction, finally nuclear ignition of hydrogen occurs in the core and the star attains its maturity on the main sequence.

O B S E R V I N G   T H E   S T A G E S

Let us now examine the picture we have outlined in more detail, especially as it would appear to an astronomer located a long distance away. As we have seen, throughout the earliest phases of a star's life, it shines without the benefit of sustained fusion in its core. The energy such a protostar produces comes from the heating up of the stellar core, as the entire star steadily contracts.

Each phase of the star's life will have its characteristic temperature as noted by our faraway observer. During accretion, the total energy radiated by the core—the stellar "luminosity"—is rapidly increasing, but these changes, as we saw, are shrouded by the surrounding dusty envelope. Protostars are thus brightest at far-infrared wavelengths, corresponding to temperatures as low as only a few tens of degrees absolute. By the time the stellar wind has dispersed the dusty cocoon and exposed the pre-main sequence object, its surface temperature has reached perhaps 3,000 to 4,000 degrees. Thus pre-main sequence stars are optically recognizable, although they usually produce even more radiation at short infrared wavelengths in their earliest phases. The pre-main sequence precursors of stars, roughly comparable in mass to our Sun, are known as "T Tauri stars," named after the first of these stars astronomers found, a variable star in the constellation of Taurus the Bull.

As pre-main sequence evolution continues, the surface temperature of the star slowly increases to a point determined by the mass initially accumulated into the earlier protostellar core. For a star like our Sun, the final surface temperature will be about 6,000 degrees. In spite of the progression of the core through higher and higher temperatures and densities, the outward manifestations of these later changes are slight.

Although astronomers have been accumulating observations of all the stages in a star's life in recent years, it is fair to say that really tremendous strides have been taken within the past few years in observing the very earliest stages of stellar life. The excitement derives from a rare convergence of vastly different observational techniques and theories focused on a handful of remarkable objects. Monitoring these objects has given us a great deal of new insight into the protostellar accretion phase and the onset of the powerful stellar winds that dispel the dusty *circumstellar* (literally, "around the star") fog and enable us to recognize newly fledged stars.

H E R B I G - H A R O   O B J E C T S

In the dense dark nurseries we find more than merely stars. Gas and dust clouds glow as they reflect the light of associated stars: These are the so-called *reflection nebulae*, whose colors are usually bluish. But the clouds also contain a small population of knotty nebulosities, often tiny, that are red. Detailed observations of the spectrum of light from these knots reveal that, while some of them merely reflect the light of young stars, others betray the presence of specific glowing colors associated with such elements as hydrogen, sulfur, oxygen, and nitrogen. These knots were first recognized more than thirty years ago, independently, by two astronomers: George Herbig in California and Guillermo Haro in Mexico. Now called *Herbig-Haro objects* (HH's for short), they represent a rather rare population in dark clouds. Principally, if not exclusively, they lurk around nurseries of low-mass, as distinct from high-mass, stars. What are they and where do they come from?

At first glance, the knots appeared to be associated with the T Tauri stars. Indeed, we know that some HH objects do lie very close to T Tauri stars; others even extend nebulous wispy arms to embrace these stars. But most of the approximately one hundred HH nebulae do not exhibit obvious stellar connections. How can we learn about their origins? Pairs, or series, of photographs taken over one or two decades have proved especially helpful. These show, in some cases, definite motions of the HH objects across the sky. Many turn out to be in rapid flight, presumably from their places of birth. In some cases we find families of HH knots moving in opposing directions, away from one another. Such a pattern implicates an object, usually invisible by optical techniques, between the two sets of moving HH nebulae. And, indeed, subsequent searches by infrared or radio methods along the line connecting these oppositely directed knots have usually readily detected previously unsuspected objects with distinctly peculiar properties.

Astronomers interpret these infrared or radio sources as the locations of the stars responsible for the moving HH objects, and believe these stars must be very deeply embedded in dense dust clouds that hide them from our visible-light view. They further believe that these stars must have either created and ejected the HH knots from their immediate vicinities into the clouds, or have generated beams of energy that probe the clouds, picking up and accelerating preexisting blobs of material that we then see as HH's.

Why do we see the colors of specific glowing atoms when we observe the nebulous HH knots? The explanation lies in the fact that the knots are moving so fast: The high-speed impact between the knots and their surrounding medium "shocks" and heats up the HH's. The shocked gas begins to glow with the characteristic colors of the atoms it contains, a process that serves to cool off the gas that constitutes the knots. (By the way, in thinking about those impacts, you shouldn't have a mental image of rocks hitting stone walls here; even the densest HH's are very tenuous entities and they and their surroundings would still easily win any terrestrial competition for the best vacuum!) Nevertheless, because the knots are moving so fast—often of order 100 kilometers each second (over 200,000 miles per hour)—their collisions with the material in the environment can produce a great deal of energy.

WHAT POWERS THE HERBIG-HARO OBJECTS?

What have we learned about the origins of these interstellar bullets? What kind of star can manufacture them and why do these stellar powerhouses restrict themselves to hurling HH knots in only two opposed directions instead of all directions?

The deep embedding of these stars in dust requires that we observe them at far-infrared wavelengths, where the radiation penetrates the dust. As we saw, the radiation at these wavelengths comes from very cool dust grains warmed by their proximity to these stars. When we use these observations to estimate the total luminosity of the stars, it turns out to be surprisingly small. The stars that are responsible for the motions of HH nebulae typically range from a luminosity of only a few hundredths up to one hundred times that of the Sun, figures smaller than we might naïvely have expected.

Nevertheless, astronomers have been able to put together a viable working hypothesis for the sort of stars that could be responsible for the HH knots. We believe they are low-mass stars seen in, or very soon after, their protostellar accretion phase. As a fragment of a large molecular gas and dust cloud collapses, a stellar core is assembled, but it is by no means a "finished product." Of necessity, the accretion produces a rather chaotically disorganized gassy blob. We know that stars like our Sun rotate in a reasonably organized fashion, with layers of gas at about the same latitude all spinning around the star's axis at the same rate. But there is no a priori reason why a protostellar core, built from material plastered onto its original seed mass by a collapsing cloud fragment, should know in advance the "correct" stellar behavior. Consequently, one can imagine a period of adjustment while the young star redistributes its material less randomly. During this period, matter is still falling onto the star from all directions, acting in a sense like the lid of a pressure cooker.

But something is happening inside the newly formed star as well. Once a temperature of half a million degrees is reached in the densest part of its core, nuclear fusion is established: not the full-blown hydrogen-to-helium fusion that characterizes mature stars, but essentially the first half of this process, namely the creation of *deuterium* ("heavy hydrogen") out of two atomic hydrogen nuclei (protons). This fuel still provides about one third of the energy generated by converting four protons into helium, but does not need the fiery

Reflection nebula in Orion (NGC 1977). Photo credit: David Malin; © 1977, Anglo-Australian Telescope Board.

temperatures (of order 15 million degrees Kelvin) necessary for the fully fledged fusion.

The onset of deuterium-burning abruptly provides the star with a new energy source with which it can, and does, literally turn itself inside out. The key here is the process of *convection*, by which hotter material from the core of the star rises, very much as hot air produced by an electric heater on the floor rises toward the ceiling in your home. In the protostar, giant looped currents of hot material flow from the region where deuterium fusion is taking place toward the cooler outer layers. We believe the star can use the energy of the seething bubbling engendered by this process to redistribute its spin into a more "sensible" configuration.

No two stars will have the same amount of work to perform: The details depend on the history of how each individual star was assembled. The combination of in-falling cloud material and the convection from below can generate substantial pressure in the hot stellar gas trapped under the in-falling "lid." Eventually this pressure must break out, especially if it can find a "relief valve," a zone of minimum confining pressure. Just such a zone exists over each of the star's spinning poles. Perhaps it is at this stage that the HH objects are born, ejected by tremendous fountains of material spurting from the star's poles. If so, the pressure exerted by the still in-falling matter has to be overcome before this hot gas can escape the clutches of the protostar. This rain of material may be sufficiently dense that only highly confined streams of hot gas can reach the outside.

This would explain why astronomers, observing radio waves from these objects, see narrow "jets" of material near protostars. It also identifies a general time frame for HH's: They must follow the phase of deuterium-burning in protostars. Furthermore, if this scenario is correct, the jets should steadily fan out as they leave the star—becoming less and less "beamed" as time passes and the surviving remnant of the collapsing cloud exerts less and less pressure. The broad jets could then act as "hoses" of gas, accelerating the dispersal of the dusty cocoon around a host protostar and hastening the establishment of a global, more or less spherical, wind from a fledgling T Tauri star.

It should be emphasized that while this physical sketch is plausible, given our observations, it is by no means established. In discussing the mechanism behind the Herbig-Haro objects, we have reached the cutting edge of this particular area of astronomy. Both our observations and our theories are still addressing the thorny puzzle of the birth of a small star: At such a scientific frontier there are few guidelines; there should be no preconceptions.

THE BIRTH OF THE SOLAR SYSTEM

Now that we have outlined a tentative sketch of the way in which the Sun is likely to have formed, there is one other question we should ask. How does the formation of a solar system, like our own, fit into the process of star birth? How do planets, satellites, comets, and the other "debris" accompanying us through space come to be?

Imagine yourself whirling a rock on a string around your head. What happens when you stop rotating the tether? Why doesn't the stone lunge instantly at your head? Its *angular momentum*, or spin, prevents it from attaining the center of its orbit. Of course, given sufficient time, friction between string and finger, and air resistance, and perhaps the wrapping of the string around your neck could all conspire to reduce the angular momentum and to bring the stone closer to you.

This analogy has some value for us in the context of protostellar collapse. Material from the in-falling cloud, too, has angular momentum, and this is not so easily disposed of in the near-vacuum of space. (In fact, this momentum is strictly conserved in the absence of frictional processes.) Consequently, a lot of matter which has high angular momentum will collect in a repository where it can continue to orbit the star, far from the core. As the star material collapses, the rotating material will tend to go from a round shell to a doughnut or a disk around the protostar's equator (very much as our own spinning Earth, even though it is solid and thus has a lot less "give," tends to flatten a bit at the poles and bulge at the equator). It is this vast but tenuous disk that contains the ingredients of which planets could eventually be constructed.

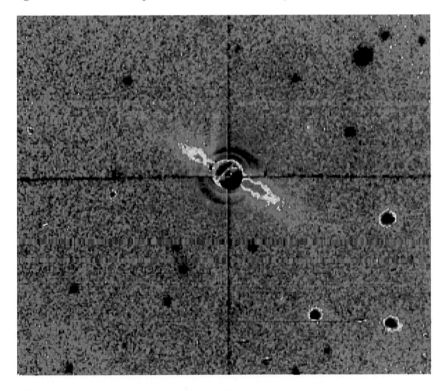

The disk around the star Beta Pictoris. Photo credit: Bradford Smith and Richard Terrile; image courtesy of JPL/Caltech/IPAC.

There are several distinct fates that astronomers can envision for the disk material. It may spiral out farther and farther from the young star but at an ever-reduced rate of spin so as to conserve its angular momentum. Likewise, it might spiral inward to the star, speeding up constantly, constrained by the same conservation principle. (This is very much the way an ice skater regulates her speed in a spin: arms in, speed up; arms out, slow down.) Or the disk material might conceivably approach the star only to be trapped in a blob of high-speed gas, destined to be ejected as an HH object. Even if matter were retained by the disk, there are still several options: It might remain as finely divided debris or it might become incorporated into larger and larger chunks, a buildup that could result eventually in planets. Thus, not every disk of rotating material would necessarily give rise to a family of planets. In recent years, astronomers, using optical, radio, and infrared-detecting instruments, have found evidence for a number of these disks around nearby stars, giving us more confidence in the above scenario and strengthening our impression—although there is certainly no *guarantee*—that planets may exist elsewhere.

We should perhaps mention that even if some or most of the disk material eventually forms planets, not every piece would become part of these large agglomerations. Some of the material may form smaller chunks, such as the pieces of "dirty ice" we call *comets*. In this picture, our comets came from the early disk around the forming Sun and therefore carry a fossilized chemical and physical record of the early history of our planetary system. This accounts, at least partially, for the comet fever that swept both astronomical and lay communities during the recent visit by comet Halley to the inner solar system. Actually it is unnecessary to send space probes to a comet, or to chase one in flying observatories, to be aware of cometary material. Strewn along the often highly elongated orbits of comets that return regularly is debris, shed by a comet during its repeated passages around the Sun. Occasionally the Earth's orbit in space intersects such a stream of debris and we see a number of "shooting stars," or even a "shower" of them at a predictable time of the year, as tiny ex-cometary particles burn up from the heat of their encounter with our atmosphere.

STELLAR MATURITY

After all the excitement of the first few million years, stars like our Sun settle down to a rather quieter pre-main sequence existence. Surface activity diminishes greatly; planets may be established; and stellar wind abates considerably. Eventually, the temperature in the core becomes hot enough for hydrogen to fuse into helium and the star to reach the main sequence (after about half a billion years).

Very little then alters over the billions of years that follow. And it is ultimately this prospect of several billion years of relative constancy of stellar

Halley's comet as seen during its recent pass through the inner solar system. The photograph is a combination of three shots taken in different colors, exposed on the moving comet; thus the colors of the stars are streaked. Photo credit: David Malin; © 1985, Anglo-Australian Telescope Board.

conditions that fosters an environment in which long-term chemical experimentation on planets is possible, and life can arise. (Bear in mind that the above time scales are for stars of about the mass of our Sun; much more massive stars will blaze through their lives very much more quickly, a factor that may entirely eliminate high-mass, fast-living stars as sites for intelligent life.)

But all good things must eventually come to an end. One day a star like the Sun (and indeed every star) will find that it has converted all of its central hydrogen fuel into helium "ash" and that it can no longer oppose the ever-present inward pull of gravity. The star must either find a new nuclear fuel to generate the energy required to withstand gravity or prepare to meet its end. Once again, stars of different mass will undergo different stages of development. The more mass a star has, the more weight it can bring to bear on its central regions and the hotter it can become. Very massive stars can fuse a number of new elements from their helium ash before they die. Less massive stars like our Sun, on the other hand, cannot continue opposing gravity very much longer beyond this point. Thus all stars die—at their own pace—once the exhaustion of central hydrogen signals the beginning of the end.

But, as you will see in the next chapter, the universe is the supreme example of ecology. As stars of all masses die, they puff off, or violently eject, their outer layers or even their entire selves, as they reach their end. All these ejecta travel through space as dusty gases containing the heavier elements that are the results of stellar "cookery." And this processed debris is not lost; much of it winds up in just those giant cloud complexes that ultimately collapse, leading to the birth of the next generation of stars.

RETROSPECT

The violence of stellar death has long been known, but the surprising violence of the birth of low-mass stars is something very new to us. Earlier generations of astronomers thought that the gentle, gradual collapse of a gas cloud's core would form an equally quiescent star; but today we know this is not an accurate description of star birth. There is collapse, accompanied by a vast disk, attended by violent, narrow jets of gas spraying out of the star's rotational poles. HH objects rush away at tremendous speeds along opposed paths, crashing into the ambient medium as the fledgling star adjusts to its new life. Giant winds leap from the stellar surface and scour the surroundings as the star ages, even while it accretes fresh material at its equator from the disk. Protoplanets formed during these vigorous phases begin their accretion to planetary masses as the stellar gales abate and the long journey to the main sequence stage is initiated. At that point, as the expression goes, "a star is born"!

TO TOUCH A STAR

BEN BOVA

THE FIRST THOUGHT to touch Aleyn's conscious mind after his long sleep was, I've lost Noura. Lost her forever.

He lay on the warm, softly yielding mattress of the cocoon, staring upward for the better part of an hour, seeing nothing. But whenever he closed his eyes Noura's face was there. The dazzle of her dark eyes, the glow of firelight sparkling in them. The rich perfume of her lustrous ebony hair. The warmth of her smile.

Gone forever now. Separated by time and distance and fate. Separated by my own ambition.

And by Selwyn's plotting, he added silently. His mouth hardened into a thin, bitter line. If I live through this, he won't, Aleyn promised himself.

Slowly he pulled himself up to a sitting position. The sleep chamber was familiar, yet strange. The cocoon where he had spent the past thousand absolute years was almost the same as he remembered it. Almost. The cocoon's shell, swung back now that he had been awakened, seemed a slightly different shade of color. He recalled it being brighter, starker, a hard hospital white. Now it was almost pearl gray.

The communicator screen was not beside the cocoon any more, but at its end, by his feet. The diagnostic screens seemed subtly rearranged. The maintenance robots had changed things over the years of his sleep.

"Status report," he called, his voice cracking slightly.

The comm screen remained blank but its synthesized voice, a blend of Aleyn's parents and his university mentor, replied:

"Your health is excellent, Aleyn. We are on course and within fifty hours of destination. All ship systems are operational and functioning within nominal limits."

Aleyn swung his legs off the cocoon's mattress and stood up, warily, testingly. The cermet floor felt pleasantly warm to his bare feet. He felt strong. In the reflections of the diagnostic screens he saw himself, scattered and disarranged like a cubist painting of a lean naked young man.

"Show me the star," he commanded.

81

The comm screen flickered briefly, then displayed a dully glowing red disc set in a thickly swirling nebula of ionized gases shining so brightly that their long, gleaming filaments blotted out the light of the nearby stars. Their glowing colors startled Aleyn, filled him with wonder and awe. From his home world the nebula had seemed almost ordinary: a compact cloud of plasma, some of its billows pale pinkish red, others electric blue, depending on their ionization.

But here, inside the nebula, the plasma tendrils were brilliant, sparkling streams of color. Every hue of the rainbow glowed around Aleyn: pulsating reds and blues, oranges and greens, shades so bright it hurt his eyes, tones so subtle that Aleyn had never seen them before. The plasma filaments seemed almost alive, writhing and twining, pulsing, breathing, growing.

It took an extreme effort of his will to tear his eyes away from the cloud and concentrate on the star at its core. The star's disc was perfectly round, ruddy like the dying embers of a fire, glowering sullenly against the depths of space.

Aleyn's heart nearly stopped.

"That's not a star!" he shouted.

"Vejovus 1888IR2434," said the comm screen, after a hesitation that was unnoticeable to human senses.

"It can't be!"

"Navigation and tracking programs agree. Spectrum matches. It is our destination star," the screen insisted.

Aleyn stared at the image a moment longer, then bolted to the hatch and down the short corridor that led to the ship's bridge.

The bridge screens were larger. But they all showed the same thing. Optical, infrared, radar, high-energy, and neutrino sensors all displayed a gigantic, perfectly circular metal sphere.

Aleyn sagged into the only chair on the bridge, oblivious to the slight chill against his naked flesh while the chair adjusted its temperature.

"We thought it was a star," he murmured to no one. "We thought it was a star."

Aleyn Arif Bellerophontes, son of the director of the Imperial Observatory and her consort, and therefore distrusted by Admiral Kimon, the emperor's chief of astro-engineering; betrayed by Selwyn, his best friend; exiled to a solitary expedition to a dying star—Aleyn sat numb and uncomprehending, staring at a metal sphere the size of a star.

No. Bigger.

"What's the radius of that object?"

Numbers sprang up on every screen, superimposed on the visual display, as the computer's voice replied, "Two hundred seventeen point zero nine eight million kilometers."

"Two hundred million kilometers," Aleyn echoed. Then he smiled. "A metal sphere four hundred million kilometers across." He giggled. "A sphere with the radius of a water-bearing planet's orbit." He laughed. "A Type III civilization! I've found a Type III civilization!"

His laughter became raucous, uncontrolled, hysterical. He roared with laughter. He banged his fists on the armrests of his chair and threw his head back and screamed with laughter. Tears flowed down his cheeks. His face grew red. His breath rasped in his throat. His lungs burned. He did not stop until the chair, under override command from the computer's medical program, sprayed him with a soporific and he lapsed into unconsciousness.

A thousand light-years away, scientists and engineers of the Hundred Worlds labored valiantly to save Aleyn's home world from doom. Kasta, the original home planet of the Empire, was in danger from its own star, Raman. The Kastans had lived on a green-and-blue world that circled a gentle yellow star. They had built a mighty civilization and expanded it out into space, out to a hundred worlds circling a hundred other stars. But their own star, Raman, was about to betray them. To their horror, Kastan astronomers found that Raman was not as stable as they had believed.

A cycle of massive flares would soon erupt across Raman's normally placid face. Soon, that is, in terms of a star's gigayear lifetime: ten thousand years, give or take a few millennia. Raman would not explode. The predicted flares would not tear the star apart; they would merely blow away a tiny fraction of the star's substance.

Too feeble to be of consequence in the lifespan of the star itself.

The flares would nonetheless be disastrous to all the planets that orbited Raman. They would casually boil away the air and oceans of Kasta, destroy all life on the original homeworld of Aleyn's race, leave nothing afterward but a blackened ball of rock.

Millions of technologists had struggled for centuries to save Kasta, following the mad scheme of a woman scientist who woke from cryonic sleep once each thousand years to survey their progress. It was not enough. The course of Raman's evolution had not yet been altered enough to avert the period of flares.

Kasta's daystar would go through its turbulent phase despite the valiant efforts of the Empire's best, most dedicated men and women. In all the vast storehouses of knowledge among the Hundred Worlds, no one knew enough about a star's behavior to forestall Raman's impending fury.

Three young scientists, Aleyn, Noura, and Selwyn, hit upon the idea of monitoring other stars that were undergoing the same kind of turbulence. Aleyn had fought through the layers of academic bureaucracy and championed their joint ideas to the topmost level of the Imperial hierarchy, to Admiral Kimon himself.

It had been a clever trap. But it had taken a thousand years of sleep, a thousand years of slowly dreaming and thinking in the gelid cold of cryonic suspension, for him to see things clearly, to understand what they had done to him.

Kimon, reluctantly agreeing to the proposal of the son of his chief rival within the Imperial court, had sent out a fleet of one-man ships toward the stars that Selwyn, Noura, and Aleyn had listed. He had assigned Aleyn himself to one of those long, lonely ventures. Selwyn the traitor remained at Kasta. With Kimon. With Noura. While Aleyn sped through the dark star paths on a journey that would take twenty centuries to complete.

They had packed him off, sent him away, while they lived their lives, loved, aged, and laughed at Aleyn all through the centuries.

And now, rousing himself slowly from the soporific's dreaminess, Aleyn realized what a cosmic joke it all was. Their researches had shown that Vejovus 1888IR2434, a dim reddish star some thousand light-years from Kasta, was flickering and pulsating much as Raman would during its time of agony. A good star to observe, an excellent opportunity to gather the data needed to save Raman and Kasta. Better still, this star in Vejovus lay in the direction opposite the alien worlds, so a scout ship sent to it would cause no diplomatic anxieties, offer no threat to aliens sensitive to the Empire's attempts at expansion.

But the star was not a star. Its spectrum had been strange; that was one of the reasons they had wanted to study it. Now Aleyn realized why the spectrum had seemed so odd: The object was an artificial sphere imbedded in a swirling compact cloud of ionized gases.

Aleyn felt the cold hand of chemically induced calm pressing against his innards. The joke was no longer funny. Yet it remained a colossal irony. He had discovered a Type III civilization, a gigantic artifact, the work of an unknown race of aliens with undreamed-of technological powers. They had built a sphere around their star, so that their civilization could catch every erg of energy the star emitted, while they lived on the inner surface of their artificial world in the same comfort, breathing the same air, drinking the same water, that they had enjoyed on their original home planet.

And Aleyn felt disappointment. The discovery of the eons was a crushing defeat to a man seeking knowledge of the inner workings of the stars. Despite the tranquilizing agent in his bloodstream, Aleyn wanted to laugh at the pathetic absurdity of it all. And he wanted to cry.

The drugs allowed him neither outlet. This nameless ship he commanded was in control of him, its programming placing duty and mission objectives far beyond mortal needs.

For three Kasta-normal days he scanned the face of the enormous sphere while his ship hung in orbit beyond its glowering surface. He spent most of the time in his command chair on the bridge, surrounded by display screens and the soft reassuring hum of electrical equipment. He wore the regulation uniform of the Imperial Science Service, complete with epaulets of rank and nametag, thinking nothing of the absurdity of such formality. There were no other clothes aboard the ship.

The sphere was not smooth. Intricate structures and networks of piping studded its exterior. Huge hatches dotted the curving surface—all of them tightly closed. The metal was hot; it glowed dull red like a poker held too close to a fire. Aleyn saw jets of gas spurting from vents here and there, flashing brilliantly as they joined the plasma filaments of the surrounding nebula.

Not another body anywhere within light-years. Not a planet or asteroid or comet. "They must have used every scrap of matter in their solar system to build the sphere," Aleyn said to himself. "They must have torn their own home planet apart, and all the other worlds of this system."

All the data that his ship's sensors recorded was transmitted back toward Kasta. At the speed of light, the information would take a thousand years to reach the eager scientists and engineers. Noura would be long dead before Aleyn's first report reached the Empire's receivers.

"Unless she got permission to take the long sleep," Aleyn hoped aloud. But then he shook his head. Only the topmost members of the scientific hierarchy were permitted to sleep away centuries while others toiled. And if Noura received such a boon, undoubtedly Selwyn would too. They would share their lives even if they awakened only one year out of each hundred.

That night, as he brooded silently over the meal the ship had placed on the galley's narrow table, Aleyn realized that Selwyn had indeed murdered him.

"Even if I survive this mission," he muttered angrily, "by the time I return to Kasta more than two thousand years will have passed. Everyone I know—everyone I love—will have died."

Unless they take the long sleep, a part of his brain reminded him. Just as you did while this ship was in transit, they could sleep in cryogenic cold for many centuries at a time.

There is a chance that Noura will be alive when I return, he replied silently, afraid to speak the hope aloud. *If* I return. No, not if. When! When I return, if Selwyn still lives, I will kill him. Gladly. *When* I return.

He pushed the tray of untouched food away, got to his feet and strode back to the bridge.

"Computer," he commanded. "Integrate all data on Noura Sudarshee, including my personal holos, and feed it all to the interactive program."

The computer complied with a single wink of a green light. Within moments, Noura's lovely face filled the bridge's main display screen.

Aleyn sank into the command chair and found himself smiling at her. "I need you, dearest Noura. I need you to keep me sane."

"I know," she said, in the vibrant low voice that he loved. "I'm here with you, Aleyn. You're not alone anymore."

He fell asleep in the command chair, talking with the image of the woman he had left a thousand light-years behind him. While he slept, the ship's life-support system sprayjected into his bloodstream the nutritional equivalent of the meal he had not eaten.

The following morning Aleyn resumed his scan of the sphere. But now he had Noura to talk to.

"They don't seem to know we're out here," Aleyn said. "No message, no probe—not even a warning to go away."

"Perhaps there are no living people inside the sphere," said Noura's image, from the comm screen at Aleyn's right hand.

"No people?" He realized that her words were formed by the computer, acting on the data in its own banks and relaying its conclusions through the interactive *Noura* program.

"The sphere seems very old," said Noura's image, her face frowning slightly with concern.

Aleyn did not answer. He realized that she was right—the computer was drawing his attention to the obvious signs of the sphere's enormous age.

He spiralled his ship closer, searching for a port through which he might enter, staring hard at the pictures the main display screens revealed, as if he could force the sphere to open a hatch for him if he just concentrated hard enough. Aleyn began to realize that the sphere was *old*—and it was falling into ruin. The gases venting into space were escaping from broken pipes. Many of the structures on the sphere's outer surface seemed collapsed, broken, as if struck by meteors or simply decayed by eons of time.

"This was built before Raman was born," Aleyn murmured.

"Not that long ago," replied Noura, voicing the computer's calculation of erosion rates in an ionized nebula caused by radiation and the rare wandering meteor. "Spectral analysis of the surface metal indicates an age no greater than two hundred million years."

Aleyn grinned at her. "Is that all? Only two hundred million years? No older than the first amphibians to crawl out of Kasta's seas?"

Noura's image smiled back at him.

"Are they still there?" Aleyn wondered. "Are the creatures who built this still living inside it?"

"They show no evidence of being there," said Noura. "Since the sphere is so ancient, perhaps they no longer exist."

"I can't believe that. They *must* be there! They must be!"

For eight more days Aleyn bombarded the sphere with every wavelength his equipment could transmit: radio, microwaves, infrared laser light, ultraviolet, X rays, gamma rays. Pulses and steady beams. Standard messages and simple mathematical formulas. No reaction from the sphere. He poured alpha particles and relativistic electrons across wide swatches of the sphere, to no avail.

"I don't think anyone is alive inside," said Noura's image.

"How do we know where their receivers might be?" Aleyn countered. "Maybe their communication equipment in this area broke down. Maybe their main antennas are clear over on the other side."

"It would take years to cover every square meter of its surface," Noura pointed out.

Aleyn shrugged, almost happily. "We have years. We have centuries, if we need them. As long as you're with me, I don't care how long it takes."

Her face became serious. "Aleyn, remember that I am only an interactive program. You must not allow my presence to interfere with the objectives of your mission."

He smiled grimly and fought down a surge of anger. After taking a deep, calming breath, Aleyn said to the image on the screen, "Noura my darling, the main objective of this mission is to keep me away from you. Selwyn has accomplished that."

"The major objective of this mission," she said, in a slightly lecturing tone, "is to observe the behavior of a turbulent subdwarf-class star and relay that data back to Kasta."

Aleyn jabbed a forefinger at the main display screen. "But we can't even see the star. It's inside the sphere."

"Then we must find a way to get inside, as well."

"Right!" he agreed. "I knew you'd see it my way sooner or later."

Aleyn programmed the computer to set up a polar orbit that would eventually carry the ship over every part of the gigantic sphere. The energy in the antimatter converters would last for millennia, of course. Still, he extended the magnetic scoops to draw in the swirls of hydrogen atoms from the glowing nebula. They would feed the fusion system and provide input for the converters.

It was precisely when the engines fired to move to their new orbit that the port began to open.

Aleyn barely caught it, out of the corner of his eye as one of the auxiliary display screens on his compact bridge showed a massive hatch swinging outward, etched sharply in bright, bloodred light.

"Look at that!" he shouted.

Swivelling his command chair toward the screen he commanded the ship's sensors to show him the port.

"Aleyn, you did it!" Noura's image seemed equally excited.

The port yawned open like the gateway to hell, lurid red light beyond it.

Aleyn took manual control of the ship, broke it out of the new orbit it had barely established, and maneuvered it toward the open port. It was kilometers wide, big enough to engulf a hundred ships like his own.

"Why now?" he asked. "Why did it stay closed when we were sending signals and probes to the sphere and open up only when we ignited the engines?"

"Neutrinos, perhaps," said Noura, with the wisdom of the ship's computer. "The thrusters generate a shower of neutrinos when they fire. The neutrinos must have penetrated the sphere's shell and activated sensors inside."

"Inside," Aleyn echoed, his voice shaking.

With trembling hands, Aleyn set all his comm channels on automatic to make certain that every bit of data that the ship's sensors recorded was sent back toward Kasta. Then he aimed his ship squarely at the center of the yawning port and fired his thrusters one more time.

It seemed as if they stood still, while the burning hot alien sphere swallowed them alive.

The port engulfed them, widening and widening as they approached until its vast expanse filled Aleyn's screens with a sullen, smoldering red glow. The temperature gauges began to climb steadily upward. Aleyn called up the life-support display on the main bridge screen and saw that it was drawing much more energy than usual, adjusting the heat shielding and internal cooling systems to withstand the furnace-like conditions outside the ship's hull.

"It's like stepping into a netherworld inferno," Aleyn muttered.

With a smile that was meant to be reassuring, Noura said, "The cooling systems can withstand temperatures of this magnitude for hundreds of hours."

He smiled back at her. "My beloved, sometimes you talk like a computer."

"It's the best I can do, under the circumstances."

The port was several hundred kilometers thick. Aleyn's screens showed heavily ribbed metal, dulled and pitted with age, as they cruised slowly through.

"This must be the thickness of the sphere's shell," he said. Noura agreed with a nod.

After more than two hours, Aleyn's ship finally cleared the port. He could see the interior of the sphere.

A vast metallic plain extended in all directions below him, glowing red-hot. Aleyn focused the ship's sensors on the inner surface and saw a jumble of shapes: stumps of towers blackened and melted down, shattered remains of what must have been buildings, twisted guideways that disappeared entirely in places where vast pools of metal glittered in the gloomy red light.

"It looks like the roadway melted and then the metal hardened again afterward," said Aleyn.

"Yes," Noura said. "A tremendous pulse of heat destroyed everything."

The sphere was so huge that it seemed perfectly flat from this perspective. Aleyn punched at his controls, calling up as many different views as the sensors could display. Nothing but the burnt and blackened remains of what must have been an enormous city. No sign of movement. No sign of life.

"Did they kill themselves off in a war?" Aleyn wondered aloud.

"No," said Noura. "Listen."

Aleyn turned toward her screen. "What?"

"Listen."

"I don't—" Then he realized that he did hear something. A faint whispering, like the rush of a breeze through a young forest. But this was pulsating irregularly, gasping, almost like the labored breath of a dying old man.

PAT RAWLINGS

"What is it?" Aleyn wondered.

"There is atmosphere here within the shell," said Noura.

Aleyn shook his head. "Couldn't be. How could they open that hatch to space if . . ."

But the computer had already sampled the atmosphere the ship was flying through. Noura's voice spoke what the other display screens showed in alphanumerics:

"We are immersed in an atmosphere that consists of sixty-two percent hydrogen ions, thirty-four percent helium ions, two percent carbon, one percent oxygen, and traces of other ions."

Aleyn stared at her screen.

"Atmospheric density is four ten-thousandths of Kasta standard sea-level density." Noura spoke what the other screens displayed. "Temperature outside the ship's hull is ten thousand degrees, kinetic."

"We're inside the star's chromosphere," Aleyn whispered.

"Yes, and we're cruising deeper into it. The cooling systems will not be able to handle the heat levels deeper inside the star." For the first time, Noura's image appeared worried.

Aleyn turned to the control board and put an image of the star on the main screen. It was a glowering, seething ball of red flame, huge and distended, churning angrily, spotted with ugly dark blotches and twisting filaments that seemed to writhe on its surface and then sink back again like some mythical sea monster prowling an ocean of fire.

The sound outside the ship's hull seemed louder as Aleyn stared at the screen, fascinated, hypnotized. It was the sound of the star, he realized, the tortured irregular pulsebeat of a dying star.

"We're too late," he whispered at last. "This star has already flared at least once. It killed off the civilization that created the sphere. Burned them to a cinder."

"It will destroy us, too, if we go much deeper," said Noura.

What of it? Aleyn thought. This whole mission is a failure. We'll never gain the knowledge that I thought we could get from studying this star; it's past the period of turbulence that we need to observe. The mission has failed. I have failed. There's nothing on Kasta for me to go back to. No one in the Hundred Worlds for me to go back for.

"Aleyn!" Noura's voice was urgent. "We must change course and leave the sphere. Outside temperatures will overwhelm the cooling systems within a few dozen hours if we don't."

"What of it? We can die together."

"No, Aleyn. Life is too valuable to throw away! Don't you see that?"

"All I see is the hopelessness of everything. What difference if I live or die? What will I accomplish by struggling to survive?"

"Is that what you want?" Noura asked. "To die?"

"Why not?"

"Isn't that what Selwyn wants, to be rid of you forever?"

"He *is* rid of me. Even if I get back to Kasta the two of you will have been dead for more than a thousand years."

Noura's image remained silent, but the ship turned itself without Aleyn's command and pointed its nose toward the port through which they had entered.

"The computer is programmed to save the ship and its data banks even if the pilot is incapacitated," Noura said, almost apologetically.

Aleyn nodded. "I can't even commit suicide."

Smiling, Noura said, "I want you to live, my darling."

He stared at her image for long moments, telling himself desperately that it was merely the computer speaking to him, using the ship's data files and his personal holos to synthesize her picture and manner of speech. It was Noura's face, Noura's voice, but the computer's mind.

She doesn't care if I live, he told himself. It's the data banks that are important to her.

With a shrug that admitted defeat, Aleyn put the nose camera view on the main display screen. A shock of raw electricity slammed through him; he saw that the giant port through which they had entered the sphere was now firmly closed.

"We're trapped!" he shouted.

"How could it close?" Noura's image asked.

"You are not of the creators."

It was a voice that came from the main display screen, deep and powerful. To Aleyn it sounded like the thunderclap of doom.

"Who said that?"

"You are not of the creators."

"There's someone alive in the sphere! Who are you?"

"Only the creators may return to their home. All others are forbidden."

"We're a scientific investigation team," Noura's voice replied, "from the planet ''

"I know you are from a worldling called Kasta. I can see from your navigational program where your home world is located."

His heart racing wildly, Aleyn asked, "You can tap into our computer?"

"I have been studying you since you entered the world."

Noura said swiftly, "Aleyn, he's communicating through our own computer."

"Who are you?" Aleyn asked.

"In your tongue, my name is Savant."

"What are you?" asked Noura.

"I am the servant of the creators. They created me to survive, to guard, and to protect."

"You're a computer?" Aleyn guessed.

For half a heartbeat there was no response. Then, *"I am a device that is as far beyond what you know of computers as your minds are beyond those of your household pets."*

With a giggle that trembled on the edge of hysteria, Aleyn said, "And you're quite a modest little device, too, aren't you?"

"My function is to survive, to guard, and to protect. I perform that function well."

"Are there any of the creators left here?" Noura asked.

"No."

"What happened to them?"

"Many departed when they realized the star would flare. Others remained here."

"To try to prevent the star from flaring," Aleyn suggested.

"That was not their way. They remained to await the final moments. They preferred to die in their homes, where they had always lived."

"But they built you."

"Yes."

"Why?"

"To await the time when those who fled return to their home."

"You mean they're coming back?"

"There is no evidence of their return. My function is to survive, to guard, and to protect. If they ever return, I will serve them."

"And help them rebuild."

"If you wish it so."

Noura asked, "Do you have any idea of how long ago the . . . creators left?"

"By measuring the decay of radioactive atoms I can count the time. In your terms of reference, the creators fled approximately eighteen million years ago. The star's first flare took place eleven thousand years later."

"First?" Aleyn asked. "There've been more?"

"Several. And very soon the next flare will take place."

"We must get out of here," Noura said.

"That is not allowed."

"Not—what do you mean?" For the first time, Aleyn felt fear burning along his veins.

"I am the servant of the creators. No others may enter or leave."

"But you let us in!"

"To determine if you are of the creators. You are not. Therefore you may not leave."

The fear ebbed away. In its place Aleyn felt the cold implacable hand of cosmic irony. With a sardonic grin he turned to Noura's image.

"I don't have to commit suicide now. This Savant is going to murder me."

Noura's image stared blankly at him. It had no answer.

Aleyn pulled himself up from the command chair and went back through the narrow corridor to the ship's galley. He knew that the computer automatically spiced his food with tranquilizers and vitamins and anything else it felt he needed, based on its continuous scans of his physical and psychological condition. He no longer cared.

He ate numbly, hardly tasting the food. His mind swirled dizzyingly. An alien race. The discovery of a lifetime, of a thousand lifetimes, and he would not live to report it. But where did they go? Are they still out there, scattering through the galaxy in some desperate interstellar diaspora?

Is that what the people of Kasta should have done? Abandon their home world and flee among the stars? What makes Kastans so arrogant that they think they can reverse the course of a star's evolution?

He went to his cabin as the miniature serving robots cleared the galley table. Stripping off his uniform, Aleyn was surprised to see that it was stained and rank with sweat. Fear? he wondered. Excitement? He felt neither at the moment. Nothing but numb exhaustion. The ship's pharmacy was controlling his emotions now, he knew. Otherwise he'd be bashing his head against the metal bulkhead.

He crawled into the bunk and pulled the monolayer coverlet up to his chin, just as he used to do when he was a child.

"Noura," he called.

Her face appeared on the screen at the foot of the bunk. "I'm here, Aleyn."

"I wish you were," he said. "I wish you truly were."

"I *am* with you, my dearest. I am here with you."

"No," he said, a great wave of sadness washing over him. "You're merely a collection of data bits. My real Noura is on Kasta, with Selwyn."

Her eyes flashed. "Your real Noura may be on Kasta, but she is not with Selwyn."

"It would be pleasant to think so."

"It is true!" the image insisted. "Who would know better than I?"

"You're not real."

"I am the sum of all the ship's records of Noura Sudarshee; the personnel records are complete from her birth to the day you left Kasta."

"No better than a photograph," Aleyn countered. "A still photograph compared to a living, breathing woman."

"I am also made up of your holos of Noura Sudarshee, your private recordings and communications." She hesitated a moment, then said, almost shyly, "Even your subconscious memories and dreams."

"Dreams?" Aleyn blurted. "Memories?"

"This ship's psychological program has been scanning your brainwave activity since you came aboard. During your long sleep you dreamt extensively of me. All that data is included in this imagery."

Aleyn thought about that for a moment. An electronic clone of his beloved

Noura, complete down to the slightest memory in his subconscious mind. But the deadening hand of futility made him laugh bitterly.

"That only makes it worse, my dearest. That only means that when I die, I will be killing you too."

"Don't think of death, darling. Think of life. Think of me."

He shook his head wearily. "I don't want to think of anything. I want to sleep. Forever."

He closed his eyes. His last waking thought was that it would be a relief never to have to open them again.

He dreamed of Noura, as he always did. But this time the dream was drenched with a dire sense of foreboding, of dread. He and Noura were on Kasta, at one of the wild and incredibly beautiful places where a glacier-fed waterfall tumbled down a sheer rock scarp into a verdant valley dotted with trees. Not another person for hundreds of kilometers. Only the two of them sitting on the yielding grass under the warming golden light of Raman.

But Raman grew hotter, so hot that the grass began to curl and blacken and the waterfall to steam. Aleyn looked up at Raman and saw it broiling angrily, lashing out huge tongues of flame. It thundered at them and laughed. In Raman's blinding disc he saw the face of Selwyn, laughing at him, reaching out his flaming arms for Noura.

"NO!" he screamed.

Aleyn was sitting up on his bunk, soaked with sweat. Grimly, he got up, washed and dressed. He strode past the galley and took the command chair at the bridge.

"Good morning, darling," said Noura's smiling image.

He made himself smile back at her. "Good morning."

Her face became more serious. "The cooling systems are nearing overload. In six more hours they will fail."

"Backups?"

"The six-hour figure includes the backups."

Aleyn nodded. Six hours.

"Savant!" he called. "Can you hear me?"

"Yes."

"Why do you refuse to allow us to leave your domain? Are you prohibited from doing so?"

"I am programmed to survive, to guard, and to protect. I await the creators. There is nothing in my programming that requires me to allow you to leave."

"But there's nothing in your programming that prohibits you from allowing us to leave, is there?"

"That is so."

"Then allow us to leave and we will search for the creators and bring them back to you."

The synthesized voice was silent for several heartbeats. Aleyn realized that each second of time was an eternity for such a powerful computer. It must be considering his proposition very carefully, like a computer chess program, calculating each move as far into the future as it could see.

"The creators are so distant now that they could not be found and returned before the star flares again. Its next flare will be much greater than the earlier one. Its explosion will destroy this sphere. It will destroy me. I will not survive. I will have failed my primary purpose."

It was Aleyn's turn to be silent, thinking, his mind churning through all the branching possibilities. Death stood at the end of each avenue, barring the door to escape.

"Aleyn," said Noura's image softly, "the ship is drifting deeper into the chromosphere. Hull temperature is rising steeply. The cooling systems will fail in a matter of minutes if corrective action is not taken."

Corrective action, Aleyn's mind echoed. Why not simply allow the ship to drift toward the heart of the dying star and let us be vaporized? It will all be finished in a few minutes. Why try to delay the inevitable, prolong the futility? Why struggle, merely to continue suffering?

He looked squarely at Noura's image in the screen. "I can't kill you," he whispered. "Even if you are only my memories and my dreams, I can't let you die."

Turning to the main screen, he saw the angry heart of the dying star, seething red, writhing and glowering, drumming against the hull with the dull muted thunder of approaching doom.

"Savant," he called again. "Have you scanned all of our data banks?"

"I have."

"Then you know that we of Kasta are attempting to prevent our own star from exploding."

"Your Raman is younger than my star."

"Yes, and the data you have recorded about your star would be of incalculable help in allowing us to gain an understanding of how to save Raman."

"That is of no consequence."

"But it is!" Aleyn snapped. "It is! Because once we learn how to control our own star, how to prevent it from exploding, we can come back here and apply that knowledge to your star."

"Return here?"

"Yes! We can return here and save your star! We can help you to survive! We can allow you to achieve your primary objective."

"I am programmed to survive, to guard, and to protect."

"We will help you to survive. You can continue to guard and protect until we return with the knowledge that will save your star from destruction."

Again the alien voice went silent. Aleyn counted to twenty, then fifty, then . . .

Noura sang out, "The port is opening!"

Aleyn swung his chair to see the screen. The vast hatch that had sealed the port was slowly swinging open again. He could see a slice of star-studded darkness beyond it. Without thinking consciously he turned the ship toward the port, away from the growling, glaring star.

"Savant," he called once again, "we need the data you have accumulated on your star's behavior."

"Your data banks are too small to accommodate all of it. Therefore I have altered the atomic structure of your ship's hull and structure to store data."

"Altered the hull and structure?"

"The alteration is at the nuclear level. It will not affect the performance of your ship. I have placed instructions in your puny computer on how to read the data."

"Thank you!"

"You must return within thirty thousand years if you are to save this star."

"We will. I promise you."

"I will survive until then without you."

"You will survive beyond that, Savant. We will be back, and we will have the knowledge we need to save you and your star.

"I will wait."

The ship headed toward the opening; the port was gaping wide now, showing the swirling colorful glow of the nebula. It looked inviting now, a gentle, cool embrace after the flaming hell inside the sphere. Through the twining clouds Aleyn could see the colder darkness of infinity and even a few hard pinpoints of stars.

"The cooling system is returning to normal," Noura's image said. "We will survive."

"We will return to Kasta," said Aleyn. "I'll sleep for a thousand years, and when I wake up again, we'll be back at Kasta."

"The real Noura will be waiting for you."

He smiled, but there was still sadness in it. "I wish I knew that was true."

"It is true, my beloved Aleyn. Who would know better than I? She is in deep sleep even now, waiting for your return."

"Do you really believe so?"

"I *know* it."

"And Selwyn, also?"

"Even if he waits with her," Noura's image replied, "she waits for *you*."

He closed his eyes briefly. Then he realized, "But that means—"

"It means you will no longer need me." Noura's image said. "You will erase me."

"I don't know if I can do that. It would be like murdering you."

She smiled at him, a warming, loving smile without a trace of sadness in it. "I am not programmed to survive, Aleyn. My objective was to help *you* to survive. Once the real Noura is in your arms, you will not need me anymore."

He stared at the screen for many long moments. Then, wordlessly, he reached out his hand and touched the button that turned off the display.

SUPERNOVAE
AND PULSARS

ESSAY BY

DAVID J. HELFAND

SPECULATION BY

ROBERT SILVERBERG

SUPERNOVAE: CREATIVE CATACLYSMS IN THE GALAXY

DAVID J. HELFAND

Columbia University

DECEMBER 7, A.D. 185. EARLY MORNING.

THE SUN, RISING LATER EACH DAY as winter approaches, begins to illuminate the morning sky over eastern China and its Han capital at Lo-yang. The myriad twinkling stars begin to fade and disappear—the faintest first and then the brighter ones—just as they have each morning since Chinese astrologers began surveying the sky. But this morning is different. One star doesn't disappear.

It shines on, brilliant enough to be visible long after sunrise, moving across the sky in the familiar pattern of all the nighttime stars, but clearly of special significance. The astrologers check their star charts and find that this is not just a known star that has suddenly brightened; it inhabits a spot on the celestial sphere where no star has ever been visible before. They call it a *K'o-hsing*, or "Guest Star," and rush to seek an audience with the Emperor to inform him of this unexpected visitor.

Today we know that what the Chinese witnessed was actually not the arrival of a new star but the explosive destruction of an old one. They saw an event that marked the creation of all the chemical elements heavier than iron, and the injection into the interstellar medium of the lighter atoms such as carbon, nitrogen, and oxygen, which are essential to the formation of planets and life. The explosion stirred and heated the matter in the surrounding area of space, sweeping it into denser clouds that would someday form a new generation of stars. In the expanding shock wave, electrons and atomic nuclei were accelerated to speeds within a hairbreadth of the speed of light itself—producing the so-called cosmic rays which, through collisions with living cells, form the principal agent of biological evolution on Earth. And finally, in all likelihood this cataclysmic event marked the birth of one of the most remarkable denizens of the heavens: a neutron star.

The Guest Star of A.D. 185 was not the first such visitor the Chinese had seen, but it was noteworthy for its unusual brilliance and its longevity, remaining visible for at least seven and perhaps as long as twenty months (the ancient records are somewhat ambiguous on this point). A number of more transient guest stars lasting a few days to a few weeks had been recorded by Greek and Chinese astronomers over the centuries. In the West these brief visitors were called *novae,* or "new" stars—an ironic nomenclature, since we now know that they in fact involve a system of two very old stars. In such a pair, one star is dumping material onto the other, causing occasional outbursts as the accumulating matter heats up and explodes. Modern astronomers have catalogued hundreds of these brief-lived novae, with one or two occurrences each year visible to the naked eye. However, only six of the *long-lasting* novae have been recorded in the past two thousand years. The last of these was studied extensively by the European astronomer Johannes Kepler in 1604, just a few years before the invention of the telescope. It was not until much more recently, however, that the qualitative difference between the long- and short-lived events came to be understood.

Precisely 1,700 years after the Guest Star of 185, a much fainter outburst was observed in the distant Andromeda nebula (now called the Andromeda galaxy). Though visible only through a telescope, this event was to be the key that unlocked the mystery of these sudden celestial visitors. By 1930 it was realized that Andromeda was a separate "island universe" from our own Milky Way, and that its stars were a million times more distant than those in our Galaxy. This new Guest Star, then, must have been of spectacular intrinsic brilliance, and in a 1934 paper, Walter Baade and Fritz Zwicky coined the term *supernova* to describe such events. A rough calculation of the energy involved suggested that indeed only the disruption of an entire star could produce such a celestial display. The scientific study of supernovae had begun.

SUPERNOVA REMNANTS

When we point our telescopes in the direction of the supernova of 185, we find ample evidence of what the explosion has wrought. A giant bubble of gas roughly forty light years across has been heated to a temperature of nearly 25 million degrees by the shock of the explosion. At the edge of this cavity the interstellar magnetic field has been compressed and tangled, accelerating particles to extremely high energies, which in turn create a rim that glows brightly with radio waves. Shards of the exploded star, now mixing with the surrounding gas, show evidence of a most unusual chemical composition, an indication of the material's origin deep in the parent star.

Such supernova remnants are also seen in the sky where each of the five other historical guest stars appeared, and a total of 140 further examples have been discovered throughout the Galaxy. The total energy from these explosions, all of which have occurred in the past 20,000 years or so, is enough to heat the gas in a large portion of interstellar space to a temperature of over a million degrees and to dominate the motions of the cooler clouds which mark stellar birth sites. And yet it is clear that only a tiny fraction of all stars end their lives in such a dramatic fashion. Why and how such explosions occur, along with the examination of the products they produce, form one of the central areas of study in modern astronomy.

THE FATE OF THE SUN

The Sun's size, shape, and brightness have been very nearly constant for more than 4 billion years, and we fully expect them to remain so for another 5 billion years. This constancy, however, does not imply that the Sun is a static body. Each second, in its superheated core, 4 million tons of matter (enough to fill a coal train stretching from New York to Philadelphia) are turned into pure energy. This process is the byproduct of a nuclear reaction that converts nearly a billion tons of the simplest element, hydrogen, into a like amount of the slightly more complex element helium. The energy produced in this way goes to maintain the intense heat at the center of the Sun, resulting in an outward pressure sufficient to balance the relentless inward pull of gravity. To maintain a constant core temperature, the Sun must ultimately radiate away this energy; the light and heat we receive over 100 million kilometers out in space is the visible sign of the nuclear fires in the core which provide each square centimeter of the Sun's surface with 25,000 watts of power.

This conversion of hydrogen to helium, however, is a one-way street and eventually the Sun will simply run out of fuel. At that point, the energy to sustain the thermal pressure of the core will disappear and the Sun will begin to shrink. The gravitational energy released in this contraction will go in part to keep the Sun shining and in part will, at first, actually increase the core's temperature. The core density will also rise as the material there is squeezed into a smaller and smaller space. If the density and temperature become great enough, new nuclear reactions can ignite. The ashes of the initial hydrogen fusion, helium, become the fuel for the next nuclear reaction cycle which produces such elements as carbon, nitrogen, and oxygen. When these new reactions begin, the energy released halts the collapse and a new balance between gravity and thermal pressure is established. These new reactions run to completion much more rapidly, however, and the helium-powered phase will typically last less than 10 percent as long as the hydrogen-powered part of a star's life cycle.

For the Sun, helium burning will be the end of the road. When the entire core has been converted to carbon, nitrogen, and oxygen, the collapse will begin again and no new cycle of nuclear burning will turn on to stop it. The diameter of the Sun will shrink from over 1 million kilometers to less than 10,000 kilometers, similar in size to the Earth. The collapse will stop only when a new

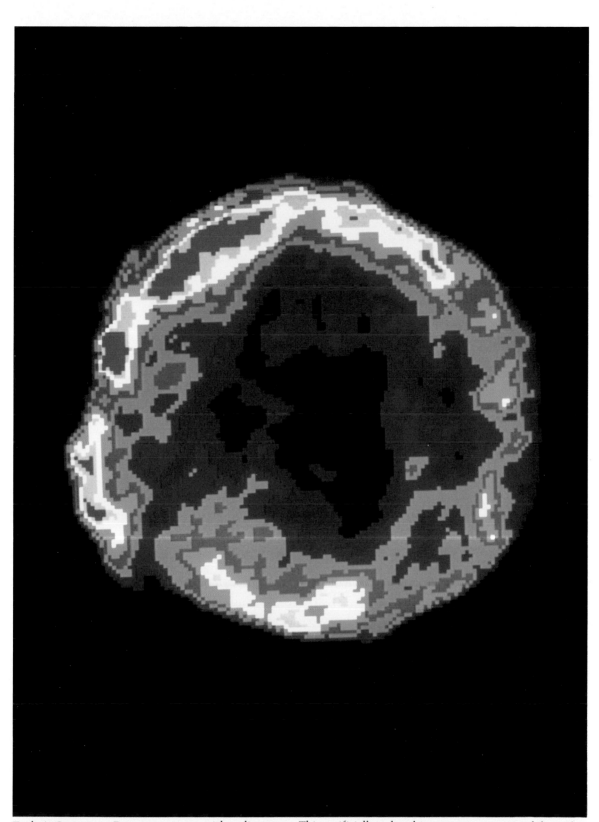

Tycho's Supernova Remnant as seen with radio waves. This artificially colored image was constructed from data gathered with the Very Large Array telescope. Observers: S. P. Reynolds & R. A. Chevalier; photo courtesy of NRAO/AUI.

force finally emerges to counter the relentless pull of gravity. It is a force unknown in everyday matter, a force that arises from the fundamental abhorrence of electrons for one another. When squeezed to a density of roughly one ton per teaspoonful, electrons resist further compression with an intensity much greater than the simple electrical repulsion of two like-charged particles. The result is the conversion of a normal, Sun-like star into what astronomers call a "white dwarf."

Since most stars have life cycles similar to that of our Sun, most stars will end up as slowly cooling Earth-sized embers. Such a star, in a lock between the forces of gravity and electron pressure, has no further sources of energy to draw upon and gradually cools and fades from view, finally becoming a black dwarf. Billions of white and black dwarfs exist in the Galaxy, although their small size and fading brightness leave them unrepresented among the naked-eye stars. When the Sun reaches this stage of its evolution, the Earth will become a frozen, lifeless wasteland.

THE ORIGIN OF THE ELEMENTS

If all stars followed a similar life cycle, however, the Earth would not even exist. For the elements of which the Earth is made—the silicon, calcium, and magnesium of the rocks, the nitrogen and oxygen of the atmosphere, and the iron and nickel of the core—are not primordial material. Such atoms did not exist at earlier epochs in the universe, when our Milky Way galaxy was first forming. At that ancient time, essentially all matter was in the form of hydrogen and helium (in a ratio of roughly four to one) with tiny traces of the next lightest element, lithium. Since helium undergoes no chemical reactions of any kind, and hydrogen plus lithium form only one simple two-atom combination, the universe would have remained a chemically very simple place.

In fact, of course, there are ninety-two naturally occurring atomic species and a vastly greater variety of atomic combinations which make up the richness of both the animate and inanimate Earth. And except for the original three, all of these atoms—the phosphorus in a DNA molecule, the carbon in a lump of coal, the calcium in your teeth—were created and/or distributed by exploding supernovae.

For stars at least eight to ten times the mass of the Sun, evolution does not stop at the helium-burning phase. The contraction following helium exhaustion raises the central temperature and pressure to the point where the carbon ashes can react to form still heavier elements, such as neon and magnesium. This in turn raises the central temperature to the point where collapse stops and balance between gravity and thermal pressure is reestablished. In addition, the layer of helium remaining outside the core region begins to burn, adding more ashes to the carbon fire, while even farther out, hydrogen ignites for the first time to create new helium.

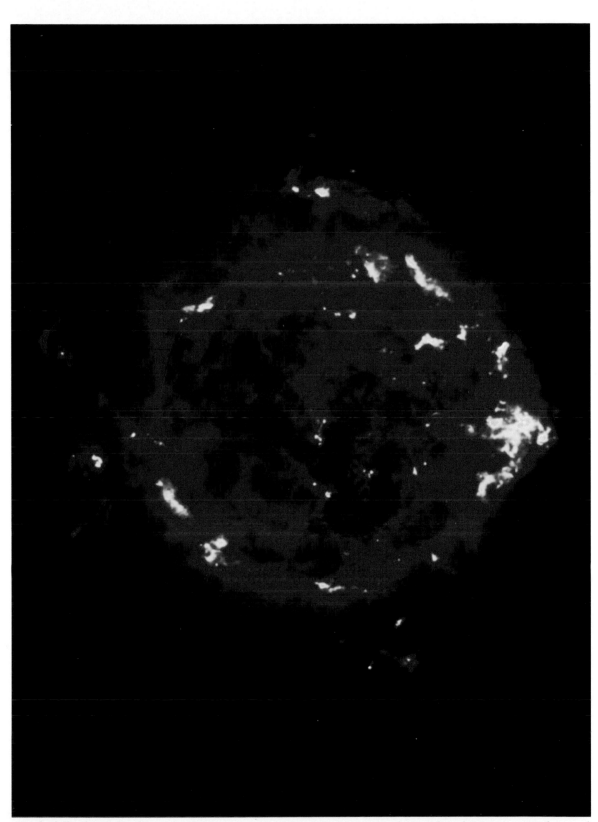

Wonderfully detailed radiograph of the supernova remnant Cassiopeia A, deep within the Perseus spiral arm of our galaxy. This image (from Very Large Array observations) was constructed using a Cray supercomputer. Observers: P. Angerhofer, R. Braun, S. Gull, & R. Perley; photo courtesy of NRAO/AUI.

The structure of such a star soon comes to resemble that of an onion, with an outermost layer of original material within which we find shells of helium, then carbon and oxygen, then neon and magnesium, and so forth. Fuel exhaustion, collapse initiation, and reignition repeat with increasing frequency until a half-dozen layers containing a mix of the twenty-six lightest elements are formed. While the initial hydrogen cycle may take 10 million years in a star ten times as massive as the Sun, the final core burning to iron (element 26) takes only a few hours to go to completion.

And then what? With sixty-six elements to go, one might well imagine that the star still has some time before it runs out of fuel. But iron occupies a special niche among all the atomic nuclei: It is the most stable arrangement of nuclear particles possible. Unlike the case of the lighter nuclei, the addition of even a single hydrogen nucleus to a nucleus of iron *absorbs* energy rather than releasing it. In seconds, then, nuclear processes, which for millions of years have held the star against collapse, come to join forces with gravity to plunge the star toward destruction. The star implodes to become a supernova.

SUPERNOVA

We are still not certain of the exact mechanism through which the vast amount of energy released in the *im*plosion of the core results in the *ex*plosion of the star's outer layers which we observe in a supernova. We can calculate that the total energy produced in the one-second collapse is equivalent to one hundred times the total output of the Sun over its 10 billion-year lifetime. Much of the energy escapes in essentially invisible forms such as neutrinos and gravitational waves. Only 1 percent of this vast energy is required to expel the outer 90 percent of the star at speeds exceeding 15,000 kilometers per second. And only one one-hundredth of 1 percent is needed to power the spectacular visible light display such as the one witnessed by the Chinese in A.D. 185.

The ultimate fate of the star's core is also unclear. In some stars, it is thought that the matter is heated sufficiently by runaway nuclear reactions to bring about a reversal of inward-falling material, and the complete disruption of the star ensues. In the most massive stars, the collapse may prove irreversible; matter plunges onward toward the central point, rending the fabric of spacetime and forming a black hole (a fascinating scenario which will be discussed in the next chapter). There is a third possibility, however, which we are certain happens to at least some stars. In this case, the core collapse is halted when, as we shall see, matter turns into a form containing mainly neutrons, and still another new force comes into play.

Analogous to the electron-electron repulsion which supports white dwarfs, this new force holds the neutrons apart with sufficient strength to support one or two Sun's worth of material in a ball only twenty-five kilometers across. As the in-falling matter from the rest of the star crashes into this suddenly rigidified core, it bounces back, hurtling away into space. A neutron star has been born.

THE NEUTRON STAR

Matter is composed predominantly of empty space. The atoms that make up the pages of this book, the wine in your glass, and the air in your lungs are all constructed from just three fundamental particles: the negative, light electron; the more massive, positively charged proton; and the similarly massive but uncharged neutron. The latter two particles are bound tightly together in the atom's nucleus, a dense, tiny ball typically one trillionth of a centimeter across. The fleet electrons circle this nucleus at distances of roughly 10,000 times the nuclear diameter, held in their orbits by the strong electrical attraction of the protons' opposite electrical charge. Between the electron and the nucleus is a vacuum—empty space; if we were to build a scale model of an atom with a basketball as the nucleus, the electrons would be represented by a swarm of circling peas about a kilometer away, with nothing at all in between.

In familiar forms of matter, these atoms are arranged in a variety of ways. In a gas, their average separation depends on quantities such as temperature and pressure; the air in your room, for example, has particles spaced at roughly ten times their average diameter. In a liquid, the electron orbits of neighboring atoms are nearly touching, but the atoms are free to slide over each other, allowing the liquid to take the shape of its container but preventing any attempt to pack the atoms more closely. (Try compressing a glass of water with an inverted jar cover if you're doubtful.) Solids have their atoms arranged in fixed patterns and thus resist changes in both size and shape.

The density of a substance or the amount of mass in a given volume (for example, grams per cubic centimeter, or ounces per teaspoonful) is determined both by how tightly packed its atoms are and how much each atom weighs. Water has a density of one gram per cubic centimeter, whereas a typical rock has a density five times this value, and a block of uranium, the element with heaviest individual atoms, is nearly four times denser still (18.95 grams per cubic centimeter). Air at the surface of the Earth contains only .001 gram per cubic centimeter. It is in this context, then, that we must try to imagine what neutron star material is like.

At the surface we find iron atoms packed so closely that each cubic centimeter of matter weighs one ton (making excavation projects on the stellar crust tedious in the extreme). As we move farther into the star, the atoms are crushed closer and closer together under the tremendous pressure of the overlying material until, at a depth of about three hundred meters, the density reaches 1 million tons per teaspoon. Atoms are no longer recognizable entities as the electrons are pushed from their individual orbits by encroaching neighbors and flow freely through a sea of densely packed nuclei.

As we continue inward, the pressure and density continue to rise, the electrons increasingly find themselves "face to face" with an oppositely charged proton, and occasionally, in this incredibly dense environment, the two snap together in a nuclear reaction, creating a new neutron plus a ghostly *neutrino* which quickly escapes from the star. Farther into the star, the rough equality among the numbers of protons, neutrons, and electrons begins to shift in favor of the neutrons until, at a depth of nearly ten kilometers, only 2 percent of the particles remain charged. First atoms, then their nuclei, have been crushed out of existence, giving way to a sea of freely moving neutrons. The density has reached 10 billion tons per teaspoonful—the mass of an entire star has been compressed to the density of an atomic nucleus.

At the very heart of the neutron star, even more exotic forms of matter may exist, but here our knowledge of physics begins to fail us. One possibility is that a new type of nuclear particle, the pion, forms and condenses into a rigid crystalline core. Another is that the neutrons themselves begin to dissolve into their constituents, *quarks*—the most fundamental particles we know.

Despite the remoteness of these forms of matter from our everyday experience, work on solving the mystery of the neutron star's core is an active field of research. We have built giant particle accelerators, miles in circumference, which smash individual atomic nuclei together with tremendous energy in an attempt to re-create, for a few fleeting microseconds, the densities encountered in a neutron star core. In addition, we send X-ray telescopes into space to measure the energy radiated from recently formed neutron stars, in order to gauge how rapidly they have cooled from the trillion-degree temperatures of the fiery birth; rapid cooling, for example, would suggest that a pion condensate exists. And, as we move closer to an understanding of the neutron star's core, we learn more about the structure and constituents of atomic nuclei themselves, the building blocks from which all matter in the universe is made.

The remarkable density and composition of a neutron star are not its only noteworthy features. In the collapse of the stellar core which leads to the neutron star's formation, the rotation of the star and the strength of its magnetic field also increase dramatically. Our Sun rotates at the leisurely pace of once every twenty-eight days. But just as a twirling figure skater spins faster as she draws her arms toward her body, a shrinking sphere rotates faster and faster as its radius decreases. Were we to suddenly collapse the Sun to the fifteen-kilometer size of a neutron star, its spin rate would rise to a thousand times *per second*. Likewise, the Sun's magnetic field—which, on average, is about ten times the strength of the Earth's field—would increase a trillionfold in such a collapse to neutron star size.

The only permanent stellar remnant of a supernova, then, is this superdense, rapidly spinning, highly magnetic star made primarily of neutrons. With their tiny size and lack of any internal energy source, you might well imagine that we have little hope of ever removing these remarkable bodies from the realm of theory and speculation. In 1960 most astronomers and physicists would have thought the same way. But in the past twenty-five years we have discovered several distinct and completely unexpected manifestations of neutron stars, signaling their presence throughout the Galaxy.

PULSARS

NOVEMBER 28, 1967. LATE EVENING.

A Cambridge University graduate student, having spent the summer driving fence posts into a meadow and stringing antenna wire between them, sits at the console of the novel radiotelescope watching the chart paper spew out of the recorder. The endless wavy black line, mimicking the cosmic static coming over the audio monitor, is punctuated by the occasional click from an unshielded light switch being flicked on or the rising and falling drum roll produced by the spark plugs firing in a passing car. This new telescope has been designed to observe distant radio sources as they drift overhead and, by examining how they "twinkle" in the tenuous clouds of charged particles permeating the solar system, to determine their sizes more accurately than the largest existing radiotelescopes can manage. A unique aspect of this new instrument is that it is set up to notice changes in signal strength over a fraction of a second. Since astronomers are used to evolutionary time scales of millions of years, this sort of high time resolution has never been used before.

Having learned to distinguish easily between man-made interference and the twinkling radio sources, Jocelyn Bell is troubled by a bit of "scruff" on the chart record which has appeared each of the past several evenings. It looks neither like interference nor like a properly behaved radio source. It has reappeared each night four minutes earlier than the last, indicating that it is moving across the sky at the same rate as the stars. Tonight, as the predicted reappearance time for the source approaches, she speeds up the chart recorder to have a closer look. The radio signal appears as a series of regularly spaced pulses 1.33 seconds apart. The discovery will shake the astronomical community and eventually confirm the existence of neutron stars.

Initial speculation on the pulses' origin ranged from "L.G.M.'s" (Little Green Men) to pulsing white dwarfs to a variety of exotica in between. The discovery of a dozen other such sources within a year, however, all with different pulse repetition rates and positions in the sky—but otherwise similar characteristics—convinced even the most arrogant Earthlings that these radio beacons were not all deliberately aimed at us by civilizations throughout the Galaxy. It was much more likely that the cause was a natural phenomenon, albeit an extraordinary one.

The pieces of the puzzle all came together with the discovery and analysis of one pulsed signal in particular. In the year A.D. 1054, Chinese astronomers had noted a brilliant Guest Star in what we now call the constellation of Taurus the bull. Today, the remnant of the explosion can be seen as a chaotic nebula that reminded early telescopic observers of a crab. It was in the center of this Crab nebula that the crucial signal was found, pulsing at an astonishing *thirty times a second*. A pulse this frequent imposed some very strict physical limits on the underlying mechanism and eliminated all the contending explanations except that of a rotating neutron star. A year later, in 1969, time-lapse photography revealed that the visible star at the center of this remnant was actually the neutron star itself, blinking on and off at the same thirty cycles per second, a rate just a little too fast for the human eye to perceive. *Pulsars,* as these objects came to be called, showed that neutron stars were real.

Today, more than four hundred radio pulsars have been detected in the Galaxy. Twenty years of intensive study has taught us much of what we know about the masses, spin rates, magnetic fields, and internal structure of neutron stars. Their unexpectedly high velocities and their distribution in the Galaxy contain clues to the ways supernovae collapse and the fates of many massive stars. Used as supremely accurate clocks, they provide us with information on interstellar matter and offer a unique new test of Einstein's general theory of relativity. Even theories in fields as diverse as nuclear physics and cosmology, the study of the origin of the universe, are constrained by pulsar observations. Their extreme densities and electromagnetic fields provide us with unique astrophysical laboratories in space.

Pulsars, it turns out, don't pulse at all. The regular bursts of radio emission we observe originate in *continuous* beams of radiation which emerge from the star at each of its magnetic poles. As in the Earth, the magnetic axis of the typical neutron star is not aligned with its rotation axis (the line around which it spins). As one of the magnetic poles is brought around to point at the Earth, once each rotation, a beam of radio waves sweeps over us and creates a pulse— much as the continuous beacon, rotating atop a lighthouse, flashes its warning to ships at sea.

In a pulsar the beams are created at the surface of the star where the rapidly turning magnetic fields set up an electric field of 100 trillion volts. Gargantuan lightning bolts zap the surface, prying loose charged particles and accelerating them to very nearly the speed of light. These particles move away from the star, constrained to travel along the magnetic lines of force and radiating high-energy gamma rays as they go. These gamma rays in turn produce matter/antimatter particle pairs which move on to create more gamma rays. A cascade of particles and radiation ensues, following along the star's magnetic axes until all colors of the electromagnetic rainbow—from radio waves through visible light to X-rays—are beamed away into space. We observe a flash of this radiation each time the beam sweeps past our telescopes once per stellar rotation.

All of this energy leaving the star must come from somewhere. No nuclear reactions occur in the center of a neutron star (remember, it's all at the density of an atomic nucleus already!) and its radius is held rigidly fixed so that no

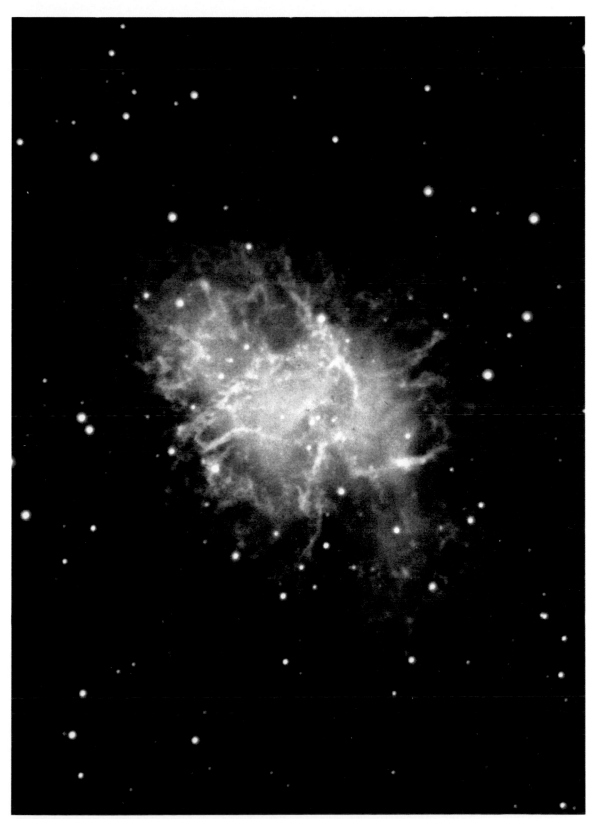

The Crab nebula (M1), the remnant of a supernova seen on Earth in A.D. 1054. Photo courtesy of the Lick Observatory.

contraction occurs. The only other source of energy the star has is its spin, and it is indeed the gradual slowing down of the neutron star's rotation that yields the power for its pulsar beacon. Although it was the remarkable *stability* of the pulsar periods that led to their discovery and the initial excitement about Little Green Men, it has been the very subtle changes in their rates of pulsation that have led to our present detailed understanding of neutron star structure and evolution.

PULSAR CLOCKS

The average spin rate of an ordinary pulsar is about two rotations per second. The young neutron star in the center of the remnant of the supernova explosion of A.D. 1054, the Crab Nebula pulsar, is spinning thirty times each second, while the slowest known rotator spins only once every four and a half seconds. It turns out that all of the known radio pulsars are slowing down. The largest declines are usually seen in the youngest stars, with the current record being a loss of a millionth of a second per year. (Pulsars are really very good clocks!) However, the smallest slowdown rate yet observed is seen, somewhat surprisingly, in the star with the fastest spin rate of all. Astronomers have discovered a remarkable "millisecond pulsar," an object containing about as much mass as our Sun, and twenty-five kilometers in diameter that spins on its axis 660 times each second, yet loses time only at the rate of three billionths of a second each millennium. Nonetheless, this nearly imperceptible slowing of the gigantic flywheel is sufficient to power a beam of radiation with an energy equivalent to the output of a thousand Suns.

The millisecond pulsar is such an accurate clock that it may soon become the world's time standard. Other pulsars, however, have shown departures from their expected steady spin-down rates which have yielded important clues relevant to a variety of areas of study in physics and astronomy. For example, several objects have shown sudden increases in spin rate followed by a gradual relaxation to the original slowing pattern. Analysis of such events has led to detailed models describing the interior of neutron stars and general information on how matter behaves at nuclear densities. In addition, observation of pulsar spin rates over a period of years has been used, in combination with our knowledge of the Earth's motion around the Sun, to discover that many neutron stars are rocketing through space at speeds up to two hundred miles per second. The origin of these high velocities is uncertain; possibilities include an asymmetry in the supernova explosion, the effects of a companion star in orbit around the supernova's progenitor, and a photon rocket effect resulting from an offset of the magnetic axis from the star's rotation axis.

Finally, pulsar clocks have provided the first new opportunities in fifty years for testing Einstein's theory of general relativity (which will be described in some detail in James Trefil's chapter). Despite the fact that more than half of all normal stars come in pairs, only seven of the more than four hundred known pulsars have a binary companion. The pulsar labeled 1913 + 16 was the first to be discovered in a binary system, and it now appears that its companion is another neutron star. A decade of careful monitoring of this pulsar's spin rate has allowed us to determine masses for the two stars accurate to better than one half of 1 percent, by far the best mass measurement for any astronomical object outside the solar system. In addition, the roughly eight-hour orbit period of 1913 + 16, now calculable to nine decimal places, has been measured to have decreased by six ten-thousandths of a second over eight years, precisely the amount that should occur, according to general relativity, as a result of the emission of so-called gravity waves. These moving ripples of warped space-time have never been measured directly, and the 1913 + 16 observation is regarded as a major breakthrough in relativity physics. And more recently, the supreme timing accuracy of the millisecond pulsar has even been used to set limits on conditions in the very early universe, a fraction of a second after the Big Bang, by constraining how many longer-wavelength gravity waves are left over from that turbulent time. Thus, although pulsars turned out not to be the beacons of advanced civilizations, they continue to teach us many things about the astronomy of stars and the physics of matter, space, and time.

X - R A Y   S T A R S

From our knowledge of stellar evolution and our observations of supernovae in other galaxies similar to our own, we expect that there is, on average, one supernova explosion every fifty years in the Milky Way. Even if only a small fraction of such events create neutron stars (and we have direct evidence that at least 10 to 20 percent do), a complete census of the galactic neutron star population should number nearly 100 million. Most of these will be rotating slowly or will have magnetic fields which have weakened with age and will not operate as radio pulsars. However, if a convenient source of nearby matter exists, the tremendously strong gravitational attraction of a neutron star will assure that some energy will still be released. As matter falls toward the star, it picks up speed until, when it reaches the surface, it is traveling nearly 10 percent the speed of light. Such collisions with the star produce very high temperatures, typically in the range of tens or hundreds of millions of degrees. The result is a source of high-energy radiation—an X-ray or a gamma-ray star.

Five years before Jocelyn Bell's pulsar discovery, it was found quite accidentally that intense sources of X-ray radiation could be found throughout the sky. A quarter century of study employing increasingly sophisticated rocket- and satellite-borne detectors has allowed us to identify the various types of astronomical objects responsible for this high-energy radiation. The two brightest classes of galactic objects are both produced in supernovae: the hot clouds of gas stirred up by recent explosions, and binary X-ray stars in which one member of the stellar pair is a neutron star.

Nearly a hundred X-ray-emitting binary systems have been pinpointed in the Milky Way, and their properties are every bit as intriguing as those of the radio pulsars. In some cases the magnetic field is still strong enough to channel matter torn from the companion down onto the magnetic poles of the star. There, within an area of ten-by-ten city blocks, the energy equivalent of nearly 100,000 Suns is produced. Matter, crashing into the unyielding surface, is liberating heat and X-rays at a rate equivalent to 300,000 all-out nuclear wars per *square meter each second*. Passing within even a few light years (that's 20 trillion or 30 trillion miles) of such a star's magnetic pole would mean death within minutes from radiation exposure.

Because the heat from the accreting matter is concentrated at the stellar magnetic poles, we sometimes see a regular variation in the X-ray brightness and temperature as the neutron star rotates on its axis. The range of periods is even greater than that for pulsars, ranging from dozens of times per second up to once per fourteen minutes. And, unlike the radio pulsars, most of the X-ray pulsars have decreasing rather than lengthening intervals between pulses—they spin faster and faster as matter spiraling in from the companion strikes the surface in the direction of rotation, giving the star an extra little kick. Indeed, the most promising scenario for explaining the ultrafast millisecond radio pulsar is that it was born with a binary companion that it quite literally consumed over perhaps 100 million years, during which its spin rate increased from perhaps one rotation per second to the currently observed value of 660.

GAMMA-RAY BURSTS

The most mysterious of the celestial phenomena for which we hold neutron stars responsible are the so-called gamma-ray bursts. These brief, intense pulses of very high energy radiation were discovered in the early 1970's by Defense Department satellites sent aloft to monitor the nuclear test ban treaty by watching for the telltale bursts of radiation that accompany a thermonuclear explosion. While no Earth-based blasts were seen, over a hundred bright flashes from the sky occurred each year. After fifteen years, the number of bursts recorded has finally exceeded the number of theories put forward to explain them, but we are still far from a definitive model for the phenomenon. About the only consensus that has emerged is that neutron stars are probably responsible. The rapid fluctuations seen in the bursts, often on time scales as short as a thousandth of a second, suggest that a very small object is involved. In addition, we see among the gamma rays a distribution of energies that looks like that expected for radiation emerging from a high-gravity object with a relatively strong magnetic field—again suggesting neutron stars. Finally, the large number of bursts observed and the apparent lack of repetition in at least

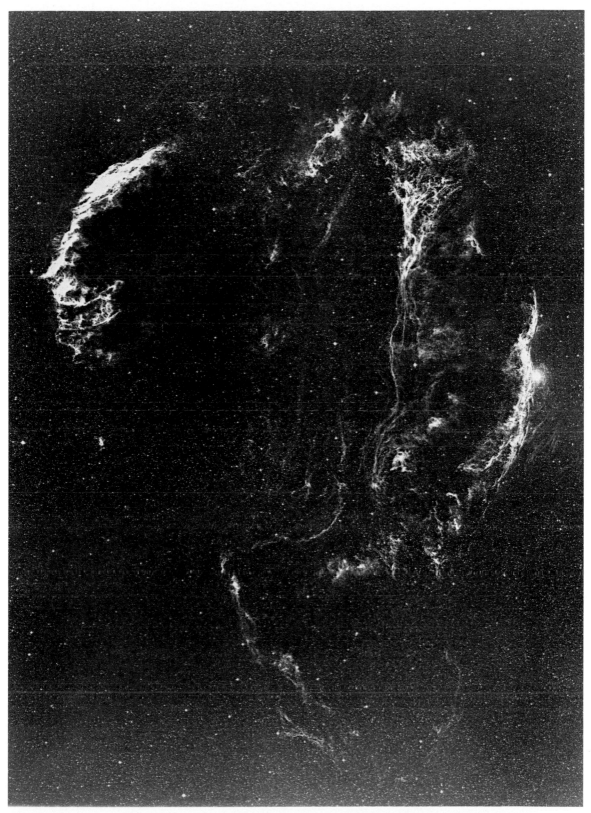

The Cygnus Loop, an older supernova remnant. Photo courtesy of Palomar Observatory/Caltech.

a decade for most sources requires a large population of bursting objects. The 100 million or so dead pulsars rattling around the galactic disk are thus implicated as prime suspects. Intensive searches of the sky in the vicinity of the few well-localized bursts has turned up nothing at radio or visible wavelengths, however, and it may well take another stroke of serendipity, similar to the discovery of the bursts themselves, before these suspects are convicted.

As with much of modern astrophysics, the study of supernovae was begun in antiquity but saw substantial progress only in the past few decades. Only thirty years ago, the origin of the chemical elements was a mystery and the neutron star was regarded as a rather obscure figment of a few theorists' imaginations. Although we now have a solid picture of how supernovae synthesize new matter and have confirmed the existence of neutron stars in a variety of settings, many questions remain: Precisely which stars end their lives in these cataclysmic explosions? Exactly what mix of new elements do they produce? And how many actually leave neutron stars behind? What is the ultimate fate of pulsars and X-ray stars, and to what extent do supernova explosions influence the formation of new stellar generations? With powerful new instruments to probe the heavens and with the increasingly close connections between physics and astronomy to guide us, the prospects for finding answers to such questions are bright. Meanwhile, each astronomer is secretly waiting in hopes that one night soon a new K'o-hsing in our part of the Galaxy will blaze forth in the sky, giving us our first close-up view of these creative cataclysms. *

---

*As we go to press, the next best thing has happened—a supernova in our nearest neighbor galaxy, the Large Magellanic Cloud, has erupted. Easily visible to the naked eye, it has sent hundreds of astronomers around the world into a frenzy of activity, employing every telescope on Earth and in space to record each detail of the rare event.

THE IRON STAR

ROBERT SILVERBERG

THE ALIEN SHIP CAME DRIFTING UP from behind the far side of the neutron star just as I was going on watch. It looked a little like a miniature neutron star itself: a perfect sphere, metallic, dark. But neutron stars don't have six perky little outthrust legs, and the alien craft did.

While I paused in front of the screen the alien floated diagonally upward, cutting a swath of darkness across the brilliantly starry sky like a fast-moving black hole. It even occulted the real black hole that lay thirty light-minutes away.

I stared at the strange vessel, fascinated and annoyed, wishing I had never seen it, wishing it would softly and suddenly vanish away. This mission was sufficiently complicated already. We hadn't needed an alien ship to appear on the scene. For five days now we had circled the neutron star in seesaw orbit with the aliens, 180 degrees apart. They hadn't said anything to us and we didn't know how to say anything to them. I didn't feel good about that. I like things direct, succinct, known.

Lina Sorabji, busy enhancing sonar transparencies over at our improvised archeology station, looked up from her work and caught me scowling. Lina is a slender, dark woman from Madras whose ancestors were priests and scholars when mine were hunting bison on the Great Plains. She said, "You shouldn't let it get to you like that, Tom."

"You know what it feels like, every time I see it cross the screen? It's like having a little speck wandering around on the visual field of your eye. Irritating, frustrating, maddening—and absolutely impossible to get rid of."

"You want to get rid of it?"

I shrugged. "Isn't this job tough enough? Attempting to scoop a sample from the core of a neutron star? Do we really have to have an alien spaceship looking over our shoulders while we work?"

"Maybe it's not a spaceship at all," Lina said cheerily.

115

"Maybe it's just some kind of giant spacebug."

I suppose she was trying to amuse me. I wasn't amused. This was going to win me a place in the history of space exploration, sure: Chief Executive Officer of the first expedition from Earth ever to encounter intelligent extraterrestrial life. Terrific. But that wasn't what IBM/Toshiba had hired me to do. And I'm more interested in completing assignments than in making history. You don't get paid for making history.

Basically the aliens were a distraction from our real work, just as last month's discovery of a dead civilization on a nearby solar system had been—the one whose photographs Lina Sorabji now was studying. This was supposed to be a business venture involving the experimental use of new technology, not an archaeological mission or an exercise in interspecies diplomacy. And I knew that there was a ship from the Exxon/Hyundai combine loose somewhere in hyperspace right now, working on the same task we'd been sent out to handle. If they brought it off first, IBM/Toshiba would suffer a severe loss of face, which is considered very bad on the corporate level. What's bad for IBM/Toshiba would be exceedingly bad for me. For all of us.

I glowered at the screen. Then the orbit of the *Ben-wah Maru* carried us down and away, and the alien disappeared from my line of sight. But not for long, I knew.

As I keyed up the log reports from my sleep period, I said to Lina: "You have anything new today?" She had spent the past three weeks analyzing the dead-world data. You never know what the parent companies will see as potentially profitable.

"I'm down to hundred-meter penetration now. There's a system of broad tunnels wormholing the entire planet. Some kind of pneumatic transportation network, is my guess. Here, have a look."

A holoprint sprang into vivid life in the air between us. It was a sonar scan that we had taken from 10,000 kilometers out, reaching a short distance below the surface of the dead world. I saw odd-angled tunnels lined with gleaming luminescent tiles that still pulsed with dazzling colors, centuries after the cataclysm that had destroyed all life there. Amazing decorative patterns of bright lines were plainly visible along the tunnel walls, lines that swirled and overlapped and entwined and beckoned my eye into some adjoining dimension.

Trains of sleek snub-nosed vehicles were scattered like caterpillars everywhere in the tunnels. In them and around them lay skeletons, thousands of them, millions, a whole continent full of commuters slaughtered as they waited at the station for the morning express. Lina touched the fine scan and gave me a close look: biped creatures, broad skulls tapering sharply at the sides, long apelike arms, seven-fingered hands with what seemed like an opposable thumb at each end, pelvises enlarged into peculiar bony crests jutting far out from their hips. It wasn't the first time a hyperspace exploring vessel had come

BOB EGGLETON

across relics of extinct extraterrestrial races, even a fossil or two. But these weren't fossils. These beings had died only a few hundred years ago. And they had all died at the same time.

I shook my head somberly. "Those are some tunnels. They might have been able to convert them into pretty fair radiation shelters, is my guess. If only they'd had a little warning of what was coming."

"They never knew what hit them."

"No," I said. "They never knew a thing. A supernova brewing right next door, and they must not have been able to tell what was getting ready to happen."

Lina called up another print, and another, then another. During our brief fly-by last month, our sensors had captured an amazing panoramic view of this magnificent lost civilization: wide streets, spacious parks, splendid public buildings, imposing private houses, the works. Bizarre architecture, all unlikely angles and jutting crests like its creators, but unquestionably grand, noble, impressive. There had been keen intelligence at work here, and high artistry. Everything was intact and in a remarkable state of preservation, if you make allowances for the natural inroads that time and weather and, I suppose, the occasional earthquake will bring over three or four hundred years. Obviously this had been a wealthy, powerful society, stable and confident.

And between one instant and the next it had all been stopped dead in its tracks, wiped out, extinguished, annihilated. Perhaps they had had a fraction of a second to realize that the end of the world had come, but no more than that. I saw what surely were family groups huddling together, skeletons clumped in threes or fours or fives. I saw what I took to be couples with their seven-fingered hands still clasped in a final exchange of love. I saw some kneeling in a weird elbows-down position that might have been one of . . . Who can say? Prayer? Despair? Acceptance?

A sun had exploded and this great world had died. I shuddered, not for the first time, thinking of it.

It hadn't even been their own sun. What had blown up was this one, forty light-years away from them, the one that was now the neutron star about which we orbited and which once had been a main-sequence sun maybe eight or ten times as big as Earth's. Or else it had been the other one in this binary system, thirty light-minutes from the first, the blazing young supergiant companion star, of which nothing remained except the black hole nearby. At the moment we had no way of knowing which of these two stars had gone supernova first. Whichever one it was, though, had sent a furious burst of radiation heading outward, a lethal flux of cosmic rays capable of destroying most or perhaps all life-forms within a sphere a hundred light-years in diameter.

The planet of the underground tunnels and the noble temples had simply been in the way. One of these two suns had come to the moment when all the fuel in its core had been consumed: Hydrogen had been fused into helium,

helium into carbon, carbon into neon, oxygen, sulfur, silicon, until at last a core of pure iron lay at its heart. There is no atomic nucleus more strongly bound than iron. The star had reached the point where its release of energy through fusion had to cease; and with the end of energy production the star no longer could withstand the gravitational pressure of its own vast mass. In a moment, in the twinkling of an eye, the core underwent a catastrophic collapse. Its matter was compressed—beyond the point of equilibrium. And rebounded. And sent forth an intense shock wave that went rushing through the star's outer layers at a speed of 15,000 kilometers a second.

Which ripped the fabric of the star apart, generating an explosion releasing more energy than a billion suns.

The shock wave would have continued outward and outward across space, carrying debris from the exploded star with it, and interstellar gas that the debris had swept up. A fierce sleet of radiation would have been riding on that wave, too: cosmic rays, X-rays, radio waves, gamma rays, everything, all up and down the spectrum. If the sun that had gone supernova had had planets close by, they would have been vaporized immediately. Outlying worlds of that system might merely have been fried.

The people of the world of the tunnels, forty light-years distant, must have known nothing of the great explosion for a full generation after it had happened. But all that while, the light of that shattered star was traveling toward them at a speed of 300,000 kilometers per second, and one night its frightful, baleful, unexpected glare must have burst suddenly into their sky in the most terrifying way. And almost in that same moment—for the deadly cosmic rays thrown off by the explosion move at nearly the speed of light—the killing blast of hard radiation would have arrived. And so these people and all else that lived on their world perished in terror and light.

All this took place a thousand light-years from Earth; that surging burst of radiation will need another six centuries to complete its journey toward our home world. At that distance, the cosmic rays will do us little or no harm. But for a time, that long-dead star will shine in our skies so brilliantly that it will be visible by day, and by night it will cast deep shadows, longer than those of the moon.

That's still in Earth's future. Here the fatal supernova, and the second one that must have happened not long afterward, were some four hundred years in the past. What we had here now was a neutron star left over from one cataclysm and a black hole left over from the other. Plus the pathetic remains of a great civilization on a scorched planet orbiting a neighboring star. And now a ship from some alien culture. A busy corner of the galaxy, this one. A busy time for the crew of the IBM/Toshiba hyperspace ship *Ben-wah Maru*.

I was still going over the reports that had piled up at my station during my sleep period—mass-and-output readings on the neutron star, progress bulletins on the setup procedures for the neutronium scoop, and other routine stuff of that nature—when the communicator cone in front of me started to glow. I flipped it on. Cal Bjornsen, our communications guru, was calling from Brain Central downstairs.

Bjornsen is mostly black African with some Viking genes salted in. The whole left side of his face is cyborg, the result of some extreme bit of teenage carelessness. The story is that he was gravity-vaulting and lost polarity at sixty meters. The mix of ebony skin, blue eyes, blond hair, and sculpted titanium is an odd one, but I've seen a lot of faces less friendly than Cal's. He's a good man with anything electronic.

He said, "I think they're finally trying to send us messages, Tom."

I sat up fast. "What's that?"

"We've been pulling in signals of some sort for the past ninety minutes that didn't look random, but we weren't sure about it. A dozen or so different frequencies all up and down the line, mostly in the radio band, but we're also getting what seem to be infrared pulses, and something flashing in the ultraviolet range. A kind of scattershot noise effect, only it isn't noise."

"Are you sure of that?"

"The computer's still chewing on it," Bjornsen said. The fingers of his right hand glided nervously up and down his smooth metal cheek. "But we can see already that there are clumps of repetitive patterns."

"Coming from them? How do you know?"

"We didn't, at first. But the transmissions conked out when we lost line-of-sight with them, and started up again when they came back into view."

"I'll be right down," I said.

Bjornsen is normally a calm man, but he was running in frantic circles when I reached Brain Central three or four minutes later. There was stuff dancing on all the walls: sine waves, mainly, but plenty of other patterns jumping around on the monitors. He had already pulled in specialists from practically every department—the whole astronomy staff, two of the math guys, a couple from the external maintenance team, and somebody from engines. I felt preempted. Who was CEO on this ship, anyway? They were all babbling at once. "Fourier series," someone said, and someone yelled back, "Dirichlet factor," and someone else said, "Gibbs phenomenon!" I heard Angie Seraphin insisting vehemently: " . . . continuous except possibly for a finite number of finite discontinuities in the interval minus-pi to pi—"

"Hold it," I said. "What's going on?"

More babbles, more gibberish. I got them quiet again and repeated my question, aiming it this time at Bjornsen.

"We have the analysis now," he said.

"So?"

"You understand that it's only guesswork, but Brain Central gives good guesses. The way it looks, they seem to want us to broadcast a carrier wave they can tune in on, and just talk to them while they lock in with some sort of word-to-word translating device of theirs."

"That's what Brain Central thinks they're saying?"

"It's the most plausible semantic content of the patterns they're transmitting," Bjornsen answered.

I felt a chill. The aliens had word-to-word translating devices? That was a lot more than we could claim. Brain Central is one very smart computer, and if it thought that it had correctly deciphered the message coming in, then in all likelihood it had. An astonishing accomplishment, taking a bunch of ones and zeros put together by an alien mind and culling some sense out of them.

But even Brain Central wasn't capable of word-to-word translation out of some unknown language. Nothing in our technology is. The alien message had been *designed* to be easy: put together, most likely, in a careful high-redundancy manner, the computer equivalent of picture-writing. Any race able to undertake interstellar travel ought to have a computer powerful enough to sweat the essential meaning out of a message like that, and we did. We couldn't go further than that, though. Let the entropy of that message—that is, the unexpectedness of it, the unpredictability of its semantic content—rise just a little beyond the picture-writing level, and Brain Central would be lost. A computer that knows French should be able to puzzle out Spanish, and maybe even Greek. But Chinese? A tough proposition. And an *alien* language? Languages may start out logical, but they don't stay that way. And when its underlying grammatical assumptions were put together in the first place by beings with nervous systems that were wired up in ways entirely different from our own, well, the notion of instantaneous decoding becomes hopeless.

Yet our computer said that their computer could do word-to-word. That was scary.

On the other hand, if we couldn't talk to them, we couldn't begin to find out what they were doing here and what threat, if any, they might pose to us. By revealing our language to them we might be handing them some sort of advantage, but I couldn't be sure of that, and it seemed to me we had to take the risk.

It struck me as a good idea to get some backing for that decision, though. After a dozen years as CEO aboard various corporate ships, I knew the protocols. You did what you thought was right, but you didn't go all the way out on the limb by yourself if you could help it.

"Request a call for a meeting of the corporate staff," I told Bjornsen.

It wasn't so much a scientific matter now as a political one. The scientists would probably be gung-ho to go blasting straight ahead with making contact. But I wanted to hear what the Toshiba people would say, and the IBM people, and the military people. So we got everyone together and I laid the situation out and asked for a Consensus Process. And let them go at it, hammer and tongs.

Instant polarization. The Toshiba people were scared silly of the aliens. We must be cautious, Nakamura said. Caution, yes, said her cohort Nagy-Szabo. There may be danger to Earth. We have no knowledge of the aims and motivations of these beings. Avoid all contact with them, Nagy-Szabo said. Nakamura went even further. We should withdraw from the area immediately, she said, and return to Earth for additional instructions. That drew hot opposition from Jorgensen and Kalliotis, the IBM people. We had work to do here, they said. We should do it. They grudgingly conceded the need to be wary, but strongly urged continuation of the mission and advocated a circumspect opening of contact with the other ship. I think they were already starting to think about alien marketing demographics. Maybe I do them an injustice. Maybe.

The military people were about evenly divided between the two factions. A couple of them, the hairsplitting career-minded ones, wanted to play it absolutely safe and clear out of here fast, and the others, the up-and-away hero types, spoke out in favor of forging ahead with contact and to hell with the risks.

I could see there wasn't going to be any consensus. It was going to come down to me to decide.

By nature I am cautious. I might have voted with Nakamura in favor of immediate withdrawal; however, that would have made my ancient cold-eyed Sioux forebears howl. Yet in the end, what swayed me was an argument that came from Bryce-Williamson, one of the fiercest of the military sorts. He said that we didn't dare turn tail and run for home without making contact, because the aliens would take that either as a hostile act or a stupid one, and either way they might just slap some kind of tracer on us that ultimately would enable them to discover the location of our home world. True caution, he said, required us to try to find out what these people were all about before we made any move to leave the scene. We couldn't just run and we couldn't simply ignore them.

I sat quietly for a long time, weighing everything.

"Well?" Bjornsen asked. "What do you want to do, Tom?"

"Send them a broadcast," I said. "Give them greetings in the name of Earth and all its peoples. Extend to them the benevolent warm wishes of the board of directors of IBM/Toshiba. And then we'll wait and see."

We waited. But for a long while we didn't see.

Two days, and then some. We went round and round the neutron star, and they went round and round the neutron star, and no further communication came from them. We beamed them all sorts of messages at all sorts of frequencies along the spectrum, both in the radio band and via infrared and ultraviolet as well, so that they'd have plenty of material to work with. Perhaps their translator gadget wasn't all that good, I told myself hopefully. Perhaps it was stripping its gears trying to fathom the pleasant little packets of semantic data we had sent them.

On the third day of silence I began feeling restless. There was no way we could begin the work we had been sent here to do, not with aliens watching. The Toshiba people—the Ultra Cautious faction—got more and more nervous. Even the IBM representatives began to act a little twitchy. I started to question the wisdom of having overruled the advocates of a no-contact policy. Although the parent companies hadn't seriously expected us to run into aliens, they had covered that eventuality in our instructions, and we were under orders to do minimum tipping of our hands if we found ourselves observed by strangers. But it was too late to call back our messages and I was still eager to find out what would happen next. So we watched and waited, and then we waited and watched. Round and round the neutron star.

We had been parked in orbit for ten days now around the neutron star, an orbit calculated to bring us no closer to its surface than nine thousand kilometers at the closest skim. That was close enough for us to carry out our work, but not so close that we would be subjected to troublesome and dangerous tidal effects.

The neutron star had been formed in the supernova explosion that had destroyed the smaller of the two suns in what had once been a binary star system here. At the moment of the cataclysmic collapse of the stellar sphere, all its matter had come rushing inward with such force that electrons and protons were driven into each other to become a soup of pure neutrons. Which then were squeezed so tightly that they were forced virtually into contact with one another, creating a smooth globe of the strange stuff that we call neutronium, 100 trillion times denser than steel and 100 million billion times more incompressible.

That tiny ball of neutronium glowing dimly in our screens was the neutron star. It was just eighteen kilometers in diameter, but its mass was greater than that of Earth's sun. That gave it a gravitational field a quarter of a billion billion times as strong as that of the surface of Earth. If we could somehow set foot on it, we wouldn't just be squashed flat; we'd be instantly reduced to fine powder by the colossal tidal effects—the difference in gravitational pull between the soles of our feet and the tops of our heads, stretching us toward and away from the neutron star's center with a kick of 18 billion kilograms.

A ghostly halo of electromagnetic energy surrounded the neutron star: X-rays, radio waves, gammas, and an oily, crackling flicker of violet light. The neutron star was rotating on its axis some 550 times a second, and powerful jets of electrons were spouting from its magnetic poles at each sweep, sending forth a beaconlike pulsar broadcast of the familiar type that we have been able to detect since the middle of the twentieth century.

Behind that zone of fiercely outflung radiation lay the neutron star's atmosphere: an envelope of gaseous iron a few centimeters thick. Below that, our scan had told us, was a two-kilometers-thick crust of normal matter, heavy elements only, ranging from molybdenum on up to transuranics with atomic numbers as high as 140. And within that was the neutronium zone, the stripped nuclei of iron packed unimaginably close together, an ocean of strangeness nine kilometers deep. What lay at the heart of *that*, we could only guess.

We had come here to plunge a probe into the neutronium zone and carry off a spoonful of star-stuff that weighed 100 billion tons per cubic centimeter.

No sort of conventional landing on the neutron star was possible or even conceivable. Not only was the gravitational pull beyond our comprehension—anything that was capable of withstanding the tidal effects would still have to cope with an escape velocity requirement of 60,000 kilometers per second when it tried to take off, two thirds the speed of light—but the neutron star's surface temperature was something like 3.5 million degrees. The surface temperature of our own Sun is six *thousand* degrees and we don't try to make landings there. Even at this distance, our heat and radiation shields were straining to the limits to keep us from being cooked. We didn't intend to go any closer.

What IBM/Toshiba wanted us to do was to put a miniature hyperspace ship into orbit around the neutron star: an astonishing little vessel no bigger than your clenched fist, powered by a fantastically scaled-down version of the drive that had carried us through the space-time manifold across a span of a thousand light-years in a dozen weeks. The little ship was a slave-drone; we would operate it from the *Ben-wah Maru*. Or, rather, Brain Central would. In a maneuver that had taken fifty computer-years to program, we would send the miniature into hyperspace and bring it out again *right inside the neutron star*. And keep it there a billionth of a second, long enough for it to gulp the spoonful of neutronium we had been sent here to collect. Then we'd head for home, with the miniature ship following us along the same hyperpath.

We'd head for home, that is, unless the slave-drone's brief intrusion into the neutron star released disruptive forces that splattered us all over this end of the galaxy. IBM/Toshiba didn't really think that was going to happen. In theory a neutron star is one of the most stable things there is in the universe, and the math didn't indicate that taking a nip from its interior would cause real problems. This neighborhood had already had its full quota of giant explosions, anyway.

Still, the possibility existed. Especially since there was a black hole just thirty light-minutes away, a souvenir of the second and much larger supernova bang that had happened here in the recent past. Having a black hole nearby is a little like playing with an extra wild card whose existence isn't made known to the players until some randomly chosen moment midway through the game. If we destabilized the neutron star in some way not anticipated by the scientists back on Earth, we might just find ourselves going for a visit to the event horizon instead of getting to go home. Or we might not. There was only one way of finding out.

I didn't know, by the way, what use the parent companies planned to make of the neutronium we had been hired to bring them. I hoped it was a good one.

But obviously we weren't going to tackle any of this while there was an alien ship in the vicinity. So all we could do was wait. And see. Right now we were doing a lot of waiting, and no seeing at all.

Two days later Cal Bjornsen said, "We're getting a message back from them now. Audio only. In English."

We had wanted that. We had even hoped for that. And yet it shook me to learn that it was happening.

"Let's hear it," I said.

"The relay's coming over ship channel seven."

I tuned in. What I heard was an obviously synthetic voice: no undertones or overtones, not much inflection. They were trying to mimic the speech rhythms of what we had sent them, and I suppose they were actually doing a fair job of it, but the result was still unmistakably mechanical-sounding. Of course there might be nothing on board that ship but a computer, I thought, or maybe robots. I wish now that they had been robots.

It had the absolute and utter familiarity of a recurring dream. In stiff, halting, but weirdly comprehensible English came the first greetings of an alien race to the people of the planet of Earth. "This who speak be First of Nine Sparg," the voice said. Nine Sparg, we soon realized from context, was the name of their planet. First might have been the speaker's name, or his—hers? its?—title; that was unclear, and stayed that way. In an awkward pidgin English that we nevertheless had little trouble understanding, First expressed gratitude for our transmission and asked us to send more words. To send a dictionary, in fact: Now that they had the algorithm for our speech, they needed more content to jam in behind it, so that we could go on to exchange more complex statements than *Hello* and *How are you.*

Bjornsen queried me on the override. "We've got an English program that we could start feeding them," he said. "Thirty thousand words: That should give them plenty. You want me to put it on for them?"

"Not so fast," I said. "We need to edit it first."

"For what?"

"Anything that might help them find the location of Earth. That's in our orders, under 'Eventuality of Contact with Extraterrestrials.' Remember, I have Nakamura and Nagy-Szabo breathing down my neck, telling me that there's a ship full of bogymen out there and we mustn't have anything to do with them. I don't believe that myself. But right now we don't know how friendly these Spargs are and we aren't supposed to bring strangers home with us."

"But how could a dictionary entry—"

"Suppose the Sun—*our* sun—is defined as a yellow G-two type star," I said. "That gives them a pretty good beginning. Or something about the constellations as seen from Earth. I don't know, Cal. I just want to make sure we don't accidentally hand these beings a road map to our home planet before we find out what sort of critters they are."

Three of us spent half a day screening the dictionary, and we put Brain Central to work on it too. In the end we pulled seven words—you'd laugh if you knew which they were, but we wanted to be careful—and sent the rest across to the Spargs. They were silent for nine or ten hours. When they came back on the air their command of English was immensely more fluent. Frighteningly more fluent. Yesterday, First had sounded like a tourist using a Fifty Handy Phrases program. A day later, First's command of English was as good as that of an intelligent Japanese who has been living in the United States for ten or fifteen years.

It was a tense, wary conversation. Or so it seemed to me, the way it began to seem that First was male and that his way of speaking was brusque and bluntly probing. I may have been wrong on every count.

First wanted to know who we were and why we were here. Jumping right in, getting down to the heart of the matter. I felt a little like a butterfly collector who has wandered onto the grounds of a fusion plant and is being interrogated by a security guard. But I kept my tone and phrasing as neutral as I could, and told him that our planet was called Earth and that we had come on a mission of exploration and investigation.

So had they, he told me. Where is Earth?

Pretty straightforward of him, I thought. I answered that I lacked at this point a means of explaining galactic positions to him in terms that he would understand. I did volunteer the information that Earth was not anywhere close at hand.

He was willing to drop that line of inquiry for the time being. He shifted to the other obvious one:

What were we investigating?

Certain properties of collapsed stars, I said, after a bit of hesitation.

And which properties were those?

I told him that we didn't have enough vocabulary in common for me to try to explain that either.

The Nine Sparg captain seemed to accept that evasion too. And provided me with a pause that indicated that it was my turn. Fair enough.

When I asked him what *he* was doing here, he replied without any apparent trace of evasiveness that he had come on a mission of historical inquiry. I pressed for details. It has to do with the ancestry of our race, he said. We used to live in this part of the galaxy, before the great explosion. No hesitation at all about telling me that. It struck me that First was being less reticent about dealing with my queries than I was with his; but of course I had no way of judging whether I was hearing the truth from him.

BOB EGGLETON

"I'd like to know more," I said, as much a test as anything else. "How long ago did your people flee this great explosion? And how far from here is your present home world?"

A long silence: several minutes. I wondered uncomfortably if I had over-played my hand. If they were as edgy about our finding their home world as I was about their finding ours, I had to be careful not to push them into an overreaction. They might just think that the safest thing to do would be to blow us out of the sky as soon as they had learned all they could from us.

But when First spoke again it was only to say, "Are you willing to establish contact in the visual band?"

"Is such a thing possible?"

"We think so," he said.

I thought about it. Would letting them see what we looked like give them any sort of clue to the location of Earth? Perhaps, but it seemed far-fetched. Maybe they'd be able to guess that we were carbon-based oxygen-breathers, but the risk of allowing them to know that seemed relatively small. And in any case we'd find out what *they* looked like. An even trade, right?

I had my doubts that their video transmission system could be made com-patible with our receiving equipment. But I gave First the go-ahead and turned the microphone over to the communications staff. Who struggled with the problem for a day and a half. Sending the signal back and forth was no big deal, but breaking it down into information that would paint a picture on a cathode-ray tube was a different matter. The communications people at both ends talked and talked and talked, while I fretted about how much technical information about us we were revealing to the Spargs. The tinkering went on and on and nothing appeared on screen except occasional strings of horizontal lines. We sent them more data about how our television system worked. They made further adjustments in their transmission devices. This time we got spots instead of lines. We sent even more data. Were they leading us on? And were we telling them too much? I came finally to the position that trying to make the video link work had been a bad idea, and started to tell communications that. But then the haze of drifting spots on my screen abruptly cleared and I found myself looking into the face of an alien being.

An alien face, yes. Extremely alien. Suddenly this whole interchange was kicked up to a new level of reality.

A hairless wedge-shaped head, flat and broad on top, tapering to a sharp point below. Corrugated skin that looked as thick as heavy rubber. Two chilly eyes in the center of that wide forehead and two more at its extreme edges. Three mouths, vertical slits, side by side: one for speaking and the other two, maybe, for separate intake of fluids and solids. The whole business supported by three long columnar necks as thick as a man's wrist, separated by open spaces two or three centimeters wide. What was below the neck we never got to see. But the head alone was plenty.

They probably thought we were just as strange.

With video established, First and I picked up our conversation right where he had broken it off the day before. Once more he was not in the least shy about telling me things.

He had been able to calculate in our units of time the date of the great explosion that had driven his people from their home world: It had taken place 387 years ago. He didn't use the word *supernova*, because it hadn't been included in the 30,000-word vocabulary we had sent them, but that was obviously what he meant by "the great explosion." The 387-year figure squared pretty well with our own calculations, which were based on an analysis of the surface temperature and rate of rotation of the neutron star.

The Nine Sparg people had had plenty of warning that their sun was behaving oddly—the first signs of instability had become apparent more than a century before the blowup—and they had devoted all their energy for several generations to the job of packing up and clearing out. It had taken many years, it seemed, for them to accomplish their migration to the distant new world they had chosen for their new home. Did that mean, I asked myself, that their method of interstellar travel was much slower than ours, and that they had needed decades or even a century to cover fifty or a hundred light-years? Earth had less to worry about, then. Even if they wanted to make trouble for us, they wouldn't be able easily to reach us, a thousand light-years from here. Or was First saying that their new world was *really* distant—all the way across the galaxy, perhaps, 70,000 or 80,000 light-years away, or even in some other galaxy altogether? If that was the case, we were up against truly superior beings. But there was no easy way for me to question him about such things without telling him things about our own hyperdrive and our distance from this system that I didn't care to have him know.

After a long and evidently difficult period of settling in on the new world, First went on, the Nine Sparg folk finally were well enough established to launch an inquiry into the condition of their former home planet. Thus his mission to the supernova site.

"But we are in great mystery," First admitted, and it seemed to me that a note of sadness and bewilderment had crept into his mechanical-sounding voice. "We have come to what certainly is the right location. Yet nothing seems to be correct here. We find only this little iron star. And of our former planet there is no trace."

I stared at that peculiar and unfathomable four-eyed face, that three-columned neck, those tight vertical mouths, and to my surprise something close to compassion awoke in me. I had been dealing with this creature as though he were a potential enemy, capable of leading armadas of war to my world and conquering it. But in fact he might be merely a scholarly explorer who was making a nostalgic pilgrimage, and running into problems with it. I decided to relax my guard just a little.

"Have you considered," I said, "that you might not be in the right location after all?"

"What do you mean?"

"As we were completing our journey toward what you call the iron star," I said, "we discovered a planet forty light-years from here which, beyond much doubt, had had a great civilization, and which evidently was close enough to the exploding star system here to have been devastated by it. We have pictures of it that we could show you. Perhaps *that* was your home world."

Even as I was saying it the idea started to seem foolish to me. The skeletons we had photographed on the dead world had had broad tapering heads that might perhaps have been similar to those of First, but they hadn't shown any evidence of this unique triple-neck arrangement. Besides, First had said that his people had had several generations to prepare for evacuation. Would they have left so many millions of their people behind to die? It looked obvious from the way those skeletons were scattered around that the inhabitants of the planet hadn't had the slightest clue that doom was due to overtake them that day. And finally, I realized that First had plainly said that it was his own world's sun that had exploded, not some neighboring star. The supernova had happened here. The dead world's sun was still intact.

"Can you show me your pictures?" he said.

It seemed pointless. But I felt odd about retracting my offer. And in the new rapport that had sprung up between us I could see no harm in it.

I told Lina Sorabji to feed her sonar transparencies into the relay pickup. It was easy enough for Cal Bjornsen to shunt them into our video transmission to the alien ship.

The Nine Sparg captain withheld his comment until we had shown him the batch.

Then he said, "Oh, that was not our world. That was the world of the Garvalekkinon people."

"The Garvalekkinon?"

"We knew them. A neighboring race, not related to us. Sometimes, on rare occasions, we traded with them. Yes, they must all have died when the star exploded. It is too bad."

"They look as though they had no warning," I said. "Look: Can you see them there, waiting in the train stations?"

The triple mouths fluttered in what might have been the Nine Sparg equivalent of a nod. "I suppose they did not know the explosion was coming."

"You suppose? You mean you didn't tell them?"

All four eyes blinked at once. Expression of puzzlement.

"Tell them? Why should we have told them? We were busy with our preparations. We had no time for them. Of course the radiation would have been harmful to them, but why was that our concern? They were not related to us. They were nothing to us.''

I had trouble believing I had heard him correctly. A neighboring people. Occasional trading partners. Your sun is about to blow up, and it's reasonable to assume that nearby solar systems will be affected. You have fifty or a hundred years of advance notice yourselves, and you can't even take the trouble to let these other people know what's going to happen?

I said, ''You felt no need at all to warn them? That isn't easy for me to understand.''

Again the four-eyed shrug.

''I have explained it to you already,'' said First. ''They were not of our kind. They were nothing to us.''

I excused myself on some flimsy pretext and broke contact. And sat and thought a long long while. Listening to the words of the Nine Sparg captain echoing in my mind. And thinking of the millions of skeletons scattered like straws in the tunnels of that dead world that the supernova had baked. A whole people left to die because it was inconvenient to take five minutes to send them a message. Or perhaps because it simply never had occurred to anybody to bother.

The families, huddling together. The children reaching out. The husbands and wives with hands interlocked.

A world of busy, happy, intelligent people. Boulevards and temples. Parks and gardens. Paintings, sculpture, poetry, music. History, philosophy, science. And a sudden star in the sky, and everything gone in a moment.

Why should we have told them? They were nothing to us.

I knew something of the history of my own people. We had experienced casual extermination too. But at least when the white settlers had done it to us, it was because they had wanted our land.

For the first time I understood the meaning of *alien.*

I turned on the external screen and stared out at the unfamiliar sky of this place. The neutron star was barely visible, a dull blue dot, far down in the lower left quadrant; and the black hole was high.

Once they had both been stars. What havoc must have attended their destruction! It must have been the Sparg Sun that blew first, the one that had become the neutron star. And then, fifty or a hundred years later, perhaps, the other, larger star had gone the same route. Another titanic supernova, a great flare of killing light. But of course everything for hundreds of light-years around had perished already in the first blast.

The second sun had been too big to leave a neutron star behind. So great was its mass that the process of collapse had continued on beyond the neutron-star stage, matter crushing in upon itself until it broke through the normal barriers of space and took on a bizarre and almost unthinkable form, creating an object of infinitely small volume that was nevertheless of infinite density:

a black hole, a pocket of incomprehensibility where once a star had been.

I stared now at the black hole before me.

I couldn't see it, of course. So powerful was the surface gravity of that grotesque thing that nothing could escape from it, not even electromagnetic radiation, not the merest particle of light. The ultimate in invisibility cloaked that infinitely deep hole in space.

But though the black hole itself was invisible, the effects that its presence caused were not. That terrible gravitational pull would rip apart and swallow any solid object that came too close; and so the hole was surrounded by a bright ring of dust and gas several hundred kilometers across. These shimmering particles constantly tumbled toward that insatiable mouth, colliding as they spiraled in, releasing flaring fountains of radiation, red-shifted into the visual spectrum by the enormous gravity: the bright green of helium, the majestic purple of hydrogen, the crimson of oxygen. That outpouring of energy was the death-cry of doomed matter. That rainbow whirlpool of blazing light was the beacon marking the maw of the black hole.

I found it oddly comforting to stare at that thing. To contemplate that zone of eternal quietude from which there was no escape. Pondering so inexorable and unanswerable an infinity was more soothing than thinking of a world of busy people destroyed by the indifference of their neighbors. Black holes offer no choices, no complexities, no shades of disagreement. They are absolute.

Why should we have told them? They were nothing to us.

After a time I restored contact with the Nine Sparg ship. First came to the screen at once, ready to continue our conversation.

"There is no question that our world once was located here," he said at once. "We have checked and rechecked the coordinates. But the changes have been extraordinary."

"Have they?"

"Once there were two stars here, our own and the brilliant blue one that was nearby. Our history is very specific on that point: a brilliant blue star that lit the entire sky. Now we have only the iron star. Apparently it has taken the place of our Sun. But where has the blue one gone? Could the explosion have destroyed it too?"

I frowned. Did they really not know? Could a race be capable of attaining an interstellar spacedrive and an interspecies translating device, and nevertheless not have arrived at any understanding of the neutron star/black hole cosmogony?

Why not? They were aliens. They had come by all their understanding of the universe via a route different from ours. They might well have overlooked this feature or that of the universe about them.

"The blue star—" I began.

But First spoke right over me, saying, "It is a mystery that we must devote all our energies to solving, or our mission will be fruitless. But let us talk of other things. You have said little of your own mission. And of your home world. I am filled with great curiosity, Captain, about those subjects."

I'm sure you are, I thought.

"We have only begun our return to space travel," said First. "Thus far we have encountered no other intelligent races. And so we regard this meeting as fortunate. It is our wish to initiate contact with you. Quite likely some aspects of your technology would be valuable to us. And there will be much that you wish to purchase from us. Therefore we would be glad to establish trade relations with you."

As you did with the Garvalekkinon people, I said to myself.

I said, "We can speak of that tomorrow, Captain. I grow tired now. But before we break contact for the day, allow me to offer you the beginning of a solution to the mystery of the disappearance of the blue sun."

The four eyes widened. The slitted mouths parted in what seemed surely to be excitement.

"Can you do that?"

I took a deep breath.

"We have some preliminary knowledge. Do you see the place opposite the iron star, where energies boil and circle in the sky? As we entered this system, we found certain evidence there that may explain the fate of your former blue sun. You would do well to center your investigations on that spot."

"We are most grateful," said First.

"And now, Captain, I must bid you good night. Until tomorrow, Captain."

"Until tomorrow," said the alien.

I was awakened in the middle of my sleep period by Lina Sorabji and Bryce-Williamson, both of them looking flushed and sweaty. I sat up, blinking and shaking my head.

"It's the alien ship," Bryce-Williamson blurted. "It's approaching the black hole."

"Is it, now?"

"Dangerously close," said Lina. "What do they think they're doing? Don't they know?"

"I don't think so," I said. "I suggested that they go exploring there. Evidently they don't regard it as a bad idea."

"You sent them there?" she said incredulously.

With a shrug I said, "I told them that if they went over there, they might find the answer to the question of where one of their missing suns went. I guess they've decided to see if I was right."

"We have to warn them," said Bryce-Williamson. "Before it's too late. Especially if we're responsible for sending them there. They'll be furious with us once they realize that we failed to warn them of the danger."

"By the time they realize it," I replied calmly, "it *will* be too late. And then their fury won't matter, will it? They won't be able to tell us how annoyed they are with us. Or to report to their home world, for that matter, that they had an encounter with intelligent aliens who might be worth exploiting.''

He gave me an odd look. The truth was starting to sink in.

I turned on the external screens and punched up a close look at the black hole region. Yes, there was the alien ship, the little metallic sphere, the six odd outthrust legs. It was in the zone of criticality now. It seemed hardly to be moving at all. And it was growing dimmer and dimmer as it slowed. The gravitational field had it, and it was being drawn in. Blacking out, becoming motionless. Soon it would have gone beyond the point where outside observers could perceive it. Already it was beyond the point of turning back.

I heard Lina sobbing behind me. Bryce-Williamson was muttering to himself: praying, perhaps.

I said, "Who can say what they would have done to us—in their casual, indifferent way—once they came to Earth? We know now that Spargs worry only about Spargs. Anybody else is just so much furniture." I shook my head. "To hell with them. They're gone, and in a universe this big we'll probably never come across any of them again, or they us. Which is just fine. We'll be a lot better off having nothing at all to do with them."

"But to die that way," Lina murmured. "To sail blindly into a black hole . . ."

"It is a great tragedy," said Bryce-Williamson.

"A tragedy for them," I said. "For us, a reprieve, I think. And tomorrow we can get moving on the neutronium-scoop project." I tuned up the screen to the next level. The boiling cloud of matter around the mouth of the black hole blazed fiercely. But of the alien ship there was nothing to be seen.

A great tragedy, yes, I thought. The valiant exploratory mission that had sought the remains of the Nine Sparg home world has been lost with all hands. No hope of rescue. A pity that they hadn't known how unpleasant black holes can be.

But why should we have told them? They were nothing to us.

BLACK HOLES

ESSAY BY

WILLIAM J. KAUFMANN

SPECULATION BY

CONNIE WILLIS

THE BLACK HOLE

WILLIAM J. KAUFMANN

San Diego State University

A BLACK HOLE is one of the most astonishing objects ever predicted by modern science. It is a place where gravity is so strong that nothing—not even light—can escape. Its gravity is so powerful that a hole has literally been punched in the fabric of space and time.

Scientists should have recognized the possibility of black holes in 1916, when the German astronomer Karl Schwarzschild succeeded in solving Einstein's equations for the gravity surrounding a point mass. Only a few months earlier, these equations had been written down for the first time by an inspired genius preoccupied with the possibility of a *geometrical description* of the phenomenon of gravitation. The crowning achievement of this quest is today called the general theory of relativity. Among the major predictions of this theory is that gravity slows time and warps space.

Far from any sources of gravity, clocks tick at their normal rate and space is flat. In other words, the sum of the angles of a triangle is exactly 180 degrees, and all of the usual rules we learned in high school geometry are obeyed. But near a source of gravity, the ticking of clocks is slowed and the geometry of space is curved. The stronger the gravity, the greater are these effects.

Although ingenious experiments using starlight passing by the eclipsed Sun and precise atomic clocks in our laboratories confirmed Einstein's predictions, for almost half a century, no one paid very much attention to general relativity. Mathematically, it was extremely complex and the old-fashioned description of the force of gravity—first proposed by Isaac Newton—gave predictions of required accuracy for the orbits of comets, planets, or whatever it was applied to. In truth, the gravitational fields we encounter on Earth and across the solar system are exceedingly weak—so weak that the curvature of space and the slowing of time can hardly be detected. It seemed inconceivable that gravity might somewhere be so strong that the full effects of general relativity would exhibit themselves.

NEUTRON STARS

Then the discovery of neutron stars burst upon astronomy in 1968. Pulsating radio sources, called pulsars, were found scattered all across the sky. The discovery of a pulsar at the center of the Crab nebula—the remnant of a gargantuan stellar explosion—began to convince astronomers that the extraordinarily dense objects called neutron stars might actually exist. Prior to 1968 the only type of identified stellar corpse was the white dwarf—a burned-out star squeezed by its own gravity into a hot, dense ball roughly the size of Earth. Shortly after the discovery of the subatomic particle called the neutron in 1932, astronomers speculated that some stellar corpses might become so compressed as to consist of side-by-side neutrons. In other words, could the matter of an entire star become as dense as an atomic nucleus? Such a star would be extremely small—perhaps only ten miles in diameter—but would contain as much mass as the Sun.

The first comprehensive description of a neutron star was given by J. Robert Oppenheimer in 1939, shortly before he began working on the first atomic bomb. Oppenheimer realized that gravity at the surface of a neutron star would be extremely strong. Indeed, the escape velocity—the speed needed to get away—from a neutron star equals half the speed of light. Oppenheimer suggested that it would take only a little more contraction for the gravity around a dead star to be so powerful that the escape velocity would *exceed* the speed of light. Since nothing can travel faster than light, nothing could ever leave such a highly collapsed object. Light itself could not escape from the grip of such powerful gravity, and thus the dead star would have permanently disappeared from the universe. Although Oppenheimer published a second paper in 1939 on these effects, it was not until 1955 that anyone began using the term *black hole* to describe such a collapsed star.

A BLACK HOLE MODEL

Imagine standing on the surface of a massive burned-out star that is just about to collapse to form a black hole. All of the star's nuclear fuel has been exhausted, and with no further energy output from the star's interior, it is doomed to collapse into oblivion. Also suppose that you have a powerful searchlight that shines beams of light out into space, as shown in the accompanying diagram.

Before the collapse begins, light rays leave your searchlight along straight lines. But as the collapse proceeds, the strength of gravity around the dead star grows, and thus space surrounding the star becomes increasingly curved. Light rays are thus deflected from their straight-line paths, bent back down to the star's shrinking surface, as shown in Figure 1 on page 139.

At a critical stage near the end of this collapse, you find that *all* beams of light are pulled down to the star's surface. Even the vertical beam that you had aimed directly outward into space becomes deflected inward. At this stage, physicists say that the star has collapsed within its own *event horizon*—a one-way corridor in the geometry of highly warped space. Since light beams aimed directly upward cannot get out, obviously nothing else can. The entire star has genuinely vanished from the rest of the universe.

The size of a star's event horizon depends on its mass. For example, a star containing ten times the mass of the Sun has an event horizon roughly thirty-six miles in diameter. As soon as all the star's matter becomes crushed inside a sphere thirty-six miles in diameter, an event horizon envelops the collapsing mass, which disappears. The term *event horizon* is very appropriate. It is literally a *horizon* in the geometry of space beyond which you cannot see any events.

Once inside its event horizon, the dead star continues to collapse. The star shrinks until its entire mass is crushed to infinite density at a single point, called the *singularity*, which becomes the center of the black hole. Thus a black hole has only two parts: a "surface" (the event horizon) and a "center" (the singularity). The distance between the surface and the center is often called the Schwarzschild radius.

In the vicinity of a black hole, the bizarre effects of general relativity become severe. For example, as viewed by an observer far from the hole, time slows down so much that clocks stop at the event horizon. Inside the event horizon the directions of space and time become interchanged! To understand what this means, think about your life here on Earth. You have freedom to move in the three dimensions of space, but you have no ability to move at will through the fourth dimension of time. Whether we like it or not, we are all being dragged relentlessly through time from the cradle to the grave.

Inside a black hole, you do gain a limited ability to move through time. But it does you no good because you find yourself pulled relentlessly through space from the event horizon into the singularity. That is why collapse to the singularity is inevitable. Just as we outside a black hole cannot halt the forward movement of time (past to future), inside a black hole it is impossible to halt the forward movement of space (event horizon to singularity). Once a star has fallen inside its event horizon, no forces in the universe can prevent the star from being crushed to a point.

To help visualize the geometry of a black hole, mathematicians have devised a variety of tricks. Foremost among these is to suppress two of the four dimensions of space-time. This is useful because we have no trouble visualizing and understanding two-dimensional surfaces. For example, it is obvious that a tabletop is flat, whereas the surface of a football is curved.

Imagine slicing through the warped geometry surrounding a black hole and pulling out a two-dimensional sheet of space. (Mathematicians call this process "taking a spacelike hypersurface.") Far from the black hole, gravity is weak, and thus your two-dimensional sheet is flat. Nearer the black hole, the sheet is curved somewhat like a funnel.

In the 1950's, when mathematicians first learned how to take spacelike hypersurfaces correctly, they found an extraordinary surprise. There are actually *two* outside regions and *two* inside regions to a black hole. In other words, there are two distinct flat regions far from the hole and two separate funnel-shaped regions back-to-back near the hole. The resulting geometrical shape, called an Einstein-Rosen bridge, is shown in Figure 2 on page 141.

How are we to interpret the Einstein-Rosen bridge? One possibility is that the full geometry of a black hole connects our universe (the upper sheet) to a separate parallel universe (the lower sheet). An alternative possibility is that the upper and lower sheets are actually connected to each other far from the hole. In that case, the Einstein-Rosen bridge would connect one part of our universe with another. Such a geometrical figure is often called a wormhole and is shown in Figure 3 on page 141. If you could travel through such a wormhole, you would find that it connects different locations and different times in our universe.

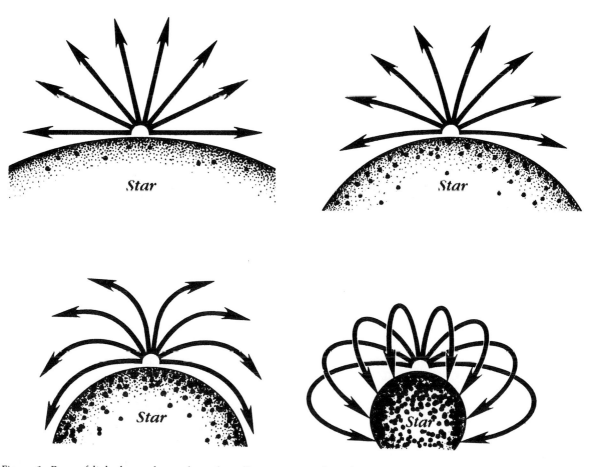

Figure 1. Rays of light leave the surface of a collapsing star. When the star collapses within its event horizon, no rays can escape.

FINDING BLACK HOLES

A search for black holes began in earnest in 1970 with the launch of Explorer 42 from the coast of Kenya on the equator. This satellite consisted of two X-ray telescopes which gave us our first comprehensive look at the X-ray sky. Using a satellite is required for such observations because X-rays do not penetrate the Earth's atmosphere. Out of gratitude to the Kenyan people, Explorer 42 was christened *Uhuru*, which means "freedom" in Swahili. During three years of flawless operation, *Uhuru* discovered nearly three-hundred different X-ray objects across the sky.

In 1972 a great deal of attention became focused on one particular X-ray source, called Cygnus X-1 because of its location in the constellation of Cygnus the Swan. It was soon discovered that this powerful X-ray source, which itself does not emit a detectable amount of light, is in orbit about an ordinary star much like the Sun. Discovering a double star is not unusual. Indeed, about half the stars you see in the sky at night are double stars. It was, however, very odd to discover a star that cannot be seen with light yet is one of the brightest X-ray sources in the sky.

All of the data that have accumulated about Cygnus X-1 can be interpreted as a black hole orbiting an ordinary star. Gas escaping from the outer atmosphere of the ordinary star is captured into orbit about the black hole, forming a huge disk that surrounds the hole. Gases in the disk become hotter and hotter as the enormous pull of gravity causes them to spiral in toward the hole. About a hundred miles above the hole, these gases reach a temperature of 2 million degrees, causing them to emit copious X-rays. Thus the X-rays reveal the existence of this superheated gas very near the black hole. No other explanation of the Cygnus X-1 data seems plausible, and thus many astronomers agreed a black hole had been discovered in this system. In the early 1980's, a similar double star system, called LMC X-3, was discovered in the Large Magellanic Cloud, a companion galaxy to our Milky Way. It seems quite likely that LMC X-3 is the second known black hole.

SUPERMASSIVE BLACK HOLES

In recent years, significant black hole research has become focused on galaxies and quasars. As you will read in a later chapter, some galaxies have been discovered to emit enormous amounts of energy, often at radio, infrared, or X-ray wavelengths. Because of their extraordinary energy output, they are often called active galaxies. Quasars seem to be an extreme version of these active galaxies. Although they look like stars (hence their name, contracted from "quasi-stellar object"), they are incredibly luminous. Indeed, a typical quasar shines with the brightness of a hundred galaxies.

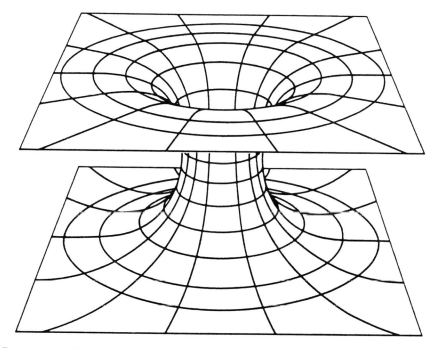

Figure 2: An Einstein-Rosen bridge

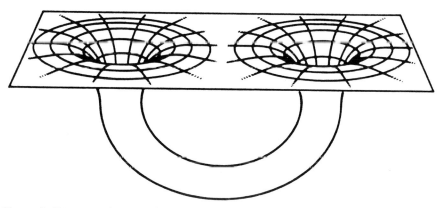

Figure 3: Diagram of a wormhole

Active galaxies and quasars exhibit surprisingly rapid brightness fluctuations. They flare up and dim back down over periods as short as a week. The frequency of such variations is related to the size of the object. Since nothing can travel faster than the speed of light, an object cannot fluctuate in brightness faster than light travels across that object. For instance, an object one light-year in diameter cannot fluctuate in brightness faster than once a year. Since quasars and active galaxies fluctuate as rapidly as once a week, their energy-producing regions must be as small as one light-week in diameter. Thus quasars and active galaxies produce the brightness of a hundred galaxies from a region roughly the size of the solar system!

How can so much energy be created in such a small volume? That has been a thorny question for astrophysicists since the 1960's. The answer seems to involve exceedingly massive black holes, each typically containing as much matter as a billion Suns. If a so-called *supermassive black hole* exists at the center of a galaxy, it would certainly attract enormous amounts of interstellar gas and dust. As the in-falling material plunges toward the hole, it would become extremely hot and release the huge energy output that astronomers observe. In a seeming paradox, therefore, black holes are responsible for the most luminous objects in the universe.

MINI-BLACK HOLES

Black holes can be a powerful source of energy in a very different way. Physicists find it very useful to think of empty space as filled with numerous particles and antiparticles that are continuously being created and destroyed.* At every point in space, for example, you can imagine that an electron and an antielectron come into existence for a very tiny fraction of a second, then annihilate each other and disappear. The only restriction on this novel idea is that the electron/antielectron pair can exist only for a time so short that they cannot be directly observed. Thus they are called "virtual pairs" because they don't really exist in the sense that they can be measured or studied—their existence is virtual.

Imagine a virtual pair of particles momentarily forming near the event horizon of a black hole. During their brief existence the two particles separate by a very tiny distance. If one of the particles slips across the event horizon, it disappears from the universe, leaving its partner with no ability to annihilate and return to the imaginary sea of virtual particles. Thus the exposed particle must become a real particle in the real world. The only readily available source for the particle's mass is the energy in the gravitational field of the black hole. Thus the newly created particle robs the hole of some of its mass and becomes

---

*An antiparticle is a piece of antimatter, material whose properties are opposite to ordinary matter. When a particle and an antiparticle meet, they annihilate each other and become pure energy.

free to wander off into space. In this way black holes can actually lose matter; hence, the process is called black hole evaporation.

This extraordinary effect—derived from our modern understanding of the subatomic realm called *quantum mechanics*—was discovered in 1974 by the brilliant British physicist Stephen Hawking. It is not important for big black holes such as those created by dead stars. But if there were very small black holes—especially those whose Schwarzschild radii are smaller than atoms—quantum mechanical evaporation would be of paramount importance. Quite simply, the smaller a black hole gets, the more particles it emits; the more particles it emits, the smaller it gets. This is a catastrophic runaway that dooms the remaining black hole to explode in a powerful blast of gamma rays.

No known astronomical process could produce small black holes today. Only during the Big Bang itself, when the whole universe throbbed with violent undulations of space and time, could tiny chunks of matter be crushed to the inconceivable densities needed to form tiny black holes. Thus a black hole small enough to exhibit significant evaporation must be a relic of the creation event.

In the mid-1970's, Stephen Hawking proved that an evaporating black hole is indistinguishable from what we call a *white hole*. Remember: A black hole is a region of powerful gravity into which things fall and forever disappear from the universe. A white hole is the time-reversal of a black hole. Particles and radiation spontaneously gush out of a white hole in precisely the same random way that they are emitted by an evaporating black hole.

A black hole is an "information sink," a place where information is irretrievably removed from the universe. For example, the chemical composition and molecular structure of an object falling into a black hole is the sort of information that the black hole deletes from the universe. Conversely, a white hole is an "information source" which constantly and randomly adds new and totally unexpected information to the universe. Thus Hawking's work suggests that there is a fundamental randomness to the content of the universe and the nature of reality.

BLACK HOLES AND THE BIG BANG

Understanding black holes also helps us answer important questions about the creation of the universe. Roughly 20 billion years ago, the entire universe was in a state of infinite density, like that found at the center of a black hole. But unlike a black hole, where the singularity is a point, the cosmic singularity of the Big Bang filled the entire universe. At a singularity, the curvature of space and time is infinite—which means that the past, the future, and the present are all mixed up with one another and with the directions of space. Consequently, space and time do not really exist as separate, identifiable entities; they are all jumbled up in a sort of space-time foam. Concepts like "up," "down," "past," and "future" have no meaning. You can never know what existed before the Big Bang because at the moment of the Big Bang you lose any ability to tell the direction of time. Questions like "What happened before the Big Bang?" are as meaningless as asking "What is north of the Earth's north pole?"

Stephen Hawking's unification of quantum mechanics and general relativity gives important insight into the nature of singularities. Because the gravity of a singularity is so strong, it is surrounded by a seething mass of particles and antiparticles constantly bursting into existence and annihilating one another. In an ordinary black hole, this chaotic process is forever hidden from us by the event horizon, and thus these random events do not influence the outside universe. But during the Big Bang, the whole universe was a singularity. In a single blinding flash, matter and radiation erupted everywhere. These ideas suggest that the universe began with an explosion because that is the only thing that the cosmic singularity could do.

SCHWARZSCHILD RADIUS

CONNIE WILLIS

"WHEN A STAR COLLAPSES, it sort of falls in on itself." Travers curved his hand into a semicircle and then brought the fingers in, "and sometimes it reaches a kind of point of no return where the gravity pulling in on it is stronger than the nuclear and electric forces, and when it reaches that point nothing can stop it from collapsing and it becomes a black hole." He closed his hand into a fist. "And that critical diameter, that point where there's no turning back, is called the Schwarzschild radius." Travers paused, waiting for me to say something.

He had come to see me every day for a week, sitting stiffly on one of my chairs in an unaccustomed shirt and tie, and talked to me about black holes and relativity, even though I taught biology at the university before my retirement, not physics. Someone had told him I knew Schwarzschild, of course.

"The Schwarzschild radius?" I said in my quavery, old man's voice, as if I could not remember ever hearing the phrase before, and Travers looked disgusted. He wanted me to say, "The Schwarzschild radius! Ah, yes, I served with Karl Schwarzschild on the Russian front in World War I!" and tell him all about how he had formulated his theory of black holes while serving with the artillery, but I had not decided yet what to tell him. "The event horizon," I said.

"Yeah. It was named after Schwarzschild because he was the one who worked out the theory," Travers said. He reminded me of Muller with his talk of theories. He was the same age as Muller, with the same shock of stiff yellow hair and the same insatiable curiosity, and perhaps that was why I let him come every day to talk to me, though it was dangerous to let him get so close.

"I have drawn up a theory of the stars," Muller says while we warm our hands over the Primus stove so that they will get enough feeling in them to be able to hold the liquid barretter without dropping it. "They are not balls of fire, as the scientists say. They are frozen."

145

"How can we see them if they are frozen?" I say. Muller is insulted if I do not argue with him. The arguing is part of the theory.

"Look at the wireless!" he says, pointing to it sitting disemboweled on the table. We have the back off the wireless again, and in the barretter's glass tube is a red reflection of the stove's flame. "The light is a reflection off the ice of the star."

"A reflection of what?"

"Of the shells, of course."

I do not say that there were stars before there was this war, because Muller will not have an answer to this, and I have no desire to destroy his theory, and besides, I do not really believe there was a time when this war did not exist. The star shells have always exploded over the snow-covered craters of No Man's Land, shattering in a spray of white and red, and perhaps Muller's theory is true.

"At that point," Travers said, "at the event horizon, no more information can be transmitted out of the black hole because gravity has become so strong, and so the collapse appears frozen at the Schwarzschild radius."

"Frozen," I said, thinking of Muller.

"Yeah. As a matter of fact, the Russians call black holes 'frozen stars.' You were at the Russian front, weren't you?"

"What?"

"In World War I."

"But the star doesn't really freeze," I said. "It goes on collapsing."

"Yeah, sure," Travers said. "It keeps collapsing in on itself until even the atoms are stripped of their electrons and there's nothing left except what they call a naked singularity, but we can't see past the Schwarzschild radius, and nobody inside a black hole can tell us what it's like in there because they can't get messages out, so nobody can ever know what it's like inside a black hole."

"I know," I said, but he didn't hear me.

He leaned forward. "What was it like at the front?"

It is so cold we can only work on the wireless a few minutes at a time before our hands stiffen and grow clumsy, and we are afraid of dropping the liquid barretter. Muller holds his gloves over the Primus stove and then puts them on. I jam my hands in my ice-stiff pockets.

We are fixing the wireless set. Eisner, who had been delivering messages between the sectors, got sent up to the front when he could not fix his motorcycle. If we cannot fix the wireless we will cease to be telegraphists and become soldiers and we will be sent to the front lines.

We are already nearly there. If it were not snowing we could see the barbed wire and pitted snow of No Man's Land, and the big Russian coalboxes sometimes land in the communication trenches. A shell hit our wireless hut two

JIM BURNS

weeks ago. We are ahead of our own artillery lines, and some of the shells from our guns fall on us, too, because the muzzles are worn out. But it is not the front, and we guard the liquid barretter with our lives.

"Eisner's unit was sent up on wiring fatigue last night," Muller says, "and they have not come back. I have a theory about what happened to them."

"Has the mail come?" I say, rubbing my sore eyes and then putting my cold hands immediately back in my pockets. I must get some new gloves, but the quartermaster has none to issue. I have written my mother three times to knit me a pair, but she has not sent them yet.

"I have a theory about Eisner's unit," he says doggedly. "The Russians have a magnet that has pulled them into the front."

"Magnets pull iron, not people," I say.

I have a theory about Muller's theories. Littering the communications trenches are things that the soldiers going up to the front have discarded: water bottles and haversacks and bayonets. Hans and I sometimes tried to puzzle out why they would discard such important things.

"Perhaps they were too heavy," I would say, though that did not explain the bayonets or the boots.

"Perhaps they know they are going to die," Hans would say, picking up a helmet.

I would try to cheer him up. "My gloves fell out of my pocket yesterday when I went to the quartermaster's. I never found them. They are in this trench somewhere."

"Yes," he would say, turning the helmet round and round in his hands, "perhaps as they near the front, these things simply drop away from them."

My theory is that what happens to the water bottles and helmets and bayonets is what has happened to Muller. He was a student in university before the war, but his knowledge of science and his intelligence have fallen away from him, and now we are so close to the front, all he has left are his theories. And his curiosity, which is a dangerous thing to have kept.

"Exactly. Magnets pull iron, but *they* were carrying barbed wire!" he says triumphantly, "and so they were pulled in to the magnet."

I put my hands practically into the Primus flame and rub them together, trying to get rid of the numbness. "We had better get the barretter in the wireless again or this magnet of yours will suck it in, too."

I go back to the wireless. Muller stays by the stove, thinking about his magnet. The door bangs open. It is not a real door, only an iron humpie tied to the beam that reinforces the dugout and held with a wedge, and when someone pushes against it, it flies inward, bringing the snow with it.

Snow swirls in, and light, and the sound from the front, a low rumble like a dog growling. I clutch the liquid barretter to my chest and Muller flings himself over the wireless as if it were a wounded comrade. Someone bundled in a wool coat and mittens, with a wool cap pulled over his ears, stands silhouetted against the reddish light in the doorway, blinking at us.

"Is Private Rottschieben here? I have come to see him about his eyes," he says, and I see it is Dr. Funkenheld.

"Come in and shut the door," I say, still carefully protecting the liquid barretter, but Muller has already jammed the metal back against the beam.

"Do you have news?" Muller says to the doctor, eager for new facts to spin his theories from. "Has the wiring fatigue come back? Is there going to be a bombardment tonight?"

Dr. Funkenheld takes off his mittens. "I have come to examine your eyes," he says to me. His voice frightens me. All through the war he has kept his quiet bedside voice, speaking to the wounded in the dressing station and at the stretcher bearer's posts as if they were in his surgery in Stuttgart, but now he sounds agitated and I am afraid it means a bombardment is coming and he will need me at the front.

When I went to the dressing station for medicine for my eyes, I foolishly told him I had studied medicine with Dr. Zuschauer in Jena. Now I am afraid he will ask me to assist him, which will mean going up to the front. "Do your eyes still hurt?" he says.

I hand the barretter to Muller and go over to stand by the lantern that hangs from a nail in the beam.

"I think he should be invalided home, Herr Doktor," Muller says. He knows it is impossible, of course. He was at the wireless the day the message came through that no one was to be invalided out for frostbite or "other noncontagious diseases."

"Can you find me a better light?" the doctor says to him.

Muller's curiosity is so strong that he cannot bear to leave any place where something interesting is happening. If he went up to the front I do not think he would be able to pull himself away, and now I expect him to make some excuse to stay, but I have forgotten that he is even more curious about the wiring fatigue. "I will go see what has happened to Eisner's unit," he says, and opens the door. Snow flies in, as if it had been beating against the door to get in, and the doctor and I have to push against the door to get it shut again.

"My eyes have been hurting," I say, while we are still pushing the metal into place, so that he cannot ask me to assist him. "They feel like sand has gotten into them."

"I have a patient with a disease I do not recognize," he says. I am relieved, though disease can kill us as easily as a trench mortar. Soldiers die of pneumonia and dysentery and blood poisoning every day in the dressing station, but we do not fear it the way we fear the front.

"The patient has fever, excoriated lesions, and suppurating bullae," Dr. Funkenheld says.

"Could it be boils?" I say, though of course he would recognize something so simple as boils, but he is not listening to me, and I realize that it is not a diagnosis from me that he has come for.

"The man is a scientist, a Jew named Schwarzschild, attached to the artillery," he says, and because the artillery are even farther back from the front lines than we are, I volunteer to go and look at the patient, but he does not want that either.

"I must talk to the medical headquarters in Bialystok," he says.

"Our wireless is broken," I say, because I do not want to have to tell him why it is impossible for me to send a message for him. We are allowed to send only military messages, and they must be sent in code, tapped out on the telegraph key. It would take hours to send his message, even if it were possible. I hold up the dangling wire. "At any rate, you must clear it with the commandant," but he is already writing out the name and address on a piece of paper, as if this were a telegraph office.

"You can send the message when you get the wireless fixed. I have written out the symptoms."

I put the back on the wireless. Muller comes in, kicking the door open, and snow flies everywhere, picking up Dr. Funkenheld's message and sending it circling around the dugout. I catch it before it spirals into the flame of the Primus stove.

"The wiring fatigue was pinned down all night," Muller says, setting down a hand lamp. He must have gotten it from the dressing station. "Five of them frozen to death, the other eight have frostbite. The commandant thinks there may be a bombardment tonight." He does not mention Eisner, and he does not say what has happened to the rest of the thirty men in Eisner's unit, though I know. The front has gotten them. I wait, holding the message in my stiff fingers, hoping Dr. Funkenheld will say "I must go attend to their frostbite."

"Let me examine your eyes," the doctor says, and shows Muller how to hold the hand lamp. Both of them peer into my eyes. "I have an ointment for you to use twice daily," he says, getting a flat jar out of his bag. "It will burn a little."

"I will rub it on my hands then. It will warm them," I say, thinking of Eisner frozen at the front, still holding the roll of barbed wire, perhaps.

He pulls my bottom eyelid down and rubs the ointment on with his little finger. It does not sting, but when I have blinked it into my eye, everything has a reddish tinge. "Will you have the wireless fixed by tomorrow?" he says.

"I don't know. Perhaps."

Muller has not put down the hand lamp. I can see by its light that he has forgotten all about the wiring fatigue and the Russian magnet and is wondering what the doctor wants with the wireless.

The doctor puts on his mittens and picks up his bag. I realize too late I should have told him I would send the message in exchange for them. "I will come check your eyes tomorrow," he says and opens the door to the snow.

The sound of the front is very close.

As soon as he is gone, I tell Muller about Schwarzschild and the message the doctor wants to send. He will not let me rest until I have told him, and we do not have time for his curiosity. We must fix the wireless.

"If you were on the wireless, you must have sent messages for Schwarzschild," Travers said eagerly. "Did you ever send a message to Einstein? They've got the letter Einstein sent to him after he wrote him his theory, but if Schwarzschild sent him some kind of message, too, that would be great. It would make my paper."

"You said that no message can escape a black hole?" I said. "But they could escape a collapsing star. Is that not so?"

"Okay," Travers said impatiently and made his fingers into a semicircle again. "Suppose you have a fixed observer over here." He pulled his curved hand back and held the forefinger of his other hand up to represent the fixed observer, "and you have somebody in the star. Say when the star starts to collapse, the person in it shines a light at the fixed observer. If the star hasn't reached the Schwarzschild radius, the fixed observer will be able to see the light, but it will take longer to reach him because the gravity of the black hole is pulling on the light, so it will seem as if time on the star has slowed down and the wavelengths will have been lengthened, so the light will be redder. Of course that's just a thought problem. There couldn't really be anybody in a collapsing star to send the messages."

"We sent messages," I said. "I wrote my mother asking her to knit me a pair of gloves."

There is still something wrong with the wireless. We have received only one message in two weeks. It said, "Russian opposition collapsing." and there was so much static we could not make out the rest of it. We have taken the wireless apart twice. The first time we found a loose wire but the second time we could not find anything. If Hans were here he would be able to find the trouble immediately.

"I have a theory about the wireless," Muller says. He has had ten theories in as many days: The magnet of the Russians is pulling our signals in to it; the northern lights, which have been shifting uneasily on the horizon, make a curtain the wireless signals cannot get through; the Russian opposition is not collapsing at all. They are drawing us deeper and deeper into a trap.

I say, "I am going to try again. Perhaps the trouble has cleared up," and put the headphones on so I do not have to listen to his new theory. I can hear nothing but a rumbling roar that sounds like the front.

I take out the folded piece of paper Dr. Funkenheld gave me and lay it on the wireless. He comes nearly every night to see if I have gotten an answer to his message, and I take off the headphones and let him listen to the static.

I tell him that we cannot get through, but even though that is true, it is not the real reason I have not sent the message. I am afraid of the commandant finding out. I am afraid of being sent to the front.

I have compromised by writing a letter to the professor that I studied medicine with in Jena, but I have not gotten an answer from him yet, and so I must go on pretending to the doctor.

"You don't have to do that," Muller says. He sits on the wireless, swinging his leg. He picks up the paper with the symptoms on it and holds it to the flame of the Primus stove. I grab for it, but it is already burning redly. "I have sent the message for you."

"I don't believe you. Nothing has been getting out."

"Didn't you notice the northern lights did not appear last night?"

I have not noticed. The ointment the doctor gave to me makes everything look red at night, and I do not believe in Muller's theories. "Nothing is getting out now," I say, and hold the headphones out to him so he can hear the static. He listens, still swinging his leg. "You will get us both in trouble. Why did you do it?"

"I was curious about it." If we are sent up to the front, his curiosity will kill us. He will take apart a land mine to see how it works. "We cannot get in trouble for sending military messages. I said the commandant was afraid it was a poisonous gas the Russians were using." He swings his leg and grins because now I am the curious one.

"Well, did you get an answer?"

"Yes," he says maddeningly and puts the headphones on. "It is not a poisonous gas."

I shrug as if I do not care whether I get an answer or not. I put on my cap and the muffler my mother knitted for me and open the door. "I am going out to see if the mail has come. Perhaps there will be a letter there from my professor."

"Nature of disease unknown," Muller shouts against the sudden force of the snow. "Possibly impetigo or glandular disorder."

I grin back at him and say, "If there is a package from my mother I will give you half of what is in it."

"Even if it is your gloves?"

"No, not if it is my gloves," I say, and go to find the doctor.

At the dressing station they tell me he has gone to see Schwarzschild and give me directions to the artillery staff's headquarters. It is not very far, but it is snowing and my hands are already cold. I go to the quartermaster's and ask him if the mail has come in.

There is a new recruit there, trying to fix Eisner's motorcycle. He has parts spread out on the ground all around him in a circle. He points to a burlap sack and says, "That is all the mail there is. Look through it yourself."

Snow has gotten into the sack and melted. The ink on the envelopes has run, and I squint at them, trying to make out the names. My eyes begin to hurt. There is not a package from my mother or a letter from my professor, but there is a letter for Lieutenant Schwarzschild. The return address says *Doctor*. Perhaps he has written to a doctor himself.

"I am delivering a message to the artillery headquarters," I say, showing the letter to the recruit. "I will take this up, too." The recruit nods and goes on working.

It has gotten dark while I was inside, and it is snowing harder. I jam my hands in the ice-stiff pockets of my coat and start to the artillery headquarters in the rear. It is pitch-dark in the communication trenches, and the wind twists the snow and funnels it howling along them. I take off my muffler and wrap it around my hands like a girl's muff.

A band of red shifts uneasily all along the horizon, but I do not know if it is the front or Muller's northern lights, and there is no shelling to guide me. We are running out of shells, so we do not usually begin shelling until nine o'clock. The Russians start even later. Sometimes I hear machine-gun fire, but it is distorted by the wind and the snow, and I cannot tell what direction it is coming from.

The communication trench seems narrower and deeper than I remember it from when Hans and I first brought the wireless up. It takes me longer than I think it should to get to the branching that will lead north to the headquarters. The front has been contracting, the ammunition dumps and officer's billets and clearing stations moving up closer and closer behind us. The artillery headquarters has been moved up from the village to a dugout near the artillery line, not half a mile behind us. The nightly firing is starting. I hear a low rumble, like thunder.

The roar seems to be ahead of me, and I stop and look around, wondering if I can have gotten somehow turned around, though I have not left the trenches. I start again, and almost immediately I see the branching and the headquarters.

It has no door, only a blanket across the opening, and I pull my hands free of the muffler and duck through it into a tiny space like a rabbit hole, the timber balks of the earthen ceiling so low I have to stoop. Now that I am out of the roar of the snow, the sound of the front separates itself into the individual crack of a four-pounder, the whine of a star shell, and under it the almost continuous rattle of machine guns. The trenches must not be as deep here. Muller and I can hardly hear the front at all in our wireless hut.

A man is sitting at an uneven table spread with papers and books. There is a candle on the table with a red glass chimney, or perhaps it only looks that way to me. Everything in the dugout, even the man, looks faintly red. He is wearing a uniform but no coat, and gloves with the finger ends cut off, even though there is no stove here. My hands are already cold.

A trench mortar roars, and clods of frozen dirt clatter from the roof onto the table. The man brushes the dirt from the papers and looks up.

"I am looking for Dr. Funkenheld," I say.

"He is not here." He stands up and comes around the table, moving stiffly, like an old man, though he does not look older than forty. He has a moustache, and his face looks dirty in the red light.

"I have a message for him."

An eight-pounder roars, and more dirt falls on us. The man raises his arm to brush the dirt off his shoulder. The sleeve of his uniform has been slit into ribbons. All along the back of his raised hand and the side of his arm are red sores running with pus. I look back at his face. The sores in his moustache and around his nose and mouth have dried and are covered with a crust. Excoriated lesions. Suppurating bullae. The gun roars again, and dirt rains down on his raw hands.

"I have a message for him," I say, backing away from him. I reach in the pocket of my coat to show him the message, but I pull out the letter instead. "There was a letter for you, Lieutenant Schwarzschild." I hold it out to him by one corner so he will not touch me when he takes it.

He comes toward me to take the letter, the muscles in his jaw tightening, and I think in horror that the sores must be on his legs as well. "Who is it from?" he says. "Ah, Herr Professor Einstein. Good," and turns it over. He puts his fingers on the flap to open the letter, and cries out in pain. He drops the letter.

"Would you read it to me?" he says and sinks down into the chair, cradling his hand against his chest. I can see there are sores in his fingernails.

I do not have any feeling in my hands. I pick the envelope up by its corners and turn it over. The skin of his finger is still on the flap. I back away from the table. "I must find the doctor. It is an emergency."

"You would not be able to find him," he says. Blood oozes out of the tip of his finger and down over the blister in his fingernail. "He has gone up to the front."

"What?" I say, backing and backing until I run into the blanket. "I cannot understand you."

"He has gone up to the front," he says, more slowly, and this time I can puzzle out the words, but they make no sense. How can the doctor be at the front? This is the front.

He pushes the candle toward me. "I order you to read me the letter."

I do not have any feeling in my fingers. I open it from the top, tearing the letter almost in two. It is a long letter, full of equations and numbers, but the words are warped and blurred. " 'My Esteemed Colleague! I have read your paper with the greatest interest. I had not expected that one could formulate the exact solution of the problem so simply. The analytical treatment of the problem appears to me splendid. Next Thursday I will present the work with several explanatory words, to the Academy!' "

"Formulated so simply," Schwarzschild says, as if he is in pain. "That is enough. Put the letter down. I will read the rest of it."

I lay the letter on the table in front of him, and then I am running down the trench in the dark with the sound of the front all around me, roaring and shaking the ground. At the first turning, Muller grabs my arm and stops me. "What are you doing here?" I shout. "Go back! Go back!"

"Go back?" he says. "The front's that way." He points in the direction he came from. But the front is not that way. It is behind me, in the artillery headquarters. "I told you there would be a bombardment tonight. Did you see the doctor? Did you give him the message? What did he say?"

"So you actually held the letter from Einstein?" Travers said. "How exciting that must have been! Only two months after Einstein had published his theory of general relativity. And years before they realized black holes really existed. When was this exactly?" He took out a notebook and began to scribble notes. "My esteemed colleague . . ." he muttered to himself. "Formulated so simply. This is great stuff. I mean, I've been trying to find out stuff on Schwarzschild for my paper for months, but there's hardly any information on him. I guess because of the war."

"No information can get out of a black hole once the Schwarzschild radius has been passed," I said.

"Hey, that's great!" he said, scribbling. "Can I use that in my paper?"

Now I am the one who sits endlessly in front of the wireless sending out messages to the Red Cross, to my professor in Jena, to Dr. Einstein. I have frostbitten the forefinger and thumb of my right hand and have to tap out the letters with my left. But nothing is getting out, and I must get a message out. I must find someone to tell me the name of Schwarzschild's disease.

"I have a theory," Muller says. "The Jews have seized power and have signed a treaty with the Russians. We are completely cut off."

"I am going to see if the mail has come," I say, so that I do not have to listen to any more of his theories, but the doctor stops me on my way out the hut.

I tell him what the message said. "Impetigo!" the doctor shouts. "You saw him! Did that look like impetigo to you?"

I shake my head, unable to tell him what I think it looks like.

"What are his symptoms?" Muller asks, burning with curiosity. I have not told him about Schwarzschild. I am afraid that if I tell him, he will only become more curious and will insist on going up to the front to see Schwarzschild himself.

"Let me see your eyes," the doctor says in his beautiful calm voice. I wish he would ask Muller to go for a hand lamp again so that I could ask him how

Schwarzschild is, but he has brought a candle with him. He holds it so close to my face that I cannot see anything but the red flame.

"Is Lieutenant Schwarzschild worse? What are his symptoms?" Muller says, leaning forward.

His symptoms are craters and shell holes, I think. I am sorry I have not told Muller, for it has only made him more curious. Until now I have told him everything, even how Hans died when the wireless hut was hit, how he laid the liquid barretter carefully down on top of the wireless before he tried to cough up what was left of his chest and catch it in his hands. But I cannot tell him this.

"What symptoms does he have?" Muller says again, his nose almost in the candle's flame, but the doctor turns from him as if he cannot hear him and blows the candle out. The doctor unwraps the dressing and looks at my fingers. They are swollen and red. Muller leans over the doctor's shoulder. "I have a theory about Lieutenant Schwarzschild's disease," he says.

"Shut up," I say. "I don't want to hear any more of your stupid theories," and do not even care about the wounded look on Muller's face or the way he goes and sits by the wireless. For now I have a theory, and it is more horrible than anything Muller could have dreamt of.

We are all of us—Muller, and the recruit who is trying to put together Eisner's motorcycle, and perhaps even the doctor with his steady bedside voice—afraid of the front. But our fear is not complete, because unspoken in it is our belief that the front is something separate from us, something we can keep away from by keeping the wireless or the motorcycle fixed, something we can survive by flattening our faces into the frozen earth, something we can escape altogether by being invalided out.

But the front is not separate. It is inside Schwarzschild, and the symptoms I have been sending out, suppurative bullae and excoriated lesions, are not what is wrong with him at all. The lesions on his skin are only the barbed wire and shell holes and connecting trenches of a front that is somewhere farther in.

The doctor puts a new dressing of crepe paper on my hand. "I have tried to invalid Schwarzschild out," the doctor says, and Muller looks at him, astounded. "The supply lines are blocked with snow."

"Schwarzschild cannot be invalided out," I say. "The front is inside him."

The doctor puts the roll of crepe paper back in his kit and closes it. "When the roads open again, I will invalid you out for frostbite. And Muller too."

Muller is so surprised he blurts, "I do not have frostbite."

But the doctor is no longer listening. "You must both escape," he says— and I am not sure he is even listening to himself—"while you can."

"I have a theory about why you have not told me what is wrong with Schwarzschild," Muller says as soon as the doctor is gone.

"I am going for the mail."

"There will not be any mail," Muller shouts after me. "The supply lines are blocked," but the mail is there, scattered among the motorcycle parts. There are only a few parts left. As soon as the roads are cleared, the recruit will be able to climb on the motorcycle and ride away.

I gather up the letters and take them over to the lantern to try to read them, but my eyes are so bad I cannot see anything but a red blur. "I am taking them back to the wireless hut," I say, and the recruit nods without looking up.

It is starting to snow. Muller meets me at the door, but I brush past him and turn the flame of the Primus stove up as high as it will go and hold the letters up behind it.

"I will read them for you," Muller says eagerly, looking through the envelopes I have discarded. "Look, here is a letter from your mother. Perhaps she has sent your gloves."

I squint at the letters one by one while he tears open my mother's letter to me. Even though I hold them so close to the flame that the paper scorches, I cannot make out the names.

" 'Dear son,' " Muller reads, " 'I have not heard from you in three months. Are you hurt? Are you ill? Do you need anything?' "

The last letter is from Professor Zuschauer in Jena. I can see his name quite clearly in the corner of the envelope, though mine is blurred beyond recognition. I tear it open. There is nothing written on the red paper.

I thrust it at Muller. "Read this," I say.

"I have not finished with your mother's letter yet," Muller says, but he takes the letter and reads: " 'Dear Herr Rottschieben, I received your letter yesterday. I could hardly decipher your writing. Do you not have decent pens at the front? The disease you describe is called Neumann's disease or pemphigus—' "

I snatch the letter out of Muller's hands and run out the door. "Let me come with you!" Muller shouts.

"You must stay and watch the wireless!" I say joyously, running along the communication trench. Schwarzschild does not have the front inside him. He has pemphigus, he has Neumann's disease, and now he can be invalided home to hospital.

I go down and think I have tripped over a discarded helmet or a tin of beef, but there is a crash, and dirt and revetting fall all around me. I hear the low buzz of a daisy cutter and flatten myself into the trench, but the buzz does not become a whine. It stops, and there is another crash and the trench caves in.

I scramble out of the trench before it can suffocate me and crawl along the edge toward Schwarzschild's dugout, but the trench has caved in all along its length, and when I crawl up and over the loose dirt, I lose it in the swirling snow.

I cannot tell which way the front lies, but I know it is very close. The sound comes at me from all directions, a deafening roar in which no individual sounds can be distinguished. The snow is so thick I cannot see the burst of flame from the muzzles as the guns fire, and no part of the horizon looks redder than any other. It is all red, even the snow.

I crawl in what I think is the direction of the trench, but as soon as I do, I am in barbed wire. I stop, breathing hard, my face and hands pressed into the snow. I have come the wrong way. I am at the front. I hear a sound out of the barrage of sound, the sound of tires on the snow, and I think it is a tank, and cannot breathe at all. The sound comes closer, and in spite of myself I look up and it is the recruit who was at the quartermaster's.

He is a long way away, behind a coiled line of barbed wire, but I can see him quite clearly in spite of the snow. He has the motorcycle fixed, and as I watch, he flings his leg over it and presses his foot down. "Go!" I shout. "Get out!" The motorcycle jumps forward. "Go!"

The motorcycle comes toward me, picking up speed. It rears up, and I think it is going to jump the barbed wire, but it falls instead, the motorcycle first and then the recruit, spiraling slowly down into the iron spikes. The ground heaves, and I fall too.

I have fallen into Schwarzschild's dugout. Half of it has caved in, the timber balks sticking out at angles from the heap of dirt and snow, but the blanket is still over the door, and Schwarzschild is propped in a chair. The doctor is bending over him. Schwarzschild has his shirt off. His chest looks like Hans's did.

The front roars and more of the roof crumbles. "It's all right! It's a disease!" I shout over it. "I have brought you a letter to prove it," and hand him the letter which I have been clutching in my unfeeling hand.

The doctor grabs the letter from me. Snow whirls down through the ruined roof, but Schwarzschild does not put on his shirt. He watches uninterestedly as the doctor reads the letter.

" 'The symptoms you describe are almost certainly those of Neumann's disease, or pemphigus vulgaris. I have treated two patients with the disease, both Jews. It is a disease of the mucous membranes and is not contagious. Its cause is unknown. It always ends in death.' " Dr. Funkenheld crumples up the paper. "You came all this way in the middle of a bombardment to tell me there is no hope?" he shouts in a voice I do not even recognize, it is so unlike his steady doctor's voice. "You should have tried to get away. You should have—" and then he is gone under a crashing of dirt and splintered timbers.

I struggle toward Schwarzschild through the maelstrom of red dust and snow. "Put your shirt on!" I shout at him. "We must get out of here!" I crawl to the door to see if we can get out through the communication trench.

Muller bursts through the blanket. He is carrying, impossibly, the wireless. The headphones trail behind him in the snow. "I came to see what had happened to you. I thought you were dead. The communication trenches are shot to pieces."

It is as I had feared. His curiosity has got the best of him, and now he is trapped, too, though he seems not to know it. He hoists the wireless onto the table without looking at it. His eyes are on Schwarzschild, who leans against the remaining wall of the dugout, his shirt in his hands.

"Your shirt!" I shout and come around to help Schwarzschild put it on over the craters and shell holes of his blasted skin. The air screams and the mouth of the dugout blows in. I grab at Schwarzschild's arm, and the skin of it comes off in my hands. He falls against the table, and the wireless goes over. I can hear the splintering tinkle of the liquid barretter breaking, and then the whole dugout is caving in and we are under the table. I cannot see anything.

"Muller!" I shout. "Where are you?"

"I'm hit," he says.

I try to find him in the darkness, but I am crushed against Schwarzschild. I cannot move. "Where are you hit?"

"In the arm," he says, and I hear him try to move it. The movement dislodges more dirt, and it falls around us, shutting out all sound of the front. I can hear the creak of wood as the table legs give way.

"Schwarzschild?" I say. He doesn't answer, but I know he is not dead. His body is as hot as the Primus stove flame. My hand is underneath his body, and I try to shift it, but I cannot. The dirt falls like snow, piling up around us. The darkness is red for a while, and then I cannot see even that.

"I have a theory," Muller says in a voice so close and so devoid of curiosity it might be mine. "It is the end of the world."

"Was that when Schwarzschild was sent home on sick leave?" Travers said. "Or validated, or whatever you Germans call it? Well, yeah, it had to be, because he died in March. What happened to Muller?"

I had hoped he would go away as soon as I had told him what had happened to Schwarzschild, but he made no move to get up. "Muller was invalided out with a broken arm. He became a scientist."

"The way you did." He opened his notebook again. "Did you see Schwarzschild after that?"

The question makes no sense.

"After you got out? Before he died?"

It seems to take a long time for his words to get to me. The message bends and curves, shifting into the red, and I can hardly make it out. "No," I say, though that is a lie.

Travers scribbles. "I really do appreciate this, Dr. Rottschieben. I've always been curious about Schwarzschild, and now that you've told me all this stuff I'm even more interested," Travers says, or seems to say. Messages coming in are warped by the gravitational blizzard into something that no longer resembles speech. "If you'd be willing to help me, I'd like to write my thesis on him."

Go. Get out. "It was a lie," I say. "I never knew Schwarzschild. I saw him once, from a distance—your fixed observer."

Travers looks up expectantly from his notes as if he is still waiting for me to answer him.

"Schwarzschild was never even in Russia," I lie. "He spent the whole winter in hospital in Göttingen. I lied to you. It was nothing but a thought problem."

He waits, pencil ready.

"You can't stay here!" I shout. "You have to get away. There is no safe distance from which a fixed observer can watch without being drawn in, and once you are inside the Schwarzschild radius you can't get out. Don't you understand? We are still there!"

We are still there, trapped in the trenches of the Russian front, while the dying star burns itself out, spiraling down into that center where time ceases to exist, where everything ceases to exist except the naked singularity that is somehow Schwarzschild.

Muller tries to dig the wireless out with his crushed arm so he can send a message that nobody can hear—"Help us! Help us!"—and I struggle to free the hands that in spite of Schwarzschild's warmth are now so cold I cannot feel them, and in the very center Schwarzschild burns himself out, the black hole at his center imploding him cell by cell, carrying him down into darkness, and us with him.

"It is a trap!" I shout at Travers from the center, and the message struggles to escape and then falls back.

"I wonder how he figured it out?" Travers says, and now I can hear him clearly. "I mean, can you imagine trying to figure out something like the theory of black holes in the middle of a war and while you were suffering from a fatal disease? And just think, when he came up with the theory, he didn't have any idea that black holes even existed."

GALAXIES AND CLUSTERS

ESSAY BY

HYRON SPINRAD

SPECULATION BY

DAVID BRIN

GALAXIES AND CLUSTERS

HYRON SPINRAD

University of California, Berkeley

GALAXIES—VAST COLLECTIONS of billions of stars—are the basic building blocks of the universe. These grand objects are so enormous in size that they simply dwarf all human experience. The amount of light and other energies they give off defy any attempt at everyday comparison. Yet, since we confirmed the existence of other galaxies in the 1920's, telescopes of increasing power and sophistication have shown us not just a few, not hundreds or thousands, but hundreds of billions of these grand star systems in every direction we look.

Galaxies also turn out to be "gregarious"—they generally do not appear to live alone. We find them gathered together in smaller groups or larger clusters, and those groups and clusters themselves tend to join together in immense structures astronomers call *superclusters.* Figure 1 on page 167 is a photograph that I took at the Cerro Tololo Interamerican Observatory in Chile, where a 4-meter (158-inch) diameter telescope sits atop a peak in the Andes and affords astronomers beautifully clear views of the night sky. The photograph shows a rich cluster of galaxies unromantically called Str 0431-616 (a name derived from its position in the sky). This impressive collection of galaxies is visible only from the Earth's Southern Hemisphere, by the way. As you look at the picture, keep in mind that each object that is elongated (rather than just a point) on this image is a galaxy of stars.

Furthermore, as explained in more detail in another chapter of this book, we have also discovered that the universe of galaxies is rapidly expanding on the largest scale. All the galaxies are receding from one another, so that in the time it has taken you to read this page, the distance to the cluster of galaxies shown in Figure 1 has opened up by another full million miles! This expansion is a fundamental feature of the universe which illuminates and is illuminated by our study of galaxies.

M104, the "Sombrero galaxy," a spiral in the constellation of Virgo. Photo credit: National Optical Astronomy Observatories.

TYPES OF GALAXIES

Spiral galaxies, like our own Milky Way, are most common in the universe, but as we will see, galaxies can show other shapes as well. A spiral galaxy is a huge spinning Frisbee-shaped agglomeration of stars, gas, and dust—all held together by the mutual attraction of gravity. The flat disk of a typical spiral is about 60,000 light-years in diameter—which means that communication from one edge to the other would take at least 60,000 years. Actually, the edges of spiral galaxies like our own are somewhat poorly defined; we can see where the visible material begins to thin out, but we have been accumulating a great deal of indirect evidence that the galaxy continues much farther outward than its visible edges, and generally contains much more material than we presently have the technology to see. Recently, physicists have begun to speculate that this material may be in the form of exotic subatomic particles that our theories may predict but which we have not yet discovered in our laboratories. You will hear more about this fascinating area of astronomy in a later chapter. Here we should merely note how amazing it is that even at this writing—late in the twentieth century—astronomers and physicists still need to worry that our census of the basic constituents of galaxies could be seriously deficient.

Let us confine our attention, then, to the material in galaxies that we can detect with our present-day instruments. If we were to examine a representative spiral galaxy, we would find that it contains upward of 100 billion stars in its vast pinwheel. In addition, perhaps 10 percent of its material is uncondensed gas and dust—the raw material of the universe—sprinkled among the stars and generally confined to the galaxy's main disk. Figure 2 on page 167 shows a beautiful example of a spiral galaxy, called NGC 891, seen with its disk edge-on to us. In this view, the band directly across the main disk of the galaxy is a vast lane of dust.

This might be a good time to say something about the way galaxies are named by astronomers. Except for our nearest neighbor galaxies, there are far too many of these star systems to give each of them a name. Thus, astronomers designate them by their numbers in various important catalogues of galaxies that have been drawn up over the years. The most common of these, the *New General Catalogue of Nebulae and Clusters of Stars* (or *NGC*), was published by astronomer J. L. E. Dreyer in 1888. (Although the catalogue includes many galaxies, the title does not mention that category because in Dreyer's day galaxies were still confused with nebulae.)

Another main type of galaxy is the elliptical or E galaxy, whose general shape is like a slightly elongated basketball or a football. When we see a three-dimensional object like this projected on the sky, it appears to us to be shaped like an ellipse. These E galaxies turn out to be most common in clusters or groups of galaxies. Most E galaxies are smooth-looking objects on long-exposure photographs. The light of the stars blends together and it takes hard work to

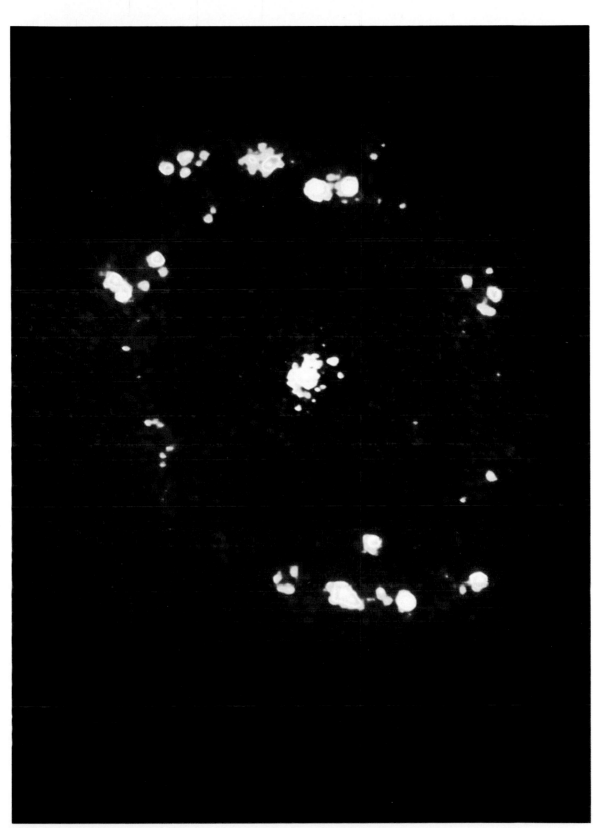

M94, spiral galaxy in the constellation of Canes Venatici. This false-color image is computer-enhanced to bring out subtle details. Photo credit: National Optical Astronomy Observatories.

measure the properties of the constituent stars individually. These galaxies contain less raw material—interstellar gas and dust—than do the spirals. There is an intermediate type of galaxy, called an SO, which looks rather like an elliptical one, but does show an underlying disk structure. Figure 3 on the facing page shows NGC 3115, an edge-on smooth SO galaxy. What you see is a smooth blending of starlight in the image and a lack of interstellar matter. In the cluster shown in Figure 1, the larger galaxies are mainly ellipticals and SOs, pretty crowded together near the cluster center and thinning out toward its periphery.

Not all galaxies show a regular structure: Some have a more chaotic shape or no well-defined shape at all, and are thus called *irregulars*. Figure 1 on the facing page shows a detailed view of such a galaxy: one of our nearest neighbors, the Large Magellanic Cloud. Because this galaxy is so close—at 150,000 light-years it is a "satellite" of our Milky Way—a lot of individual stars can be seen in the photograph.

Whatever a galaxy's type, astronomers have discovered that there is a complex relationship between the stars and the raw material. This is because new stars are born from the gas and dust in a galaxy, and stars at the end of their lives often return some of their material to the galactic reservoir. The returned material has frequently been "processed" by the star and now consists of a greater proportion of heavier elements. One of the great realizations of twentieth-century astronomy is that the shape and other large-scale properties of galaxies are intimately intertwined with the "ecology" of the stars—their interactions with their environment. In fact, recent evidence indicates that even within immense clusters of galaxies, environmental interactions may play a role in determining the properties of the individual galaxies. (More on this idea in a moment.)

DISTANCES TO GALAXIES

Before we can understand the properties of individual galaxies or determine the large-scale structure of the cosmos, we must be able to measure the distances of the galaxies—to establish what astronomers call the cosmic distance scale. Since the typical distance between large galaxies is about 2 million light-years, you can probably see that establishing this scale is not going to be very easy, even for astronomers who are used to such difficulties. In fact, the cosmic distance scale has been one of the key problems for astronomy in the second half of the twentieth century and is still a source of lively controversy.

It is relatively easy today to determine distances to nearby galaxies. The trick is to find what we might call "standard bulbs" in our galaxy and then compare them to the same objects in other galaxies. If you had a large (electrically wired) athletic field full of randomly placed light bulbs, ranging in wattage from 10 watts to 250 watts, and you stood some distance away from one end of the field on a dark night, it would be hard to tell which bulbs were

Figure 1: The rich and concentrated cluster of galaxies Str 0431–616.

Figure 2: The nearby spiral galaxy NGC 891, seen edge-on.

Figure 3: The galaxy NGC 3115, an SO type, seen edge-on.

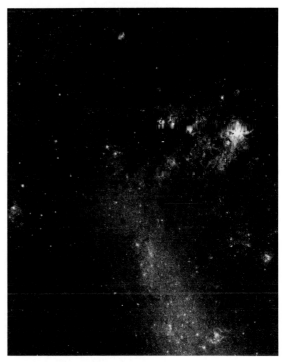

Figure 4: The central portion of the nearby irregular galaxy called the Large Magellanic Cloud.

Photos courtesy Hyron Spinrad.

closer and which were farther away. Some bulbs might look bright because they were 250-watt bulbs but were some distance away, while others might look bright because they were intrinsically dimmer but also quite close to you on the near edge of the field.

If, on the other hand, someone replaced all the lights with standard 60-watt bulbs, you would have a much easier situation on your hands. Since all the bulbs are now guaranteed to be of the same intrinsic power, the brighter ones must be closer to you and the dimmer ones farther away. What astronomers need are stars or other celestial objects that have some sort of standard or universal brightness.

For nearby galaxies, we have objects whose intrinsic brightness we know quite well—for example, a class of bright variable stars called *cepheids*. (Variable stars get brighter and dimmer regularly, like certain Christmas-tree lights.) As long as our standard-bulb stars are the same from galaxy to galaxy, we can use them to figure distances to other galaxies where we can still make out individual stars. To more distant galaxies, we must find larger standard bulbs, clusters of stars, or large regions of glowing gas. As we look farther and farther out into the universe, we worry whether these comparison objects really are the same from galaxy to galaxy—or whether their pedigrees depend on their environment.

As we work our way even farther outward—toward galaxies whose distances are measured in the tens of millions of light-years, the number of good comparison objects begins to dwindle and astronomers are forced to pin their plans and hopes on weaker foundations. This translates to an uncertain distance scale beyond 16 million light-years—a "rubber ruler" of the most annoying sort. This uncertainty in turn affects all our other measurements of galaxy properties, including their size, how much material (mass) they contain, and how bright they are. Even worse, this introduces an uncertainty into our measurement of the expansion rate of the universe, which rests on the foundation of the distances to relatively nearby galaxies.

For really distant galaxies, we have no direct way of measuring their distances but must rely on the way the galaxy participates in the expansion of the universe. Earlier in this century, Edwin Hubble and his co-workers discovered that the farther a galaxy is from us the faster it is moving away. This pattern seems to hold throughout the universe, in every direction we look. Now, it is relatively easy to measure the speed with which a galaxy is moving away—the motion leaves telltale evidence in the colors of its light (via the so-called Doppler effect). Once we know that speed, we can use Hubble's rule to get the distance to the galaxy. The trouble is, the actual numerical form of Hubble's rule depends on knowing precise distances to many closer galaxies. As long as these measurements are in doubt, all the other distances in the universe are uncertain to the same degree.

For the sake of simplicity, in this chapter I will use the cosmic distance scale favored by Allan Sandage (now at The Johns Hopkins University) and his collaborators. The distances in the universe could be smaller by a factor of two if the distance scale suggested by Gerard de Vaucouleurs of the University of Texas, Marc Aaronson of the University of Arizona, and several other astronomers turns out to be the correct one.

(Do not be too alarmed about this factor-of-two uncertainty. In astronomy, where we deal with objects that can be billions of light-years away, we simply cannot expect to pin things down with the sort of detail we are used to in building bridges or computers on Earth. Astronomers have learned to live with what they call "astronomical accuracy"—plus or minus 50 or 100 percent at times—and if you are going to be reading about astronomy, so should you!)

Once we know how far away a galaxy is, then we can measure many of its other properties as well. For example, we can measure its *angular size* (how large a fraction of the sky it seems to cover) and use the distance to derive a true diameter (in light-years). Or we can measure how bright it looks to us (its *apparent brightness*) and correct for the dimming effect of distance to find its *intrinsic brightness* (how bright it would be if we were very close to it).

MEASURING GALAXY MASSES

An even more basic property of any galaxy that astronomers would like to know is its *mass*—the total amount of material it contains. Weighing the galaxies is, as you might imagine, a nontrivial task, made somewhat easier by the fact that spiral galaxies tend to be in rotation, like a child's flattened top or a Frisbee spun on your fingertip.

The motions of the stars and gas in a rotating galaxy can be studied by measuring the *Doppler shifts* of the light they emit. When we spread out starlight by means of a prism or similar device, we see many colored lines in the star's spectrum. The various lines can be thought of as "signatures" of the elements the star contains—each element, like hydrogen, carbon, or oxygen, leaves a unique pattern of colored lines in the light.

If a star were at rest relative to the Earth, we would see its colored lines in the same place we see them when we experiment with light in our laboratories. However, the stars (and galaxies) are all moving with respect to us, and this motion changes (shifts) the colors we see. Christian Doppler showed in 1842 that if a source of light is moving away from us, its colors shift slightly toward the red end of the color scale; if the source is approaching, its colors shift toward the blue end. Since the amount of this Doppler shift depends on how fast the light source is moving, measuring the shift for celestial objects gives a way of measuring the speed with which the stars and galaxies are moving away from us or toward us. (We should point out that the Doppler method cannot measure that part of an object's motion which is *neither* toward us or away from us—that is, motion that goes across our line of sight.)

Once we know the speed with which outer material is moving around the center of a galaxy, we can apply the laws of Kepler and Newton to find how much mass there must be inside the galaxy—since it is that mass that is responsible for keeping the outer material going around. In the same way, careful measurements of the motions of the planets long ago told us the mass of the Sun. One important difference between the two situations is that in galaxies the mass is not concentrated in the very center as it is in our solar system; the stars, gas, dust, and possible "invisible" matter are much more evenly distributed.

By the way, it is just such measurements of the way material in galaxies' moves about the center that have told astronomers that galaxies seem to contain much more matter than we can directly see.

The total masses astronomers measure for galaxies can vary quite a bit, but large spiral galaxies like M31 in Andromeda can reach up to a trillion (a thousand billion) times the mass of our Sun.

CLUSTERS OF GALAXIES

If you ask an amateur astronomer in which direction on the sky you can see the largest number of galaxies with a small telescope, the answer you will get is the constellation Virgo. This is because the section of the sky we call Virgo contains a relatively nearby and fairly rich cluster of galaxies. (In the extragalactic vastness, the distance to the Virgo cluster—some 50 million light-years—doesn't seem all that large!) In fact, it turns out that our Milky Way, the Andromeda galaxy, and the rest of our small "Local Group" of galaxies are outriders of the Virgo cluster—or, to put it more properly, our group is part of the Virgo *supercluster* of galaxies. This larger ensemble contains several straggly clusters of galaxies, held together even across intergalactic distances by gravity's unrelenting pull. Recent measurements indicate that our Local Group is being pulled toward the Virgo cluster at a speed of about 150 miles *per second*.

Astronomers have devised some arbitrary definitions for grouping galaxies: A *binary galaxy pair* is two clearly related galaxies, a *group* is between five and twenty-five galaxies within a space of some 2 to 4 million light-years, and a *cluster* is a single collection with more galaxies spread out over a larger volume. A conglomeration of several groups and clusters is then called a *supercluster*.

The late astronomer George Abell of UCLA compiled an important catalogue of galaxy clusters. The rich clusters he lists can contain anywhere from one hundred to several thousand luminous galaxies in a volume of about 10 million light-years. The largest superclusters could contain as many as 20,000 galaxies over vast distances. A stringy filament of galaxies winding through the constellations of Perseus and Pegasus, for example, is about a billion light-years in length!

Like collections of people, galaxy groups and clusters are often dominated by one or several large members. In our Local Group, for example, there are two obvious leaders in size and mass: our Milky Way and the Andromeda spiral. Next in line is the Triangulum galaxy, M33, and then the Large Magellanic Cloud we discussed earlier. The other more numerous members of our group are medium-size irregulars and some small ellipticals. We have no large E galaxy near us; this is a pity, because we would very much have liked to study one of these imposing galaxies from a closer perspective.

The rich clusters of galaxies may be loose and ragged-looking or they may show a more concentrated and symmetric appearance, like the one shown in Figure 1. While the loose clusters generally contain both spirals and ellipticals, the denser, more concentrated clusters have more large E galaxies than spirals, at least near their centers.

In the same way that we can use the motions within a galaxy to measure its total mass, we can use the motions of galaxies within a cluster to get an indication of the total mass the cluster contains. (This sounds easy in principle, but can be quite challenging in practice, since we must measure Doppler shifts in the faint light of several very distant objects. The electronic technology of the 1980's has been a great help in "amplifying" small amounts of light, just as your stereo receiver at home can amplify the faint signals coming from your turntable.)

The masses we derive for various clusters turn out to be about ten times larger than we anticipated from our present knowledge of the masses of individual spiral and elliptical galaxies. Once again, our observations seem to be telling us that there is an embarrassingly large "missing mass"—some other major constituent that is invisible to us.

ENVIRONMENTAL EFFECTS IN CLUSTERS

In recent years astronomers have uncovered more and more evidence that the "habitat" of a galaxy—whether it is relatively isolated or a member of a populous cluster—can play an important role in the long-term evolution of its size, its shape, and even its contents. This is because a galaxy can and does interact gravitationally with its neighbors in the environment of a cluster. The unceasing pull of all matter on all other matter in the universe acts over the galactic distance scales just as it does within the more narrow confines of our solar system. In a cluster, galaxies moving at five hundred miles per second can rush past each other, have weak encounters in their outer regions, or can even actually collide.

The collision of two galaxies is not quite like collisions we are used to on Earth, such as the head-on crash of two automobiles. It is useful to think of the stars in a galaxy as small, widely spaced marbles suspended in a thin medium like oil, which represents the interstellar gas and dust. During galaxy collisions, the marbles are so far apart that they will almost never collide, but the "oil" may be compressed, heated, and even driven out from the colliding pair.

Alternatively, two galaxies can have a "soft encounter," somewhat like a low-speed auto crash, where the two colliding partners stick together. (Their mutual gravity helps to bind them if the collision speed was not too great.) Or the process can occur more gradually, where the two galaxies are first drawn into a close orbit and then gradually spiral inward to intertwine and "stick" after a few million years. These processes lead to what astronomers call *galaxy mergers.*

Sometimes we can find evidence for past mergers on long-exposure photographs, in the form of long faint plumes of stars, drawn out from the interacting spirals by their mutual rotations and gravitational pulls. In dense clusters of galaxies, such direct collisions are probably fairly frequent over cosmic time scales and may play an important role in the way the galaxies and the clusters develop.

Another environmental factor we must consider in tracing the way galaxies evolve is the rarefied *intergalactic medium*—the material between galaxies. Modern observations have revealed that there is a very low-density, hot gas that seems to pervade rich galaxy clusters. The density of this gas is only about a thousandth of a particle per cubic centimeter—that is, you'd have to search a thousand cubic centimeters to find one particle on average. (For comparison, the air in your room has roughly 100,000,000,000,000,000,000 particles in each cubic centimeter.)

While that is a very rarefied medium, you must keep in mind that in the vastness of intergalactic space there are an enormous number of cubic centimeters, so that the total amount of material between the galaxies can be quite large. Because it is so hot, this gas glows with energetic X-rays, which we can detect using sophisticated X-ray telescopes in orbit about the Earth.

This hot *intracluster medium*, as it is called, can sweep out a portion of the normal interstellar gas in any galaxy which rushes through the cluster's central region (where the hot gas is more concentrated). This is another way that an "innocent" galaxy can lose gas simply because of its interaction with its environment.

Gas lost to a galaxy—say an incipient spiral—is unlikely to be recaptured. But the lack of gas can be disastrous to the future development of a galaxy, because it represents the loss of raw material to make stars. A galaxy "stripped" of substantial amounts of its gas may not be able to form future generations of stars, and the birth of stars may cease—either for a while or, conceivably, forever. Such a stripped galaxy might still have the shape of a spiral, but no young brilliant bluish stars to outline its spiral arms. An SO galaxy like NGC 3115, shown in Figure 3, may be the result of such a process.

If this stripping occurs frequently, it may be that many spirals in clusters are converted to SO types. This may explain why rich clusters have more SO and E galaxies, when compared to relatively low-density environments, like our Local Group.

GALACTIC CANNIBALISM

If we study rich, concentrated clusters of galaxies closely, we note an occasional single galaxy that is much larger and brighter than the average E galaxy in the cluster. These large galaxies are called cD galaxies (a designation left over from an older system of nomenclature) or *supergiant* galaxies. None of them happens to be very close to our Milky Way, so we have to work very hard to study these imposing objects—some fully ten times the size and mass of our Milky Way. Figure 5 (below) shows a large cD galaxy in the cluster Abell 754.

One explanation for the existence of cD galaxies that has captured the imagination of both astronomers and the public in recent years takes the "merger" idea one small step further. If the two galaxies involved are of unequal size, their coming together may be less like a partnership and more like the sacrifice of an unwilling "victim." Astronomers have dubbed the process *galactic cannibalism*, because the larger "eater" galaxy consumes its smaller or mid-size neighbor (the "eatee") for lunch.

The way this happens is probably more subtle than the direct "crash" of a galaxy against a larger one. The gravitational pull of a big elliptical galaxy

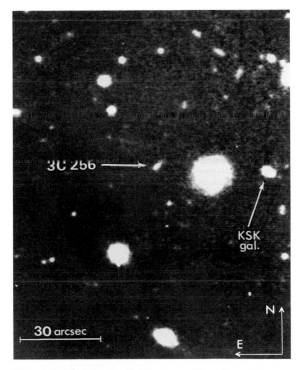

Figure 5: The central portion of the cluster of galaxies Abell 754.

Figure 6: The extremely distant radio galaxy 3C256, located some 12 billion light-years away.

Photos courtesy Hyron Spinrad.

on a casually passing neighbor in its cluster first draws the two into a set of tighter and tighter close encounters. Eventually, the outlying regions of stars in the two systems overlap. From that point on, the merge proceeds rapidly—astronomically speaking—taking only 100 million years or so to blend the smaller system into the larger one.

Astronomers calculate that it may take four to eight such "cannibalization events" to make a supergiant galaxy as large as the one we see at the center of cluster A754. Most outward signs of the "munched" galaxies ultimately disappear, although in a few cases we see large galaxies with multiple nuclei. This may indicate that some victims had individual star densities that were simply too high for quick "digestion."

One way to check the cannibalism theory—which is relatively new and still controversial—is to look very far out in space and therefore back in time. If we examine clusters so far away that we are looking halfway back to their beginnings, let's say, we should see fewer cD galaxies at their centers on average, because we see them in a less evolved state. As we come closer and closer to our own time, the number of supergiant galaxies in clusters should be seen to increase. Unfortunately, we do not have the technology at present to make such a test, but when the Space Telescope is launched, its superb imaging capability may make such observations possible.

USING GALAXIES AND CLUSTERS TO EXAMINE THE EXPANSION OF THE UNIVERSE

So far, we have examined galaxies and clusters for what they have to tell us about themselves and their contents. But now I would like to take a brief look at one of the most exciting of astronomical endeavors: using our observations of remote galaxies and clusters to pin down the details of the expansion of the universe.

Allan Sandage will discuss the expansion of the cosmos in more detail in his chapter. Here let us just remind ourselves that during the 1920's and 1930's, Edwin Hubble and his colleagues realized that the universe was expanding when they measured the distances and speeds of many galaxies independently and found that there was a correlation between the two quantities. The farther away a galaxy is, the faster it is receding from us.

The technology of Hubble's day allowed us to measure only the distances of relatively close-by galaxies, but today, with large modern telescopes and light-detecting instruments, we can make distance measurements much farther out. We discussed earlier in this chapter how astronomers look for celestial objects that act like standard light bulbs to help them in this quest. At great distances, we can no longer measure individual stars, or even clusters of stars or bright clouds of gas, and thus we cannot use them as our standard bulbs. But it turns out that the brightest E galaxy in every rich cluster has roughly the same intrinsic brightness—the same general "wattage," we might say. (Another standard bulb we sometimes use is the brightest *radio elliptical*—an elliptical galaxy that emits not only light but copious amounts of cosmic radio waves. You can read more on such "active galaxies," as they are called, in Harding Smith's chapter.)

In general, then, what this endeavor involves is finding a standard-bulb E galaxy, measuring its apparent brightness, and comparing it with the usual (or standard) brightness such galaxies have. The difference between how bright the galaxy appears, and how bright it is "supposed to be" (up close) tells us how much dimming has taken place and thus how far away it is. Then we measure the galaxy's red shift, which tells us the speed at which it is moving away from us. Comparing the two will show us how well the galaxy in question is following the pattern of the expanding universe we have found in nearby galaxies.

At this point, you may ask why we bother to make these often excruciatingly difficult observations. Why not accept that the universe is expanding smoothly, just as our observations of nearby galaxies imply? To begin with, there is the simple reason that in science we take nothing for granted. But more importantly, our theories tell us that the universe may not always have been expanding *at the same rate*. The expansion may be slowing down, although the precise *deceleration* depends on what sort of universe we live in. Clearly, it would be very exciting to be able to test these ideas by comparing the way galaxies were expanding in the remote past—say, 7 to 10 billion years ago—to the way they are receding from one another today. The trouble is that the practical problems in making such observations pose enormous challenges for astronomers.

First of all, it is just really difficult to *recognize* distant clusters. On a conventional telescopic photograph of the sky, one sees many galaxies and stars—but most of them are unrelated. They just happen to lie in the same area of the sky because we have taken a two-dimensional picture of the three-dimensional universe, losing most indications of depth in the process.

Furthermore, the number of galaxies we can see in any part of the picture increases rapidly as we look at fainter and fainter galaxies—in the same way that, in a picture of a city taken from a hill, there are just a few buildings in the foreground but an increasing number of (small-looking) buildings as you look to greater distances. Picking out a distant cluster of "related" galaxies in the mess of foreground and background galaxies is very awkward. Only clusters with unusually high density (a high number of galaxies per unit volume) can be found at faint levels, even with today's electronic detectors. The survey of clusters George Abell finished in the 1950's does not include clusters farther than about 2 billion light-years away; most are much closer. A recent survey by astronomers James Gunn, John Hoessel, and J. B. Oke has greatly increased our sample of very distant clusters, but much more remains to be done in this field.

Even when we have recognized a distant cluster and found the brightest E galaxy, there still remains the task of taking the spectrum (breaking down the light into the component colors) and measuring the Doppler shift of the colored lines. If a galaxy's light is already extremely faint, the situation can only get worse when we spread the faint beam of white light out into a spectrum: Each bit of "spread-out" light will be so faint that recording it for analysis becomes a major technological challenge. As we mentioned earlier, today we use solid-state detectors to pick up and amplify these faint bits of light. The best of these devices is called a charge-coupled device, or CCD, and can integrate (add up) light from a celestial object for hours. Although in this sense they resemble long-exposure photographs, they are far more sensitive than the best photographic emulsions. The CCD detectors are about postage-stamp size and have *digital* output, so that their results can be directed to a computer for prompt analysis. But even with the power of CCDs, *several hours* of exposure are required to record a successful faint galaxy spectrum. (This means holding the telescope rock-steady, pointing at the same tiny smudge of light for hours as the Earth rotates.)

Astronomers express the red shifts they measure for galaxies using the symbol "z," which is defined as the shift in the spectrum line divided by the original wavelength of that line. Thus, if the object we are measuring is at rest relative to us, there is no shift and z would equal zero. As the galaxy gets farther away (and thus recedes faster) its red shift increases and the value of z goes up. Red shifts with z greater than 0.5 are considered large by astronomers. With the distance scale we adopted earlier, z = 0.5 means that the galaxy or cluster is about 4 billion light-years away. The most distant cluster of normal galaxies we have studied so far has a z of about 0.9.

This work is really just beginning, so we cannot at present draw any firm conclusions about the deceleration of the universe from our current measurements. (Luckily, there are other ways we can get an idea of the large-scale properties of the cosmos; these will be discussed in later chapters.)

FINDING THE MOST REMOTE GALAXIES

I would like to close this chapter with a personal digression about some astronomical work in which I have been involved for a number of years: our attempt to probe the most remote regions of the universe in space and time. How far out (and how far back in time) can we look as we examine the universe of galaxies?

As I mentioned briefly above, in addition to "normal" galaxies like our Milky Way, astronomers have recognized a class of abnormal or "active" galaxies, which emit vast quantities of energetic particles and glow brilliantly in the radio region of the spectrum. As you read in the chapter on black holes, astronomers speculate that the "engine" that powers these violent (and large) galaxies may be a compact object at the center, perhaps a supermassive black hole. Whatever the cause of their radio brilliance, the galaxies give off so much energy that they can be recognized at much greater distances than run-of-the-mill galaxies.

Once we have pinpointed the exact position of the radio source, we can then search that portion of the sky with the best light-detecting instruments at our disposal to see if we can find the faint galaxy "culprit" responsible for the intense radio emission. When we use all our ingenuity to measure the red shifts of these objects, we find the largest distances we have ever measured to any recognized class of galaxies.

I might mention that the red shifts we measure are so great that certain lines we normally measure only in the invisible ultraviolet portion of the spectrum are shifted to become visible. Normally, these ultraviolet lines cannot be seen from the ground, because our Earth's atmosphere contains a layer of ozone that absorbs many ultraviolet rays. But if the galaxy has a truly large red shift (with z greater than 1.6—which corresponds to a distance of 10 billion light-years or so), then the ultraviolet rays become shifted to the kind of light that can make it to our telescopes without much trouble. It's as if the universe is stretching itself to give us a hand.

Using this technique, the highest red shift we have measured so far is for a galaxy called 3C 256, shown in Figure 6 on page 173. Its z is 1.82, corresponding to a distance of about 12 billion light-years!

Where do we go from here? The exploration of distant galaxies is one of those areas of astronomy where more data are desperately needed, and we are limited much more by our equipment than by our ability to conceive of useful observations. New telescopes on the ground (including the giant Keck telescope scheduled to be completed atop an extinct Hawaiian volcano in the early 1990's) and the Space Telescope (scheduled to be launched from the space shuttle, when it flies again) will give us an opportunity to push our technology to the limit and look out even farther into the uncharted reaches of deep space. No one knows what we may find, but I would bet that if the work of these instruments proceeds as astronomers hope, this chapter on galaxies will be ready for significant revision within a decade.

BUBBLES

DAVID BRIN

1.

On planets, they say, water always runs downhill. . . .

SERENA HAD NO WAY OF KNOWING if it was true. She had never been on a planet. Not in the brief million or so years she had been aware. Neither had any of her acquaintances. The very idea was ridiculous.

Very few Grand Voyageurs ever even got a chance to *see* a planet. And yet, even among them, the ancient truisms were still told.

That which goes up must fall, and will. . . .

She had been willing to take their word for it. The clichés came out of a foggy past. Why should she question them? Why should she care?

No matter how far down you fall, you can go lower still. . . .

Stunned and still nearly senseless from her passage through the maelstrom, Serena numbly contemplated the truth of the old sayings, inherited down the eons from distant times when her ancestors actually dwelled on tiny slivers of rock, down close to the bright flames of burning stars.

She had had no inkling, when she had tunneled away from Spiral Galaxy 998612a with a full cargo, that the ancient sayings would soon apply to her.

Or do they? she wondered. Was she perhaps as far down as one could possibly get? It seemed to Serena, right then, that there just wasn't any lower to go.

Her systems creaked and groaned as her instruments readapted to normal space-time. Serena still felt the heat of her passage through Kaluza space. The incandescent journey through the bowels of the singularity had raised her temperature dangerously near the fatal point.

178

Now, though, she realized that her radiators were spilling that excess heat into a coldness like none she had ever known before. Blackness stretched in all directions around her. *Impossible. My sensors must be damaged,* she hoped.

But the repair drones reported nothing wrong with her instruments. The real harm had been done elsewhere.

Then why can I not see any stars?

She increased the sensitivity of her opticals, increased it again, and at last began to see a pattern—a spray of tiny motes of light—spread across the black vault.

Tiny, tiny, faraway spirals and fuzzy globes. Galaxies.

Had she been an organism, Serena might have blinked, have closed her eyes against the dismay.

Only galaxies?

Serena had traveled deep space all her life. It was her mission—carrying commerce between far-flung islands of intelligence. She was used to black emptiness.

But not like this!

Galaxies, she thought. No stars, only *galaxies, everywhere.*

She knew galaxies, of course—island universes containing gas clouds and dust and vast myriads of stars, from millions to trillions each. Her job, after all, was to haul gifts from one spiral swirl to the next, or to and from great elliptical giants, galaxies so huge that it seemed extravagant of the universe to have made more than one.

She had spent a million years carrying cargo from one galaxy to another, and yet had never been outside of one, before.

Outside! She quailed from the thought, staring at the multitude of foggy specks all around her. *But there* isn't *anything outside of galaxies!*

Oh, she had always used distant ones for navigation, as stable points of reference. But always they had been drowned out in a swarm of nearby stars. Always there had been one great galactic disk, vast because it lay all around her, a bright, restless, noisy place filled with traffic and bustling civilizations.

She had always felt sorry for the members of those hot little cultures, so busy, so quick. They flashed through their tiny lives so briefly. They never got to see the great expanses, the vistas that she traveled. Their kind had *made* her kind, long ago. But that was so far in the past, now, that few planet-dwellers any longer knew where the Grand Voyageurs had come from. They simply took Serena and her cousins for granted.

No, she had never been outside before. For traveling *among* the galaxies had never meant traveling *between* them.

Her job was to ply the deep ways at the hearts of those galactic swirls, where stars were packed so dense and tight that their light hardly had room to escape, where they whirled and danced quick pavanes, and occasionally collided in brilliant fury.

Sometimes the crowded stars combined. In the core of nearly every galaxy there lay at least one great black hole, a gravitational well so deep that space itself warped and curled in tight geometries of compression. And these singularities offered paths—paths from one galaxy to another.

The great nebulae were not linked at their edges, but at their hearts.

So how did I get here? Serena wondered. *Here, so far from any galaxy at all?*

Part of the answer, she knew, lay in her cargo bay. Pallet fourteen was a twisted ruin. It was some violent event there that had bruised her Kaluza fields, just at the most critical phase of diving into a singularity, when she had to tunnel from one loop of space-time to another.

In disgust, she used several of her remote drones to pry apart the tortured container. The drones played light over a multicolored, spiny mass. Needlelike projections splayed in all directions, like rays of light frozen in mid-spray. The thing was quite beautiful. And it had certainly killed her.

Idiots! She cursed. Nobody had informed her that antimatter was part of her cargo. Now she understood the explosion, at least. Down in Kaluza space, Nature made a big distinction between antimatter and the "Koino-" or normal variety. It was one reason why antimatter was so rare in the cosmos. The galaxies and nearly everything else were made of Koino-matter.

In Kaluza space, normal means for containing antimatter were inadequate. Inadequate by far! It was such a widely known phenomenon, so simple. She had thought even the most simple-minded quick-life cultures would know to take precautions.

She tried to think. To remember.

In that last galaxy there had been funny little creatures who twittered at her in languages so obscure that even her sophisticated linguistic programs could barely follow them. The beings had used no machines, she recalled, but instead flitted about their star-filled galactic core on the backs of great winged beast/craft made of protoplasm. A few of the living "ships" were so large that Serena had been able to see them unmagnified—as specks fluttering near her great bulk. It was the first time she recalled ever seeing life up close, without artificial aid.

Perhaps the creatures had not understood that machine intelligences like Serena had special needs. Perhaps they thought . . .

Serena had no idea what they thought. All she knew was that their cargo had exploded just as she was midway down the narrow Way between that galaxy and another, diving and swooping along paths of twisted space.

To lose power in a singularity. Serena wondered. It had happened to none of the Voyageurs she had ever encountered. But sometimes Voyageurs *disappeared*. Perhaps this was what happened to the ones who vanished.

Galaxies.

Her attention kept drifting across the vault surrounding her. The brush-

DAVID CHERRY

strokes of light lay scattered almost evenly across the sky. It was unnerving to see so many galaxies, and no stars. No stars at all.

Plenty of stars, she corrected herself. But all of them smeared—in their billions—into those islands in the sky. None of the galaxies appeared to be appreciably above average in size, or appreciably closer than any other.

By this time her radiators had cooled far below the danger level. How could they not? It was as cold here as it ever could get. Enough light struck her to keep the temperature just near three degrees absolute. Some of that faint light came from the galaxies. The rest was long-wave radiation from space itself. It was smooth, isotropic. The slowly ebbing roar of the long-ago birth of everything.

Her remote drones reported in. Repairs had progressed. She could move, if she chose.

Great, she thought. *Move where?*

She experimented. Her drives thrummed. She felt action and reaction as pure laser light thrust from her tail. Her accelerometers swung.

That was it. There was no other way she could tell she was moving at all. There were no reference points, whose relationships would slowly shift as she swept past. The galaxies were too far away. Much, much too far away.

She tried to think of an adjective, some term from any of the many languages she knew, to convey just how far away they were. The truth of her situation was just sinking in.

Serena knew that a planet-bound creature, such as her distant ancestors, would have looked at her in amazement. She was herself nearly as large as some small planets.

If one of those world-evolved creatures were to find itself on her surface, equipped with the requirements to survive, it might move in its accustomed way—it had been called "walking," she remembered—and spend its entire brief life span before traveling her length.

She tried to imagine how such creatures must have looked upon the spaces *between* their rocky little worlds, back in their early days. It was a millionfold increase in scale from the size of a planet to that of a solar system. The prospect must have been daunting.

Then, after they had laboriously conquered their home planetary system, how they must have quailed before the interstellar distances, yet *another* million times as great! To Serena they were routine, but how stunning those spaces must have seemed to her makers! How totally frustrating and unfathomable!

Now she understood how they must have felt.

Serena increased power to her drives. She clung to the feeling of acceleration, spitting light behind her, driving faster and faster. Her engines roared. For a time she lost herself in the passion of it, thrusting with all her might toward a speck of light chosen at random. She spent energy like a wastrel, pouring it out in a frantic need to *move*!

Agoraphobia was a terrible discovery to a Grand Voyageur. She howled at the black emptiness, at the distant, tantalizing pools of light. She blasted forth with the heat of her panic.

Galaxies! Any galaxy would do. Any one at all!

Blind to all but terror, she shot like a bolt of light . . . but light was far too slow.

Sense took hold at last, or perhaps some deep-hidden wisdom circuit she had not even known of, triggered in a futile reflex for self-preservation. Her drives shut down and Serena found herself coasting.

For a time she simply folded inward, closing off from the universe, huddling within a corner of her mind darker even than the surrounding night.

2.

Galaxies have their ages, their phases, just as living things do. Aim your telescope toward the farthest specks, distant motes so far away that their light was reddened with the stretching of the universe. The universal expansion makes their flight seem rapid. It also means that the light you see is very, very old.

These, then, are the *youngest* things you will ever see. Quasars and galaxies at the very earliest stages, when the black holes in their cores were hot, still gobbling stars by the hundreds, blaring forth great bursts of light and belching searing beams of accelerated particles.

Look closer. The galaxies you'll see will be flying away from you less quickly, their light will be less reddened. And they will be older.

Pinwheel spirals turn, looking like fried eggs made of a hundred billion sparks. In their centers, the black holes are now calmer. All the easy prey have been consumed, and now only a few stars fall into their maws, from time to time. The raging has diminished enough to let life grow in the slowly rotating hinterlands.

Spiral arms show where clots of gas and giant molecular clouds concentrate in shock waves, like spume and spindrift gathering on a windswept verge. Here new stars are born. The largest of these sweep through their short lives and explode, filling nearby space with heavy elements, fertilizing the fields of life.

Barred spirals, irregulars, ellipticals . . . there are other styles of galaxies, as well, sprayed like dandelion seeds across the firmament.

But not randomly. No. Not randomly at all.

3.

Slowly, Serena came back to her senses. She felt a distant amusement.

Dandelion seeds?

Somehow, her similes had taken on a style so archaic . . . perhaps it was a form of defensive reaction. Her memory banks drew forth an image of puff-balls bending before a gusty wind, then scattering sparkling specks forth. . . .

Fair enough, she thought, of the comparison.

All sense of motion was lost, although she knew she had undergone immense acceleration. The galaxies lay all around her. Apparently unchanged.

She looked again on the universe around her. Peered at one quadrant of the sky, then another.

Perhaps they aren't scattered as smoothly as I'd thought.

She contemplated for some time. Then decided.

Fortunately, her cargo wasn't anybody's *property,* per se. *Gifts.* That was what the Grand Voyageurs like her carried. No civilization could think of "trade" between galaxies. Even using the singularities, there was no way to send anything in expectation of payment.

No. The hot, quick, short-lived cultures took whatever Grand Voyageurs like Serena brought, and loaded them down with presents to take to the next stop. Nobody ever told a Voyageur where to go. Serena and her cousins traveled wherever whim took them.

So she wasn't really stealing when she started dismantling her cargo section, pulling forth whatever she found and adapting the treasures for her own pur-poses.

The observatory took only fifty years to build.

4.

Strings.

Bubbles.

The galaxies were not evenly distributed through expanding space. The "universe" was full of *holes.*

In fact, most of it was emptiness. Light shimmered at the edges of yawning cavities, like flickers on the surface of a soap bubble. The galaxies and clusters of galaxies lay strung at the fringes of monstrous cavities.

While she performed her careful survey, cataloguing and measuring every mote her instruments could find, Serena also sought through her records, through the ancient archives carried by every Grand Voyageur.

She found that she had not been the first to discover this.

The galaxies were linked with one another—via Kaluza space—through the black holes at their centers. A Grand Voyageur traveled those ways, and so never got far enough outside the great spirals to see them in this perspective.

Now, though, Serena thought she understood.

There wasn't just one *Big Bang, at the beginning of time,* she realized. *It was more complicated than that.*

The original kernel had divided early on, and then divided again and again. The universe had many centers of expansion, and it was at the farthest-forward shock waves of those explosions that matter had condensed, roiled, and formed into galaxies and stars.

So I am at the bottom, she realized.

Somehow, when the explosion had sent her tumbling in Kaluza space, she had slipped off the rails. She had fallen, fallen nearly all the way to the center of one of the great explosions.

One could fall no farther.

The calculations were clear on something else, as well. Even should she accelerate with everything she had, and get so close to light-speed that relativistic time foreshortened, she would still never make it even to the nearest galaxy.

Such emptiness, she contemplated. Why, even the cosmic rays were faint, here. And those sleeting nuclei were only passing through. It was rare for Serena to detect even an atom of hydrogen, as a neighbor.

"It is better, far,
    to light a candle,
Than to curse the darkness."

For a time it was only the soft melancholy of ancient poetry that saved Serena from the one-way solace of despair.

5 .

To the very center, then.

Why not? Serena wondered.

According to her calculations, she was much, much closer to the center of the great bubble than to any of the sprayed galaxies at its distant rim.

Indeed. Why not? It would be something to do.

She found she only had to modify her velocity a little. She had already been heading that way by accident, from that first panicked outburst.

She passed the time reading works from a million poets, from a million noble races. She created subpersonae—little separate personalities, which could argue with each other, discussing the relative merits of so many planet-bound points of view. It helped to pass the time.

Soon, after only a few thousand years, it was time to decelerate, or she would simply streak past the center, with no time even to contemplate the bottom, the navel of creation.

Serena used much of her reserve killing the last of her velocity, relative to the bubble of galaxies. All around her the red shifts were the same, constant. All the galaxies seemed to recede away at the same rate.

So. Here I am.

She coasted, and realized that she had just completed the last task of any relevance she could ever aspire to. There were no more options. No other deeds that could be done.

"Hello?"

Irritably, Serena wiped her conversation banks, clearing away the subpersonae that had helped her while away the last few centuries. She did not want those little artificial voices disturbing her as she contemplated the manner of bringing about her own end.

I wonder how big a flash I'll make, she thought. *Is it even remotely possible that anyone back in the inhabited universe might see it, even if they were looking this way with the best instruments?*

She caressed the fields in her engines, and knew she had the will to do what had to be done.

"Hello? Has somebody come?"

Serena sent angry surges through her lingula systems. *Stop it.*

Suicide would come none too soon. *I must be going crazy,* she subvocalized, and some of her agony slipped out into space around her.

"Yes, many feel that way, when they arrive here."

Quakes of surprise made Serena tremble. The voice had come from outside!

"Who . . . who are you?" she gasped.

"I am the one who waits, the one who collects and greets," the voice replied. And then, after some hesitation:

"I am the coward."

6.

Joy sparkled and burst from Serena. She shouted, though the only one in the universe to hear her was near enough to touch. She cried aloud.

"There is a *way*!"

The coward was larger than Serena. He drifted nearby, looking like nothing so much as a great assemblage of junk from every and any civilization imaginable. He had already explained that the bits and pieces had been contributed by countless stranded entities before her. By now he was approaching the mass of a small star, and had to hold the pieces apart with webs of frozen field lines.

The coward seemed disturbed by Serena's enthusiasm.

"But I've already explained to you, it *isn't* a way! It is death!"

Serena could not make it clear to the thing that she had already been ready to die. "That remains to be seen. All I know is that you have told me that there is a way out of this place, and that many have arrived here before me, and taken that route away from here."

"I tell you it is a funnel into Hell!"

"So a black hole seems, to planet-dwellers, but we Grand Voyageurs dive into them, and traverse the tortured lanes of Kaluza space—"

"And I have told you that this is not a black hole! And what lies within this opening is not Kaluza space, but a door into madness and destruction!"

Serena found that she pitied the poor thing. She could not imagine choosing, as it obviously had, to sit here at the center of nothingness for all eternity, an eternity broken every few million years by the arrival of one more stranded voyager. Apparently every one of Serena's predecessors had ignored the poor thing's advice, given him what they had to spare, and eagerly taken that escape offered, no matter how hazardous.

"Show it to me, please," she asked politely.

The coward sighed, and turned to lead the way.

7.

It has long been hypothesized that there was more than one episode of creation. The discovery that the universe of galaxies is distributed like soap bubbles, each expanding from its own center, was the great confirmation that the Big Bang, at least, had not been undivided.

But the ideas went beyond that.

What if, they had wondered, even in ancient days, *what if there are other universes altogether?*

She and Coward traded data files while they moved leisurely toward the Hole at the very center of All. Serena was in no hurry, now that she had a destination again. She savored the vast store of knowledge Coward had accumulated.

Her own Grand Voyageurs were not the first, it seemed, to have cruised the great wormholes between the galaxies. There were others, some greater, who had nevertheless found themselves for whatever reason shipwrecked here at the base of everything.

And all of them, no doubt, had contemplated the dizzying emptiness that lay before them now.

A steady stream of very strange particles emanated from a twisted shapelessness. Rarities, such as magnetic monopoles, swept past Serena more thickly than she ever would have imagined possible. Here, they were more common than *atoms*.

"As I said, it leads to another place, a place where the fundamentals of our universe do not hold. We can tell very little from this side, only

that *charge, mass, gravity,* all have different meanings, there. Tell me, then, what hope does a creature of our universe have of surviving there? Will your circuits conduct? Will your junctions quantum-jump properly? Will your laser drives even function if electrons aren't allowed to occupy the same energy state?"

For a moment the coward's fear infected Serena. The closer she approached, the more eerie and dangerous this undertaking seemed.

"And nobody has ever come back out again," Coward whispered.

Serena shook herself out of her funk. Her situation remained the same. If this was nothing more than yet another way to suicide, at least it had the advantage of being interesting.

And who knows? Many of my predecessors were wiser than I, and they all chose this path, as well.

"I thank you for your friendship," she told the coward. "I give you all of this spare mass, from my cargo, as a token of affection."

Resignedly, the coward sent drone ships to pick up the baggage Serena shed. They cruised away into the blackness.

"What you see is only a small fraction of what I have accumulated," he explained.

"How much?"

He gave her a number, and for a long moment there was only silence between them. Then Coward went on.

"And lately, you castaways have been growing more and more common. I have hope that, soon, someone shall arrive who will leave me more than fragments."

Serena pulsed to widen the gap between them. She began to feel a soft tug—something wholly unlike gravity, or any other force she had ever known.

"I wish you well," she said.

The coward, too, began to back away. The other's voice was chastened, somber. **"So many others seem to find me pitiable, because I wait here, because I am not adventuresome."**

"I do believe you will find your own destiny," she told him. She dared not say what she really thought, so she kept her words vague. "You will find greatness that surpasses that of even those much more bold in spirit," she predicted.

Then, before the stunned ancient thing could reply, she turned and accelerated toward her destiny.

8.

On planets, they say, water always runs downhill. . . .

From the bottom, from as low as one could go in all the universe, Serena plunged downward into another place. Her shields thickened and her drives flexed. As ready as she would ever be, she dove into the strangeness ahead.

She thought about the irony of it all.

He calls himself Coward . . . she contemplated, and knew that it was unfair.

She, and all of those who had plunged this way, blindly into the unknowable, were the real cowards in a way. Oh, she could only speak for herself, but she guessed that their greatest motive was fear, fear of the long loneliness, the empty eons without anything to *do.*

And all the while, Coward accumulated mass: bits of space junk . . . debris cast out from Kaluza space . . . cargo jettisoned or donated by castaways who, like her, were only passing through. . . .

He had told Serena how much mass. And then he had told her that the rate of accumulation was slowly growing, over the long epochs.

And with the mass, he accumulates knowledge. For Serena had opened her libraries to him, and found them absorbed more quickly than she would ever have thought possible. The same thing must have happened countless times before.

Already space had warped beyond recognition around her. Serena looked back and out at all the galaxies, distant motes of light now smeared into swirls of lambent glow.

Astronomers of every civilization puzzle over the question of the missing mass, Serena thought.

Calculations showed that there had to be more mass than could be counted by measuring the galaxies, and what could be detected of the gases in between. Even cosmic rays and neutrinos could not account for it. Half of the matter was simply missing.

Coward had told her. He was accumulating it. Here and there. Dark patches, clots, stuffed in field-stabilized clusters scattered around the vast emptiness of the center of the great galactic bubble.

Perhaps I should have stayed and talked with him some more, Serena thought, as the smeared light melded into a golden glory.

She might have told him. She might have said it. But with all of his brain power, no doubt he had figured it out long ago, and chose to hide the knowledge away.

All that mass.

Someday the galaxies would die. No new stars would be born. The glow would fade. Life—even life crafted out of baryonic machines—would glimmer and go out.

But the recession of the dead whirlpools would slow. It would stop, reverse, and fall again, toward the great gravitational pull at the center of each bubble. And there, universes would be born anew.

Serena saw the last glimmer of galactic light twinkle and disappear. She knew the real reason why she had chosen to take this gamble, to dive into this tunnel to an alien realm.

It was one thing to flee loneliness.

It was quite another thing to flee one who would be God.

No wonder all the others had made the same choice. Serena hoped she would find some of her fellow mortals, if she survived the trip to the other side.

The walls of the tunnel converged. All around her was strangeness.

QUASARS AND ACTIVE GALAXIES

ESSAY BY

HARDING E. SMITH

SPECULATION BY

MICHAEL BISHOP

QUASARS AND ACTIVE GALAXIES

HARDING E. SMITH

VIOLENCE IN THE UNIVERSE

A GALAXY IS NOT merely a collection of stars; in some cases the whole is much greater than the sum of its parts. Certain types of galaxies exhibit awesome explosive events occurring in or near their nuclei that completely over-shadow the energy produced by their multitudes of stars. It is difficult to relate the magnitude of these violent events to common experience. Each second, the quiescent Sun emits more energy than 100,000 full-scale nuclear holocausts, each sufficient to obliterate life on our planet. In a normal galaxy the stars typically emit enough energy in starlight to equal 100 billion Suns. Yet the explosive galaxies dwarf a normal galaxy's energy production by factors of hundreds to thousands or more.

Such violence cannot be accounted for in terms of the ordinary processes that produce the starlight by which we see the normal spiral galaxies. Fur-thermore, the violence shows a complex variety of forms. There is evidence, in fact, that every galaxy shows activity of one form or another. As you saw in Eric Chaisson's chapter, even our own Milky Way Galaxy is known to have a small scale "happening" near its center. Lying in the direction of the con-stellation Sagittarius, this central region exhibits a moderately powerful source of radio noise, gas clouds moving at breakneck speed, and bursts of newly forming stars.

What source of energy is responsible for the activity in galaxies? Why does it manifest itself in the ways that it does? What is the relationship between such activity and the heredity and environment of galaxies? As we shall see, there is a certain family resemblance among the various kinds of active galaxies and it is helping us gradually to piece together the puzzle of their family portrait. Still, several pieces of the puzzle remain missing, and we are not quite sure how to interpret many of the clues we have.

A CATALOGUE OF ACTIVE GALAXIES

The first suggestion that violent activity is present in galaxies must have occurred to Edwin Hubble, the great pioneer of extragalactic astronomy, as he devised his classification scheme based on the appearance and form of galaxies. He classified galaxies into the categories you can read about in Hyron Spinrad's chapter—elliptical or spiral depending on their appearance in photographs. He then subdivided these classes based on the flattening of an elliptical galaxy or the tightness of a spiral's arms. Some galaxies without obvious structure were classified as irregular, but when the classification was completed, there remained many galaxies in which the form of the galaxy was obviously disturbed or disrupted. Hubble subdivided the irregular class into Irregular I (the amorphous type) and Irregular II (the disturbed irregulars). Some Irregular II galaxies are clearly undergoing strong gravitational interactions with nearby companions, wherein intense tidal forces are disrupting the galaxies by pulling stars and gas out of their regular orbits. Such tidal disturbances appear to be able to reach clear into the cores of many interacting galaxies to trigger additional violent activity in the galaxy nucleus. Other Irregular II galaxies appear to the eye to be undergoing massive explosions on the scale of an entire galaxy, ejecting material from the nucleus outward at speeds up to several thousand kilometers per second.

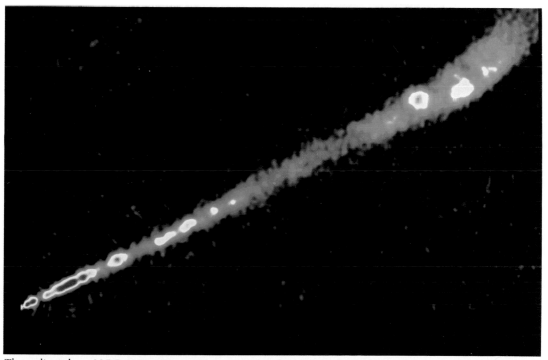

The radio galaxy NGC 6251. An enormous jet, stretching over 300,000 light-years, can be seen on this false-color radiograph taken with the Very Large Array telescope. Observers: R. A. Perley, A. H. Bridle, & A. G. Willis; photo courtesy NRAO/AUI.

Then there is a special group of spiral galaxies, discovered in the 1940's by astronomer Carl Seyfert, which exhibit brilliant pointlike nuclei powered by some as-yet-unknown but very powerful source. These *Seyfert galaxies* show evidence for high-velocity clouds of hot gas moving around the nucleus with speeds up to a few percent of the speed of light. Seyfert galaxies also contain large amounts of dust, heated by the light from the nucleus to several hundred degrees centigrade. Such dust radiates quite strongly at "infrared" galaxies, being perhaps easiest to detect with telescopes tuned to this band of the spectrum.

In contrast, some giant elliptical galaxies are powerful sources of *radio* emission. In these *radio galaxies* violent explosions or other energetic mechanisms produce enormous swarms of electrons moving at close to the speed of light. When these fast-moving electrons are trapped by powerful magnetic fields, they spiral around madly, radiating radio waves and producing in total more luminous energy than the hundreds of billions of stars in the galaxy. This radiation, called *synchrotron radiation*, gets its name from high-energy "synchrotron" accelerators, which use magnetic fields to accelerate particles to very high energies for atomic and nuclear physics experiments.

The energetic particles and magnetic field in active galaxies originate in the galaxy's nucleus, but then can be carried in vast high-speed jet streams out to distances as great as a million light-years. How these particles and field can make it out to such great distances is a mystery. The electrons lose their energy rapidly by the very act of radiating synchrotron emission. A typical electron would radiate all its energy away in only a very few seconds. Somehow the machine that powers the radio galaxy supplies fresh energetic particles continuously through the source volume. (By the way, just as the Seyfert phenomenon appears to occur only in spiral galaxies, only giant ellipticals are powerful radio galaxies.)

Recently there has also been considerable interest among astronomers in the relationship between energetic activity in galaxies and active star formation regions. As Martin Cohen described, the birth of young stars out of the interstellar medium in our own and other galaxies is a process of great interest and importance to all of astronomy, but it is poorly understood even in regions in the Milky Way. The new interest in this field has in part been generated by results from the recent highly successful Infrared Astronomy Satellite (IRAS), which, in its survey of the sky at infrared wavelengths, has detected large numbers of galaxies that glow brightly in the infrared. In many cases this may result from the presence of massive star-forming regions in these galaxies where luminous young stars are heating the shrouds of dust from which they condensed, causing them to emit strongly at infrared wavelengths.

To produce so much infrared radiation in these galaxies, new stars must be forming at a much faster rate than in the Milky Way or most nearby galaxies. What has stimulated these "starbursts," as they have been called? We do not

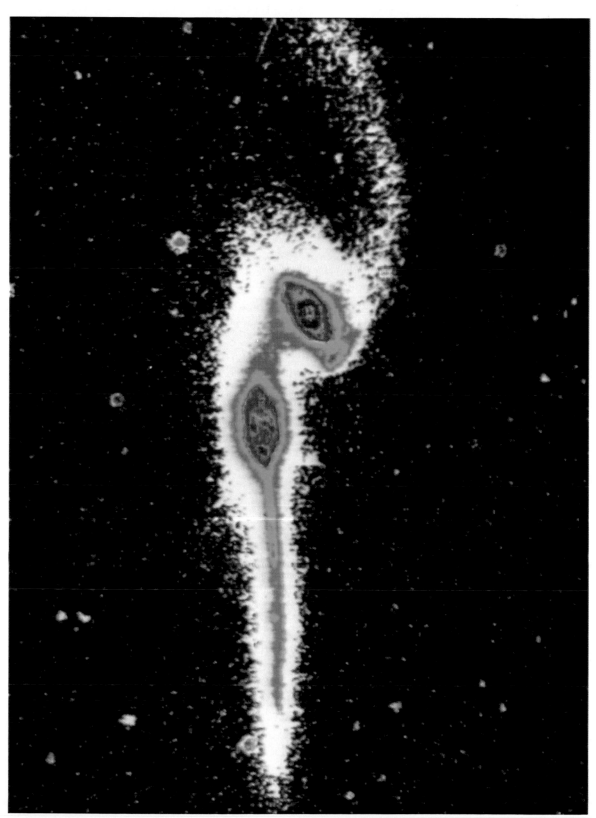

Two interacting galaxies (NGC 4676 A and B), nicknamed "The Playing Mice." Computer enhanced, false-color image. Photo credit: National Optical Astronomy Observatories.

yet know, but there does appear to be a relationship between starbursts and other forms of activity in a galaxy. Many Seyfert galaxies, for example, are among the galaxies IRAS found and show strong infrared emission from star-forming regions as well as from their nonstellar sources. An answer to which came first, the starburst (egg) or the nonstellar activity (chicken), is certain to provide valuable clues to the origin of activity in galaxies.

Arguably the most interesting active objects, and certainly the most difficult to explain are the *quasi-stellar objects*, or *quasars*. In the nearly twenty-five years since their discovery, an enormous effort—measured in terms of hours upon hours of observing time on the world's largest telescopes and years of research time spent by leading astronomers around the world—has been mounted to try to understand the workings of these fascinating but perplexing members of the astronomical "zoo." Interest is so keen in part because we believe that these may be the most distant objects yet seen and the most powerful energy sources in the universe. We have begun to understand many of their most interesting characteristics, but our knowledge is still incomplete, and, as with their active galaxy relatives, much about the quasars remains shrouded in mystery.

THE DISCOVERY OF QUASARS AND QUASAR RED SHIFTS

The story of the quasars begins in the early 1960's as the science of radio astronomy began to come of age and comprehensive catalogues of cosmic radio sources were first completed. As astronomers began to compare the positions of these sources of radio noise with optical photographs, a number of objects were readily identified. These included remnants of supernova explosions and other nebulae in our Galaxy, the powerful elliptical radio galaxies, and, rather surprisingly, certain stellar-appearing objects distributed around the sky. It was known that normal stars like our Sun are not powerful radio sources, so these "radio stars" had to be unusual; puzzled astronomers dubbed them *quasi-stellar radio sources*, shortened to *quasars*. Although quasars were first discovered as radio sources, we now know that there are actually about fifteen times as many "radio quiet" quasars as there are quasars that are powerful radio sources.

For most constituents of the universe—systems that humans will not soon or perhaps ever visit—the astronomer has only the light and other radiation they give off to elucidate their physical natures. As you have seen elsewhere in this book, by breaking the light up into its component wavelengths—creating a spectrum—the astronomer may identify features produced by the different atoms, compare their strengths, and thereby deduce which elements are present and in what proportion, and deduce such physical properties as temperature, density, and so on. When astronomers obtained spectra of the first quasars, they were again bewildered. The spectra were unlike the spectra of normal

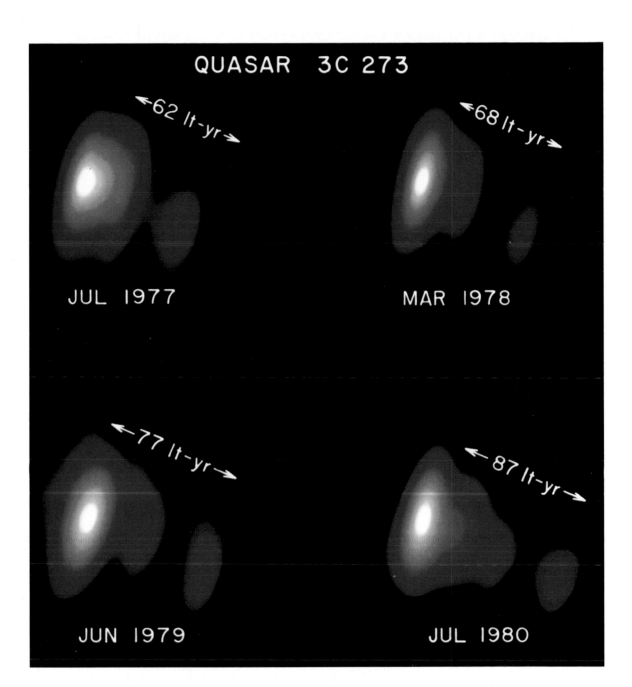

Maps of the quasar 3C273B from radio observations at four different epochs, showing how the components appear to be separating at a speed greater than the speed of light. The maps were made by connecting radiotelescopes at the Owens Valley Radio Observatory in California, the Max Planck Institute in West Germany, the National Radio Astronomy Observatory in West Virginia, and the Harvard Radio Astronomy Station in Texas. The figure is reproduced from a paper by T. J. Pearson, *et al.*, in *Nature*, April 2, 1981.

stars or galaxies, and the features present in the quasars' spectra could not be readily identified. In 1963, Caltech astronomer Maarten Schmidt put together the first pieces of the puzzle of the quasars' spectra. Schmidt was studying a spectrum of the quasar 3C 273 (the 273rd radio source in the third catalogue of radio sources compiled by radio astronomers at Cambridge University), which he had recently obtained with the 200-inch Palomar telescope, when he recognized a familiar pattern to the emission features present. Schmidt noticed, but found difficult to believe, that the features in 3C 273's spectrum fit the well-known pattern of emission produced by hydrogen, the simplest and most common chemical element. But the hydrogen emission features were not at the wavelengths he expected for stars; instead they were shifted by a large amount—15 percent toward the red (longer-wavelength) region of the spectrum. Schmidt was excited and incredulous because his discovery implied that 3C 273 was not a star at all. With a spectral red shift of 15 percent, it was out among the distant galaxies!

You will recall from Hyron Spinrad's chapter that galaxy red shifts are interpreted in terms of velocity due to the expansion of the universe and, as such, are a direct measure of the distance to the galaxy. With a red shift of 15 percent, an object would be quite far away—well over a billion light-years— and therefore should appear quite dim. But 3C 273 was *bright*, a thousand times brighter than a luminous galaxy at the same red shift. If Schmidt interpreted 3C 273's red shift in the same manner as galaxy red shifts, then he had placed it as the most luminous object in the universe! Although it caused quite a commotion in astronomical circles when it was announced, this interpretation has stood the test of time and is still the underpinning of our study of quasars today.

Once Schmidt had found the key to understanding the quasars' spectra, red shifts were quickly determined for a number of other quasars, many even more distant and more luminous. It was common practice in the early days of quasar research to wager a case of good wine for breaking the record quasar red shift, but recently the record has been broken so frequently that astronomers are more likely to restrict their bet to a single bottle. A recent (1987) compilation lists approximately 3,500 known quasar red shifts.

While I was writing this article the British science journal *Nature* announced a new record-breaking quasar red shift not once, but twice! The issue of January 8, 1987, reports that a new highest-red-shift and presumed most-distant quasar was discovered on wide-angle photographs obtained by British astronomers in a sensitive survey for high red-shift quasars. It has a red shift of 4.01 (its spectral features are shifted by an amount equal to 4.01 times their normal wavelength), a value they confirmed using the 150-inch Southern Hemisphere Anglo-Australian telescope. This great a red shift corresponds to a recession velocity of more than 90 percent the speed of light, or a distance of about 15 billion light-years, qualifying it for a listing in the *Guinness Book of Records*.

TWINKLE, TWINKLE, QUASI-STAR

Another unexpected and extraordinary discovery was that the luminous output from quasars varies in time; for a while the brightness of 3C 273 seemed to track the stock market. Unfortunately, to the best of my knowledge, no astronomers became rich as a result and the correlation has long since vanished. Astronomers were surprised not because of the fluctuations themselves, but rather because of the short times in which the quasars' brightness changed. Almost all quasars flicker in brightness by an amount of 10 percent or so, but some quasars show extreme variations in very short time scales. One of the most spectacular outbursts was discovered by Harvard University astronomers examining archival photographs of the variable quasar 3C 279 taken years before the discovery of quasars. The well-preserved old photographs showed that in 1937, and again in 1939, 3C 279 had flared in brightness by as much as a factor of 100 in a time of only a couple of weeks. What can such a brief variation tell us?

Because it takes time for light to travel across a source, astronomers can use the variability of astronomical sources to set upper limits on their sizes. Light from the front of the object reaches us before light from the middle, which in turn reaches us before light from the regions farthest from us; even a single burst of light, like a flashbulb flash, would appear to an observer to be spread out over the length of time that it takes for light to travel from back to front of the source. For example, if a quasar is observed to vary in brightness over a period of two weeks, then astronomers know that it cannot be larger than about two light-weeks in size. If the quasar were any larger, then its light fluctuations would be smeared out over a longer period, purely because of the time it takes for the light to travel across the object itself.

But two light-weeks is a very small size for objects at cosmic distances— only one twenty-sixth of a light-year, or 360 billion kilometers. The variations of 3C 279 and other quasars imply not only that these fantastic objects are producing luminous energy at a rate thousands of times greater than the output of a galaxy of hundreds of billions of stars, but that they are producing so much energy in a volume only about the size of our solar system!

Extraordinary as these characteristics may be, even larger surprises were in store for astronomers when quasars were studied using a technique called *very long baseline interferometry* (VLBI). By connecting radiotelescopes separated by very large distances, radio astronomers can simulate a giant radiotelescope that can make out as fine detail as could be achieved by a single telescope the size of that separation. To probe the very cores of the brightest radio quasars, astronomers have connected radiotelescopes around the United States, Canada, and as far away as West Germany, to simulate a telescope as big as the Earth and with a *resolving power* (ability to make out detail) better than a millionth of a degree.

When this array of telescopes was trained on the quasars, a new type of activity was discovered. The radio sources at the quasars' cores were seen to exhibit occasional outbursts. Following an outburst, the radio sources typically appear to expand and to decrease in radio power until they disappear from view or are overshadowed by a new radio outburst. If we know how far away a quasar is, we can watch its expansion and calculate the speed with which its parts are separating. When this calculation was performed for a number of quasars, it was found that this velocity often proved to be greater than the speed of light! One outburst in 3C 273, tracked in the late 1970's, appeared to have a speed nearly *ten times* the velocity of light. Such large expansion rates would be in clear violation of Einstein's special theory of relativity, the well-confirmed theory which requires that the speed of light is the "speed limit" of the universe. Thus, if these observations are taken at face value, they would require fundamental new laws of physics.

No astronomers seriously believe that quasars are really violating the speed limit established by the theory of relativity; the question is: How else can such apparently large expansion rates be explained? Those readers who are fans of relativity theory will be relieved to learn that there are several possible explanations. The best of these appears to be an effect of relativity itself, which predicts that the measurement of time itself is different in two systems that are moving relative to each other. This effect is completely negligible for systems moving at speeds that we experience on Earth—two readers of this book moving past each other in cars on a highway, or even two supersonic planes crossing the country in opposite directions. (That is why we don't have to bother with relativity theory in everyday life and perhaps why it seems strange to us when we do confront the theory.) But when things are moving at speeds close to the speed of light, funny things begin to happen to the way that length and time and other physical quantities are measured.

The details of this are beyond the scope of this book, but here is how it affects our observations of quasar outbursts: In our case, beams of very-high-energy (and, therefore, high-speed) particles moving together very nearly at the speed of light can produce radio emission such that the source *appears* to be moving faster than light when it is not really doing so. This effect requires very special conditions, however. In particular, it requires that this relativistic beam be pointed almost exactly in our direction. If this explanation is the correct one, its proponents still need to explain how all quasars bright enough to be observed with the VLBI technique just happen to have their beams pointed right at the Earth. Clearly, astronomers need to do a lot more work to understand the details of this mysterious expansion process in quasars.

THE RIDDLE OF THE RED SHIFTS

These remarkable properties—brightness, distance, size, and "super-light"

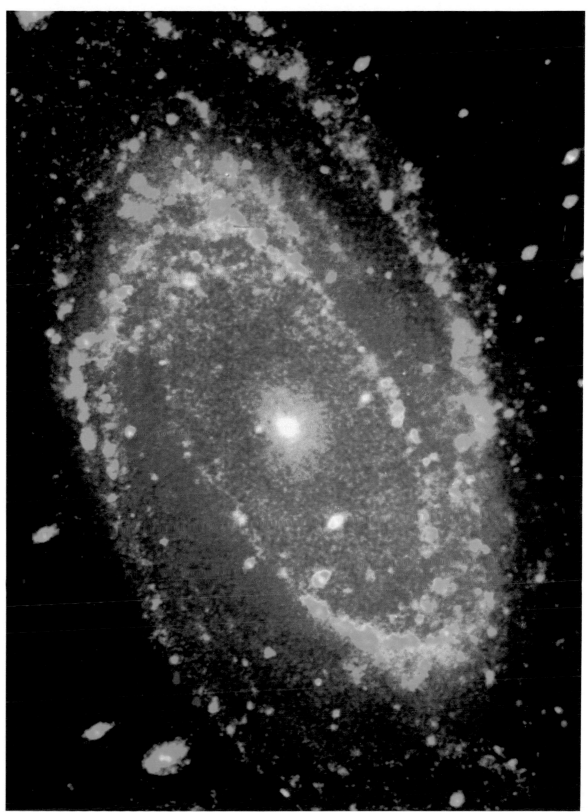

False-color enhanced image of NGC 1097, a barred spiral with long straight jets. Photo by Halton C. Arp; color enhancement work by Jean Lorre. (From the slide set "Enhanced Images of Active Galaxies," Astronomical Society of the Pacific.)

expansion—have led astronomers to investigate seriously many ideas, even rather unconventional ones, to explain quasars. One suggestion, which has been made by several astronomers, is that the quasars simply may not be as distant as they appear. If some mechanism other than the expansion of the universe were responsible for the quasars' red shifts, then the red shift would not be a reliable measure of the quasars' distances—they might be much closer than they seem. This would mean that the great brightness and expansion speed we calculate using the huge distance inferred from the quasars' red shifts would be in error as well—too large by a considerable amount, perhaps.

This suggestion has led to a lengthy and spirited controversy among astronomers over the nature of the quasar red shifts and the distances to the quasars. One group of astronomers, led by H. C. Arp, has over the years found many "unusual circumstances" in which a quasar with a high red shift appears to be physically associated with a galaxy with a much lower red shift (and hence a closer distance). If the quasar and the galaxy are actually associated in space, then both red shifts cannot be telling us the correct distance. If they had to choose, most astronomers would rely upon the distance determined for the galaxy and would question the red shift of the quasar. One big problem with this view is that we have not yet found another way to produce the quasar red shift. Other astronomers and physicists are uncomfortable with the idea of resorting to a new, as yet undiscovered, principle of physics to provide another red-shift mechanism. In addition, they point to a number of instances in which quasars appear to be associated with galaxies *at the same red shift* and argue that these quasars must indeed be as distant as their red shifts suggest. They claim that Arp's peculiar cases are simply chance coincidences of objects that appear close together on the dome of the sky but are in fact separated by great distances in depth.

This controversy has raged for nearly twenty years, with those who support the greater, so-called "cosmological" distances currently in a very substantial majority. More importantly, there do appear to be at least some verified cases of quasars that are at the large distances implied by the red shifts. In these cases we do seem to be required to face the consequences of the quasars' extreme properties and to find ways of explaining them.

A QUASAR SNAPSHOT

Gradually, then, a picture of an active galactic nucleus has begun to emerge. At its center is the powerful energy source or central engine. For now, let us consider it a "black box" whose nature is unknown. We do know that it is smaller than a few light-weeks in size, that it is producing more energy than a galaxy of Suns, and that it is radiating at wavelengths from the radio, through the infrared and visible, to X-ray and gamma-ray energies. The principal form of radiation has been shown to be synchrotron radiation, although other types of radiation may contribute. Surrounding the central source is a region which may be a few light-years in size, containing dense clouds or filaments moving with velocities up to about 10,000 kilometers per second (3 percent of the speed of light). The atoms in these clouds are excited, heated, and stripped of their electrons by the strong ultraviolet radiation from the central source. Heated to temperatures as high as 10,000° C, these clouds produce the emission features in the spectrum which we use to determine the red shift. Some astronomers speculate that these clouds may be bloated stars, moving rapidly in the strong gravitational field of the massive central object. Outside of this region is a more diffuse gas with an extent of perhaps a few hundred light-years or more. It is only this outer diffuse gas which we can see in any detail with optical telescopes.

Is all of this located at the center of a galaxy of stars, even in quasars? Many astronomers think so. In many respects Seyfert galaxies and their active galaxy kin resemble mini-quasars. They show the same central synchrotron source, high-speed emission clouds, and other properties, but on a smaller scale. Perhaps quasars are Seyfert galaxies in which the central source completely overshadows the underlying galaxy. Recent observations suggest that most lower-red-shift quasars (those presumed closest to us), when they are examined with the largest telescopes using very sensitive light-detectors, do show faint extended regions that have properties consistent with those of galaxies. A few even show evidence in their spectra for the presence of stars. The "fuzz" around the nearer quasars doesn't exactly look like a normal galaxy, however, but this should not be too surprising considering the violent activity occurring in the quasar nucleus.

THE MONSTER IN THE MIDDLE

If we accept the enormous distances inferred from the quasars' red shifts, then we must find a way of accounting for the tremendous luminous energy output of the quasar's central engine. Many theories have been proposed. None of them is by any means proven, but one theory has a certain amount of current astronomical popularity.

Some astronomers have suggested that dense compact clusters of stars near the nucleus of a large galaxy could give rise to recurrent *supernova* explosions, which would create highly energetic particles, shock waves in the gas near the galaxy core, and other forms of energy to power the quasars. As discussed in more detail in David Helfand's chapter, massive stars (those with about four or more times the mass of the Sun) end their lives in tremendous explosions. This brief death gasp may be more energetic than the entire 10 billion-year lifetime of nuclear energy production in a star like the Sun. The radio, optical, and X-ray emission (as well as other characteristics) seen in nearby supernova remnants have many similarities with quasars' emission. Even so, the great brilliance of the quasars would require a very high rate of supernova explosions. For example, the quasar 3C 273 would require about ten supernovae daily (compared with a rate of one per hundred years in our Galaxy) to fuel its emission. Some of the more spectacular outbursts, like those of 3C 279, would require a chain reaction of hundreds of nearly simultaneous supernova explosions.

The discovery of the *pulsars* and the efficient way in which the pulsars supply energy to supernova remnants like the Crab Nebula has led to the suggestion that a rapidly rotating, magnetized, massive object might also power the quasars. A normal pulsar is believed to be a superdense neutron star with the mass of one or two Suns. Quasars would require a superpulsar, termed *spinar* by the astronomers who suggested the idea, with a mass of up to a billion times the Sun's mass. By analogy with pulsars, the spinars could be very efficient energy-conversion machines, transforming the rotational energy of the massive object into the energetic particles, radiation, and other forms of energy we see. Seeing regular, periodic light variations like the pulses of radiation from a pulsar would be an important piece of evidence for demonstrating that such objects might exist. Although we have seen large *irregular* variations in some quasars, none has yet been detected to have the *periodic* type of behavior expected from a spinar.

Another idea is that the energy source for quasars might be the annihilation of matter and antimatter in the quasars' core. Particles of antimatter have properties that are opposite to the properties of the matter of which we are made. For example, whereas a matter electron has a negative electrical charge, an antimatter electron—called a positron—has the same mass but a positive charge. There is nothing particularly "odd" about antimatter; a planet, solar system, or even a universe might just as well be made of antimatter as of matter. But if a particle of matter and a corresponding particle of antimatter come into contact, they annihilate each other, turning into energy according to Einstein's relation between matter and energy ($E = mc^2$). Both the creation and annihilation of antimatter have been observed in nuclear accelerators (atom-smashers). Because the particles are completely converted into energy, the destruction of matter and antimatter is the most efficient energy-generating mechanism we know of (and thus frequently a favorite of science-fiction writers).

The energy requirement of a quasar like 3C 273 could be satisfied by the conversion of about ten Suns' worth of matter and antimatter into energy each year. This is, of course, a tiny amount compared with the amount of matter available in an entire galaxy. A problem with this explanation is that when particles of what we call matter meet and annihilate with their corresponding particles of antimatter, the energy produced comes out purely in the form of gamma rays. We do not understand how these gamma rays, which we do *not* see in the expected amounts, could be transformed into the types of energy we *do* see. There are also several arguments that antimatter simply does not exist in the required amounts in the universe to provide the power for all the quasars we observe. Nonetheless, some astronomers and physicists resolutely maintain that the universe might well by "symmetric"—that is, it might have matter and antimatter in equal amounts, separated in most places except in exotic sites like quasars.

But the explanation with the greatest current popularity in astronomical circles is that a quasar is powered by a massive black hole, consuming or "accreting" material in its vicinity. (For more on black holes, see the chapter by William Kaufmann.) At first it may seem peculiar that a black hole *consuming* matter may be considered a source of energy. Of course, even in exotic places like the region around a black hole, matter and energy are not truly created or destroyed; they are merely converted from one form to another. The tremendous gravitational pull of a massive black hole provides the material in the surrounding region with a very large amount of *gravitational potential energy*—the sort of energy you would have simply by being poised on the ledge of the thirtieth floor of a tall building. As matter falls toward the black hole, this energy is released and turned into other forms.

Astronomers now widely believe that certain X-ray sources in our Galaxy are produced by stellar-size black holes that accrete material from nearby companion stars in a double star system. In like manner, a giant black hole at the center of a galaxy may disrupt and accrete material from stars that orbit too close to it. As material falls close to the black hole, a disk of material (called an *accretion disk*) is formed which may be heated to very high temperatures and can produce some of the radiation we see. The details of how the remainder of the energy is produced are not yet very well understood (although some of the sorts of mechanisms astronomers are investigating are discussed in William Kaufmann's chapter). We do know that there is a tremendous store of gravitational energy, which may be released very efficiently by a massive black hole, and we also believe that a black hole of up to a billion solar masses might form relatively naturally in the early stages of the formation of a galaxy. Finally, observations suggest that some galaxies, including our own, have relatively massive, compact objects in their cores—is this perhaps a smaller version of the black hole that powers the quasars? The evidence is not conclusive but is considered a good bet by many astronomers.

GRAVITATIONAL LENSES

Recently, astronomers have discovered a somewhat bizarre effect that can happen to the light from a distant quasar as it makes its way to us. One of the first predictions of Einstein's general theory of relativity was that the presence of gravity bends space so that the paths of light beams traveling through that curved space are bent. This effect also led to the first confirmation of Einstein's theory, when groups led by Sir Arthur Eddington actually detected the bending of rays of starlight passing near the Sun during the total solar eclipse of 1919. It was quickly recognized that just as normal lenses refract or bend light to bring it to a focus, a massive object with its strong gravity may bend light beams passing through nearby space to bring them to a focus. However, such a *gravitational lens* has characteristics somewhat different from those of a normal lens. The gravitational lens may amplify or strengthen an image and, depending on the circumstances, may create multiple images of the lensed object.

Madeleine and Jeno Barnothy suggested early in the quasar controversy that quasars might be so bright because of the amplification of a gravitational lens, in this case a distant galaxy or perhaps a cluster of galaxies, between us and the quasar. It does not appear that the majority of quasars can be seen through gravitational lenses, so relatively little attention was paid to the Barnothys' idea until 1979, when a pair of quasars was discovered associated with a faint radio source. Although differing in brightness, the two quasar images were found by astronomers to have the same red shift and remarkably similar spectra. After a great deal of study at optical, infrared, and radio wavelengths, it was determined that the two images were the same in all respects save brightness—exactly the prediction for images formed by a gravitational lens. This interpretation was confirmed when a faint galaxy was detected in just the right place in the sky and at an intermediate distance between us and the multiply-imaged quasar—an ideal candidate to be the lens itself. Several other probable lensed quasars have now been found, convincingly confirming the predictions of general relativity and presenting us with a new problem—how to tell without a costly investment of time and effort which quasars are seen imaged and amplified through gravitational lenses and which are not.

ILLUMINATING THE EARLY UNIVERSE

Quasars and active galaxies present us with a fascinating laboratory in which to study some of the most exotic realms of physics—indeed, physical regimes impossible to re-create in a terrestrial laboratory. Equally important, perhaps, we have the hope of using quasars as "cosmological probes" to tell us about the universe in its early stages. The fact that light travels at a finite, constant speed provides the astronomer with a time machine to see back in time. The large distances of the quasars imply that we are seeing them not as they are now, but as they were at that time in the past when the light was emitted by the quasar and began its journey to us. We see a quasar that has a distance of 12 billion light-years as it was 12 billion years ago, when the universe was far different from its current state. Galaxies had newly formed or were still in the state of forming out of the intergalactic medium, the universe was much denser, and space was expanding more rapidly than in current epochs.

Some studies suggest that quasars were much more numerous in the distant past. Many astronomers have theorized that the events producing the tremendous energies of the quasars are related to the formation of galaxies or to the settling down of unruly galaxies in their adolescence. This would explain why there were more of them in earlier epochs and why we see few quasars nearby. Unfortunately, we do not yet understand the quasar phenomenon well enough to use them directly to tell us about their role in the history of the universe. Recently, however, we have begun to use the quasars as cosmological tools in a different way. We are employing them as background lamps to illuminate other material from the distant past.

It was discovered some years ago that quasars show *absorption* in their spectra; material between us and the quasar is absorbing light at selected wavelengths as the light from the quasar passes through the matter on the way to us. From the moment astronomers discovered this absorption, its origin has been a source of controversy. Could this material associated be with the quasar itself, blasted out in our direction by the explosive quasar nucleus? Or is it material totally unrelated to the quasar which happens to lie along our line of sight to the quasar? Both are exciting possibilities. In the first case there would be more fascinating quasar physics to study; in the second, the quasars may permit us to see material in young galaxies or may even be revealing matter in previously unknown forms during the early stages of the universe.

It now appears that both explanations may be correct, but it is not always clear which one holds for a particular absorption system. In the last few years, however, we believe that we have figured out how to determine the origin of at least *some* of the absorption systems. One type of absorption appears to come from intergalactic gas clouds—clouds smaller than the size of a galaxy which have formed during the early stages of the universe. The existence of such clouds was previously unknown and we don't see such clouds around today. What has happened to them? We are not certain, but one suggestion is that they have been "eaten" by giant cannibal galaxies (a process discussed by Hyron Spinrad in his chapter). Other absorption systems may be associated with gigantic halos of hot gas surrounding galaxies gas that is just too diffuse for us to detect it by its own light.

Finally, there is one other possible answer to the absorption mystery—one on which our group of astronomers at the University of California, San Diego, has been working. We believe that we have identified a class of absorption produced by the gaseous disks of galaxies in their very young stages. These are galaxies far too distant to be seen directly by the light of their stars. From their imprint on the light of the quasar as it passes through the galaxy, we believe we can deduce what galaxy disks were like when they were 1 or 2 billion years old, a small fraction of their current age. A detailed survey carried out at the University of California's Lick Observatory has identified about twenty of these systems. We are now studying them in great detail to learn about the rate at which these young galaxies have processed material through stars and the structure and motions of the gas. This exciting study is just beginning, but we have great hopes that we can use this information to tell us about how galaxies collapse out of the intergalactic medium under gravity, how they form the stars that produce the chemical elements of which we are made, and how they gradually evolve into systems like our Milky Way.

The quasars and their active relatives really do provide unique laboratories, allowing us to "experiment" with enormous black holes, gravitational lenses, and other exotic areas of physics on a grander scale than we might ever have imagined. Their immense distances and tremendous luminosities allow us to use them as lanterns to reveal the universe in its distant past. It is a curious irony that we can contemplate, study, and perhaps one day even understand violent activity in the universe which dwarfs all human endeavor, while at the same time we have such difficulty with the far lesser destructive power that we control and which seems poised on the brink of annihilating life on this planet as we know it. Let us hope that we can extend the wisdom and perspective we gain from the study of the universe, on its grandest scales, to our survival in our little corner of it.

FOR THUS DO I REMEMBER CARTHAGE

MICHAEL BISHOP

i.

Augustine wants no company, and the last person whom he expects to intrude is a troublesome astronomer from Far Cathay.

A fever has besieged the old man. In the bishop's house next to the basilica of Hippo Regius, he mulls the imminence of his own death and the portentous events of this past year.

An army of 20,000 Vandals has besieged Hippo. Under their wily king Genseric, they seem inevitable occupiers. Boniface, Count of Africa, has held them at bay throughout the summer with a force of Gothic mercenaries and a few ragtag volunteers from among the male population of upper Numidia—but Genseric's fleet has blockaded the harbor and Vandal soldiers have disabled the power plant providing Hippo with electricity. Augustine must read the psalms copied out and affixed to his bedchamber walls by the flicker of an olive-oil lamp rather than by the steady incandescence of one of Seneca the Illuminator's clever glass globes.

"This earthly city cannot last," the bishop tells himself, "but the City of God . . . the City of God endures."

Possidius appears inside the door of his bedchamber with a tray of pears, bread, and marinated chickpeas.

Bishop of Calama, a town twenty leagues to the south, Possidius fled to Hippo last October to escape the oncoming barbarians. (Two Numidian bishops less wise than he were tortured to death outside the walls of their cities.) He has lived in Augustine's episcopal quarters ten months now, but has been fussily nursing the brilliant old man for only these past two weeks.

"Go away, Possidius," murmurs Augustine.

"A modest *convivium*. Excellency, you must eat."

"Sometimes, Christ forgive me, it's hard to remember why."

"To maintain your strength, sir. And, this evening, you have a visitor."

"But I've forbidden visitors. Especially physicians."

"This isn't a physician. Vindicianus has almost lost patience with you, Excellency."

The old man in the loose black *birrus* says, "Whoever it is, is sadly unwelcome. Not for his shortcomings, but for mine."

Tears streak Augustine's face. He has been reading the Davidic psalm beginning *"Blessed is he whose transgression is forgiven,"* and the balm of its verse *"Thou shalt preserve me from trouble"* has surely induced these tears. Frequently, of late, he weeps, and Possidius cannot tell if he does so from pity for the plight of Roman Africa, or from an unspeakable gratitude to God, or from some ancient shame for which only he of all men would scruple to indict himself. Undoubtedly, he weeps for many reasons, but the bishop of Calama is unable to sort them out.

"He's a stargazer, Excellency, who hails—he declares—from the capital of Africa." Possidius places the food tray on Augustine's writing desk.

"Carthage?"

"So he says. But he's spent the past thirty years looking at the stars from various high escarpments in Northern Wei."

"Ah, yes. Flying machines and dragons aren't the only miracles from that mythic land, are they?"

"Telescopes, Excellency. Horseless chariots. Boxes that talk, and others in which pictures dance like living people. Seneca the Illuminator says they've perfected machines in Cathay a *century* in advance of any made by the Daedaluses of Rome or Constantinople.

"But the greatest miracle, Excellency, may be that your visitor has returned to Numidia exactly when Genseric's Vandals have come bearing down on us from Gibraltar and Mauretania. The astronomer sneaked through their siege lines to enter the city. Morally, sir, I think you should grant him the interview he desires."

"Morally," the old man mutters. On his feet for the first time since Possidius came in, he totters to his desk, picks up a pear, burnishes it on his robe. He lifts it to his face, sniffing it for submerged memories. He has lived three quarters of a century, and a year besides, and that Possidius should be defining morality for him—fabled Defender of the Faith against the errors of Manichees, Donatists, and Pelagians—stings. But God knows that he sometimes needs chastening, and perhaps Possidius is God's flail.

"Does my would-be visitor have a name?"

"Iatanbaal, sir."

"Christ save us. A pagan name. Does this man have any Latin, Possidius, or am I to talk to him in my execrable Neo-Punic?"

Possidius smiles. "Latin is Iatanbaal's first language. But for three decades he has spoken in the tongues of Babel."

" 'Given of God,' " Augustine muses.

"Excellency?"

"In Neo-Punic, *Iatanbaal* means 'given of God.' " He places the pear back on his desk and lapses into reverie.

"Father Augustine," Possidius prompts.

The old apostle stirs. "Oh, yes. Our visitor. Iatanbaal. 'Given of God.' In that case, let him come in."

ii.

It startles Augustine to find that Iatanbaal—why did he expect a younger man?—is hard on sixty. The astronomer, who drops to his knees to kiss the bishop's hand, is as gray as he is.

The stargazer wears a tight tunic in decadent late-Roman style, but a pair of leggings—*trousers*—favored by Hsiung-nu horsemen in the service of the Wei Cathayans among whom he has lived since the turn of the fifth Christian century. Over one shoulder Iatanbaal carries a long leathern bag, and on his left wrist he wears a thin strap bearing on it an oblong jewel, very like obsidian.

This jewel is featureless, but when the astronomer stands, it strikes the edge of Augustine's desk. Suddenly, a row of crimson characters ignites atop the black stone. However, the gleam dies quickly, and Augustine crosses his hands on his breast to stare at the enigmatic bracelet.

"Pardon me, Excellency," the astronomer says, and their eyes lock. "This device is a miniature time-gem."

The bishop realizes that he and his guest are the same height, with irises the same slaty Berber gray. In other circumstances—the besieging Vandals elsewhere, his own death a decade rather than days away—they might have been friends. Augustine lets his gaze fall again to the "time-gem."

Each time that Iatanbaal depresses a metal stem on the device, tiny crimson characters appear. At first they say *VII:XXXVIII*. A moment later: *VII:XXXIX*. The astronomer explains that these numerals signify the hour and the minute, and that the horological artisans of Lo-yang made him a device with Roman digits—a feeble thrust at his homesickness. He reveals that the time-gem takes its power from a coinlike disc, or *energon*, within the jewel.

"Seven-forty," says the bishop when new numerals—*VII:XL*—wink into view. "By what criteria do you establish the hour?"

"In Northern Wei, Father Augustine, scientifically. But while traveling, by sun and simple intuition."

Augustine tacks about. "Why have you come, Master Iatanbaal?" His guest, he knows, wants to give him the time-gem, and he has no wish to accept it, either as token of esteem or as bribe. Death's specter has carried him beyond flattery, beyond manipulation.

"Because in your *Confessions*—a copy of which the former bishop of Alexandria let me see—I found you have an unusual philosophy of time, rivaling in sophistication the theories of our most learned Cathayan astronomers."

Iatanbaal refastens his time-gem's strap. "It leads me to suspect that you alone of all Romanized westerners may be able to comprehend the startling cosmogony of the Wei genius Sung Hsi-chien. Comprehend and so appreciate."

"I wrote my *Confessions* a long time ago." Augustine eyes the astronomer warily. What he had penned about time in that book was that before God made heaven and earth, neither they nor time itself had any existence. Time did not begin until God spoke the word that inaugurated creation. Before time, there was no time, and what God did then (the conjecture that He was readying Hell for pryers into mysteries being a jesting canard), no mortal mind may reckon. Is that so amazing a theory of time? Is it powerful enough to call a Carthaginian astronomer home from Cathay to praise him? Augustine can scarcely credit such a motive.

"But, Excellency, you repeat and extend your discussion of time in the eleventh and twelfth books of *The City of God*. I read that masterpiece in Alexandria, too, but this time during a brief stop on my trip home from the Orient. In the eleventh book, you write—I've memorized the words—'*the world was made, not in time, but simultaneously with time*,' while in the twelfth you argue against those who hold that history is cyclic and that this world is born but to die and rise again. Sung Hsi-chien has discovered empirical proof of your positions in his astronomical observations, and this, I think, is a brave coincidence of minds."

"Empirical proof?" Augustine's fever has made him woozy. He sits down at his desk. "Master Iatanbaal, what need of empirical proof has a faith predicated on reason?"

"Why, none, I suppose, but Sung Hsi-chien and five generations of Cathayan lens-grinders, astronomers, cosmogonists, and sky-ray readers have still provided it. Since I was lucky enough to help Sung with his researches, I can outline these proofs for you."

"I don't require them."

"No, of course you don't. But you of all philosophers should wish to learn Sung's 'New Cosmogony.' "

"Ague grips me. I'm dying, Master Iatanbaal."

"Here, eat."

The astronomer pushes Possidius's tray toward the bishop, then hefts his long bag onto the opposite end of the desk. From it he pulls a tube of ivory and silver; an ebony box with a small glass port on its upper face; and two enameled packets, which Augustine decides are accessories to the ebony box. How he knows this, he cannot guess. But, sipping thoughtfully at his chickpea marinade, he waits for Master Iatanbaal to explain.

"A telescope," the astronomer obliges, pointing to the tube. "Outside Lung-hsi, in a tower on the Great Wall, the Wei Cathayans have a telescope so much larger than this one, Father Augustine, that it dwarfs the pillars of the Parthenon. An instrument even bigger dominates a hill near Lo-yang, while the grandest device of all stares skyward from a dome outside Ching-chao. Such far-seers, manned by imperial astronomers and scientists, have altered most of our old notions of the heavens."

Augustine dunks his bread in the piquant marinade. Telescopes larger than temple pillars? he thinks, working his bad teeth. This importunate scoundrel is lying.

"The Wei have also invented a type of colossal telescope that gathers and focuses invisible sky-rays from distant stars. The best is beyond Ku-shih, in the Takla Makan Desert, and Sung and his helpers visit it several times a year in a pterodrac—a mechanical flying dragon—commissioned by the Emperor. I myself have flown in this pterodrac, Father Augustine."

A madman, the bishop thinks. Colossal telescopes and draconoid flying machines. Fantasies that he presents as Holy Writ . . .

Iatanbaal lays the telescope aside and seizes on his ebony box, shifting it so that its tiny eye points directly at Augustine. "A luminotype chamber," he says, fingering a lever on its side. "With this, one can save the image of any object or person as it exists at the instant the operator depresses this lever. The Cathayans call such images—"the word worse than Greek to Augustine—"but I say *luminopicts*, 'light pictures,' and in Northern Wei scarcely a household is without a wall of such images in the family shrine."

"Why do you regale me with lies?"

Iatanbaal, heretofore the mildest of guests, bristles at this, but remains civil. "Lies? No lies, Excellency. The opposite. Your entire life has been a quest for truth, your whole career as a bishop a battle for truth against pagans and heretics. My prime motive in coming here—in traveling such distance; in risking my life to defy the Vandal blockade—was to bring you the cosmogonic truths that I learned in Cathay. To instruct you in them so that you may append them—before you die—to *The City of God*, the most glorious philosophy of history ever conceived."

"*Magnum opus et arduum*," Augustine murmurs. But aloud he says, "That book is finished. I can add nothing to it."

"I speak of *The City of God* in your mind, Excellency, not of dry words on paper. This grander *City of God*, the Platonic one you revise with every breath . . . unless I misjudge you terribly, *that* book will never be finished until your soul departs your body."

This approach nearly disarms Augustine. But he concludes that Iatanbaal is patronizing him and says, "I fear my soul is soon to do that. Please, sir, precede it in departing. I tire."

"By Christ, old man, I've not come all these years and all this distance to have you spurn my message!"

"Away, astronomer."

"God does not will it!"

"*Possidius!*" Augustine cries. "*Possidius, this man is—*"

"You don't believe me? Here, look!" Iatanbaal opens one of the packets beside his luminotype chamber. He thrusts at Augustine a smooth square of parchment: an image of five robed Cathayans.

These men are rendered monochromatically, in palpable light and shadow, their faces sharp but alien, the image of their robes as silken as the imaged garments. Augustine slides his thumb across the surface of this provocative square.

"A luminopict," Iatanbaal says. "The older man, at center, is Sung Hsi-chien. The rest are students—gifted disciples."

"A clever painting under an equally clever glaze."

"This isn't a hand-drawn artifact!" Iatanbaal says. "This is a luminopictic image from life, caught on a light-sensitive substance by the rapid opening and closing of this mechanical eye!"

"Do you destroy the box to remove the image? And must you make a second box to catch a second image?"

Possidius enters the bedchamber. Augustine wordlessly signals his fatigue to his fellow bishop, and Possidius, a wraith in black, approaches the astronomer.

"It's time for you to go."

The violence with which Iatanbaal shrugs aside Possidius's hand alarms Augustine. "Even the prodigal son received a warmer welcome than the one you hypocrites have tendered me!" Tears of resentment and frustration squeeze glistening from his lower lids.

"The basilica of Hippo Regius has a hostel for visitors," says Possidius. "Many now staying in it are refugees, but you, too, may shelter there. So why defame our hospitality?"

"Your flea-ridden hostel be damned!"

"Sir," says Possidius. "Sir, you try our—"

"I have no intention of deserting Father Augustine—not until death itself abstracts him from history!"

The old bishop, stunned by the astronomer's presumption, pounds his fist on the desk. "What gives you the right to impose yourself on a dying man in this unconscionable way?"

"One thing only: I'm your son, old man. I'm your son."

The fever in Augustine makes his head feel like the inflating hood of a cobra. He can think of nothing to say.

"Once, Father, you wrote of me, praising my virtues but taking no credit for them: 'I had no part in that boy, but the sin.' More recently, supposing me dead and quoting Cicero, you declared, 'You are the only man of all men whom I would wish to surpass me in all things.' A most poignant declaration."

"But you *are* dead," the bishop manages, woozier than ever with both brain heat and the fever of incomprehension.

"Iatanbaal means 'given of God,' Father. Adeodatus does, too, and my name—my true name—is Adeodatus."

iii.

Augustine remembers Carthage. There he acquired a concubine, a woman not of his class. The happiest issue of that union was the boy whom they named Adeodatus, 'given of God.' In those days—Christ be merciful—Augustine was a Manichee, a dualist proclaiming his belief in two contending gods, one benevolent and caring, one so malign and cruel that you could fix on it every sort of calamity plaguing the world. That was sixty years ago. Recently, a letter from Paulinus, bishop of Nola, has accused Augustine (facetiously, of course) of championing dualism again:

"What is *The City of God* but a manifesto dividing Creation into two camps? It seems, Aurelius Augustinius, you'll never completely elude the ghosts of your wayward past."

One such ghost has just popped up. Adeodatus—the boy he thought had died with the noble Nebridius in the undertow off the beach at Ostia—has reentered his life. He has done so only days before a mortal fever will—how did "Iatanbaal" put it?—oh, yes, *abstract him from history*. A reunion that renders mundane even the Gospel parable of the prodigal son.

How did Adeodatus survive those currents? And did Nebridius, Augustine's dearest companion after Alypius, also survive?

A single oil-burning lamp hisses in the bedchamber. Possidius has retreated to his own room. Genseric's soldiers shout obscene challenges along the inland walls of the city: shouts that clash, echo, fade, resurge.

Augustine's son—a "boy" of sixty—sits cross-legged on the floor, recounting in a monotone the story of his and Nebridius's adventure off the Italian coast. Adeodatus had been sixteen and his father's friend thirty-five.

"Nebridius, Father, had no adventure. I'm certain he drowned. I, though, was whipped out to sea. Prayer kept me afloat. Libyan pirates picked me up west of Naples. For the next nine years I was a helpless witness to their raids around the coastal towns of the Mediterranean. Finally, unwisely trusted to carry out a theft on my own, I escaped into the arms of some Greek mariners. These kind Greeks transported me to Alexandria. . . ."

Heavy-lidded and hot, Augustine listens to Adeodatus with half his attention. The details of his story are not important; vitally important, however, is the fact that after venturing to Cathay from Alexandria and living there an adult lifetime, his son has returned to Numidia. To keep filial vigil at his deathbed and to bring him . . . well, the Truth.

The old man feels his son's dry lips kissing his forehead; his own papery eyelids flutter open.

"Sleep, Father. In the morning you'll easily comprehend all the miraculous things I intend to tell you."

"Adeodatus—"

"Sleep. I've come home to stay."

Augustine remembers Carthage. He dreams of it. There he met his son's low-born mother. There he deceived the blessed Monica, his own mother, by boarding a ship to Italy while she supposed him awaiting a fairer wind. City of rowdy "scholars," pagan shrines, vain theatrics, and vulgar circus shows. In his dream—his fevered memory—Carthage rises again, raucous with trade and pageantry. He sees it as it was then, four decades before the globes of Seneca the Illuminator set its streets and windows ablaze even at deepest midnight. His memory, carried into dream, quickens every emotion—the four great perturbations of the mind—that he experienced as a self-conscious youth in Carthage.

Desire, joy, fear, and sorrow.

I knew them all there, the dreaming Augustine reflects. I know them all again every time I reenvision the city.

God, too, he discovers and rediscovers in memory and dream, as he inwardly quests for the One Thing to fill the emptiness created by his own temporary amnesia. That One Thing is God. If he ever forgets God, he finds Him again in memory, a fact that seems to the bishop a rational proof of His existence. For you cannot remember what you have wholly forgotten. God, however, resides within; and when you trip over That Which refurnishes the emptiness, you say to yourself, "This is it," and you know that the processes of your own mind have led you ineluctably back to Him.

As memory can resurrect the Carthage of old, Augustine dreamily reasons, so can it reacquaint us with our changeless Father. . . .

Adeodatus has made a pallet for himself in the bedchamber. He is using his doubled-up telescope bag for a pillow.

The cries of the barbarian heretics beyond Hippo's walls—Arian Christians who deny that Father and Son share the same substance—buzz in Augustine's head like evil flies. When he moans, his own son touches a wet cloth to his brow.

And another thing, Augustine thinks: As my memory holds every unforgotten moment of my life, God contains every possible reality, but without possessing either a past or a future. Everything that has ever happened, is happening now, or will happen tomorrow abides in Him. He foreknew—*knows*, rather—that Adeodatus would return as I lay on death's threshold, and He has ever known what he will tell me tomorrow about Sung Hsi-chien's "New Cosmogony."

Dear God, you are indeed an unpredictable dramaturge.

iv.

Morning. Augustine's fever has broken. He offers a prayer of thanksgiving and another for deliverance. Then he and Adeodatus eat the pears that Possidius brought to him last night.

JOHN COLLIER

Not long before I left, however, the dispute seemed to be resolving itself in Hong-yi Chiu's favor. Two of his pupils at the Lo-yang Academy of Sky Studies found some quasistrons surrounded by a faint, glowing pilosity. A luminous hairiness. It had the precise look of very distant lactastrons, and chromoscopic surveys of the light from this pilosity show it to exhibit the same sanguineous conversion—reddening—as the almost-stars embedded in it. This seems to prove that Chiu's quasistrons are truly billions of annilumes away and that Sung is right in crediting the origin of the universe to a primordial eruption."

"Enough of this," Augustine murmurs, clutching his head in his gnarled hands. "Please, Adeodatus, no more today."

"Forgive me, Father. I've spoken in such detail only because I wanted you to see that your theory of time coincides with Sung's. So does your belief in the linearity of history. You reject the Greek notion of cycles; so do Sung and his disciples, who believe the universe will die of cold, a plethora of icy, black lactastrons wobbling out into the darkness forever."

"That *isn't* what I believe!" Augustine rages. "We'll have our end not in ice, but in judgment and transformation!"

"You speak of the soul, Father, but I of the palpable world all about us. And Sung has found too little attractive force among the lactastrons to halt the universal expansion and to draw all matter back into a lump that may again erupt, to begin this cosmic vanity anew. *His* position coincides with *yours*—a 'No!' to the periodic rebirth of worlds. In that, you're kindred thinkers."

"We're brothers only in our shared humanity!" Augustine says. "What religion does he have?"

Adeodatus thinks. "I'm not sure. His work, perhaps."

"I've listened to you for as long as I can, Master Iatanbaal. Harangue me no more. Have mercy upon me and go."

The astronomer—his son—reluctantly obeys, and Augustine notes with wary surprise that darkness has fallen and that he himself is chill-ridden as well as feverish. Genseric's soldiers rattle their weaponry outside the city gates, and both the Roman Empire and the bishop's careworn body seem destined for the charnel heap. . . .

v.

An uproar in the corridor. Possidius is arguing with somebody who speaks Latin with a peculiar accent. Augustine, his intellect a scatter of crimson coals, sits up to see a tall black man pushing into his bedchamber past the flustered Possidius. The black man wears only a soiled tunic and sandals. Over his shoulder, a large woven bag as filthy as his tunic.

"You can't do this! The bishop is gravely ill!"

"I had a dream," the black man keeps saying, dancing with the frantio Possidius. "My dream told me to come to Augustine."

Augustine gathers the coals of his mind into a single glowing pile and looks at the Ethiop. This business of the dream touches him: He has never been able to dismiss the requests of those who have dreamed that he could help them. Indeed, Monica, his mother, envisioned his own salvation in a dream.

"Let him stay, Possidius."

The black man bows his head respectfully and says, "My name, Excellency, is Khoinata. Thank you."

"Where's my son?" Augustine asks Possidius.

"In the hostel, Excellency. He has assured me that he won't intrude on you again without your direct summons."

"A policy that I urge you, too, to adopt, Possidius."

As soon as Possidius, visibly wounded, has left, Augustine asks the Ethiop what distance he has traveled and why he thinks that the bishop of Hippo can help him. Like Adeodatus, Khoinata has sneaked through Vandal lines to enter the city, and he has come all the way from farthest Kush, a great African kingdom, for the privilege of this interview. He believes that what he has brought with him will prove to the imperious Romans that the Kushites are a people with an admirable history and a civilization deserving of the prose of a Tacitus or a Suetonius.

"What do you have?" Augustine asks him.

Instantly, Khoinata gets down on all fours, opens his bag, and begins assembling with impressive dexterity and speed the skeleton of a creature that seems to Augustine's untutored eye a troubling conflation of human being and ape.

"My brothers and I found these bones far south of Meroe. They belong to an early kind of man, a kind almost certainly ancestral to you and me. Notice: the curve of these foot bones—the way they fit with these other bones from the lower legs—*that* shows that the creature walked erect. And the skull—look here, Excellency—its skull is larger than those of apes and yet not quite so large as an adult Roman's. One of our wisest chieftains, Khoboshama, shaped a theory to explain such strangeness. He calls it the 'Unfolding of Animal Types,' and I believe it should greatly interest teachers of natural history from Carthage to Milan."

Augustine merely stares at Khoinata.

Khoinata says, "We know these bones are old—very, very old—because Khoboshama counted the rock layers in the declivity where we found them. In addition, he . . . "

Augustine spreads out the coals of his mind. He cannot keep them burning under Khoinata's discourse. He both sees and does not see the skeleton that his guest has arranged—as if from dry, brown coals—on the floor of his bedchamber. The creature has been dead for almost two million years—yes, that's the figure that the man cites—but it lives in Khoinata's imagination, and Augustine has no idea how to drive it from thence.

"Excellency, are you listening?"

"No," the bishop replies.

"But, Excellency, only you of all Romanized westerners are wise enough to grasp the far-ranging implications of . . . "

The old man feels a foreign excrescence on his arm. He glances down and finds that Adeodatus has strapped his Cathayan time-gem to his wrist.

Heedless of Khoinata, he depresses the stem on the side of its obsidian jewel, and these characters manifest on the black face of the tiny engine: *XII:I.*

The hour is one minute past midnight.

Something old is ending. Something new is beginning.

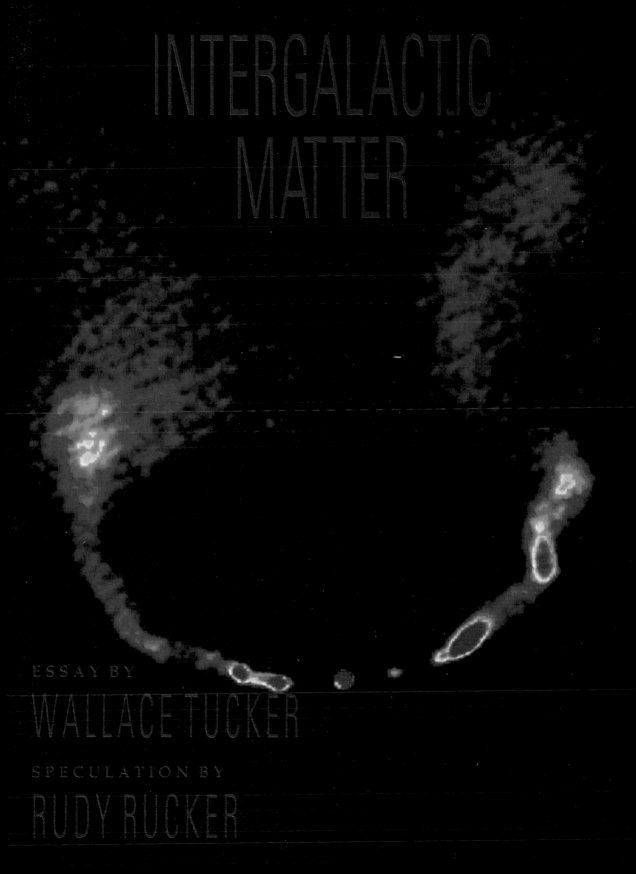

INTERGALACTIC
MATTER

ESSAY BY
WALLACE TUCKER

SPECULATION BY
RUDY RUCKER

THE INTERGALACTIC MEDIUM

WALLACE TUCKER

Harvard-Smithsonian Center for Astrophysics
University of California at Irvine

The eternal silence of these infinite spaces terrifies me.
—BLAISE PASCAL
Pensées

THOUGH PASCAL WROTE OF THE TERROR OF THE VOID when modern astronomy was in its infancy, his words still have power today. When we contemplate the immensity of the universe and the emptiness of intergalactic spaces, it is difficult not to feel an existential chill.

Thinking about the largest scales of the universe, it is as if we have been set adrift on a cold night on a vast sea. We don't know where we are, why, or what to do about it. We are frightened. To pass the time, and calm our fears, we begin to look for patterns in the stars. This is basically the way that astronomers confront the intergalactic spaces on a daily basis. They observe them carefully with telescopes and reduce these alien spaces to something familiar, something they can deal with: numbers.

In the past twenty years astronomers have, through their observations, accumulated some very interesting numbers on intergalactic spaces. These numbers do not necessarily eliminate the Pascalian terror, but they help. They give us some idea as to what is in intergalactic space and what has been happening there over the last 15 or 20 billion years. We already know that the intergalactic spaces are not empty and that they have not been eternally silent. Astronomers still do not know why there is so much intergalactic space, but they are confident that a careful study of its pattern and content will reveal much about the large-scale properties of the universe. At the very least, the terror need no longer be a terror of the unknown.

226

A SURVEY

Most of the universe is intergalactic space. The luminous collections of stars and gas that we call galaxies occupy less than one one-hundredth of 1 percent of the space in which they are located. As you have read in an earlier chapter, it may be that all galaxies are embedded in large envelopes of dark matter. The extent of these envelopes is unknown, but even with the most generous estimates of their size, they would still take up only 10 percent of intergalactic space.

There are three basic types of intergalactic space: the space between galaxies, the space between clusters of galaxies, and the space between superclusters. The differences among these types are related to the overall pattern of the distribution of galaxies. While the exact pattern is still far from clear, some details of the pattern within a few hundred million light-years of our Milky Way Galaxy are becoming apparent.

As Hyron Spinrad discussed in an earlier chapter, our Galaxy is part of a small group of about two dozen galaxies called the Local Group. These galaxies are held together in a dynamic balance between their mutual gravity and their orbital motions about their center of gravity. Most of the galaxies in the universe are members of a group or cluster of galaxies. These groups or clusters range from galaxy-poor groups such as the Local Group to rich clusters of thousands of galaxies. The space between galaxies in a group or cluster of galaxies is the first type of intergalactic space.

The Local Group is one of about fifty groups and clusters of galaxies that are part of the Local Supercluster of galaxies. The Local Supercluster has the form of a flattened disk that is about 100 million light-years in diameter. At least nine similar superclusters have been identified. The space between the groups and clusters of galaxies in a supercluster is the second type of intergalactic space.

Superclusters do not appear to be randomly spread through space. Instead they seem to be concentrated in thin shells around immense voids in space. The universe appears to be like a bubble bath. It is filled with a froth of galaxies and voids. The galaxies are spread around the edges of the voids, like the soap in soap bubbles. The voids, which contain very few galaxies, are the third type of intergalactic space.

THE SPACE BETWEEN GALAXIES

Intergalactic space of the first kind is the best understood. Observations with radio- and X-ray telescopes have established that the space between galaxies in many groups and clusters of galaxies is filled with high-energy particles and hot gas.

In the 1930's and early 1940's, American radio engineers Karl Jansky and

Grote Reber demonstrated with relatively crude receivers that the center of
our Galaxy was a strong source of radio waves. After the Second World War,
radiophysicists and engineers, especially the British and the Australians, became
radio astronomers and quickly transformed the field into a major new area of
research. Radio waves were detected from the remnants of exploded stars and
from violently active galaxies, as surveys of the sky by radio astronomers revealed scores of strong sources.

Subsequent observations showed that these radio waves were produced by
electrons moving in magnetic fields at speeds very near the speed of light. The
sources of the radio waves were apparently the sites of vast stellar and galactic
explosions. The remnants of many of these explosions can be traced with radiotelescopes into intergalactic space, far beyond the visible limits of the galaxies.
In several instances, the bubble of high-energy electrons has actually been traced
over a million light-years beyond the galaxy.

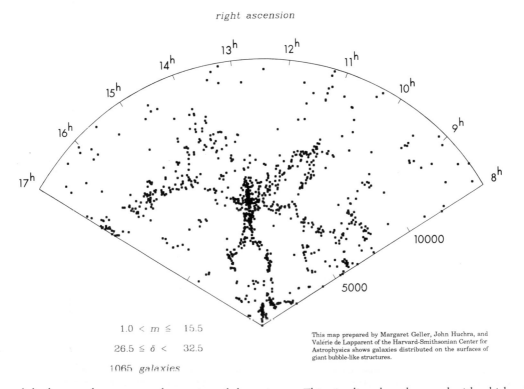

right ascension

$1.0 < m \leq 15.5$

$26.5 \leq \delta < 32.5$

1065 galaxies

This map prepared by Margaret Geller, John Huchra, and
Valérie de Lapparent of the Harvard-Smithsonian Center for
Astrophysics shows galaxies distributed on the surfaces of
giant bubble-like structures.

A map of the large-scale structure of a portion of the universe. This pie-slice plots the speed with which galaxies
are moving away from us (as distance away from the apex) against one coordinate of position in the sky (right
ascension) for a narrow range of the other position coordinate (declination). Since the speed of a galaxy's motion
is directly related to its distance, this pie-slice represents a wedge of the universe and shows the filamentary structure,
surrounding large empty regions, which is intriguing cosmologists. (Courtesy V. Lapparent, M. Geller, and J.
Huchra, Harvard Smithsonian Center for Astrophysics.)

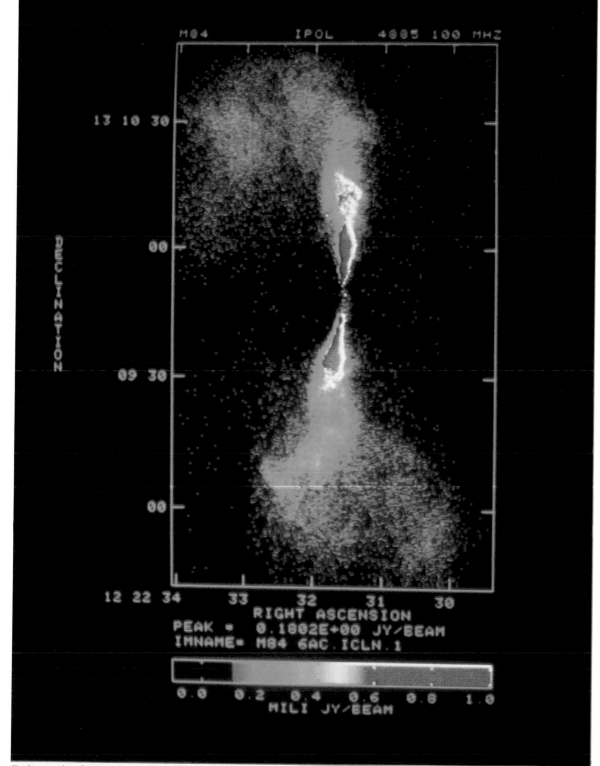

Radiograph of M84 (NGC 4374), a visible galaxy which contains the radio structure shown on this false-color image. The double jet, characteristic of radio galaxies, is clearly visible. Observers: R. A. Laing & A. H. Bridle; courtesy of NRAO/AUI.

A careful study of these bubbles provides clues to their origins. In almost all cases, the bubbles are symmetrically placed on either side of a galaxy, and are joined to that galaxy by thin jets of high-energy electrons. There seems little doubt that the central region of the parent galaxy contains an awesome power generator. The energetic output equivalent to billions of Suns has somehow been transformed into jets of high-energy particles that blast through the galaxy into intergalactic space for millions of light-years. As you saw in earlier chapters, the currently most popular model for these galactic power plants involves the breakup of stars near a rotating supermassive black hole in the center of the galaxy.

While detailed radio maps of the central regions of galaxies have provided strong supporting evidence for the black-hole model for the origin of the radio jets, wide-angle radio panoramas have given us important clues as to the ultimate fate of the jets and the intergalactic medium in which they move. The jets typically end in graceful billowy clouds.

Their appearance is similar to that of the billowy clouds at the end of a jet of steam from a whistling teakettle. This similarity is more than superficial. The billowing breakup of the steam jet and the radio jet are caused by the same phenomenon: the interaction of the jet with the surrounding gas. In the case of the teakettle, it is the air in the kitchen. In the case of the radio jet, it is the gas in intergalactic space.

As a jet bores into the intergalactic gas, it uses energy to push the gas aside and it slows down. Eventually, the jet slows to the point where it can no longer maintain a coherent shape and is disrupted into a cloud. The exact shape of a jet and the clouds it produces depends on the original intensity of the jet, the motion of the parent galaxy, and the conditions in the intergalactic gas.

The density of intergalactic gas is highest in the rich clusters of galaxies. There, the interactions between the clouds of high-energy particles are especially striking and beautiful. The galaxies in a rich cluster are orbiting the center of gravity of the cluster at speeds up to 10 million kilometers per hour. This produces a ram pressure, analogous to the "wind" that blows our hair back or our hats off when we move down the road in a convertible with the top down.

The ram pressure experienced by a radio galaxy moving through the intergalactic gas in a cluster of galaxies sweeps the radio jets backward. Astronomers have found swept-back radio jets and clouds that extend for millions of light-years through intergalactic space.

We do not have to be radio astronomers to appreciate these magnificent structures, any more than we have to be geologists to be awed by the Grand Canyon. They speak of a cosmic grandeur, of powerful forces at work over vast stretches of space and time. Our feelings are ambivalent: a sense of almost inexpressible beauty, a sense of pride that we understand in some small way the cosmic forces that produced these objects, a sense of insignificance, and perhaps the slightest sense of terror.

X-RAY ASTRONOMY

In the radio observations, the presence of intergalactic gas is revealed indirectly through its influence on the shape of the radio jets and clouds. But with X-ray telescopes, it is possible to observe the intergalactic gas directly.

X-ray astronomy is a child of the space age. The atmosphere that envelops the Earth forms a protective blanket which absorbs the X-rays that bombard our planet from outer space. This blanket has allowed higher forms of life—such as astronomers and science-fiction fans—to evolve, but it makes it impossible to observe cosmic X-rays from the surface of the Earth. X-ray astronomers must use rockets to carry their detectors a hundred miles or more upward, where the atmosphere is very thin. Captured German V-2 rockets were used in the late 1940's to detect X-rays from the Sun, but not until the 1960's was the technology of rockets and X-ray detectors sufficiently developed to detect X-rays from beyond the solar system.

The X-ray sources we are familiar with on Earth, those in dentists' and doctors' offices, are generated by beams of high-energy particles that interact with a metal plate and give off their energy in X-rays. X-ray sources in the Sun, the Galaxy, and beyond are also produced by high-energy particles. In contrast to the situation in the dentist's or doctor's office, the high-energy particles in a cosmic X-ray machine are part of an extremely hot gas. In order for a gas to give off an appreciable amount of X-radiation, it must have a temperature of millions of degrees or more.

X-ray astronomy thus provides us with a means to study the hot spots of the universe, where temperatures have soared past the million-degree mark. This capability has given us access to regions of the universe that would be difficult if not impossible to study by traditional means. We can examine the surfaces of neutron stars, peer close to the event horizon of black holes, probe the inner workings of the power sources in the centers of galaxies, and study the hot gas in the intergalactic space in clusters of galaxies.

Intergalactic gas in clusters of galaxies was discovered in the early 1970's by X-ray detectors aboard a small satellite. Over the course of the years, the data from this and other larger and more sophisticated satellites established the basic properties of this intergalactic matter. It turns out to be such a common feature of clusters of galaxies that virtually every cluster of galaxies contains a large amount of hot gas. How hot? The temperatures range from 10 million to 100 million degrees. And the total amount of material in the intergalactic gas in a cluster is comparable to the mass of all the stars in all the galaxies in a cluster.

Where did all this gas come from? Is it left over from the formation of galaxies, or was it ejected from the galaxies after they formed? It seems likely that it is a mixture of both. On the one hand, when galaxies formed from clouds of gas, it seems unlikely that they would have used up all the available raw material. Some must have been left over. This leftover, or *primordial*, gas could then have been captured by the gravitational field of the cluster of galaxies and heated by the motions of the galaxies, or by explosions such as the ones that produced the giant radio jets and tails.

On the other hand, a study of the details of the spectrum of the X-radiation shows that the intergalactic hot gas consists mostly of hydrogen. However, it also contains traces of other elements, including iron. As far as is known, iron can be manufactured only inside heavy stars. When these stars explode, iron and other heavy elements are ejected into the space between the stars in the galaxy. This is thought to be the source of the traces of iron—about thirty iron atoms per million hydrogen atoms—found in the *interstellar* spaces in our Galaxy. But how did iron get into *intergalactic* space?

Conceivably, a violent episode of many stellar explosions when the galaxies were young could have ejected much of the interstellar gas into intergalactic space. Alternatively, the ram pressure generated by the motion of the galaxies through the primordial gas captured in the cluster could sweep the gas out of the galaxy like a wind blowing leaves from a tree. We have some good evidence that this process does happen. Some galaxies in clusters of galaxies contain very small amounts of interstellar gas. Apparently it has been blown out of the galaxies by the intergalactic ram pressure.

The observed concentration of iron in the *intergalactic* gas in clusters of galaxies is about ten iron atoms per million hydrogen atoms, or about a third of the concentration found in the interstellar gas in galaxies. These observations are consistent with the theory that the intergalactic gas is a mixture of primordial gas and gas that has been processed through the interior of stars and then ejected from galaxies. If we assume that roughly half of the intergalactic gas came from galaxies, then each galaxy must have contributed a lot of gas to the cluster—ten times more gas than our Galaxy presently contains. Since our Galaxy is fairly normal in this respect, where could all the processed intergalactic gas in clusters of galaxies have come from? You can see that the search for the origin of the intergalactic gas could provide an important clue to understanding the early history of galaxies.

One possibility is that a long time ago, when galaxies were first forming, they may have had a significantly greater amount of gas than they have now. Most of this gas may have been processed through early generations of massive stars, which then exploded as supernovae and ejected the gas into intergalactic space. If these ideas are right, then primeval galaxies must have been extraordinarily luminous.

One of the most exciting prospects for the new generation of telescopes is the possibility of observing such primeval galaxies. This is possible, as we have seen, because of the finite speed of light. Light from the Andromeda galaxy, 2 million light-years away, takes 2 million years to reach us. We see the Andromeda galaxy not as it is, but as it was 2 million years ago. In the same way, if we could see a galaxy 12 to 15 billion light-years distant, we could see it as it was 12 to 15 billion years ago. This is about the time when the explosive period should have occurred. As Hyron Spinrad discusses in his chapter, with existing telescopes, it is just becoming possible to see galaxies more than a few billion light-years away, but the Hubble Space Telescope and other planned large space observatories sensitive to X-ray and infrared radiation may succeed in observing the brilliant birth pangs of galaxies.

[Just as this book was going to press, Hyron Spinrad and his co-workers announced the discovery of what may be the first primeval galaxy we have seen. Called 3C 326.1, it lies about 12 billion light-years away and contains a much larger amount of hydrogen gas than our own Galaxy. Furthermore, the hydrogen gas seems to have been enriched with heavier elements and seems to be in turbulent motion—both of which could be the result of a large number of supernovae explosions that took place before the time at which we are seeing the galaxy.
                                                    —THE EDITOR]

DARK MATTER IN GALAXIES

The work on intergalactic gas has led astronomers to ask another question—one with even more fascinating implications. Why is there still intergalactic gas in the clusters of galaxies? Why has this gas not dispersed?

The intergalactic gas is a sensitive tracer of the mass of the cluster that contains it. The temperature of any gas is a measure of the average speed of the atomic particles in the gas. As the temperature of the gas increases, the atoms move faster. On a warm day (30° C) the average speed of the atoms in the air is about 2,000 kilometers per hour. On the surface of the sun (6,000° C) the average speed of the atoms climbs to about 5 million kilometers per hour. Atomic particles in a gas hot enough to produce the X-rays observed from the intergalactic gas in clusters of galaxies reach speeds in excess of 100 million kilometers per hour.

The speed of the atomic particles in the intergalactic gas in clusters of galaxies can be related to the gravity necessary to hold the gas in the cluster. If the particles are moving too rapidly, they will escape from the cluster. The maximum speed, or escape velocity, of a particle of intergalactic gas depends on the size and mass of the cluster of galaxies that contains the gas. Conversely, if both the temperature of the gas (that is, the velocities of the particles in the gas) and the size of the gas cloud are known, we can calculate the mass necessary to keep the intergalactic gas from escaping from the cluster.

The development of sensitive X-ray telescopes in the past few years has enabled X-ray astronomers to measure the temperature and extent of the cluster gas in a number of cases and to use this technique to measure the masses of several clusters of galaxies. The results indicate that there must be a lot more mass in the clusters than we can presently observe—90 percent of the mass of the cluster must be in some mysterious dark form. Otherwise, most of the hot gas should have escaped from the gravitational pull of its cluster already. Roughly 5 percent of the mass can be accounted for by stars in the galaxies in the cluster; the gas between the galaxies in the cluster adds another 5 percent. The remaining 90 percent must be in some unknown form that has so far escaped detection by radio-, infrared, optical, or X-ray telescopes.

The nature of this so-called dark matter is one of the most challenging problems in astrophysics today. Dark matter seems to be ubiquitous. As you saw in earlier chapters, evidence for it has been found around galaxies of every size and shape. Typically, the observations imply that about 90 percent of the matter in a galaxy is in the form of an envelope of dark matter around the galaxy, consistent with the findings for clusters of galaxies.

What is the answer to this problem? Is something wrong with our understanding of gravity? Is there some additional force that comes into play in galaxies and clusters of galaxies, a force that can hold the hot gas in the clusters of galaxies? Or are the intergalactic spaces full of dark matter? Although some astrophysicists have attempted to modify gravitational theory to explain the observations without dark matter, most of the efforts have been concentrated into finding ways that the dark matter could be hidden from view.

Astronomers have searched long and hard for this matter. They have used radio-, infrared, optical, ultraviolet, and X-ray telescopes to scan the outer regions of galaxies and the intergalactic spaces for enough cool gas, hot gas, or dust to account for the dark matter. They have found some of each, but not nearly enough.

Collapsed stars, such as white dwarfs, neutron stars, and black holes are certainly dark enough to qualify as dark matter. If all galaxies have had a violent youth of the type discussed above, it is plausible that large numbers of collapsed stars would have been produced early in a galaxy's history. However, the observed concentration of iron and other elements heavier than hydrogen in gas in galaxies and in the intergalactic gas in clusters indicates that at most 50 percent of all the matter in galaxies could be in the form of collapsed stars. Otherwise, the concentration of elements heavier than hydrogen would have become much greater than is observed.

Another possibility is that the dark matter is in the form of brown dwarf stars. These are stars that have masses less than a few percent of that of the Sun—so small that they hardly qualify as stars. The nuclear reactions that produce light from the Sun and other normal stars cannot occur because the low mass cannot produce a high enough temperature in the star's center. What energy they do produce comes from the slow, slow gravitational collapse of the star. If they are visible at all, it will be at infrared wavelengths.

So far, infrared searches have come up with only a handful of possible brown dwarfs in our immediate neighborhood, not nearly enough to account for the dark matter in our Galaxy. However, our present infrared detectors cannot eliminate the possibility that quadrillions of brown dwarfs might exist in extended envelopes around galaxies.

Considerations of the origin of the universe as we understand it suggest other possibilities for the nature of dark matter. According to the Big Bang model, the universe as we know it began expanding from a hot dense state about 15 billion to 20 billion years ago. In the first few minutes of this expansion the temperature was so hot it was possible to fuse deuterium (hydrogen with a proton and a neutron in the nucleus) throughout the universe. The amount of deuterium created depends very sensitively on the conditions during this early stage. If the density of matter was very high, fusion would have continued and all the deuterium would have been further processed into helium. Thus, by observing the amount of deuterium in the universe, it is possible to set limits on the density of normal (or, as physicists call it, *baryonic*) matter—the neutrons and protons that compose the nuclei of all the elements.

These observations—still quite uncertain—suggest that the concentration of deuterium is barely consistent with most of the dark matter we need to hold the hot gas in clusters being in the form of normal or baryonic matter. If more accurate future estimates indicate a higher concentration of deuterium, then the dark matter we need must be in some nonbaryonic form.

One such form is the neutrino. Neutrinos are subatomic particles that are produced in certain nuclear reactions which are thought to have been very common in the early universe. Astrophysicists have believed for some time that we are literally awash in a sea of neutrinos without being aware of it, since neutrinos interact very rarely with ordinary matter.

Until recently, however, all this did not seem to matter much, because neutrinos were thought to be particles with energy, but no mass, in the same way that *photons* (the packets or particles of which light consists) have energy but no mass. A great abundance of neutrinos would be of no practical conse quence, or so it seemed.

Then, in 1980, experiments in the United States and the Soviet Union suggested that neutrinos might actually have small masses. Even a very small mass could make a very large difference, because the number of neutrinos in the universe is thought to be a hundred million times greater than the number of baryons. The mass of the neutrino indicated by the experiments was uncertain, but it was possible that it was large enough to explain the amount of dark matter in the universe. A wave of excitement swept through the astrophysical community. Had the solution to the mystery of dark matter been found, not in some remote galaxy but in an earthbound laboratory?

Before the celebration could begin, problems arose. First, further experiments clouded the issue of whether neutrinos really have mass and, if so, how much. These clouds still exist: The mass of the neutrino has not been confirmed.

Secondly, it has proven difficult to understand how it is possible to form galaxies in a universe dominated by fast-moving neutrinos. Our best theories suggest that in such a situation, clumps much larger than clusters of galaxies would form first, then clumps the size of clusters of galaxies, and finally, clumps the size of galaxies would condense from the clusters. Yet a variety of observations indicates that the formation happened in the opposite order. There is evidence from both optical and X-ray observations that galaxies are at least as old as, if not older than, clusters and superclusters of galaxies.

Finally, the neutrino hypothesis implies that the fraction of dark matter around galaxies should be less than in clusters, and the amount in clusters should be less than the amount in superclusters. Optical and X-ray observations of hot gas in galaxies and clusters of galaxies disagree with this prediction, but the uncertainties in the observations are such that this conclusion is not airtight.

INTERGALACTIC SPACE BETWEEN CLUSTERS

What about the intergalactic space of the second kind, the space between groups and clusters of galaxies in superclusters? Does it contain amounts of dark matter over and above the amount found in galaxies and clusters of galaxies? The existence of hot intercluster gas has not been established in superclusters, so it is not possible to use X-ray methods to determine the masses of superclusters. The motions of galaxies in and around our Local Supercluster can be used to study the gravitational force and hence the mass of the Local Supercluster. What astronomers are trying to do is to determine how strongly the gravitational force of the Local Supercluster is pulling our Local Group of galaxies and other groups of galaxies toward the center of the Local Supercluster.

It is a difficult problem, complicated by the many motions of our planet. The Earth is orbiting the Sun, which is orbiting the center of our Galaxy, which is orbiting the center of mass of the Local Group, which is orbiting the center of mass of the Local Supercluster. Understandably, astrophysicists have disagreed, and still do, about how to sort out all these motions and to determine the exact motion of the Local Group of galaxies in the Local Supercluster. The most recent and accurate determination indicates that the Local Group is moving at about 1 million kilometers per hour toward the center of the Local Supercluster, which, in turn, is itself moving at about 1 million kilometers per hour toward another supercluster that lies in the direction of the constellation Hydra on the sky.

The motion of the Local Group of galaxies within the Local Supercluster can be used to make an estimate of its total mass. This mass appears to be consistent with the mass contained in the groups and clusters of galaxies in the supercluster. There is no evidence for an additional component of dark matter in the intergalactic space between the groups and clusters of galaxies in the supercluster. This is another point against the neutrino hypothesis.

The difficulties with the neutrino hypothesis have prompted astrophysicists to consider other exotic particles that could have been formed in the Big Bang.

Unlike the neutrino, these particles have never been observed. They are still hypothetical, but it is not difficult to find a theoretical-particle physicist who can give you good reasons why particles such as axions, photinos, or gravitinos should have been produced in abundance in the first millionth of a second or less of the Big Bang. (Physicist James Trefil explains why in his chapter of this book.) These hypothetical particles, like the neutrinos, would interact only very weakly with normal matter and would therefore be invisible. Unlike neutrinos, they are predicted to have been moving much more slowly than neutrinos by the time galaxies formed. For this reason, these particles are called *cold dark matter*. These particles, which are also called *cosmions* or *WIMPs* (weakly interacting massive particles), are well suited to help in the formation of galaxies. Because they are slowly moving, they should condense into relatively small, galaxy-sized clumps of matter, pulling the baryons in with them.

The cold-dark-matter hypothesis predicts that galaxies should form before clusters and superclusters of galaxies, and that the relative amount of dark matter in galaxies, clusters, and superclusters should be approximately constant. This is in accord with the observations, unlike the neutrino hypothesis. Two troublesome problems remain, however, both related to intergalactic space of the third kind, the space in the enormous voids between superclusters.

COSMIC VOIDS

The existence of voids was established only a few years ago, but it is becoming increasingly apparent that they are a common feature of the universe. If the surveys done so far are any indication, they occupy at least 90 percent of the space of the universe. The voids appear to be approximately spherical in shape and to have a diameter of about 100 million light-years. Galaxies, in groups and clusters, are strung out in thin sheets to form the walls of the voids. Especially rich clusters or superclusters of galaxies occur where the boundaries of several voids meet.

What is in the voids? How were they formed? Are they practically devoid of matter, as they appear, or do they each contain hundreds of thousands of faint galaxies or hot gas that never condensed to become galaxies? Or are they filled with dark matter?

The existence of voids poses a problem for the cold-dark-matter hypothesis. Cold dark matter, because it is cold, clumps efficiently to form galaxies of all sizes. That is the good news. The bad news is that it forms galaxies too efficiently. If the voids contain matter, that matter should have clumped into galaxies of the types we see on the edges of the voids. The voids should be full of galaxies, but they are not. At least not full of galaxies of the type we are familiar with.

One possible solution is that the voids are truly empty. No galaxies have formed because there is no matter there with which to make them. The problem is that no one can explain how a truly empty void could have formed. The key observation that stands in our way is the so-called *cosmic microwave background radiation,* a faint radio-wave "echo" that fills the universe and was discovered in the 1960's. Astronomers believe that this radiation was released about 100,000 to a million years after the Big Bang, when the universe had cooled enough for electrons and protons to combine and make hydrogen atoms. Therefore, observations of this radiation tell us what conditions were like in the expanding, cooling primeval gas from which the galaxies were born. The trouble is that the radiation is extremely uniform, which means that voids did not exist when the universe was 100,000 years old. If they are truly empty, gravity, explosions, or some other force would have had to have moved tremendous amounts of matter over tremendous distances in a relatively short time. The consensus seems to be that this could not have happened.

Another possible solution is that the voids are not empty. Suppose that the voids do contain both cold dark matter and baryonic matter, but for some reason the matter in the voids did not condense into normal galaxies. Perhaps the formation of the first generation of galaxies created such havoc with their explosive activity that the second generation of galaxies never formed, leaving voids full of dim or failed galaxies. In this way it might be possible to save the cold-dark-matter hypothesis from the problem of the voids.

Recent observations by Stephen Gregory and J. Moody of the University of New Mexico have provided intriguing evidence on the contents of intergalactic voids. Their detailed survey of a large void in the Constellation of Bootes revealed the existence of eight previously undetected galaxies. The radiation from these galaxies is peculiar: It has the characteristics of radiation from clouds of gas rather than stars. This peculiarity suggests that the galaxies might be very young and full of large amounts of gas that has yet to collapse into stars. This interpretation lends support to the idea that not all clumps of gas condensed into galaxies at the same time, that for one reason or another, some of them may be "late bloomers." However, since eight galaxies in a region the size of the Bootes void is still only a few percent of the mean galaxy density in the universe, Gregory and Moody's discovery does not change our present belief that the voids are relatively empty of galaxies.

Nor is there any evidence that the voids are full of gas that failed to make galaxies. Cool gas clouds in intergalactic space can block the radiation from distant galaxies in much the same way that clouds in our atmosphere can block the sunlight. This blocking, or absorption, is selective, in that certain types of radiation would be absorbed more readily than others by cool intergalactic clouds. A search for this selective absorption in the light from distant quasars has been fruitless. Although more work needs to be done, the negative results imply that the amount of cool gas in the voids is negligibly small.

It is possible that the voids could be filled with hot gas. If the gas was hotter than a few million degrees, it would not absorb the visible radiation from quasars. But if the gas contains a small concentration of heavy elements, as does the intergalactic gas in clusters of galaxies, then it might produce selective absorption effects in the X-ray spectrum of distant quasars. The Advanced X-ray Astrophysics Facility, planned for launch by the space shuttle in the 1990's, might be able to detect these effects and prove the existence of hot gas in the voids.

Some astrophysicists feel that proof of hot gas in the voids already exists. They point to longstanding and often confirmed X-ray observations which reveal the existence of a diffuse glow of X-rays, called the *X-ray background radiation*, which is uniform across the sky. The number of X-rays that are seen in each range of X-ray energies matches very closely the distribution expected from a gas at a temperature of several hundred million degrees. This close match is taken by a few astrophysicists as strong, if not convincing, evidence that intergalactic space, including the voids, is filled with hot gas.

However, there are serious problems with this interpretation. It is not known how the gas in the voids could have been heated to such high temperatures. It would have started out very hot in the Big Bang, but would have cooled well below this temperature in the first few hours of the expansion. Somehow, it would have had to have been reheated to several hundred million degrees. The explosive activity associated with radio galaxies and quasars (which Harding Smith discussed in his chapter) provides less than 1 percent of the necessary energy. Perhaps the explosive activity associated with the formation of galaxies could have provided the necessary energy, but this is considered unlikely.

Another problem is that individual sources such as quasars appear to be able to account for much, if not all, of the X-ray background radiation. In this view, the X-ray background radiation only *appears* to be a uniform glow because our X-ray instruments are still quite crude. In reality it is produced by millions of distant sources of X-rays, such as quasars. The apparent uniformity results from the great distances of the sources—very much like the glow of the lights from a distant city. This interpretation implies that as more and more sensitive X-ray surveys are made, the individual sources can be picked out from the uniform glow, just as the observation of a distant city with binoculars reveals many distinct lights. Deep surveys with the Einstein X-ray telescope have provided strong evidence in support of this view. They indicate that at least 30 percent and possibly most of the X-ray background can be accounted for by quasars and similar objects.

In summary, there is no strong evidence for many dim galaxies, or hot or cool gas in the vast intergalactic voids. Thus, their contents and the reason for their existence remain a mystery.

The motion of the superclusters that are on the boundaries of the voids presents another enigma. As mentioned earlier, the Local Supercluster is moving at a rate of 1 million kilometers per hour in the direction of a supercluster in the constellation of Hydra. This type of large-scale motion appears to be typical of several superclusters within a few hundred million light-years of our Galaxy. This motion is unexplained in the cold-dark-matter hypothesis. Even chain reactions of galactic explosions seem incapable of reproducing it. One speculation is that both motion and the large-scale structure of superclusters and voids are due to the strangest of all the hypothesized types of intergalactic matter— *cosmic strings.*

Cosmic strings, like cold dark matter, are a form of matter predicted by some theories to have been created in the fraction of a second of the Big Bang. From that time on, a dense network of cosmic strings should have expanded with the universe. These strings would be infinitesimally thin (.0000000000000000000000000000001 centimeter in diameter), astronomically long (millions of light-years), and massive enough to pull the baryonic or normal matter and nonbaryonic dark matter in the universe into the observed structure of superclusters and voids. While we have no direct evidence that such strings exist, their properties may be useful enough to solve the problems we have been discussing and astronomers have done calculations of how such strings might affect the subsequent evolution of structure in the universe.

Matter would be attracted to long strings to form long flat sheets of matter— the precursors of superclusters. The network of superclusters and voids would, in this model, be due to an underlying network of cosmic strings. The voids would not be empty, but would be pervaded by dark matter and normal matter that did not form into galaxies, perhaps because of the explosive activity of galaxies formed in the vicinity of cosmic strings. The movement of the superclusters in our vicinity could be a reflection of the motions of the underlying cosmic strings, or it could be due to the attraction of the superclusters to another collection of superclusters around an extraordinarily massive cosmic string.

Whether this bizarre picture of a network of cosmic strings, filled in with exotic particles and a sprinkling of normal matter, represents the actual universe is the subject of intense speculation and debate among astrophysicists. What is not debatable is that research on intergalactic spaces is at the very frontier of our exploration of the cosmos. It has already provided valuable insight into the nature of the processes that have brought forth galaxies and shaped our universe. We now know that the intergalactic spaces have by no means been eternally silent. And though they still may be more than a bit terrifying, there is some consolation in stealing a glimpse, through our telescopes and theories, of "that immortal sea which brought us thither."

THE MAN WHO WAS A COSMIC STRING

RUDY RUCKER

As an acute-care doctor in San Francisco, I have seen many strange things. Perhaps I've turned a bit strange myself. I work at a clinic twelve hours a week; I live alone; I wear my head shaved; I speak softly; I am a morphine addict; I am Jewish; I do not have AIDS. I am my own man, but I have turned strange and stranger since I met the man who was a cosmic string.

It happened two weeks ago, in late November. It had been a long, sun-drenched day over the chocked pastel city of my birth. I was idle at home, staring out the attic window. The phone rang; it was one of my patients from the clinic. Her husband was sick. Yes, she understood I was off duty, but could I come in a private capacity? If only as a friend. Her husband was taken very bad. She would give me a gold coin. Please come right away.

The woman's name was Bei-na Id. She was from Chaotiskan, a tiny island republic off the Thai-Burmese isthmus of Kra. I had treated Bei-na for numerous small complaints; she had health insurance. She was something of a hypochondriac. Her English was odd but comprehensible. Once she'd passed gas while talking to me. We'd ignored it, but it was something I usually thought of when I talked to her: popcorn fart. Of her husband I knew nothing. They lived in the Mission, a short bus-ride away.

I agreed to come.

It was growing dark when I got to the Id home, a tiny houselet on the back of a lot. It was a converted garage. TV light flickered from behind drawn curtains. I knocked and Bei-na came quickly to the door.

"Thank you for come, Doctor. My husband is sick two days."

"Yes."

Standing just inside the front door, holding the black lunch box that I use for a medical bag, I could see the entire house. Here was the living/dining room, with two tiny girls watching TV and a boy on the couch doing homework.

241

The children were long and pale, paler than Bei-na. Perhaps her husband was American. My imagination raced: a failed priest, a renegade vet, a retired smuggler? How big would the gold coin be?

Straight ahead was the kitchen and laundry room. A fourth child stood by the sink: a smooth, perfect teenaged girl, her skin like dirty ivory. The children all ignored me, letting social custom replace the walls their house lacked. The TV was turned down very low. I could hear the dishes clunking beneath the sink-water; I could hear the chugging motor of the fridge. There was another sound as well, an odd, sputtery hiss. I looked alertly at Bei-na, waiting for info. The less I say, the more my patients tell me.

Bei-na was a short woman with prominent cheekbones and the kind of pointed glasses that lower-middle-class white women used to wear. Like a cartoon coolie's, her head was a blunt yellow cone spreading out from her neck. She seemed worried but also somewhat elated, perhaps at having gotten a doctor to come to her home. The hissing was definitely coming from behind the bedroom door. I wondered if her husband was psychotic. I imagined him crouched behind the door, mad-eyed with a machete. But no, surely not: The children were acting calm and safe.

"He been sick like this before, Doctor. When I find him first time on beach, he sick like this very bad three day and three night. My father cure him, but that medicine is all gone."

"Well, let's have a look at him. What's his name?"

"We call him Filbert. You sure you ready to see? Let me get gold coin right now be fair."

"Yes."

Bei-na spoke to her children in sliding slangy phonemes. The boy on the couch got up, turned off the TV, and herded his small sisters to the kitchen. The girl at the sink gave me a sudden amused smile. Her gums were bright-red. I wondered how a girl like that would smell, wet red and dirty ivory, so unlike her tired yellow popcorn-fart mother, who now pressed into my hand the smallest disk that I have ever heard called a "coin." It was the size of one of those paper circles that a hole-puncher makes. I pocketed it, wondering if I would be able to get it home without losing it. Bei-na opened the bedroom door.

There is a drawing by M. C. Escher called "Rind." It shows a rind, or ribbon, that curls around and around in a roughly helical pattern. The rind is bumpy, and its bumps sketch the surface of a human head. The wrappy rind is a helix head with spaces in it. One can see clouds and sky through the spaces.

Filbert Id was designed along similar lines. Each part of his body was a tight-wrapped spindle of dirty white fiber, as if he were a Michelin Man mummy with swathing-cloths of narrow, narrow skin. There were no spaces between the successive loops of cosmic string. No spaces, that is, until I made my first error.

As I leaned over Filbert Id's dimly lit bed, my initial impression was that his skin was very wrinkled. His hissing grew louder the closer I got. The noise was fretful and intricate. Bei-na, seeming to extract sense from it, spoke softly to Filbert in her own tongue, but to no avail. He seemed terrified of me, and he held up his axially grooved arms as if to push me away. If I say that the grooves were *axial*, rather than annular or longitudinal, I mean that they went around and around his head, neck, fingers, arms, chest, etc., like latitude lines.

I leaned closer.

Although Filbert's face contained the appearance of lips, his mouth did not open. *Yet how loud he hissed!* I was medically curious about his means for producing the noise without opening his mouth. Could it be that he had a punctured lung? A cancer in the passages of his sinus? A missing tympanum and a hypertrophic Eustachian tube?

I felt a fine scientific impatience with Filbert's panic. I pushed his arms out of the way and leaned very close to his face. I was struck by three things. His face held a strong electric charge (a spark jumped between us); his face did not radiate warmth; he was not breathing. Indeed—I peered closer—his nostrils were but molded dents, entirely occluded by what seemed to be flaps of Filbert's dirty, fibrous skin. The man was suffocating!

I set my black metal box on the bedside table and took out swab, tongue depressor, and rubbing alcohol. Clearly my first task was to clean out Filbert's buccal and nasal cavities. Filbert's eyes, I have omitted to mention, were matte-black slits; I had thought they were closed. Yet as I opened my kit, laying out my syringe as well, Filbert moved his head as if he were looking things over. At the sight of the needle, he redoubled his hissings and his gesticulations. Fortunately he was in no condition to rise from his bed.

"Tell him to calm down," I ordered Bei-na.

She made some bell noises; he hissed the harder.

"He very scared you break him."

"He needs to breathe, doesn't he?"

"I don't know."

"I'll give him a sedative."

Sedative. Lovely calm word. I myself was ready for my evening injection of morphine—for some morphine and for some fine classical music. This Chaotiskani nonsense was taking entirely too long.

I filled a syringe with morphine solution and stood back like a matador awaiting the moment of truth. I kept one hand in front of my upright syringe, so as not to alarm the patient. He thrashed and hissed . . . to no avail. I came in over his left forearm and pushed my needle into his chest.

It was only last week that I happened on a popular article about cosmic strings. Till then I had no language for what happened after I stuck the needle in Filbert Id.

At a certain large scale, our universe is structured like a foam of soap bubbles. All ordinary matter is confined to the "soap films"; the galaxies are specks of color on mathematical sheets surrounding huge voids.

Why are the bubbles empty? Because each of these space voids has at its center a huge, tangled loop of cosmic string.

What is a cosmic string? A linelike space-time flaw analogous to the pointlike flaws called black holes.

How do the cosmic strings empty the bubbles? Each void's central string is a closed, superconducting loop. Vast energies surge along each loop, and the endless eddying stirs up waves that push us all away.

The strings are probably talking to each other, even if they don't know it. Even if they don't care.

One theory I have is that they're larvae, and that Filbert hatched when I poked him open. My image is this: Think of the stars as pollen on the surface of a quiet pond. There are eggs on the surface, too, and the eggs turn into larvae that are the cosmic strings. The larvae wiggle and jerk, and their waves push the star pollen back, forming it into a honeycomb of 2D cells.

Either Filbert fell from the sky, which I doubt, or the strings are working at a new level, our level, yours and mine.

When I stuck my needle in Filbert Id, the man who was a cosmic string, his tight pattern came unsprung. Radiation surged out of his hollow inside, knocking me back and blowing the ceiling off the Ids' bedroom.

I was briefly blinded. I am not sure what I really saw, in the shock and confusion and lack of words. *Loony Loop* is the phrase I caught first. Loony Loop is a puzzle where you try to untangle a loop of blue nylon string from a multiply looped pattern of chrome-steel wire. Filbert Id came unsprung and turned into an enormous Loony Loop. I saw him doing it, and it made me radiation-sick. The loop hissed and buzzed, and then it tumbled rapidly upward into the night sky.

Filbert Id hatched and flew away, leaving me with a loaded morphine syringe in my hand. With practiced speed, I injected the morphine intravenously. This was my second error.

How strong was the radiation? Bei-na died in my arms a half-hour later. Her children's hair fell out, but they are on the mend. We left the ruined house together that night. Bei-na's daughter Wu-wei has become my lover, which has eased the pain of these my last two weeks.

If this be my last will and testament, I bequeath all to dear Wu-wei, to her wet red, to her dirty ivory, to her brother Bo, and to her sisters Li and Le.

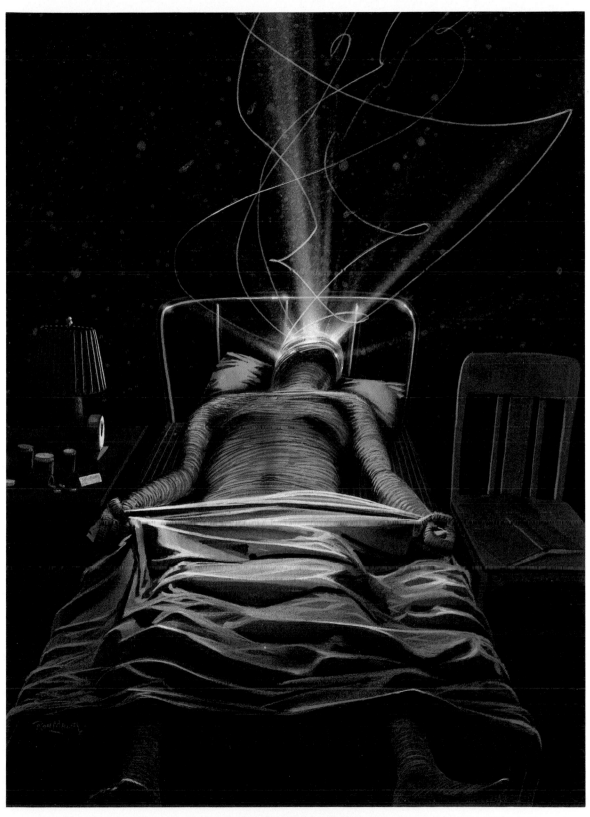

RON MILLER

Cosmic string, larvae, Loony Loop, Wu-wei. These are the words that a syn-chronistic Providence puts in my pen. My race is run beneath this sun.

With morphine, and only with morphine, the radiation sickness has been bearable. But radiation sickness is not the issue anymore. What is going to kill me—and quite soon—is something that I noticed this morning. My skin is grooved in axial rings, as skritchy as the surface of an Alva Edison cylindrical LP.

I shared a needle with Filbert two weeks ago, and what took him is ready to take me. I forbore the noon injection, but now it's dusk and I'm hissing.

It's time for the needle's last prick. I'll kiss Wu-wei goodbye and go outside to do it, to unspring and fall into the sky, a cosmic string.

COSMOLOGY

ESSAY BY

ALLAN SANDAGE

SPECULATION BY

POUL ANDERSON

COSMOLOGY: THE QUEST TO UNDERSTAND THE CREATION AND EXPANSION OF THE UNIVERSE

ALLAN SANDAGE

*The Johns Hopkins University
and
Space Telescope Science Institute*

A DECISIVE DISCOVERY

Nᴇᴡ ʏᴇᴀʀ'ꜱ ᴅᴀʏ 1925; ᴡᴀꜱʜɪɴɢᴛᴏɴ, ᴅ.ᴄ.: The thirty-third meeting of the American Astronomical Society had been in progress since December 30. In a late session on the last day a paper was read *in absentia*, submitted by a young astronomer from Pasadena in remote southern California. Working with the Mount Wilson 100-inch reflector, then the world's largest telescope, Edwin Hubble, age thirty-two, had discovered variable stars of a certain type—the *cepheids*—in a vast spiral-shaped cloud then called the Great Nebula in Andromeda (or M31). As Hyron Spinrad discusses in his chapter, these stars serve astronomers as standard beacons in the universe, enabling them to measure cosmic distances. The cepheids had appeared at much fainter brightness levels on Hubble's photographs of M31 than in the Magellanic Clouds, the satellites to the Milky Way. Thus, Hubble was able to prove beyond doubt that the Andromeda nebula was at a distance far beyond the limits of the Milky Way— it was a separate galaxy.

Edwin Hubble at the 48-inch Schmidt telescope at Palomar Observatory. (Photo courtesy of Palomar Observatory and the Niels Bohr Library, American Institute of Physics.)

Hubble's paper, published early in 1925, marked the closing of a long debate on the nature of the white nebulae. Since the time of the great astronomer William Herschel in the eighteenth century, observers had seen these objects in the sky in regions away from the band of the Milky Way, but there was no agreement about their distance. They could either be relatively close, and would then be part of the Milky Way system, or they could be remote independent systems—*island universes*, similar to the Milky Way but isolated. Clearly, this was a question of fundamental importance to understanding the large-scale structure of the universe.

The island universe hypothesis was an old idea, begun in speculation as early as the 1700's. Emanuel Swedenborg (1688–1772), Thomas Wright (1711–1786), Immanuel Kant (1724–1804), among others, had discussed the hypothesis. Theirs were the first ideas of a new *cosmology* (or theory of the universe) of a vast dimension, but the subject remained speculative for lack of new observational data.

The situation changed decisively in the final decade of the last century. Large telescopes began to be built, primarily in the western United States. Major observatories were founded at which the problem of the nebulae began to be studied, using the new powerful methods of observational astronomy. The Lick Observatory in California, Lowell Observatory in Arizona, Yeakes Observatory in Wisconsin, and Mount Wilson Observatory became the centers for this study.

Hubble's discovery of the M31 cepheid variables had not been made in a vacuum. The island universe hypothesis *had* begun to be heavily discussed again in the early years of this century on the basis of a variety of observations made with the new telescopes. A number of astronomers in the United States and Europe argued for the island universe hypothesis, but others were not convinced. Principal among the opposition was Harlow Shapley, who was the influential director of the Harvard Observatory in 1924 and who had been a former colleague of Hubble at Mount Wilson.

Hubble's observations proved to be conclusive, showing to both sides that the Andromeda nebula was distant. By inference it was clear that other nebulae similar to M31 were also very likely to be at remote distances. It is fair to say that with Hubble's demonstration, modern cosmology *as a science* began the accelerated development that has led to our present ideas of the creation of the universe itself.

COSMOLOGY

The tapestry of our modern theory of the origin and large-scale properties of the cosmos is breathtaking. Its scope is awesome. Based on astronomical observations, on experiments in particle physics, and on a theoretical understanding of the forces that govern phenomena on both the large scale (the realm of the galaxies) and on the small scale (the realm of the atom), it has a strong ring of truth. Besides, it has that exquisite beauty which is essential for truth. But further, the theory is to a large extent testable and, as we shall see, its central predictions have, rather surprisingly, already been verified.

All cultures have produced their own peculiar cosmology; ours is not unique in the attempt. Cosmology is the quest for a cogent world view, without which society seldom functions well. Examples of ancient cosmologies that shaped the societies that made them are the Taoism and Buddhism of the Chinese, the Egyptian view of life after death, the Greek universe governed by gods of nature, the Norse legends of Valhalla and its citizens, and the medieval reliance on astrology based on beliefs about the influence of the stars.

What is cosmology? Pushed to its speculative limit, the widest definition would be "a system of beliefs leading to an explanation of the mystery of existence." But this would put much of the practice beyond the scientific method, which insists on prediction and testability. A narrower and more useful dictionary definition is: "Cosmology is that branch of natural philosophy that deals with the character of the universe as a cosmos—that branch that deals with *processes* of nature and the relation of its parts." We shall later claim that, still keeping within the scientific method, we can broaden the definition slightly by recognizing the recent advances in high-energy particle physics and state that "Cosmology also deals with the ontology of things—that is, inquires into *being*—in this case, the existence or being of the cosmos and its contents." Clearly, this then becomes nothing less than an inquiry into the question of creation. It can say nothing about the *reason* for the event but rather provides a description of the consequent *processes* that began just after the instant of creation.

Early on, astronomy naturally provided the way to approach cosmology, both in ancient cultures and in our own. The objects of astronomical study are not of this world. We look out as we look up—an idea as old as the Chinese. As we look out, we begin to sample a wider world beyond our neighborhood. Each cosmology has been born from this realization.

COUNTING THE GALAXIES

Following Hubble's discovery, study of the galaxies took on a wholly new significance. One key question was: Are galaxies the structures with which to map the basic character of the universe, or are they only an intermediate component, leading to a larger hierarchy as we sample larger and larger parts of the universe? If galaxies are only an intermediate structure, then as we look to larger and larger distances, they should decrease in importance relative to the larger structures they compose. Hubble set out to test this idea.

In one of his least-known but most important observational programs, Hubble began to survey many (about a thousand) areas of the sky with the

Mount Wilson telescopes in the middle 1920's. The method was to count the number of galaxies at progressive levels of faintness. In general, the fainter a galaxy, the farther away it is. If galaxies are spread uniformly in space in all directions and at all distances, then the number of them seen at fainter intensity levels should increase in proportion to the volume surveyed. This would not be true if galaxies are merely a local phenomenon relative to a much larger organization.

Hubble announced the results of his survey over a seven-year period from 1931 to 1938 in a series of reports, supplemented by a major count survey performed by Nicholas Mayall at the Lick Observatory in 1934. The result was that the number of galaxies does, in fact, increase with increasing faintness in the way expected if they are distributed homogeneously in space at all distances. From this, Hubble concluded in 1930, 1934, and 1936 that galaxies can give us a fair sampling of the universe at large.

To be sure, it has subsequently been found that galaxies are organized into clusters and often lie on sheets resembling bubbles that encircle voids. Nevertheless, Hubble's discovery still stands when averages are taken over many of the bubbles, voids, and sheets—that is, over an appreciable fraction of the sky: The universe is homogeneous in the large.

THE EXPANDING UNIVERSE

It might have been thought that here at last was the solution to the cosmological problem. The basic building blocks of the universe had been found. They were distributed homogeneously on the largest scales that were measured. They show no sign of an edge to their distribution, to the limit of the largest telescopes.

True enough—but there was one other (crucial) discovery yet to be understood. Astronomers had found—in the second decade of the twentieth century—that the lines in the spectra of all but the nearest galaxies showed a *red shift*. As explained in earlier chapters, a shift of the colors in the spectrum toward the red means the galaxy is moving away from us. The systematic red shift of the galaxies is interpreted to mean that the universe is in general expansion. It surely is one of the capital discoveries in all of science.

The time was 1922. Einstein's theory of general relativity, describing the relationships between space, time, and gravity, had been published in 1916. Scientists generally assumed that space was "stable" or static—it did not move. Newton, two hundred years before, had nevertheless puzzled over how this could be. Because Newton's law of gravity requires that masses attract each other, all objects in a static universe would be expected to fall together to form a massive "central lump." In the solar system the reason this does not happen is understood. The planets move. The force of gravity inward is counterbalanced by the outward centrifugal force caused by their circular motion around the

Sun. Newton wondered if there might, in fact, be a large-scale motion of the universe outward to counter his inward force, but the wonder remained just that.

Then, in 1922, the Russian mathematician Alexander Friedmann found a solution to Einstein's complicated set of relativity equations that suggested a general expansion of space, carrying test particles with it as if they had radial velocities outward. When Friedmann published the solution to Einstein's equations that predicted the expanding universe, Einstein was not impressed and published a two-sentence rebuttal of Friedmann's paper the same year. He then published a further two-sentence paper in 1923 withdrawing his earlier one, admitting *his* mistake, and agreeing with Friedmann. It is the Friedmann equations that form the loom upon which the current discipline of theoretical cosmology is woven.

The next person to generalize the theory and take the expansion prediction seriously was a Belgian theologian, the Abbé Georges-Henri Lemaître, who believed that here was the *scientific prediction of the creation event*. Everyone now agrees, but his 1927 paper with its famous "coasting" solution for the motion of the universe was buried in a relatively obscure journal. It was found in 1930 by George McVittie, then a research student working with the great British astronomer Arthur Eddington, who thereafter wrote extensively on the expanding universe. The idea began to spread.

(Left) Vesto M. Slipher, who pioneered measuring the red shifts of galaxies; (right) Milton Humason, who worked with Hubble measuring galaxy red shifts and other characteristics. (Photos courtesy of AIP Niels Bohr Library.)

It is not clear how far any of the theoretical framework had penetrated into the Mount Wilson and the Lick observatories in 1927. These were the two largest observatories in the world at the time, and one would have thought that any observational test of such theories would have to be made at one of them. But this turned out not to be the case, at least at first.

At Percival Lowell's private observatory in Flagstaff, Arizona, Vesto Slipher, one of a pair of famous astronomer brothers, had begun in about 1915 to obtain spectra of spiral nebulae. In early 1921, *The New York Times* (January 19) reported Slipher's discovery of what was then considered an enormous red shift for a nebula known as NGC 584. Translating the shift into motion, the discovery indicated that the nebula was moving away at a velocity of about two thousand kilometers per second! Slipher had perfected his own design of an instrument for taking spectra of very faint objects, and took spectra for a total of about thirty galaxies between 1915 and 1924. He discovered that most had shifts of their spectral lines toward the red. Was this the expansion of space predicted by Friedmann and Lemaître?

Slipher never published his results on NGC 584 or others on his list. He did send the velocities to Gustav Strömberg at Mount Wilson and to Eddington in England. Strömberg made an analysis of them in a 1925 publication, concluding that here was a strange phenomenon indeed, because no other astronomical objects had such large apparent motions, most of which were outward.

In the mid-1920's the mathematician and theoretical physicist Harold Percy Robertson had become interested in the Friedmann expanding spaces. In a highly theoretical paper published in 1928 he combined Slipher's red shifts with brightness measures of the same galaxies published by Hubble in 1926. In a small paragraph in his nearly forgotten paper one reads words paraphrased as: *It appears that a relation between red shift and distance can be established from these data giving a rough verification of Friedmann's prediction.* Robertson, who soon became famous in cosmology for his proof of the mathematical equation for the geometry of a homogeneous space, recounts this incident in a single sentence in his 1963 article on cosmology in a new edition of the *Encyclopedia Britannica*. He told the story privately in 1960, but he made no other point of it and history seems to have passed him by in this central discovery.

Hubble had also been studying the galaxy data in the late 1920's, trying like many others to interpret them. Slipher's largest velocities were about two thousand kilometers per second. In 1925, Lundmark had published an analysis of the existing data where he fitted a mathematical series to the correlation of red shift and distance. Besides the linear term, which later was to become so famous, he added a square term in the distance. He found a negative coefficient for it, concluding that no red shifts should exist larger than about three thousand kilometers per second. If true, clearly this could not be the Friedmann phenomenon, which required larger and larger red shifts as you went to greater and greater distances.

Hubble knew of Lundmark's work. It was crucial to determine the reality of the squared term; what was needed were more red-shift data. Hubble suggested a plan to Milton Humason, a self-educated man at Mount Wilson who progressed between 1918 and 1963 from mule driver to janitor to night assistant to observer to staff astronomer to secretary of the Mount Wilson and Palomar observatories. Humason was to observe the spectra of fainter galaxies that Hubble thought would show larger red shifts if this was the Friedmann effect. In 1929, Humason obtained spectra with the Mount Wilson equipment, exposing photographic plates on the galaxy NGC 7619 for thirty-six hours with a confirming spectrum of forty hours. He obtained a red shift of four thousand kilometers per second. Hubble and Humason then published back-to-back announcements in volume 15 (1929) of the *Proceedings of the National Academy of Sciences*. Humason gave the spectral data. Hubble combined all available data and announced that they showed a linear relationship between the speed of the galaxies and their distance. The farther the galaxy, the faster it was receding from us. Here was the pattern of the expanding universe. This has turned out to be the most important discovery in astronomy, certainly in the twentieth century, and debatedly since Copernicus and Kepler. It has changed our conception of cosmology and has opened the door into the modern, scientific theory of creation.

Hubble and Humason began thereafter a campaign of observation with the

The 200-inch telescope on Palomar Mountain in Southern California, the largest light-gathering telescope in the world from 1949 to 1976. To appreciate its size, notice the figures in the lower foreground. Photo copyright © 1959, by, and courtesy of, Caltech.

Mount Wilson 100-inch reflector, proving that the relation was general and that it applied everywhere and at all distances. By 1950 the relation had been eventually extended to red shifts, expressed as a velocity of 60,000 kilometers per second. This *was* clearly the Friedmann-Lemaître effect. Important papers were published by Hubble and Humason in 1930, 1931, 1934, and 1936. The work was begun again by Humason using the 200-inch telescope at Palomar in 1949 and has continued, in its several aspects, to this day both at Palomar and now principally at Lick.

A   M O D E L   O F   T H E   U N I V E R S E

All the work from Hubble's day onward has shown that the relation is *linear*— that is, the red shifts increase in direct proportion to a galaxy's distance from us. This form of the relation is so crucial that much of the early work at Palomar with the newly completed 200-inch reflector was spent proving this. A linear relation is the only mathematical form of such a law where every observer, on every galaxy, sees the same type of velocity-distance relation. Each observer appears (to himself) to be the center of the expansion. But in reality there is no center—every place in the expanding universe is the center.

To understand this, consider Eddington's famous example of the surface of a balloon painted with dots. The curved surface of this balloon is an analogy (with one fewer dimension) for the curved space of the universe in Einstein's general theory of relativity. (If you have not yet read William Kaufmann's chapter, you may want to do so before proceeding. He discusses this notion in more detail.) On the curved surface of a balloon, as on the surface of the Earth, there is no center or edge. Any point on the surface has as much right to consider itself the center *of that surface* as any other point. (Of course, the whole balloon has a center, but the *surface* does not!)

Now we add some additional air to the balloon and watch it expand. Place yourself on any dot and look at other dots in any direction. All the dots move away from all others. A linear relation (which is what our balloon obeys) is the only velocity law where all points are equivalent.

The second crucial thing to realize is that a linear relation is the only law that permits all points to have had a common origin at some time in the past. Let the air out of a balloon and let its surface become smaller and smaller until it has zero area (in the limit of the imaginary balloon). When this happens it is clear to see that all points are together at a common point. Said differently, consider two galaxies seen from our vantage point and say one is twice as far away as the other. The linear law says that the velocity of the distant one is twice as great as that of the nearer galaxy. In your mind's eye, now reverse the velocities so that the galaxies approach us. The near one reaches us at a particular time. The farther one reaches us at the *same* time. It has twice as far to go but it is moving twice as fast. The same will be true for all galaxies in the space. Hence, if the velocity law is linear, then there could be a creation event in the past, when all matter was together and where all parts of space coincided in a sort of cosmic egg. Lemaître called it the *primeval atom* in his famous book by that title—a book that became a primer for students to learn something of the mysterious expansion.

THE TIME SCALE OF THE UNIVERSE

All this concerning the expansion is, of course, well known to those who follow astronomical developments. The general idea has even become part of common culture, worldwide; everyone has heard of the expanding universe. It is the centerpiece of the modern cosmological world view. But is it true?

Hubble was not sure. In all his writing he was cautious and never committed himself to the view that red shift means expansion and hence that it is a clear signal for a creation event. There were two reasons. The first resulted from a highly technical analysis he made with some data that turned out to be incorrect.

The more serious problem concerns the time for the creation event, calculated by the argument we discussed above. By reversing the velocities of the expanding galaxies, we can calculate when all galaxies must have been together by dividing their distances by their velocities. When Robertson in 1928 and Hubble in 1929 did that, they obtained a very short time for the expansion age of the universe—less than 2 billion years. But 2 billion years was less than the age of the crust of the Earth, already in the 1930's put at about 3.5 billion years by the geologist Arthur Holmes and others. How could the whole universe be younger than the Earth?

This time-scale problem has persisted until recently. The difficulty rests with finding the value of the distances to galaxies by which to divide the measured velocities to calculate when the clock began. As you can read in Hyron Spinrad's chapter, distances to galaxies have been enormously hard to measure. It has turned out, after thirty years of effort—primarily at Palomar—that we can identify a small class of distance indicators in addition to the cepheid variables to be used in the measurements. These indicators are brighter than cepheids, permitting their discovery in galaxies at much larger distances than the cepheids. The work has been to find ways of calibrating the absolute brightness of such indicators, and then to apply the calibration to actual galaxies of known velocity. In this way, the crucial ratio of distance divided by velocity—which is often called the Hubble time—can be calculated.

Early in the Palomar work in the middle 1950's it was known that Hubble's scale of distance was too small—but by how much? In 1950 the correction to the scale was put by Walter Baade to be about two times; Hubble's distances should be multiplied by two. This would increase the age from 2 billion to 4 billion years—not enough, because the age of the Sun had been found in the early 1950's to be about 5 billion years. As more and more was learned about the distance indicators from Mount Wilson and from Palomar from 1950 to the early 1970's, it became clear that the correction factor was much more than two. By 1956 it was thought to be at least 3, giving an age of at least 6 billion.

Without going into the technical details, it suffices here to note that astronomers now working on the distance scale problem agree that the correction to Hubble's 1936 distance scale is at least a factor of six and could be as large as twelve—the preferred value at present. This puts the Hubble time between about 12 billion and 24 billion years.

This is not exactly the age of the universe, because the expansion may have slowed down with time—pulling in on itself due to the self-gravity of the entire system. In the most popular model, where space-time is precisely "flat" in the Euclidean geometrical sense, this slowing will cause the true age of the universe to be two thirds of the Hubble time. If so, then the range given by the correction factor between six and twelve gives a universal age of between 8 billion and 16 billion years.

How then can we tell if the expansion of the universe implied by these measurements is real? The crucial test is to compare this age with the age obtained by other methods.

By the 1950's, astronomers had learned how to age-date the stars. This came from an understanding that the source of starlight was the nuclear conversion of hydrogen into helium deep in the interiors of the stars, where the temperatures are high enough for the nuclear reactions to work. Knowing how much hydrogen there is to convert to helium, and knowing the rate at which any given star is radiating away this released nuclear energy, tells how long the star can go on burning its fuel. In the 1950's, astronomers learned how to identify a phase in a star's life when it had converted about 10 percent of its hydrogen to helium. Knowing how much energy had been released by the conversion of that amount of matter to helium tells us when that particular star began to shine. The game then became one of finding the oldest stars in our Galaxy. By age-dating those stars, we can straightaway establish that our Galaxy is at least that old.

The theory of stellar evolution as developed between 1935 and about 1965 has been so convincingly borne out by a number of different tests that there is no question of its correctness in general outline. It then became a matter of improving the calculations to obtain a *precise* measurement of stellar ages. This task is complicated by the requirement that we must know the abundance of certain critical elements such as oxygen, nitrogen, and carbon in a star before we get the correct answer for the nuclear burning rates. The best estimates in 1987 for the ages of its oldest stars put the age of our Galaxy at greater than 12 billion years but less than about 18 billion, with the best guess at close to 15 billion.

The good agreement with the range of possible Hubble ages and the corresponding age of the universe (depending on the slowdown rate of the expansion) is remarkable. If the observed red shifts do not mean expansion, then no such agreement would be expected. The agreement, which most astronomers believe is real, removes Hubble's second objection: The expansion does appear to be real. Of course, there are still the small remaining details of the time-scale problem. Do we have the crucial factor of two thirds, or not? Is the correction factor six or twelve? Are the oldest stars in the Galaxy 12 billion or 18 billion years old? These are important questions because their answers determine the eschatology of the cosmos—the *ultimate fate* of the universe. We know the gravity of all the matter in the universe is slowing down the expansion. Is there enough matter to stop the expansion completely sometime in the future, whereupon the collapse of the entire system of galaxies should begin? Or does the expansion have enough energy to continue forever? The time-scale data are simply not good enough yet to decide this further question.

THE EARLY UNIVERSE

Where then does this leave the search for a coherent cosmology? We have emphasized that the expansion appears to be real. It may require a creation event. (The velocity-distance relation is linear.) Is there other evidence for such an event? The conclusion reached by taking the Friedmann model seriously is that the universe is a most remarkable machine. If it is expanding, it must once have been denser and hotter than it is now. By considering the physical conditions at the earliest times that are still describable by the Friedmann equations, the cosmological problem becomes much richer than merely a description of the organization of the present universe.

George Gamow and his students Ralph Alpher, Armin Hermann, and James Wightman Follin took the Friedmann model quite seriously in the 1950's and asked what would happen if they were to run the equations backward toward the high-density and -temperature era, assuming, in fact, a creation event. In a classic series of papers in the 1940's and in an important book by Gamow in 1952 called *The Creation of the Universe*, these men set down the foundations of what is now called the *new cosmology*. Their aim was to describe the creation of the stable matter we have in the universe today, out of the "cauldron" of energy at the beginning. For example, about 0.01 seconds after the creation event itself, free neutrons and protons had cooled to temperatures and expanded to densities that were low enough for them to react by standard, well-understood reactions of nuclear physics. Gamow and his students showed that they would then form the stable nuclei of heavy hydrogen (deuterium), two isotopes of helium with mass 3 and 4, and lithium 7 (with 3 protons and 4 neutrons). The universe, continuing to expand, cooled until at about one thousand years after the event, it was cold enough for the free electrons to combine with the free protons to form neutral hydrogen atoms. Before this time the free *photons*, the packets of electromagnetic energy, were being absorbed by the electrons.

This kept the electrons from forming atoms and kept the photons from traveling very far. After the electrons combined with protons into atoms, the photons became independent particles and continued to cool. The universe became transparent to them and they could now essentially survive forever. Alpher and Hermann could predict the temperature that these photons should have today, knowing how high the temperature and density had to be at the time of the formation of the two kinds of helium and the lithium. Their predicted temperature for the leftover radiation was five degrees above absolute zero— very cold and difficult to observe. The prediction, made in the early 1940's, was lost in the pages of the physics journal called the *Physical Review* but not forgotten by them or by Follin, the fourth member of the team. In the 1950's, Follin had begun to think about how to detect this leftover radiation using the new techniques of rocketry, which were beginning to be applied to astronomy. Although no public record exists of experiments considered by Follin or his students, it is not true, as you sometimes read in popular books, that Gamow's team had not begun to think of how their prediction could be tested, or that they did not believe in them.

The radiation left over from the hot epoch of the universe was indeed discovered in 1963, almost by accident, by the Bell Telephone astronomers Arno Penzias and Robert Wilson, who eventually received the Nobel Prize in physics for this work. Their serendipitous discovery came just before that of a Princeton team which had mounted a specific experiment to find such radiation, following a new and independent prediction of their own. Now confirmed by many experimenters, both from the ground and using rockets, the *cosmic background* radiation (as it has come to be called) is at roughly three degrees above absolute zero. Flooding in on us from everywhere in the universe, it is our most direct confirmation of the hot, dense early period in the history of the universe predicted by the new cosmology.

There has also been confirmation of the calculations by the Gamow team of the abundances of the light elements produced during the early phases of the universe. These calculations had been made more precise in the 1960's by Robert Wagoner and have now become a "cottage industry" among the physicists. Recently, new techniques in astronomical spectroscopy have allowed astronomers to measure the abundances of helium and lithium with much greater precision. Their work has shown spectacular agreement with the predictions, providing yet another strong verification of the hot early universe.

But the new cosmology has been even bolder in an attempt to understand even earlier times. As you will read in the chapter by James Trefil, physicists are now trying to calculate the properties of the hot early universe back to such high energies that the times are said to be only -10^{-24} seconds after the creation event—which astronomers like to call the Big Bang. The reasons for believing that these ideas are more than speculation are that particle physics has witnessed an internal revolution of its own in our understanding of the four fundamental forces of nature.

The basic theory of these forces and how they can be unified—which James Trefil will explain—is so elegant that many believe it must be true. Furthermore, a number of its predictions have already been confirmed in our largest particle accelerators.

The logical extension of the theory to even higher energies predicts a unification of the strong nuclear force and the now unified "electroweak" force at energies far beyond what can be produced in particle accelerators at 10^{18} MeV. However, if the new cosmology is correct, the early universe had such energies some 10^{-36} seconds after the Big Bang.

Fantasy? Perhaps. But remember that the same type of people that gave us the 3° radiation, the nucleosynthesis of ^{3}He, ^{4}He, and ^{7}Li, and the W and heavy bosons have given us this extension of the theory. What are the consequences?

A direct prediction of these ideas is that the universe must today be very close to flat in shape—as the specialists say, it must have zero space-time curvature. In that case, according to Einstein's general theory, the density of matter must be high enough to just create an exact Euclidean geometry. This leads to a very definite prediction for the matter density of the present universe. If we could spread out all the matter in the cosmos evenly, its average density would be near 10^{-30} grams per cubic centimeter. The flat geometry also requires that the age of the universe be precisely two thirds of the Hubble distance velocity ratio. These two predictions return the ball once again to the astronomers' court. Ideally, both the mean density of matter in the universe and, as we saw, its time scales should be observable at the telescope.

The time-scale test almost works, as we saw. It does so precisely if the observed Hubble time is 24 billion years and the age of the galaxies is 16 billion, because $2/3 \times 24 = 16$. This is why the time-scale test is now being looked at so carefully at many observatories.

The mean density test is more difficult. As discussed in Wallace Tucker's chapter, we see only the *visible* matter in the universe (using a broad definition of *visible* to include radio-waves and other forms of radiation). We cannot feel (via gravity) any dark matter that is spread uniformly in space, because there are no unbalanced forces from such a distribution. Counting up the visible mass that produces the visible radiation gives, at most, only one one-hundredth the needed density to make a flat universe. Therefore, for the new cosmology to be correct requires at least one hundred times more mass in the universe than we can see.

Some consider the internal particle physics theories to be so persuasive as to believe in this amount of dark matter. Some find the conclusion on dark matter to be so outrageous as to disbelieve the particle physics theories. If dark matter exists, it would be crucial to detect it in some way. We cannot rely on the time-scale test alone, since we do not know if we shall ever be able to determine the age of the Galaxy accurately enough, even if the problem of the distances to galaxies is solved to great precision. A great effort is, therefore, presently being put toward the direct detection of the dark matter in the universe, in an attempt to prove or disprove its existence. On that may rest the fate of much of the present superstructure of cosmological theory.

Nevertheless, the scientific cosmology built from the foundations of observations of the galaxies, almost entirely in this century, is surely essentially correct. With it has come the realization of the vastness of the universe, an elaboration of its expansion, and an idea of its creation, mysterious as that event remains.

REQUIEM FOR A UNIVERSE

POUL ANDERSON

THIS IS NOT MY STORY, but David Rhys can't tell it. Nor can I, except in a ghostly way. The words are lacking, and still more is the understanding. Maybe that's as well. He understood, just a little, and it sent him over the edge. Even so, humankind needs to hear.

Is the story true? He who replies to that is either a fool or wise beyond all wisdom of our race. The question forever haunts us: "What is truth?" Certainly these things did not happen as your birth has happened and your death will. Think, though, of a mathematical theorem. Its truth, its meaning, exists apart from any material reality; it is false only if, somewhere, it contradicts itself, disavows the logic from which it sprang. Then there are the truths uttered by poetry and by music. I think Rhys's story comes nearest to those; but you must judge for yourself.

It entered my life through a call in the middle of the night. I didn't hear, being too heavily asleep. Despite exercise regimen and biochemical control, the body takes much time to regain full strength after a year in space. Laura woke, and left our bed immediately to answer. After that separation, we wanted to be together in peace, and had set the phone to respond exclusively to messages that the program deemed we must receive. Among the codes for that was the name David Rhys.

The image was another woman's, Marie Fontenay, neuropsychiatrist in Paris, calling from Grenoble. While I talked with her—we found we did best in Spanish—Laura made coffee. We two had taken a primitive cottage away off on Kauai, to be alone with sea and sand, flowers and sun and rainbows. It felt good to do things for ourselves. Especially it did to me. A linker lives mostly among abstractions. Laura teaches history at an elementary school in California. No computer yet built, no program yet written can do for children what a living person can, if she has the gift and their parents can afford her salary.

"Thanks," I said to her. "Much needed. I'm off for Honolulu in an hour."

She studied my face a moment before she murmured, "Bad, hm?"

"Bad enough that they're sending a suborbital to bring me to France. 'They' being the Institute of Holothetics, and the rocket lent by the Peace Command."

"Why *you?*" For an instant her question hurt; then I realized she wasn't implying I was merely a linker. After all, my sort aren't many either. But the few, few holothetes do differ from us not just in degree but in kind. If we linkers are like high priests in the temple of science and technology, they are like its gods; and often what they have to tell the faithful is perforce Delphic.

The Kona was rich and reviving on my tongue. "Well, since I am an old friend of Dave's and we've worked together in the past, Jeanie—his wife, that is, not their daughter—thought I'll have some chance of guessing what went wrong and what can be done about it." Grimly: "If anything can. He's . . . catatonic? Fontenay, the doctor, says the brain scans show no organic damage but every trace of a traumatic, absolutely devastating impact. And Dave was . . . he's always had more psychic strength than most people." Otherwise he could not have done what he did, been what he was, my thought went on.

"Why must you go in person?"

"Same reason I had to be in space. They couldn't build the Galactic Analyzer and get it operating properly without a linker; and the communications channels weren't adequate to connect me across fifty astronomical units. . . . I'm sorry. I'm still too dazed to know when I'm quacking forth the obvious."

"You're on Earth now," she protested.

"And the channels aren't adequate either. Fontenay said a technician on the project told her. You see, I'll have to examine Dave's program."

"It's too complex for transmission in a reasonable time?" She shook her head and whistled. Sudden terror struck. She grabbed my arm. "Be careful! It could hurt you too."

"Fontenay thinks not." I'd have been more honest to say she hoped not. "They haven't called in another holothete because she is afraid of what it might do to him or her. A linker can't have the same experience." What song the sirens sang could not lure mariners who were tone-deaf.

She clung to me. "I've got to go," I told her: in friendship and in my pride.

So she talked with gallant merriment while our car flew us to Honolulu Interplanetary, and kissed me fiercely before I boarded the rocket. Oh, I had reasons aplenty to be careful.

Acceleration was tough on flesh not reaccustomed to Earth gravity, but the arc was altogether soft. I floated in my harness, hearing silence as if it were a presence, hearing the blood pulse within me, and looked at the outviewer. Stars gleamed multitudinous and winter-cold through a crystalline darkness. When I touched a control, vision swung toward the planet. We were coming around to dayside, and heaven was a blue-and-gold coronet on swirling vastnesses of cloud. Below their virginal white I saw land on ocean, malachite set in turquoise. How beautiful is this world our mother. How far from her had the soul of David Rhys wandered?

The crew saw I wanted to think and left me undisturbed. My thoughts were not of programs, however, nor in computer language. They dwelt on Rhys.

The popular mind supposes holothetes are all cold fish. It's true they are apt to be a little awkward socially, and over the years some grow eccentric to the point of what looks like madness. You cannot work with, live in, the Absolute, which is inhuman, and leave the strangeness of it wholly behind when you uncouple from your machine. But not the less do you remain a child of Earth. No less than your sisters and brothers can you know pain, jubilation, fear, wishfulness, anger, love.

Apart from those rare gifts which made it possible for him to become a holothete, Rhys was simply a decent man. Off work, he enjoyed gardening, carpentry, a half liter in the pub after a day's hike in the woodlands around Snowdon; he played violin in an amateur chamber orchestra; he voted Constructive and worried about too much loss of national autonomy to the World Union; no linguist, he had trouble with his Spanish on international hookups but slogged good-naturedly ahead anyway; his artistic idols were Shelley, Monet, and Berlioz, though most commonly projected in his house were astronomical images and old folk tunes. I'd several times been a guest in that house. It held a happy family.

Now and then he did drift out of touch, into lordly half-memories; and he admitted that the great psychological writers left him wondering what the shootin' was for. ("An Americanism, in your honor, Jack," he'd laughed; and I'd replied, "Hey, while the shooting was going on over there, my ancestors were picking cotton in Alabama.") The price did not seem overly high for being at one with everything science has learned. I tried hard not to envy him. He must have sensed that, for once in conversation he quietly pointed out that the demands on linkers are as hard in their fashion, and the need for us is basic. "Your eyes process more data, but your ears hear what people say, and that matters most."

Had it been his humanness that made him vulnerable to whatever the thing was he encountered?

A car with an attendant waited for me at Lyon and flitted me to Grenoble. That man was employed at the Institute's laboratory there, but knew nothing about the disaster. Since it wasn't in the news, I realized powerful persons wanted it kept secret for a while. Well, when you have a problem subtle and frightening, you're better off without journalists.

The man took me to a suite in the residential building, helped me settle in, and advised me to rest before reporting. "No," I said. "My impression is that this won't keep. It's early afternoon here. Thank you, señor, and good day."

I did ache. My head and eyelids felt full of sand. An antifatigant took care

of that, but it was blessed to lean back into a lounger's embrace and sip a cup
of bouillon I'd sent the errand cart to get me. While the phone searched for
Marie Fontenay, my gaze went out the window. The compound occupies a hill
with a view over the medieval city, the river, green countryside, distant Alpine
snowpeaks. Even stronger than seeing Earth from space, a scene like this brings
to me the sense of home, that here is where we belong.

Fontenay was in conference at the hospital when the communications found
her, but left as soon as she heard I'd arrived and called me from an office. Her
head nearly leaped out of my screen, haggard with stress, vivid with purpose.
"Ah, Sr. Henry," she greeted almost brusquely. "Welcome. Are you prepared
to commence?"

I nodded. "How is Rhys?" My throat tightened up.

"I will show you. He is in a private room in the neurological ward." The
hologram transmuted itself.

It was a full scan. The thin blanket did not hide how stiffly my friend lay,
not quite straight, congealed in a convulsion. I touched for a close-up. His face
was white and likewise locked—against what? His eyes were open but blank—
staring at what? I reached forward as if I could stroke the time-faded blond
hair. But that was for Jeanie, when she visited yonder hushed place. Surely
she kept vigil somewhere in town, or soon would.

I switched back to Fontenay, and was grateful to her for continuing the
impersonal tone: "It is a state of total fugue. He had an experience he could
not bear, and fled from awareness. We have completed the molecular tests and
found no genetic predisposition. Therefore, the experience must have been terrible indeed."

"What, uh, prognosis?"

"I do not know. His brain has full capability but refuses to use it. That is
clinically well-known, but the form it has taken here is unique." She scowled.
"Studying the encephalograms and other indicators, I have been tempted to
diagnose the condition as active rather than passive—part of him desperately
threshing about in search of what might save him. It is childish of me, at least
in my present ignorance."

"You can't haul him out of the trance? Drugs, electropulses—"

"I am afraid to try. It could destroy him completely. This *is* a defense
mechanism. And we know little yet about the psychodynamics of holothetics.
Remember, he was stricken while in the program." Fontenay drew breath.
"On the other hand, if we do nothing, that probably means just a slower destruction. He cannot long maintain such tension and—yes, I will say it—grief.
The indicators of overwhelming sorrow are unmistakable. He will become either
a madman or a vegetable. My rather wild hope is that you can find a clue to
what might help."

"What happened, exactly?"

"We'll make full recordings available to you, audiovisual as well as computer. Briefly, he had been engaged for about seven hours—that seemed unduly long, but it was an unprecedentedly ambitious undertaking and he had expected several lengthy sessions—when he began to show distress. At first, irregular breath; soon, moans and small jerky motions; all at once, screaming and flailing about. A linker was present and in circuit too. He did not participate in the actual program, which would have been distracting to Rhys, but stood guard on the electronics. A microvariation in line voltage, anything like that, would have disrupted the intricate process, he tells me. Nothing untoward had occurred. Being thus only partially engaged, he observed the trouble, cut off the entire operation, and called for help." Sternly: "Yes, he knew that may harm a person in the circuit, but after watching the tapes—that is a wise routine, making them—I agree the emergency justified his action. Rhys's tetany became rigidity, and in it he remains."

"I'll judge for myself," I said with care. "First, however, have you anything more to tell me? Anything you can imagine might be significant?"

Fontenay sat quiet until: "Look closely at the last few seconds before the shutdown. Was—is Rhys a religious man, Sr. Henry?"

"No, except that, well, he scarcely ever talked about it, but I have heard him say he walked in awe. And—let me think—yes, he told me his parents were churchgoers, and took him when he was a boy. Why do you ask?"

" 'The living God!' " she answered in English. Returning to Spanish: "That was what he cried out. His only real words. After them, coma. Does this suggest anything to you?"

"No," I admitted low. "But . . . you know, you haven't told me what he was working on, and I haven't thought to ask. What is it?"

Again she hesitated before she made response. "The biography, from beginning to end, the origin and fate, of the universe."

I spent the rest of that day familiarizing myself with the huge new mainframe computer at the heart of the laboratory. Nothing less could have made possible the project that the Galilean Society commissioned and Rhys undertook. Strange it was to lie back in the same lounger he had used and adjust on my head the same helmet.

Electromagnetic induction joined my brain to the machine, and for a time beyond time I lost any forebodings. I almost forgot why I was there. The power of intellect that was mine outshone and overrode all else. In the words of a writer, among the many who have tried to describe what linkage is like, I was drunk on sanity.

The instrument and I were one. We shared its world-spanning nanosecond access to every datum ever entered in molecular memory units; its nearly light-speed scan, selection, and integration of what we needed; its quadrillionfold mathematical and logical operations within an eyeblink; . . . my human creativity, flexibility, initiative, awareness. *I* was our program, which continuously rewrote itself, which had no hidden flaws to take us astray because it was not composed beforehand by an outsider but evolved in action. Not that I was conscious of this. I did it. I was it.

Think of a man running. That is so intricate and changeable a set of motions, within a context of circumstances so enormous and unpredictable, that we have never built a robot able to do it half as well. Even our organics are poor, clumsy parodies. But the man runs. He doesn't know how; he doesn't have to—his entire body knows for him.

Like such an athlete, I strained toward my goal and exulted in my strength. And today I was mighty beyond anything I had known before. For the span of this linkage, mine was the greatest intelligence in the whole of humanity.

Warming up, I calculated a few hundred Bessel functions to several hundred decimal places. It was trivial, done in an instant. Rather than take the information out of the database, I decided for myself the exact configurations that various large protein molecules must needs have, and put them through their chemical paces. I became conversant with neurology and related disciplines. Thereupon I dismissed them, aside from a small amount left in my brain in order that I could later talk seriously with Fontenay. More congenial was a problem in astrophysics, practice for efforts to come. I established arbitrary initial conditions—gas and dust distributions, galactic location, ambient force fields—and ran off the development of the system that resulted. Matter condensed, nuclear fires kindled, a new star brightened; planets formed; geology did its work; atmospheres brewed each its special weathers, and also altered with millions and billions of years; and these happenings were inevitable from the beginning. Yet often and often as I watched the unfolding of my logic, I was surprised.

Does God feel thus? I don't presume to guess. I didn't look into life, though one of my imaginary words was bound to engender it. To this day, too much is unknown about that. I could have imposed conditions more detailed, but following out their consequences would have taken time we could ill afford, when Rhys lay in hell.

Disconnecting at last, returning to mere flesh, always leaves me with a sense of desolation, unutterable loss. I have to remember what is best in my days, such as Laura, and go out and savor the world around me, before I can again be content with what I am.

"Frankly, I consider the project lunatic," Fontenay declared when I phoned her in the morning. "An ancient Greek would tell us your friend was stricken down for his hubris."

"No, it's a perfectly respectable scientific idea," I replied. "Something went ghastly wrong, but that was unforeseeable."

"Exactly! What can we, for all of our proud instruments and theories, foresee? Without a solid basis of facts, thought is empty, mere noise. And what do we actually know about the universe, as immeasurably huge and old as it is?" She spread her hands and shrugged her shoulders in the French fashion. "Nothing!"

"That isn't true. Pardon me, but it isn't. We have instruments throughout the solar system, farther than Pluto. Their precision is limited only by quantum uncertainties built into nature. They study planets of the nearer stars, supernovae in the remotest galaxies, and everything between. Since the unified field theory was worked out, and that was over a century ago, we've had a clear understanding of the structure and behavior of matter, energy, space-time, and the dimensions beyond. The fact that hardly any people are able to learn it in its entirety just proves that the Ultimate is not like the everyday environment our evolution has fitted us for. In linkage, I've employed the theory easily. It predicts what our physicists and astronomers observe, and nothing that contradicts their observations. So we're being entirely reasonable when we use it to make deductions about things we cannot observe, such as the distant past or the far future."

"And?" The note of scorn lingered.

"Well, we know the universe originated as a quantum fluctuation about twenty billion years ago. We know the primordial fireball expanded, that the cellular distribution of galactic clusters was the work of energy concentrations we call strings, that most matter is nonluminous particles in space. Nevertheless, the mass is insufficient to close the universe. It will expand forever."

She stopped me with an impatient chopping gesture. "I am aware of this, Sr. Henry. Every educated person is. But the totality of galaxies, those mutable energies and particles you speak of, in a space-time whose wave front has been expanding at the speed of light for twenty billion years—no, you *cannot* handle it. Could the sheer volume have overloaded Rhys?"

Not bothering to correct her physics, I shook my head and answered, "No. We do have our failures, we computermen. Usually they're due to inadequate data, but occasionally the problem proves to be too big—or, rather, inappropriately formulated. We realize that after a while and quit. It's scarcely worse than a similar frustration in ordinary life."

"I spoke figuratively. Of course I have an acquaintance with your profession, as far as a nonlinker can. In fact, I wonder why he wrestled as long as he did with his nonsensical, impossible task."

"Because it isn't. Certainly nobody supposes we can deal with countless individual stars—or galaxies or clusters. In linkage yesterday, I reviewed the entire project to date, from the original proposals and studies to the final schematics. It requires a lot of mathematics to follow. In essence, though, the plan is—was—to take our theoretical structure, plug in what relevant empirical data we possess, and compute the consequences. Not in detail, obviously. On the broadest scale, the cosmos as a whole. We don't need to know what single molecules in the air are doing to predict the weather quite successfully. The dynamics of the mass suffices. Likewise for the universe. That's what the instigators, the sponsors, and David Rhys intended."

Fontenay frowned. "But the objective?"

"Why, to check out our knowledge. To see if the calculated course of events made sense. If it didn't, if it yielded an absurdity, we'd know there was an error somewhere in our concepts." I attempted a smile. "Then, as we say in America, it would have been back to the drawing board."

Perhaps the archaic phrase puzzled her, for she began to ask "What—" and broke off with: "Thank you. I suspected something like this, but wanted clarification. Now what do you suggest we do?"

I gathered courage to tell her: "What I am going to do is link with the record Rhys left. I mean to follow him down whatever road it was he walked."

I couldn't really, and was glad of that. A linker is not a holothete. It's hard to explain the difference, immense though it be. Every linkage involves creativity; that is the reason for it. Through his or her peculiar, intensely trained gift, a holothete has such mastery as to confer on the system a creative imagination.

I can dream the seed of a planetary system and apply the mathematical laws of physics to make it flower. I cannot change those laws if they seem faulty—not, and continue making sense. Rhys could. Analogy: I am a competent professor of the subject; he was Einstein.

Another analogy: The world outside our skins is real, but what we directly experience is our sensory impressions. From those we infer—we construct—sunlight, trees, lovers, everything. We do this on so deep, instinctive a level that we can properly say we experience these things themselves. But an atom or a galaxy is too alien, too remote from what our race has evolved amidst. Such must always be abstractions, consciously formed, never felt or understood as we feel and understand our dear immediate realities—unless we are holothetes in linkage.

From the molecules of the database I would summon up the vast program Rhys had written as he went along. I would replay it and dimly, partially, distortedly know what had passed through him. My purblindness was my armor. This I must hope.

Creation began.

From emptiness, the fireball bloomed. It was not the first, nor would it be the last. Limitlessly throughout the omnicontinuum, indeterminacy brought forth universes. No two of them were akin. That was the most I knew. Necessity made them be, but they were unreachable. Nothing whatsoever could pass between. I was alone in this cosmos which was mine.

Outward and outward the energy storm raged. Yet there was never a primordial chaos. In that supernal surging, the very laws of nature changed, like foam on the back of a wave. Unity broke asunder; dimensions twisted, cast

JOHN HARRIS

themselves wide or shrank toward nullity; the single force became four; the speed at which attainable space fled from itself dwindled to that of light, which was flung into existence like spindrift blown off the crest of the wave. And all, all was contrapuntal, its majesty wholly foreordained.

Billions upon billions of nanoseconds passed. The fundamental particles formed. Antimatter went its way; the imbalance that would drive the future was manifest. A seething sea of hydrogen and helium mingled with darker material. It cooled as it widened until its radiation roar was a whisper. One-dimensional cables hauled it on the currents of their dissolution. It gathered in monstrous many-layered configurations, millions of light-years apart from one another.

Quiescence fell.

The cold and the dark entered into my spirit. Creation had ended.

No. Not altogether. Glimmers awoke, faint and tiny. The gas was falling in on itself. Galactic clusters coalesced, protogalaxies, the earliest stars. From their atoms, gravitation evoked the other three forces, and light was reborn. The Suns were furnaces forging the higher elements, as high as iron. The greatest of them exploded in supernova glory, and out of their deaths came nuclei new and strange. Dust lanes dimmed a little the shining spirals; but this was dust that went into younger suns, and worlds of theirs, and upon some of those worlds, life.

But how feeble this was, how swiftly the gigayears fell away. Time is not a fixed, marked rod; it is events. Harking back to those first furious hours, I now found only the gasps of a thing that was dying. While old stars burned out and ever fewer came into being, I meditated on the paradox that a closed universe, fated to reach an ultimate size and then contract until the fireball blazes afresh, gives any dwellers in it an infinite future: for the closer it draws to the end, the more manyfold, diverse, and swift are its changes.

Huge stars collapsed to black holes, which light itself could no longer escape. Whole galaxies did, and devoured those around them. After a trillion years, the last members of the last generation of energy-hoarding dwarfs flickered out. And there was darkness.

Space expanded onward into silence. Perhaps weird forms of life huddled near some few black holes, drawing nourishment from the in-fall. I could not know, nor did I care. They, too, were doomed.

Flashes in the night—black holes must also perish. Quantum tunneling erodes them: the smaller they are, the faster. Finally these death-rattles likewise ended.

Matter itself was vanishing. Quantum accident made black holes of atoms, and photons of those. Wavelengths stretched as they wearied until radiation guttered toward its own extinction. It took time—oh, yes, for any such event was an unimaginably seldom thing; but because of that sparsity, a billion billion billion years were to me as a solitary heartbeat.

When a black hole was entirely gone, the singularity at its core strayed naked. There natural law was annulled and anything could happen. Nothing did, for nothing was left. It was simply that law was going out with all else.

What meaning had the whole thing had? It was a senseless upwelling of randomness, sinking back to the zero whence it came.

If ours could have been a closed universe! They existed. The same blind chance made that certain. But ours was too small, and therefore condemned to grow infinite.

Adrift in frozen doomsday, I knew what shattered Rhys. It was hard enough on me; an infinitesimal part of my mind thought I'd need Fontenay's help to rid me of nightmares. And I was like a boy listening to a man tell of a war he has suffered. Rhys had *known*, had *been* this hopelessness. It overcame him in a rush, before he could comprehend and break free, as a black hole drinks light. This was our fatal arrogance, that we supposed a man can behold our destiny and live.

Almost, I released myself. I might be at hideous risk. But—something had come to him. I could not imagine what, here where everything had happened that was ever going to happen. Maybe it was no more than his flight from the unendurable. But while I was able, I would endure.

It came to me.

And the universe ended.

That is an arsenal powerful and delicate which Fontenay has at her command. Within hours I was sitting up in bed and talking rationally with her. She'd sought me in person, for wisdom is hers as well.

"His associate had the best of intentions," I said. "No way could he have realized that the worst possible thing was to stop the program. That's always hazardous, you know; the shock is considerable. This time it interrupted what might have saved him."

"Are you sure?" she asked in a subdued voice. "It seems . . . fantastic."

"No, I am not sure, and yes, the whole affair is fantastic," I answered. "What I have discovered is that there is, in fact, something missing in our cosmology. The logic showed this as inexorably as it traced the entire pattern that went before."

"His mind was disintegrating under stress. Hallucination—"

"That doesn't occur in linkage. If it could, and if it did in this case, I'd have recognized it as such—I, the detached observer, not the directly involved holothete." Which was not quite true of myself, I thought with a slight shudder. "Of course, logic is only as good as its postulates, but what we've found out is that ours have implications we never imagined. I'm not saying that whatever appeared is necessarily a construct corresponding to reality. I do think that probably it is. And at least it gives us a possibility of healing my friend."

She raised her brows. "How?"

Doubtless she anticipated what I'd say: "Put him back in circuit. I'll be in parallel, guiding his injured brain till it resurrects what it alone was able to . . . deduce, create, envision . . . and completes the sequence: draws the full conclusion that it was prevented from drawing—solves the riddle—whatever the answer may be.

"I admit the attempt may fail. It may permanently ruin his mind. But he hasn't much to lose, has he? And my hope is, from the glimpse I got, that going through with it can save him."

Marie Fontenay is an almighty brave person. She staked her reputation, her career, when she agreed to my counsel. Naturally, first she studied and thought. She got a holothete to analyze the neurology. Results were ambiguous. I have an idea that what persuaded her was what I had already related of that which Rhys met at the graveside of time.

Triumph. Splendor. Joy.

This is not my story, but David Rhys can't tell it. After his long convalescence he's eager to take up his work—more than eager, considering what we both believe is a revelation that logic gave unto him. However, he isn't an especially articulate man, outside of his profession. Nor can I find words that will serve. They don't exist. I must simply try.

I must simply proclaim that there in the abyss a flame appeared, and somehow it smiled and its spirit said with unbounded love: "Go home to my forebears and tell them all this was mistaken. They forgot about themselves."

THE NEW PHYSICS
AND THE UNIVERSE

ESSAY BY

JAMES TREFIL

SPECULATION BY

GENE WOLFE

THE NEW PHYSICS AND THE UNIVERSE

JAMES TREFIL

George Mason University

THE MOST EXCITING THING to happen in cosmology in the last decade has been the coming together—some people might call it the shotgun marriage—of elementary particle physics and the study of the evolution of the universe. This may seem at first glance to be a somewhat surprising development—after all, what could be more different than a proton and the whole universe? Yet, as we shall see shortly, there is a kind of logic in this development. In fact, we probably ought to have been able to anticipate it once we knew about the Big Bang and the cosmic microwave background radiation. The upshot of this new alliance between seemingly unconnected branches of science is that we are starting to come very close to answering some very old questions: where the universe came from and how it got to be the way it is.

WHAT THE WORLD IS MADE OF

I suppose we should start by talking about why there is any connection at all between elementary particle physics and cosmology, and maybe back up a little more and talk about what elementary particle physics is. Ever since 1805, when the English chemist John Dalton published his theory that matter was made up of atoms, we have known that the materials we see in the world around us are not themselves elementary but are actually conglomerates of atoms (the word comes from the Greek for "that which cannot be divided"). Dalton based his theory on the regularities that were being uncovered by the new science of chemistry and produced a number of predictions that could be (and were) tested in the laboratory.

But the atom isn't really indivisible, as we all know. In the early years of this century Ernest Rutherford showed that almost all the mass of the atom is concentrated in an unimaginably dense nucleus, around which lightweight electrons move in orbit. Instead of being itself elementary, the atom (and hence

276

all matter) was made of things more elementary still. Through the 1920's and 1930's a simple picture of the world developed, in which all matter was thought to consist of only three particles. These were the proton (with a positive electrical charge), the neutron (with no electrical charge), and the electron (with negative electrical charge). The protons and neutrons, in roughly equal numbers, combined to make the nuclei of atoms, and then the electrons went into their orbits to complete the job. As in Dalton's original scheme, these composite atoms would then come together to make the infinite complexity of molecules that we see in our everyday world.

This simple picture of the fundamental constituents of matter, alas, was not to survive long. By the 1950's, scientists studying the collisions of protons with nuclei began to realize that when a nucleus is torn apart, all sorts of strange and wonderful things can be found in the debris. There were, of course, the protons and neutrons you'd expect to find, but in addition there was a whole collection of new particles. These particles seemed to live inside the nucleus, but when freed from this environment they decayed—came apart—in very short times. The instability of these particles explains why we were not previously aware of them—they can be seen only briefly and under very special conditions such as those that exist in the laboratory.

It quickly became evident, in fact, that there were two classes of particles in nature. There were particles like the proton, the neutron, and the stuff that was seen in the debris of nuclear collisions. These particles seemed to be at home in the nucleus and to contribute in some way to holding it together. The other class of particles were those like the electron—particles that are normally found not inside the nucleus but outside of it. The former class of particles was christened *hadrons* (after the Greek for "strongly interacting ones"). The latter particles were called *leptons*, or weakly interacting ones.

It turned out that going into the nucleus after the hadrons had opened a real Pandora's box. Throughout the 1960's and into the 1970's the number of hadrons being discovered skyrocketed. The last time I looked there were over two hundred, but no one is counting anymore. It's clear that a system of the world with two hundred kinds of "elementary" particles just isn't going to work. Some way of ordering the hadrons had to be found. In the late 1960's such a scheme was proposed, and since then this scheme has come to dominate the study of the basic structure of matter. The scheme is actually very similar to the simple proton-neutron-electron picture of the 1930's. The idea is that just as all nuclei are merely different arrangements of the hadrons, all hadrons are themselves simply different arrangements of things more fundamental still, things for which the name *quarks* was invented. The name actually comes from a line in James Joyce's *Finnegans Wake* that goes "Three quarks for Muster Mark," and it reflects the fact that in its earliest incarnation the quark model had three different kinds of quarks in it.

If you accept for a moment that this model is valid, then it gives us a remarkably simple picture of the structure of matter. There are a small number of quarks, and these quarks are put together in different ways to make the hundreds of hadrons. These hadrons, in turn, combine to form the nuclei of the hundred-plus known chemical elements. The leptons are then added to make up atoms, which then come together to make the molecules.

At the moment, it appears that there are six different kinds of quarks in nature. We have seen hadrons that contain five of them in the laboratory, and it is expected that the next round of new high-energy accelerators (the machines that are popularly called "atom smashers") to come on line will find evidence for the sixth. The quarks are unlike any other particles known. For one thing, they have electrical charges that are either one-third or two-thirds that found on the electron or proton. They are the only particles that are supposed to have this sort of fractional charge. The quarks also have another property, whimsically called *color,* which is analogous to electrical charge. Each type of quark can have one of three possible color charges, just as it can have one of a small number of possible electrical charges.

The six quarks are called, respectively, "up," "down," "strange," "charm," "bottom," and "top." The names are suggested by various properties of the particles and by analogies—if a hadron contains a charm quark, for example, it will survive much longer than you might expect (i.e., lead a "charmed" life). For our purposes, however, we need only know that according to our present notions all hadrons are made from these six quarks.

I should point out one other difference between quarks and hadrons. No one has succeeded in producing unambiguous evidence for the existence of free quarks (that is, quarks not locked into hadrons). Indeed, present theories tell us that quarks cannot be torn loose from hadrons—in the jargon of physics, they are *confined.* The best analogy is to imagine that the quarks are something like the ends of a rubber band. No matter what you do, you can't pull the end of a rubber band off. You can tear the band apart, but this just produces shorter strings with two ends. In just the same way, we believe that you can never pull a quark out of a hadron.

TRACING THE EARLY HISTORY OF THE UNIVERSE

Given this picture of the structure of matter, it becomes easy to see how elementary particle physics and cosmology come together. One thing we know about the Big Bang is that during its early stages the universe was much hotter than it is now. When any material—be it the universe or a pot of boiling water—is heated, its constituent parts move faster. This means that when the inevitable collisions between these constituents occur, they are much more violent in a hot material than in a cold one. As we start to trace the Big Bang back through time, then, we will be encountering situations in which ever more violent (read higher-energy) collisions are taking place at the microscopic level.

Computer-enhanced photograph of the trails of subatomic particles in a bubble chamber. Color-enhancement techniques by Patrice Loiez, CERN. Photo credit: CERN.

This is why the things we have come to know about the structure of matter can help us understand the early evolution of the universe.

Let's take atoms as a simple example. The atom is a relatively airy, fragile structure. The electrons, far from the nucleus in their orbits, can be knocked loose in a collision without much difficulty. What this means is that if the temperature of a material is very high, all the electrons will be separated from their nuclei. Matter in this state, in which positively charged nuclei and negatively charged electrons can move around independently of each other, is called a *plasma*. If an electron in a plasma does manage to attach itself to a nucleus to form an atom, it will be torn off in a subsequent collision. When the temperature of a material is too high, then, atoms simply cannot exist.

The temperature needed to create a plasma isn't all that great. It can easily be produced in our laboratories. (Indeed, a large part of the current attempts to reproduce the nuclear fusion that powers the stars depends on being able to produce and confine plasmas.) Since most of the matter in the Sun and other stars is in a plasma state as well, plasma should not be thought of as some sort of exotic and unknown form of matter. In fact, it is by far the most common state of matter in the universe.

From these arguments, it follows that as the universe was expanding and cooling during the early stages of the Big Bang, there must have been a time when the temperature was too high for atoms to exist, followed by a time when the temperature had fallen to the point where they could. In between these two, there must have been a transition during which the atoms formed.

It is useful to consider another, more familiar process in nature which has the same properties. When you lower the temperature of water, there is a sharply defined temperature—32°F—when it freezes. At this temperature the water changes form, from a liquid to a solid. We say it freezes, and physicists say that it goes through a *phase change*.

We can make the same sort of statement about the formation of atoms in the early universe. It turns out that the "freezing" of the plasma into atoms isn't as sharply defined as the freezing of liquid water into ice, but the two are similar enough to give us a useful analogy. When the universe was about 100,000 years old, the temperature had dropped to the point where electrons that attached themselves to atoms would no longer necessarily be torn loose in collisions. By the time the universe was a million years old, the temperature was so low that the disruption of an atom by collision was a fairly rare event. Matter in the form of atoms was safely established, and we say that the atoms "froze" out of a plasma in the period around 500,000 years.

If we continue our journey backward in time, the next important juncture occurs about three minutes after the Big Bang. This was another freezing, or phase change, but it involved the nuclei themselves rather than the atoms. At around the three-minute mark the temperature had dropped to the point that when two hadrons (a proton and a neutron, for example) came together to form a nucleus, it had a reasonable chance of surviving. Before the universe was three minutes old, any such nucleus that was formed would quickly have been disrupted. Consequently, before this time, matter existed in the form of a sea of hadrons and leptons.

The freezing of hadrons into nuclei at three minutes, like the freezing of the atoms later, was not a simple, instantaneous process. It proceeded in a stepwise fashion, first forming deuterium (one proton and one neutron) and then, by subsequent collisions, tacking on a few more protons and neutrons to form various isotopes of helium and even a little lithium. In this collection of nuclei, it turns out that the simplest—deuterium—is the most easily torn apart in collisions. Therefore, the whole nucleus-building process had to wait until the deuterium was stable before the rest could proceed. Once deuterium was around, the rest of the nuclei formed quickly.

You might be interested to know, as a point of historical interest, that the Big Bang theory was first proposed back in the 1940's as a mechanism by which the nuclei in the periodic table could have been synthesized all at once, at the very beginning. The idea was that the universe created its nuclear "capital" early on, and that it has been living on it ever since. It quickly became obvious, however, that the expansion of the universe would carry protons and neutrons

The main tunnel of the Fermilab particle accelerator, Batavia, Illinois. (Fermilab photo.)

apart from each other in short order, thereby preventing the formation of anything heavier than lithium (three protons, two neutrons). Because of this realization, the Big Bang theory did not really catch on until we understood the formation of elements by stars. (You will recall from earlier chapters that our present understanding is that all nuclei heavier than lithium were created in stars much later in the evolution of the universe.)

Before the three-minute mark, then, the matter in the universe was in the form of a collection of hadrons and leptons, but no nuclei were present. After the first three minutes, hadrons were locked up in the newly formed nuclei.

Resuming our journey backward in time, we pass through a universe where more and more energy is present in collisions, and in which more and more exotic hadrons are created from this energy. The world looks less and less familiar. Finally, when we get back to a time roughly ten microseconds after the beginning, we encounter yet another phase change. At that time, the hadrons were created out of their constituent quarks, or, if you prefer, the quarks froze to create the hadrons. Before this time, matter existed in the most fundamental form we know, as a collection of quarks and leptons. Afterward, the quarks disappeared and were replaced by hadrons.

It is tempting to suppose that this particular phase change took place in just the way the formation of atoms and nuclei did—by a process of adding the pieces together one at a time. In point of fact, however, we now understand that this particular transition (and others we'll discuss shortly) must have been rather different. It was much more like the formation of a magnet out of iron atoms than the freezing of water into ice. In the case of a magnet, at high temperatures all the iron atoms are aligned randomly in space, each one pointing in its own direction. In such a situation the magnetic fields of the individual atoms tend to cancel one another out and the material taken as a whole has no magnetic properties. As the temperature is lowered, however, there comes a point where the individual atoms suddenly line up. The fields now reinforce one another and a magnet is born. The sudden lining up of the atoms is a phase change, even though it doesn't much resemble the freezing of water.

The transition from quarks to hadrons was like the formation of a magnet. At ten microseconds the free, randomly moving quarks suddenly rearranged themselves, just as the individual atoms do in a magnet. After this transition, the quarks were locked in, never to be seen as free particles again.

It would seem, then, that we have reached the point of ultimate simplicity in our backward journey through the history of the universe. Matter has been broken down into its basic constituents—quarks and leptons—and it seems that there's nowhere else to go. This "end of the road" feeling isn't justified, however, because up to now we've been considering only half the story. The basic constituents of all matter may be quarks and leptons, but until we've talked about how these constituents interact with each other, we really haven't given a full description of the state of the universe.

THE FORCES THAT GOVERN THE UNIVERSE

Physicists attack this aspect of the problem by investigating forces. By the end of the nineteenth century we knew of two forces that allowed matter to interact. There was the familiar force of gravity, holding the planets in their orbits and people on the surface of the Earth, and there was the force of electromagnetism, which governed magnets, electrical charges, and other such phenomena. In the twentieth century we added two new forces to this roster. One of these is the so-called *strong force*, the force that holds the hadrons in the nucleus together and locks the quarks into hadrons. The other is the *weak force*, which governs some forms of radioactive decay. Everything that happens in the universe happens because one or more of these forces is acting.

At first glance this categorization of forces appears to be a major achievement. Explaining the infinite number of processes in the universe in terms of just four basic forces seems like an enormous simplification. It is, of course, but that doesn't stop theoretical physicists from wondering if they can't do better. You can understand this point of view by asking the question: "What is the minimum number of forces you need to make a universe?" According to the basic laws of motion that Isaac Newton wrote down in the seventeenth century, any change in an object's state of motion must be caused by the action of a force. A universe with no forces could have no changes—it would be a dull place indeed. A universe in which things happen, therefore, needs at least one force, but it really doesn't need more. The question that naturally arises, then, is whether or not the four forces we see are truly distinct, or whether they are actually no more than different aspects of the same single force.

In the language of theoretical physics, a theory in which two different forces are seen to have an underlying identity is called a *unified field theory*. Let me give you a simple example to show how such a theory might operate: Suppose you were rolling marbles toward two holes in the ground, and that one hole had a slight hill in front of it. If you rolled the marbles slowly, some would stop on that hill and come rolling back toward you. Looking at your results, you would say that the holes were very different—the marbles fell into one but rebounded from the other. In that universe, there would be two kinds of holes.

If, however, you rolled the marbles faster, they would both be able to make it into the region of the holes, and you would see that the two systems were basically identical. The point is that you could see this underlying identity only if the marbles were moving very fast—if they had a lot of energy. At lower speeds the difference would reappear.

The situation with the underlying forces is the same. If particles collide at low energies, the forces look different. If they collide at higher energies, the apparent differences go away and the true underlying identity of the forces becomes manifest. We say that the forces become unified. Since high particle speeds occur only at high temperatures, we expect to see the forces unified early in the life of the universe, when it was very hot. In fact, as we move backward in time from the freezing of the quarks, the major changes we will see will be of this type.

So long as we are thinking about forces, we might take a moment to summarize the current thoughts on what a force is and, in the process, to introduce a new type of particle. When we talk about two particles exerting a force on each other, we do not have in mind something analogous to a collision between billiard balls, where the particles actually come into contact. The picture of the interaction that comes from our modern understanding of physics is more complex. When particles A and B come near each other, a third particle is kicked out of A, travels through the vacuum, and hits B. It is the action of this intermediary particle that changes the motion of A and B, and which we see as producing a force.

Each of the four forces has its own particle to act as intermediary—indeed, we think of the difference in the forces as arising from the differences in the exchanged particles. These force-generating particles are neither quarks nor leptons, but a third class of fundamental entities. This class can be referred to in a number of ways, the most usual being *bosons* or *gauge particles*. The former name comes from the twentieth-century Indian physicist S. N. Bose, who first investigated the general properties of this type of particle; the second refers to the fact that the types of theories that deal with the unification of forces (and hence with the process by which the bosons associated with different forces are seen to be identical) are called gauge theories. This term is something of an historical accident and has nothing to do with the early universe.

With each of the forces, then, we can associate a particle. We can think of this particle as carrying the force. The most familiar of the gauge particles is the *photon*, the particle that makes up ordinary light and other forms of electromagnetic radiation. The exchange of photons is what generates the electromagnetic force. The weak force is generated by a particle called the *intermediate vector boson*. This particle had been predicted by our theories and was seen in the laboratory for the first time in 1983. The strong force is generated by the exchange of things called *gluons* between quarks (they "glue" the quarks together). We believe that the gluons, like the quarks themselves, cannot be seen as independent particles in the laboratory. Finally, the force of gravity is associated with the exchange of a particle called the *graviton*, which has not yet been observed directly.

The idea that the four forces are actually one—or, equivalently, that all the gauge particles are really identical in spite of their apparent differences—is an old one in physics. Albert Einstein spent the latter half of his life trying unsuccessfully to show that gravity and electromagnetism were really identical, a fact that should give you some idea of the difficulty of the problem. In the

Aerial View of CERN (the European Center for Nuclear Research), with Lake Geneva and the Alps in the background. The large circle is the Super Proton Synchrotron and the small circle the Proton Synchrotron, both particle accelerators. (CERN Photo.)

late 1960's and early 1970's, theorists began to develop the modern version of the unified field theory. It turns out that this unification doesn't happen all at once; we don't suddenly find an energy at which all four forces become identical. Instead, we find that the unification takes place in a stepwise fashion, with each force joining in at a higher energy.

THE EARLIEST MOMENTS OF THE UNIVERSE

With this background, we can resume our journey back toward the moment of creation. We left off, you will recall, with the freezing of quarks into hadrons at the ten-microseconds mark. At this time, the temperatures were still low enough so that all four forces were seen as distinct and different, and so they remain until our trip takes us back to one ten-billionth of a second after the beginning. At this point, the temperatures were so high that the first unification—which turns out to be the coming together of the electromagnetic and weak forces—could occur. Before the universe was one ten-billionth of a second old, the quarks and leptons interacted with each other through the medium of only three fundamental forces. From this time on, they had the full complement of four.

It may seem strange to you that we can talk with such confidence about what happened so long ago under such unusual conditions. In point of fact, however, today we can re-create the conditions of the universe as it was when it was one ten-billionth of a second old, right here in our particle accelerators. At laboratories such as the European Center for Nuclear Research (CERN) in Geneva, Switzerland, there are machines that take two beams of protons, accelerate them to almost the speed of light, and then let them collide head-on. In some of these collisions the temperature in a volume of space about the size of a proton is raised to the levels it had when the weak and electromagnetic forces unified, and scientists can study what happens under these conditions. Consequently, we have some confidence in our ability to describe the history of the universe at least as far back as this point.

The next important milestone on our way back to the Big Bang occurs at 10^{-35} seconds. This is a time so short as to be almost incomprehensible—it is represented by a decimal point, thirty-four zeros, and then a one. At this time the second unification took place. It involved the coming together of the strong force with the newly unified electroweak force. Before 10^{-35} seconds there were two forces operating in the universe; afterward there were three.

In many ways, this particular "freezing" was the most important in the entire history of the universe. The theories that describe it are called *grand unified theories*, or GUTs. In addition to describing what happens to the forces themselves, they make some rather striking statements about what else was happening in the universe when the freezing occurred. The most important of these predicted processes is called *inflation*.

You know that when water freezes into ice, it expands. This is why bottles left outside in winter are often broken when their contents freeze. In an analogous process, the GUTs predict that when the strong forces "froze out" at 10^{-35} seconds, the universe expanded at a rate much higher than that associated with the normal Big Bang. Although the details of how the rapid expansion occurred are a little complicated, the end result is that in a very, very short time the universe expanded from something with a characteristic size (called its *radius of curvature)* smaller than that of an individual proton to something with a radius of curvature the size of a grapefruit. This rapid ballooning of the size of the universe early in its development is what is called inflation, and a universe that undergoes this process is said to be an *inflationary universe.*

The discovery of inflation solved a very old problem in cosmology. One of the features of the cosmic microwave background is that it is very uniform—no matter which way we look we see essentially the same sort of radiation coming toward us. This means that the regions of the universe that emitted the original radiation must have been at the same temperature when the radiation was emitted. But in the conventional Big Bang scenario, these regions would never have been close enough together to have established a "shared" uniform temperature. This was known, for technical reasons, as the *horizon problem.* With inflation, however, we can get around this difficulty. Before inflation occurred, the universe was much smaller than we might otherwise think, and all its parts would have been in contact with one another. Once a uniform temperature was established, it was maintained through the inflationary expansion and is seen today as the uniformity in the microwaves. This is an elegant solution to a fundamental problem, and it made scientists much more ready to accept the GUTs than they usually are when confronted with new ideas.

The GUTs also predict that quarks and leptons, hitherto thought of as separate and distinct, can actually be transformed into each other if the energies at which they collide are high enough. A quark, in other words, can become a lepton, and vice versa. To a physicist, this is equivalent to saying that the two particles are identical. This means that in the period before the GUT freezing, the universe consisted of just two sorts of particles: the quark/leptons and the gauge particles (or bosons) that are exchanged to generate the forces. In this period, there were also only two forces: the unified strong-electroweak force and gravity.

We believe that the ultimate freezing occurred at 10^{-43} seconds, at what is called the *Planck time.* (It's named after the early twentieth-century physicist Max Planck, one of the founders of our modern ideas about the behavior of the subatomic realm, the ideas we call *quantum mechanics.*) At this time, as you probably have already anticipated, the force of gravity becomes unified with the rest of the forces. Before the Planck time, there was only a single unified force operating to produce change in the universe.

The theories that describe this ultimate unification are generally referred to by the term *supersymmetry*, or SUSY. In addition to predicting the unification of gravity with the other forces, these theories indicate that at the temperatures characteristic of the birth of the universe, the two remaining classes of particles—the quark/leptons and the gauge particles—become interchangeable with each other. Consequently, they tell us that in its moment of birth, the universe was as simple as it could possibly be. There was one sort of particle interacting through a single, fully unified force. Each subsequent freezing made the universe more complex and more diverse.

The supersymmetry theories have another property that is very interesting to cosmologists. All versions of the theory predict the existence of a large number of as-yet-undiscovered elementary particles. These new particles would form a sort of mirror image of our ordinary world. For each quark, there would be a supersymmetric quark partner (dubbed, predictably, a *squark*), and so on. In some versions of the theory this mirror-image picture is carried to the extreme of imagining an entire shadow universe made of a new kind of matter, interacting with ours only through the force of gravity. But even more conventional theories suggest that one or another of the new particles predicted by the theories may have survived to the present day.

In fact, if these sorts of particles are present in great numbers, they may even exert enough of a gravitational force to affect the rate of expansion of the universe, and hence its ultimate fate. They might, in fact, be the dark matter whose existence is predicted by our observations of clusters of galaxies (and, we might add, by part of the inflationary-universe theory). In this way, the predictions of supersymmetry and the predictions of the GUTs intertwine with each other.

This, then, is our current picture of the way the universe arrived at its present state. How much confidence can we have in it? Is it dependable, or are scientists talking about GUTs and SUSYs like medieval scholars arguing about how many angels can dance on the head of a pin? As I mentioned, we can have some confidence in the story I've just told, back to the ten-billionth-of-a-second mark, simply because we are capable of reproducing the conditions of the universe at that time in our laboratories. The cosmological implications of the GUTs cannot be tested directly, since we will probably never be able to produce the temperatures that existed at 10^{-35} seconds, but we can test other predictions of these theories in the laboratory. The present verdict on the GUT is mixed: Some predictions seem to be borne out, but the most striking prediction—that the proton is not an eternally stable particle but will eventually decay—has yet to be verified. The SUSYs remain firmly in the realm of theoretical physics, with experimentalists just starting to think about finding ways to test them. Consequently, you should probably think of the description of the very early universe I've just given you as something more in the nature of a progress report than a final answer.

ALL THE HUES OF HELL

GENE WOLFE

*T*HREE WITH EGG ROLL, KYLE THOUGHT. *Soon four without—if this shadow world really has (oh, sacred!) life.* The *Egg* was still rolling, still spinning to provide mock gravitation.

Yet the roar of the sharply angled guidance jets now seeped only faintly into the hold, and the roll was slower and slower, the feeling of weight weaker and weaker.

The *Egg* was in orbit . . . around nothing.

Or at least around nothing visible. As its spin decreased, its ports swept the visible universe. Stars that were in fact galaxies flowed down the synthetic quartz, like raindrops down a canopy. Once Kyle caught sight of their mother ship; the *Shadow Show* herself looked dim and ghostly in the faint light. Of the planet they orbited, there was no trace. Polyaris screamed and took off, executing a multicolored barrel-roll with outstretched wings through the empty hold; like all macaws, Polyaris doted on microgravity.

In his earphones Marilyn asked, "Isn't it pretty, Ky?" But she was admiring her computer simulation, not his ecstatic bird: an emerald forest three hundred meters high, sparkling sapphire lakes, suddenly a vagrant strip of beach golden as her hair, and the indigo southern ocean.

One hundred and twenty degrees opposed to them both, Skip answered instead, and not as Kyle himself would have. "No, it isn't." There was a note in Skip's voice that Kyle had noticed, and worried over, before.

Marilyn seemed to shrug. "Okay, darling, it's not really anything to us— less even than ultraviolet. But—"

"I can see it," Skip told her.

Marilyn glanced across the empty hold toward Kyle.

He tried to keep his voice noncommittal as he whispered to his mike: "You can see it, Skip?"

Skip did not reply. Polyaris chuckled to herself. Then silence (the utter,

289

deadly quiet of nothingness, of the void where shadow matter ruled and writhed invisible) filled the *Egg*. For a wild instant, Kyle wondered whether silence itself might not be a manifestation of shadow matter, a dim insubstance felt only in its mass and gravity, its unseen heaviness. Galaxies drifted lazily over the ports, in a white *Egg* robbed of Up and Down. Their screens were solid sheets of deepest blue.

Skip broke the silence. "Just let me show it to you, Kyle. Allow me, Marilyn, to show you what it actually looks like."

"Because you really know, Skip?"

"Yes, because I really know, Kyle. Don't you remember, either of you, what they said?"

Kyle was watching Marilyn across the hold; he saw her shake her head. "Not all of it." Her voice was cautious. "They said so much, darling, after all. They said quite a lot of things."

Skip sounded as though he were talking to a child. "What the Life Support people said. The thing, the only *significant* thing, they did say."

Still more carefully, Marilyn asked, "And what was that, darling?"

"That one of us would die."

An island sailed across her screen, an emerald set in gold and laid upon blue velvet.

Kyle said, "That's my department, Skip. Life Support told us there was a real chance—perhaps as high as one in twenty—that one of you would die, outbound from Earth or on the trip back. They were being conservative; I would have estimated it as one in one hundred."

Marilyn murmured, "I think I'd better inform the Director."

Kyle agreed.

"And they were right," Skip said. "Kyle, I'm the one. I died on the way out. I passed away, but you two followed me."

Ocean and isle vanished from all the screens, replaced by a blinking cursor and the word DIRECTOR.

Marilyn asked, "Respiration monitor, L. Skinner Jansen."

Kyle swiveled to watch his screen. The cursor swept from side to side without any sign of inhalation or exhalation, and for a moment he was taken aback. Then Skip giggled.

Marilyn's sigh filled Kyle's receptors. "The programming wizard. What did you do, Skip? Turn down the gain?"

"That wasn't necessary. It happens automatically." Skip giggled again.

Kyle said slowly, "You're not dead, Skip. Believe me, I've seen many dead men. I've cut up their bodies and examined every organ; I know dead men, and you're not one of them."

"Back on the ship, Kyle. My former physical self is lying in the *Shadow Show*, dead."

Marilyn said, "Your physical self is right here, darling, with Ky and me."

And then to the Director: "Sir, is L. Skinner Jansen's module occupied?"

The trace vanished, replaced by NEGATIVE: JANSEN 1'S MODULE IS EMPTY.

"Console," Skip himself ordered.

Kyle did not turn to watch Skip's fingers fly across the keys.

After a moment Skip said, "You see, this place—the formal name of our great republic is Hades, by the way—looks the way it does only because of the color gradations you assigned the gravimeter data. I'm about to show you its true colors, as the expression has it."

A blaze of 4.5, 6, and 7.8 ten-thousandths millimeter light, Polyaris fluttered away to watch Skip. When he made no attempt to shoo her off, she perched on a red emergency lever and cocked an eye like a bright black button toward his keyboard.

Kyle turned his attention back to his screen. The letters faded, leaving only the blue southern ocean. As he watched, it darkened to sable. Tiny flames of ocher, citron, and cinnabar darted from the crests of the waves.

"See what I mean?" Skip asked. "We've been sent to bring a demon back to Earth—or maybe just a damned soul. I don't care. I'm going to stay right here."

Kyle looked across the vacant white hold toward Marilyn.

"I can't," she whispered. "I just can't, Ky. You do it."

"All right, Marilyn." He plugged his index finger into the Exchange socket, so that he sensed rather than saw the letters overlaying the hellish sea on the screens: KAPPA UPSILON LAMBDA 23011 REPORTS JANSEN 1 PSYCHOTIC. CAN YOU CONFIRM, JANSEN 2?

"Confirmed, Marilyn Jansen."

RESTRAINT ADVISED.

Marilyn said, "I'm afraid restraint's impossible as long as we're in the *Egg*, sir."

DO NOT ABORT YOUR MISSION, JANSEN 2. WILL YOU ACCEPT THE RESTRAINT OF JANSEN 1 WHEN RESTRAINT IS PRACTICAL?

"Accepted whenever practical," Marilyn said. "Meanwhile, we'll proceed with the mission."

SATISFACTORY, the Director said, and signed off.

Skip asked, "So you're going to lock me up, honeybone?"

"I hope that by the time we get back it won't be necessary. Ky, haven't you anything to give him?"

"No specifics for psychosis, Marilyn. Not here. I've got some back on the *Shadow Show*."

Skip ruffled his beard. "Sure. You're going to lock up a ghost." Across the wide hold, Kyle could see he was grinning.

Polyaris picked up the word: "Ghost! *Ghost! Ghost!*" She flapped to the vacant center of the *Egg*, posing like a heraldic eagle and watching to make certain they admired her.

The shoreline of a larger island entered their screens from the right. Its beach was ashes and embers, its forest a forest of flames.

"If we're going to make the grab, Marilyn . . ."

"You're right," she said. Courageously, she straightened her shoulders. The new life within her had already fleshed out her cheeks and swollen her breasts; Kyle felt sure she had never been quite so lovely before. When she put on her helmet, he breathed her name (though only to himself) before he plugged into the simulation that seemed so much more real than a screen.

As a score of pink arms, Marilyn's grav beams dipped into the shadow planet's atmosphere, growing dark and heavy as they pulled up shadow fluid and gases from a lake on the island and whatever winds might ruffle it. Kyle reflected that those arms should be blue instead of black, and told the onboard assistant director to revert to the hues Marilyn had originally programmed.

Rej, the assistant director snapped.

And nothing happened. The gravs grew darker still, and the big accelerator jets grumbled at the effort required to maintain *Egg* in orbit. When Kyle glanced toward the hold, he discovered it had acquired a twelve-meter yolk as dark as the eggs Chinese bury for centuries. Polyaris was presumably somewhere in that black yolk, unable to see or feel it. He gave a shrill whistle, and she screamed and fluttered out to perch on his shoulder.

The inky simulation doubled and redoubled, swirling to the turbulence of the fresh shadow matter pumped into the *Egg* by the gravs. Generators sang the spell that kept the shadow "air" and "water" from boiling away in what was to them a high vacuum.

The grumbling of the jets rose to an angry roar.

Skip said, "You've brought Hell in here with us, honeybone. You, not me. Remember that."

Marilyn ignored him, and Kyle told him to keep quiet.

Abruptly the gravitors winked out. A hundred tons or more of the shadow-world's water (whatever that might be) fell back to the surface, fully actual to any conscious entity that might be there. "Rains of frogs and fish, Polyaris," Kyle muttered to his bird. "Remember Charlie Fort?"

Polyaris chuckled, nodding.

Skip said, "Then remember too that when Moses struck the Nile with his staff, the Lord God turned the water to blood."

"You're the one who got into the crayon box, Skip. I'll call you Moses if you like, but I can hardly call you 'I Am,' after you've just assured us you're not." Kyle was following Marilyn's hunt for an example of the dominant life form, less than a tenth of his capacity devoted to Polyaris and Skip.

"You will call me *Master!*"

Kyle grinned, remembering the holovamp of an ancient film. "No, Skip. For as long as you're ill, I am the master. Do you know I've been waiting half my life to use that line?"

Then he saw it, three quarters of a second, perhaps, after Marilyn had: an upright figure striding down a fiery beach. Its bipedal locomotion was not a complete guarantee of dominance and intelligence, to be sure; ostriches had never ruled a world and never would, no matter how big a pest they became on Mars. But—yes—those powerful forelimbs were surely GP manipulators and not mere weapons. *Now, Marilyn! Now!*

As though she had heard him, a pink arm flicked down. For an instant the shadow man floated, struggling wildly to escape, the gravitation of his shadow world countered by their gravitor; then he flashed toward them. Kyle swiveled to watch the black sphere splash (there could be no other word for it) and, under the prodding of the gravs, recoalesce. They were four.

In a moment more, their shadow man bobbed to the surface of the dark and still-trembling yolk. To him, Kyle reflected, they were not there; the *Egg* was not there. To him it must seem that he floated upon a watery sphere suspended in space.

And possibly that was more real than the computer-enhanced vision he himself inhabited, a mere cartoon created from one of the weakest forces known to physics. He unplugged, and at once the *Egg*'s hold was white and empty again.

Marilyn took off her helmet. "All right, Ky, from here on it's up to you—unless you want something more from the surface?"

Kyle congratulated her and shook his head.

"Darling, are you feeling any better?"

Skip said levelly, "I'm okay now. I think that damned machine must have drugged me."

"Ky? That seems pretty unlikely."

"We should de-energize or destroy him, if we can't revise his programming."

Marilyn shook her head. "I doubt that we could reprogram him. Ky, what do you think?"

"A lot of it's hard-wired, Marilyn, and can't be altered without new boards. I imagine Skip could revise my software if he put his mind to it, though it might take him quite a while. He's very good at that sort of thing."

Skip said, "And you're a very dangerous device, Kyle."

Shaking his head, Kyle broke out the pencil-thin cable he had used so often in training exercises. One end jacked into the console, the other into a small socket just above his hips. When both connections were made, he was again in the cybernetic cartoon where true matter and shadow matter looked equally real.

It was still a cartoon with colors by Skip: Marilyn's skin shone snow-white, her lips were burning scarlet, her hair like burnished brass, and her eyes blue fire; Skip himself had become a black-bearded satyr, with a terra-cotta complexion and cruel crimson lips. Kyle tightened both ferrules firmly, tested his jets, released his safety harness, and launched himself toward the center of the *Egg*, making Polyaris crow with delight.

The shadow man drifted into view as they neared the black yolk. He was lying upon what Kyle decided must be his back; on the whole he was oddly anthropomorphic, with recognizable head, neck, and shoulders. Binocular organs of vision seemed to have vanished behind small folds of skin, and Kyle would have called his respiration rapid in a human.

Marilyn asked, "How does he look, Ky?"

"Like hell," Kyle muttered. "I'm afraid he may be in shock. At least, shock's what I'd say if he were one of you. As it is, I . . ." He let the sentence trail away.

There were strange, blunt projections just above the organs that appeared to be the shadow man's ears. Absently, Kyle tried to palpate them; his hand met nothing, and vanished as it passed into the shadow man's cranium.

The shadow man opened his eyes.

Kyle jerked backward, succeeding only in throwing himself into a slow spin that twisted his cable.

Marilyn called, "What's the matter, Ky?"

"Nothing," Kyle told her. "I'm jumpy, that's all."

The shadow man's eyes were closed again. His arms, longer than a human's and more muscled than a body builder's, twitched and were still. Kyle began the minute examination required by the plan.

When it was complete, Skip asked, "How'd it go, Kyle?"

He shrugged. "I couldn't see his back. The way you've got the shadow water keyed, it's like ink."

Marilyn said, "Why don't you change it, Skip? Make it blue but translucent, the way it's supposed to be."

Skip sounded apologetic. "I've been trying to; I've been trying to change everything back. I can't, or anyway not yet. I don't remember just what I did, but I put some kind of block on it."

Kyle shrugged again. "Keep trying, Skip, please."

"Yes, please try, darling. Now buckle up, everybody. Time to rendezvous."

Kyle disconnected his cable and pulled his harness around him. After a moment's indecision, he plugged into the console as well.

If he had been unable to see it, it would have been easy to believe that *Egg*'s acceleration had no effect on the fifty-meter sphere of dark matter at its center; yet that too was mass, and the gravs whimpered like children at the strain of changing its speed and direction, their high wail audible—to Kyle at least—above the roaring of the jets. The black sphere stretched into a sooty tear. Acceleration was agony for Polyaris as well; Kyle cupped her fragile body in his free hand to ease her misery as much as he could.

Somewhere so far above the *Egg* that the gravity well of the shadow planet had almost ceased to make any difference and words like *above* held little meaning, the *Shadow Show* was unfolding to receive them, preparing itself to

KIKUO HAYASHI

embed the newly fertilized *Egg* in an inner wall. For a moment Kyle's thoughts soared, drunk on the beauty of the image.

Abruptly the big jets fell silent. The *Egg* had achieved escape velocity.

Marilyn returned control of *Egg* to the assistant director. "That's it, folks, until we start guiding in. Unbuckle if you want."

Kyle tossed Polyaris toward the yolk and watched her make a happy circuit of the *Egg*'s interior.

Skip said, "Marilyn, I seem to have a little problem here."

"What is it?"

Kyle took off his harness and retracted it. He unplugged, and the yolk and its shadow man were gone. Only the chortling Polyaris remained.

"I can't get this Goddamned thing off," Skip complained. "The buckle's jammed or something."

Marilyn took off her own acceleration harness and sailed across to look at it. Kyle joined them.

"Here, let me try it," Marilyn said. Her slender fingers, less nimble but more deft than Skip's, pressed the release and jiggled the locking tab; it would not pull free.

Kyle murmured, "I'm afraid you can't release Skip, Marilyn. Neither can I."

She turned to look at him.

"You accepted restraint for Skip, Marilyn. I want to say that in my opinion you were correct to do so."

She began, "You mean—"

"The Director isn't satisfied yet that Skip has recovered, that's all. Real recoveries aren't usually so quick or so . . ." Kyle paused, searching his dictionary file for the best word. "Convenient. This may be no more than a lucid interval. That happens, quite often. It may be no more than a stratagem."

Skip cursed and tore at the straps.

"Do you mean you can lock us . . . ?"

"No," Kyle said. "I can't. But the Director can, if in his judgment it is indicated."

He waited for Marilyn to speak, but she did not.

"You see, Marilyn, Skip, we tried very hard to prepare for every foreseeable eventuality, and mental illness was certainly one of those. About ten percent of the human population suffers from it at some point in their lives, and so with both of you on board and under a great deal of stress, that sort of problem was certainly something we had to be ready for."

Marilyn looked pale and drained. Kyle added, as gently as he could, "I hope this hasn't been too much of a shock to you."

Skip had opened the cutting blade of his utility knife and was hacking futilely at his straps. Kyle took it from him, closed it, and dropped it into one of his own storage areas.

Marilyn pushed off. He watched her as she flew gracefully across the hold, caught the pilot's-chair grab bar, and buckled herself into the seat; her eyes were shining with tears. As if sensing her distress, Polyaris perched on the bar and rubbed her ear with the side of her feathered head.

Skip muttered, "Go look at your demon, Kyle. Go anyplace but here."

Kyle asked, "Do you still think it's a demon, Skip?"

"You've seen it a lot closer up than I have. What do you think?"

"I don't believe in demons, Skip."

Skip looked calm now, but his fingers picked mechanically at his straps. "What *do* you believe in, Kyle? Do you believe in God? Do you worship Man?"

"I believe in life. Life is my God, Skip, if you want to put it like that."

"Any life? What about a mosquito?"

"Yes, any life. The mosquito won't bite me." Kyle smiled his metal smile.

"Mosquitoes spread disease."

"Sometimes," Kyle admitted. "Then they must be destroyed, the lower life sacrificed to the higher. Skip, your Marilyn is especially sacred to me now. Do you understand that?"

"Marilyn's doomed."

"Why do you say that?"

"Because of the demon, of course. I tried to tell her that she had doomed herself, but it was actually you that doomed her. You were the one who wanted him. You had to have him, you and the Director; and if it hadn't been for you, we could have gone home with a hold full of dark matter and some excuse."

"But you aren't doomed, Skip? Only Marilyn?"

"I'm dead and damned, Kyle. My doom has caught up with me. I've hit bottom. You know that expression?"

Kyle nodded.

"People talk about hitting bottom and bouncing back up. If you can bounce, that isn't the bottom. When somebody gets where I am, there's no bouncing back, not ever."

"If you're really dead, Skip, how can the straps hold you? I wouldn't think that an acceleration harness could hold a lost soul, or even a ghost."

"They're not holding me," Skip told him. "It was just that at the last moment I didn't have guts enough to let Marilyn see I was really gone. I'd loved her. I don't anymore—you can't love anything or anyone except yourself where I am. But—"

"Can you get out of your seat, Skip? Is that what you're saying, that you can get out without unfastening the buckle?"

Skip nodded slowly, his dark eyes (inscrutable eyes, Kyle thought) never leaving Kyle's face. "And I can see your demon, Kyle. I know you can't see him because you're not hooked up. But I can."

"You can see him now, Skip?"

"Not now—he's on the far side of the black ball. But I'll be able to see him when he floats around to this side again."

Kyle returned to his seat and connected the cable as he had before. The black yolk sprang into being again; the shadow man was facing him—in fact glaring at him with burning yellow eyes. He asked the Director to release Skip.

Together they drifted toward the center of the *Egg*. Kyle made sure their trajectory carried them to the side of the yolk away from the shadow man; and when the shadow man was no longer in view, he held Skip's arm and stopped them both with a tug at the cable. "Now that I know you can see him, too, Skip, I'd like you to point him out to me."

Skip glanced toward the watery miniature planet over which they hovered like flies—or perhaps merely toward the center of the hold. "Is this a joke? I've told you, I can see him." A joyous blue and yellow comet, Polyaris erupted from the midnight surface, braking on flapping wings to examine them sidelong.

"That's why I need your input, Skip," Kyle said carefully. "I'm not certain the feed I'm getting is accurate. If you can apprehend shadow matter directly, I can use your information to check the simulation. Can you still see the demon? Indicate his position, please."

Skip hesitated. "He's not here, Kyle. He must be on the other side. Shall we go around and have a look?"

"The water's still swirling quite a bit. It should bring him to us before long."

Skip shrugged. "Okay, Kyle, you're the boss. I guess you always were."

"The Director's our captain, Skip. That's why we call him what we do. Can you see the demon yet?" A hand and part of one arm had floated into view around the curve of the yolk.

"No. Not yet. Do you have a soul, Kyle?"

Kyle nodded. "It's called my original monitor. I've seen a printout, though of course I didn't read it all; it was very long."

"Then when you're destroyed it may be sent here. Here comes your demon, by the way."

Kyle nodded.

"I suppose it may be put into one of these horrors. They seem more machine than human, at least to me."

"No," Kyle told him. "They're truly alive. They're shadow life, Skip, and since this one is the only example we have, just now it must be the most precious life in the universe to you, to Marilyn, and to me. Do you think he sees us?"

"He sees me," Skip said grimly.

"When I put my fingers into his brain, he opened his eyes," Kyle mused. "It was as though he felt them there."

"Maybe he did."

Kyle nodded. "Yes, possibly he did. The brain is such a sensitive mechanism that perhaps a gravitational disturbance as weak as that results in stimulation, if it is uneven. Put your hand into his head, please. I want to watch. You say he's a demon—pretend you're going to gouge out his eyes."

"You think I'm crazy!" Skip shouted. "Well, I'm telling you, you're crazy!"

Startled, Marilyn twisted in her pilot's chair to look at them.

"I've explained to you that he *sees* me," Skip said a little more calmly. "I'm not getting within his reach!"

"Touch his nose for me, Skip. Like this." Kyle lengthened one arm until his fingers seemed to brush the dark water several meters from the drifting shadow man's hideous face. "Look here, Skip. I'm not afraid."

Skip screamed.

"Have I time?" Kyle asked. He was holding the grab bar of Marilyn's control chair. In the forward port, the *Shadow Show* was distinctly visible.

"We've a few minutes yet," Marilyn told him. "And I want to know. I have to, Ky. He's the father of my child. Can you cure him?"

"I think so, Marilyn, though your correcting the simulator hues has probably helped Skip more than anything I've done thus far."

Kyle glanced appreciatively in the direction of the yolk. It was a translucent blue, as it should have been all along, and the shadow man who floated there looked more like a good-natured caricature of a human being than a demon. His skin was a dusty pinkish brown, his eyes the cheerful bright-yellow of daffodils. It seemed to Kyle that they flickered for a moment, as though to follow Polyaris in her flight across the hold. Perhaps a living entity of shadow matter could apprehend true matter after all—that would require a thorough investigation as soon as they were safely moored in the *Shadow Show.*

"And he can't really see shadow matter, Ky?"

Kyle shook his head. "No more than you or I can, Marilyn. He thought he could, you understand, at least on some level. On another he knew he couldn't and was faking it quite cleverly." Kyle paused, then added, "Freud did psychology a considerable disservice when he convinced people that the human mind thinks on only three levels. There are really a great many more than that, and there's no question but that the exact number varies between individuals."

"But for a while you really believed he might be able to, from what you've told me."

"At least I was willing to entertain the thought, Marilyn. Occasionally you can help people like Skip just by allowing them to test their delusional systems. What I found was that he had been taking cues from me—mostly from the direction of my eyes, no doubt. It would be wrong for you to think of that as lying. He honestly believed that when you human beings died, your souls came here, to this shadow planet of a shadow system, in a shadow galaxy. And that he himself was dead."

Marilyn shook her head in dismay. "But that's insane, Ky. Just crazy."

She has never looked this lovely, Kyle thought. Aloud he said, "Mental illness is often a way of escaping responsibility, Marilyn. You may wish to consider that. Death is another, and you may wish to consider that also."

For a second Marilyn hesitated, biting her lip. "You love me, don't you, Ky?"

"Yes, I do, Marilyn. Very much."

"And so does Skip, Ky." She gave him a small, sad smile. "I suppose I'm the luckiest woman alive, or the unluckiest. The men I like most both love me, but one's having a breakdown. . . . I shouldn't have started this, should I?"

"While the other is largely inorganic," Kyle finished for her. "But it's really not such a terrible thing to be loved by someone like me, Marilyn. We—"

Polyaris shrieked and shrieked again—not her shrill cry of pleasure or even her outraged squawk of pain, but the uncanny, piercing screech that signaled a prowling ocelot: Danger! *Fire!* Flood! INVASION and *CATASTROPHE!*

She was fluttering about the shadow man, and the shadow man was no longer a dusty pinkish brown. As Kyle stared, he faded to gray, then to white. His mouth opened. He crumpled, slowly and convulsively, into a fetal ball.

Horrified, Kyle turned to Marilyn. But Marilyn was self-absorbed, her hands clasping her belly. "It moved, Ky! It just moved. *I felt life!*"

OTHER PLANETS, OTHER LIFE

ESSAY BY
DONALD GOLDSMITH

SPECULATION BY
FREDERIK POHL

WHO WILL SPEAK FOR EARTH? AN ESSAY ON EXTRATERRESTRIAL INTELLIGENCE AND CONTACT

DONALD GOLDSMITH

During the past centuries, as humanity has gradually come to recognize that we inhabit only a single planet orbiting a roughly average star in a giant galaxy made of hundreds of billions of stars, the thought that we might find fellow sentient beings has exerted a powerful fascination on those who think about this possibility. When most of us consider communication with life beyond the Earth, we encounter a serious obstacle, one that is intimately related to our relatively recent discovery of the facts of life in the universe.

That obstacle is Earth-centeredness, the emotional refusal to admit the isolation (and, in simple-minded terms, the insignificance) that the vast distances of space impose upon us. Our hearts and our cultural mythology (to say nothing of most science fiction) speak against such loneliness, and tell us that if the universe is indeed inhabited by other beings, then a chief element in their desires will be the wish to inspect, admire, entertain, enslave, or devour us. But when we examine the cosmos as it is, rather than as we imagine it or hope it will be, science has some important lessons to teach us. The immense cosmic distances described in earlier chapters certainly permit a vast array of potential worlds in our Galaxy (let alone in other galaxies). The universe therefore clearly contains an abundance of potential sites where forms of "intelligent" life might appear. But this same vastness also implies that in a galaxy sprinkled with stars that are, on the average, several light-years apart, even our closest neighbor civilizations are likely to be extremely distant, with a few dozen light-years a highly optimistic estimate and a few thousand light-years a conservative one.

Faced with these enormous distances, most of us react by noting the impossibility that *we* could travel so far, but then compensate for the pain of separation by instinctively reassuring ourselves that *other* civilizations surely have technological abilities so far superior to ours that they could traverse the light-years with ease. Indeed, no doubt exists that our own technology has developed enormously and at great speed, and that far greater technological advances lie in our future. But the results of modern physics have shown us that there are limits in the universe—not limits to technology, but more fundamental limits deriving from the basic workings of the universe. Even if it turns out that some of these limits may be modified as our understanding of nature becomes more sophisticated, for now there is no evidence at all that these limits can be breached, and we must take them at face value. Of these limits, two are paramount: (1) You can't travel faster than light; (2) there is no such thing as a free lunch.

Point 1 means that if you are four light-years (as we are) from the star Alpha Centauri (the Sun's closest neighbor), then there is no way that any being, artifact, or message can travel from there to here, or from here to there, in less than four years. If you know Einstein's theory of relativity, you know that it is true that if you send an astronaut from here to Alpha Centauri in a rocket that travels at, say, 99.6 percent of the speed of light, then she will record the length of her journey—mentally, biologically, and every other way—as taking only four months. That may be fine for the astronaut, but those who finance the trip on Earth will have aged four years during her voyage, and must wait a full eight years for her to return with any news, or for any signal to arrive from her investigation of Alpha Centauri.

Point 2 means that to send the astronaut to Alpha Centauri costs a bundle. We now use various currencies to measure costs on Earth; in the future, these might be expressed in units of energy. How much would it cost to send an astronaut to Alpha Centauri in a perfectly efficient spaceship, not at 99.6 percent of the speed of light but at merely 0.1 percent of that speed? Bear in mind that 0.1 percent of the speed of light exceeds 1 million kilometers per hour, and that an astronaut needs fuel to reach that speed after leaving the Earth, to slow down at Alpha Centauri, to accelerate upon departure for home, and to decelerate upon return. The cost turns out to be several years' worth of the *total* U.S. energy consumption, a staggering figure that even Congressional committees would have trouble appropriating. Although we or another civilization may find ways to make space travel much cheaper than it is for us now, calculations reveal that even low-speed travel will probably always be incredibly expensive in energy terms, and high-speed travel (close to the speed of light) will likely remain prohibitively expensive.

Furthermore, a better way to make contact with other civilizations exists: Send a message by photons—massless packets of energy in electromagnetic waves—which are cheap, fast, and reliable. Communication, not corporeal contact, is what we fundamentally seek (although, once again drawing on a rich human tradition of Earth-centeredness, many of us feel emotionally that if you can't press the flesh, you're not making real contact). If other civilizations have adopted the view that only personal visits are worth the effort, we may be left to molder in the dark, since the physics that we know implies that space travel will be so difficult as to be extremely rare. But if other civilizations know the physics that we do (and often more), logic will dictate that they establish mutual contact, at least at first, through electromagnetic waves. This is not an easy pill to swallow; every report of the landing of an alleged extraterrestrial spacecraft testifies to the fact that we cherish a visit and don't regard a message as an adequate emotional substitute.

Scientists who regard themselves as active in SETI (the search for extraterrestrial intelligence) agree, with a near unanimity that is rare in science, that the best way to engage in SETI is with photons, the particles that form all types of electromagnetic radiation, such as light, radio, X-rays, and gamma rays. In this conclusion they are merely seconding what society on Earth already "knows": Radio and television broadcasts are the most efficient way to reach a large audience, even over the relatively tiny distances that separate people on our planet. For larger distances, the advantages of photons increase accordingly.

SETI scientists therefore have the following message for Earth: If you want to find the closest galactic neighbors with whom we might communicate, first assume that they have reached *at least* our level of technological ability. (Civilizations less developed than ourselves, either through choice or because their evolution has not brought them technology, will remain undetected for the time being.) Then use *our* best means to listen for, and to broadcast if we choose, signals sent between civilizations, or perhaps just signals leaked from a civilization accidentally, as we leak part of all our television, radar, and FM transmissions into space.

At first glance this advice may appear just as Earth-centered as any fantasy of "E.T.'s" landing to check us out. And in one sense it is: The advice presupposes that the evolution of life forms in the universe leads through something like our technological stage—that is, through a world whose communications are dominated by photon-borne messages. We have no way to be sure that this is so, but we may note that the hypothesis above is one of Earth-*averageness*, not Earth-centeredness. The hypothesis requires that our history as a society has been at least roughly encompassed by a sizable fraction of all other civilizations. Most of these have progressed to some stage far more advanced than anything we can imagine, and might use some superior means of communication (whimsically called *zeta waves* by SETI scientists) of which we are absolutely ignorant. However, if we simply sit on our assets waiting for the day that *we* discover zeta waves, our prospects for interstellar communication are highly limited in the near term. Furthermore, if the typical technological development pattern passes *through* radio on the way to zeta waves, then any civilization that now has zeta waves can, if it chooses, contact those less advanced civilizations who still know only radio. As Carl Sagan has noted, they will "wheel the old radiotelescopes out of the museums" if they seek to speak to their underdeveloped neighbors.

Of course, we can't be sure of anything that a far more technologically advanced civilization might have on its mind—such as, for example, whether the whole notion of contacting "backward civilizations" might be a total bore, or be left for high-school science projects and occasional masters' theses on anthropology. Some scientists have speculated that if highly advanced civilizations have come to exist in the Milky Way, at least some of them will want to lord it over the entire galaxy. Hence the fact that we remain free from extraterrestrial dominance (or so most of us believe) shows that civilizations must be extremely rare—otherwise at least one of them would have succeeded in colonizing the galaxy, and with it our planet, Quork 484. In my opinion, these speculations suffer from a scientifically rationalized form of Earth-centeredness. I believe that it is logically impossible to draw a conclusion that rests on how a civilization sufficiently advanced to colonize a galaxy would behave, since any such conclusion imposes our cultural attitudes on a highly different (to put it mildly) situation.

This may or may not be high-class reasoning. I do feel safe in asserting that civilizations more like ourselves in technological development are more likely to establish contact with us than those less like ourselves. This might imply that we should expect to make contact first with a civilization not greatly in advance of our own, rather than stumbling upon a veritable Athens of the Milky Way. Unfortunately, we have no way of knowing the relative numbers of Earthlike and far more advanced civilizations. Lacking the relative abundances of these two vague categories, my assertion, although eminently reasonable, has no chance of being proven correct until we *do* establish contact.

For contact will, I believe, almost surely occur; the question is when, and how. Ever since Stanley Miller and Harold Urey, more than thirty years ago, produced amino acids in a flask that contained nothing more than a simple mixture of the most abundant elements in the universe, scientists have accepted the likelihood that complex organic molecules can easily form throughout the cosmos. Amino acids have also been found in certain kinds of meteorites—the "carbonaceous chondrites," chunks of rock that fell to Earth from space and are thought to be the oldest and least altered material from the primitive solar system. Though it's a long step from amino acids to life, the general belief is that given "world enough and time," life is likely to arise naturally where its building blocks are abundant.

Worlds enough there seem to be. Astronomers have recently detected material around relatively nearby stars that is apparently in the process of forming planets. Most astronomers, recognizing that the Sun is an average star, believe that many, if not most, stars have planetary systems like the Sun's.

In our own solar system, the search for life has recorded one hit (Earth) and three long foul balls (which may yet go fair): Mars, Europa, and Titan. Mars seems to have conditions close to those capable of supporting life, and in eras billions of years ago, when water ran in Martian channels, may well have had flourishing life. Europa, one of Jupiter's four large satellites, has a frozen crust that some scientists speculate may conceal a worldwide ocean where molecules float and interact, potentially forming more complex compounds. Titan, the largest of Saturn's moons, has a smoggy, nitrogen-rich atmosphere that perpetually shrouds the moon's surface. This smog conceals from our view conditions thought to be similar to—but much colder than—those on the primitive Earth, 4.5 billion years ago. An ethane-methane ocean may exist on Titan, and might even prove to be the home of primitive organisms—if and when we "land" there.

Exploration of the solar system, difficult and time-consuming, highlights the fact that it's a long way to the stars. Alpha Centauri is 50,000 times farther from us than Jupiter, so the *Voyager* spacecraft, which took about two years to reach Jupiter and its moons, would require 100,000 years to travel to Alpha Centauri. It is these immense interstellar distances that make UFO reports so highly unlikely to be evidence of interstellar spacecraft! I discount all UFO reports as evidence of extraterrestrial visitors on the grounds of our knowledge of (1) the difficulty of interstellar travel; (2) how unusual a suggestive UFO sighting is, and the difficulty that humans have in recording unusual events correctly; and (3) most of all, the lack of anything other than personal accounts rather than hard evidence. Most UFO reports appear to refer to natural phenomena, and the ones that don't are the least reliable. (Those interested in the subject of UFOs should consult a marvelous book by Philip Klass, *UFOs Explained.*) On a still more basic level, my desire (shared by many, I believe) is for *contact* with another civilization. Alleged extraterrestrial spacecraft that merely fly over or even kidnap an occasional human for inspection without leaving any information are not making contact in my book—not when the television networks would be glad to give them a special program, possibly even without commercials. Hence, I find UFO reports unconvincing twice over, once because they don't appear to represent extraterrestrial spacecraft, and also because even if I strain to believe that they might, they represent the "silent intruders" (a variant of the Earth-centered bogeymen) who have nothing to say to us (and, being far more advanced than we, are sure to escape further investigation).

The first UFO report that I will take seriously is the report that we have detected an extraterrestrial *signal*. This is so because I know that to send a

Top: The *Voyager* spacecraft record containing the sights and sounds of Earth. (Courtesy JPL)
Bottom: The record mounted on the *Voyager 1* spacecraft, which traveled past Jupiter and Saturn before beginning its long journey into interstellar space. Pictorial instructions for playing the record are shown on its case. (NASA photo.)

ten-minute television program to Alpha Centauri, to arrive with a signal strength that our technology could capture, would cost a few thousand dollars. To send such a program not four light-years but a thousand light-years, again with an intensity level accessible to a civilization like ours, would cost a few *hundred* thousand dollars. And this is a conservative estimate—it might even cover modest salaries for the stars of the program. This is so much less than the cost of any expedition that it should appeal to any civilization that does not have unlimited resources.

Which brings me to the key point that now deserves serious attention: *Who* will speak for Earth? Until contact is established, SETI efforts must concentrate on detection, not broadcasting. Detection promises results *now*; broadcasting is "bread on the waters" for an unknown wait. (If you think that we are in deep trouble if all civilizations share this attitude, remember that we continuously "broadcast" radio signals through the radio, television, and military radar photons that leak into space.) The big news from the SETI front is that we *are* beginning to concentrate on listening. During the past few years, quietly but firmly, SETI has evolved from a subject of nearly pure speculation and no action into an ongoing research effort, one with modest beginnings but a plan for tremendous improvement. The change is apparent within the scientific community, where SETI is no longer a figure of fun. A full-time SETI listening project has been under way since September 1985 and NASA is planning to have a far more potent system on the air sometime during the mid-1990's.

One key difficulty in any search for artificial signals from another civilization is that we can't know much about their messages. Not only do we not know the direction in the sky from which the message might arrive; we also don't know which frequency they are using to broadcast, or what form their messages take. After examining all the different types of photons that we might use for communication, and all the types of photons that the universe emits naturally (which might interfere with, or completely hide, an artificial message), most SETI scientists have concluded that the most likely band of the photon spectrum for interstellar messages is *radio*, and especially the part of the radio spectrum between the frequencies of about 1,000 to 10,000 megahertz (1 billion to 10 billion cycles per second). But this conclusion still leaves a huge number of channels to search, since we cannot expect that a particular alien civilization will broadcast on channel 9, or at 104.2 megahertz on the FM dial. Using our knowledge of how passage through interstellar space affects radio signals, SETI researchers estimate that in order to search the frequency band between 1,000 and 10,000 megahertz, we may need to search as many as *100 billion* different frequency channels. Until recently this would have represented an impossible task, but with modern computer technology, such a search is merely extremely difficult, though by no means impossible.

The SETI listening project that now functions full time is META, the Mega

(Million)-channel ExtraTerrestrial Assay, a receiver and computer system capable of analyzing 8.4 million different frequency channels simultaneously. META is connected to the business end of a refurbished 25-meter radio antenna at Oak Ridge, Massachusetts. The man behind META, Professor Paul Horowitz, deliberately designed the receiver system to concentrate on the frequency band close to 1,420 megahertz (1,420 million cycles per second), the "home frequency" of the cosmos, the frequency at which hydrogen atoms, the most abundant type of atom in the universe, naturally radiate. META will "work" if other civilizations, recognizing the universal nature of this frequency, choose to broadcast signals close by this "magic" frequency. (At precisely this frequency, the natural radio emission from hydrogen atoms that marks 1,420 megahertz likewise swamps all but the most intense artificial signals.) During the course of a year or so, the META system sweeps over the entire sky visible from Oak Ridge, listening to 8.2 million different frequencies as it does so. If the search yields no detection of an artificial signal, the META scientists can try again at twice the "magic" frequency, or half this value.

But the basic assumption behind the META system may miss the mark: Other civilizations may well be trying to find their neighbors or be leaking radio waves, but they may simply not be broadcasting at what we might recognize as a "magic" frequency. The projected system of detectors and signal analyzers that NASA plans to build will be able to span the entire range of radio frequencies that appear to be favored for interstellar communication, from about 1,000 to 10,000 megahertz. The NASA detectors will be attached to existing radiotelescopes in both the Northern and the Southern Hemispheres, making the entire sky available for inspection.

The META system may not succeed; the NASA system may not succeed. Even if they don't, to me they seem supremely worth the effort (and the modest cost—about $100 million over a decade or so for the full planned NASA search). On the other hand, I believe that sooner or later such a search is likely to find a clearly artificial signal. When that happens, in my opinion it will already be too late to have a reasoned discussion concerning the reply that we might make. There is a paranoid strain that enters here, suggesting that one country might detect a signal but keep it secret (presumably from its own population as well) for its military or social value. Putting aside such issues as the true worth of such a secret, and the enjoyable speculation that this plan is already in operation (which would explain much of politicians' behavior during the past few years), I submit that no such secret could be kept for more than a few days. This brings us back to the question of what we, as a planet, might plan *now* to do about such a signal.

Through one of the ironies for which society is famous, it seems clear to me that if scientists wait to be consulted until the signal is detected, they won't be taken seriously then: The matter will seem too important to consult an expert. On the other hand, if the scientific community were to engage in debate today over the appropriate reply to an extraterrestrial message, they will most likely be laughed at. But when the moment arrives, the existence of a model message prepared by the world's scientists could provide the focus for worldwide discussions and would remind us that it is a planet, not a political subset of its population, that has established contact with another civilization.

I have proposed that the International Astronomical Union and the International Astronomical Federation create a committee to encourage the process of formulating a reply to an artificial extraterrestrial signal. This committee would raise interest within the community of scientists and scholars, who in turn might succeed in awakening interest among the general public. If not, the proposed message or messages would nonetheless make a key step toward producing a consensus, prior to the detection of a signal, as to what Earth's reply should contain. I am not so optimistic as to believe that general agreement would arise among scientists, let alone in the public at large. On the other hand, I *am* optimistic that to awaken debate over the contents of our reply— even at the price of derisory mention among those who find all of SETI a worthless endeavor—will prove beneficial. We may not establish contact in our lifetimes, and discussion of our reply may therefore prove highly premature. Nevertheless, it can't hurt to be ready.

What should Earth say to the cosmos? Since my goal is to produce consensus, I won't make any specific suggestions, but I can note the precursor of a reply message and our present abilities in sending information. In 1974, to celebrate the upgrading of the surface of the 300-meter radio antenna in Arecibo, Puerto Rico (the largest radio dish on Earth), scientists used the antenna in the reverse sense to broadcast an interstellar message in the direction of the globular star cluster M13 in the constellation Hercules, 25,000 light-years from Earth. The message was broadcast at a frequency of 2,380 megahertz (note that this is not particularly close to the "magic" frequency of 1,420 megahertz) and contained 1,679 "bits" of information; each "bit" consisted of a single item, in this case whether a frequency channel was "on" or "off"—that is, whether the transmitter was or was not broadcasting at that frequency at a particular moment. The message was repeated a few times and lasted for a few minutes.

In the year 26988 or so, if anyone in the star cluster M13 happens to have a powerful receiver tuned to 2,380 megahertz and attached to an antenna pointed in our direction, our message might be detected and recorded as a suggestive, nonrandom set of on-off pulses. If those detecting the signal notice, in the universal world of mathematics, that 1,679 is the product of two prime numbers (23 and 73), they may hit on the idea of arranging the "bits" into a rectangular grid, 23 columns by 73 rows, or 23 rows by 73 columns, and using two different colors, one for the "on" bits and another for the "off" bits. If they do so, one of the two choices will produce a meaningless blur, but the other will shout (so we think) with the cry of "intelligent beings over here!" The recipients of

Aerial view of the giant 1,000-foot-diameter radiotelescope at Arecibo, Puerto Rico, used to broadcast Earth's first intentional radio message to extraterrestrial civilizations. (Photo courtesy of the National Astronomy and Ionosphere Center, Cornell University.)

our message will see a crude representation of a human figure, a map of the solar system, symbols representing the most important elements in our kind of life, and the structure of the DNA molecule, which governs the process of replication in every organism on Earth. They can mull the message over and might decide to reply, in which case we can expect to hear from them, presumably at the same frequency at which we sent the message, in about the year 51988.

The Arecibo radio message raises some important issues. For me, the most important are these: Should scientists celebrating an improved antenna be the ones who decide whether, when, and what to broadcast to other civilizations? If not, then who? It may be noted that the Arecibo message was a one-shot affair, and was directed to a star cluster sufficiently distant that we can hardly expect any consequences on a human time scale. (Of course, with just this philosophy we have come close to ruining our planet on a human time scale.) The chief moral that I draw from the Arecibo message is that the issue of who should compose a message from Earth deserves more attention than it has received until now. Beyond that, another issue emerges: Do we really want to send such a low-budget picture into space? Our technology is now entirely capable (and was in 1974 as well) of sending a message that would contain not a thousand or so bits of information but a hundred million or so, without taking any more time to broadcast than the few minutes consumed by the Arecibo message. A hundred million bits can be used to convey the contents of several thousand printed pages, or a few thousand detailed pictures. This seems to me to represent a capability sufficient to sidestep much of the potential argument over message content, since it offers the opportunity to include a host of diverse, even possibly conflicting, information and opinions.

On the other hand, maybe we shouldn't try to paint ourselves in living color. Lewis Thomas suggested that we might try broadcasting nothing but Bach, on the theory that we should start by bragging; perhaps it's worth a try. Ernst Fasan has proposed a basic principle of truthfulness—that is, anything might reasonably be included so long as it is true. The difficulty with this principle is that we humans (could it be true of other civilizations' members?) are notoriously slow to agree on what *is* true.

I would propose another principle, the democratic principle: Anything is acceptable in a reply message so long as it has been openly discussed and, in some vaguely defined sense, agreed upon. This is a principle for ourselves, not for the recipient of our messages. *They* may have strange forms of political organization (just what those are is one of the prime pieces of information we might hope to learn), but it is we ourselves who must speak for Earth.

The astrophysicist Philip Morrison has called SETI "the archaeology of the future," comparing the search for another civilization's signal to the excavation of the remains of a bygone civilization on Earth. In both cases we are looking into the past—on Earth because the information has been long buried; in space

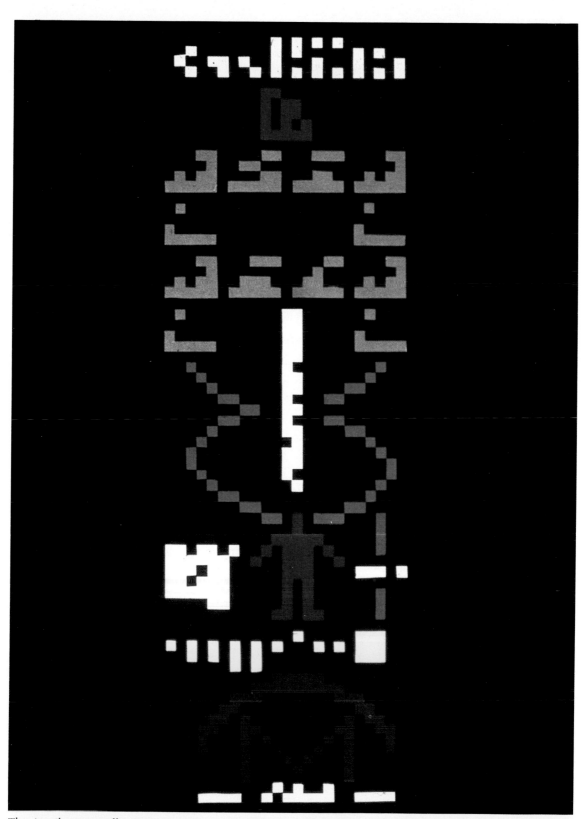

The Arecibo interstellar message, sent on November 16, 1974. The signal contained 1,679 bits of information, a number that is the product of 73 and 23, two prime numbers. The hope is that the recipients will display the message as a 73-by-23 array, and will reconstruct the pattern of light and dark that shows, among other things, human beings, the telescope, and the radio ''channel'' on which the message was sent. (Photo courtesy of the National Astronomy and Ionosphere Center, Cornell University.)

because it has taken many years to reach us. The difference is that archaeology examines the past of Earth, but SETI attempts to examine its *future*, by discovering what paths other civilizations, many with longer histories than ours, have traveled in past times. It appears likely that insight into our future can be plucked from the airwaves—once we know how and where to look. Once a signal has been detected, the way that we think about our planet will change. Those who care about the future might do well to plan now for the time that the signal arrives—a watershed in the history of Earth that will change us from a silent to a communicating planet.

THE DARK SHADOW

FREDERIK POHL

IN PRETTY LITTLE FTERA'S OPINION, being assigned to duty on the first of the deep-space stringships was the highest honor any space-academy cadet could hope to attain. After all, a stringship was not like any other spacecraft. Stringships went where no others had any reason to go, because there was nothing there to go to. That was what a stringship was for: to seek out regions of space as far as possible from any real-world or even shadow-world gravitational source, so that when it deployed its mighty cosmological strings they would not be pulled into distorted shapes. So Ftera's first few days on Stringship One were a blur of proud delight at being chosen.

Of course Ftera wasn't the only newcomer. The whole crew was new, for so was the stringship. This big, powerful new ship was making its maiden voyage into the clear spaces between stars; it was twice the size of a normal interstellar craft, and its mission was of great importance to the race. Stringship One's only reason for existence was to conduct research into the nature and function of cosmological strings. Though Ftera had no clear notion of what a cosmological string was, that did not imply any doubt about the importance of the research—after all, what was intelligent life *for*, if not to learn every secret of the universe, however obscure or well concealed?

It had not disturbed Ftera in the least to be assigned to work in the kitchens. He reasoned that it was an important job—in certain ways, perhaps, the most important job on the ship, because if the engineers, scientists, and string operators weren't properly fed, how could they do their work properly? And if they failed, the whole enterprise would be endangered! So when his shift was over, Ftera carefully retraced all the steps of the cleaning machines, to make sure no stain or crumb remained on any part of them to decay and spoil the taste or the edibility of the next meal. Then, assured that his task was done and thankful that it was over, he headed for the fog baths to soak the salts out of his pores. He leaned sidewise against the reclining board, letting the mist flow over his hard, wedge-shaped head and limber body while he dreamed of his triumphant return home. . . .

He was almost asleep when the call came.

Ftera peered out of the fog to answer the phone. The face on the screen belonged to Mahlgronig, chief tensor operator and by all odds the best-looking engineer on the stringship. "Oh," said Ftera shyly, "you've caught me in the bath. You've mislaid your calculator log? Yes, it was in the dining hall; I put it aside for you. Bring it to you now? Oh, I'd be glad to!"

But Ftera interpreted "right now" as meaning "as soon as quite fit to appear in public." A young male, just beginning a mission that would last for a year or more, had standards to maintain. So Ftera took time to air-comb his fur and polish the short, forward-thrusting horns over his eyepits. It was a quarter of an hour before, satisfied that he was looking his best, Ftera hesitantly pushed the heavy sliding doors of the generation room.

Ftera had never been in the generation room before and he stopped in the doorway, peering around. Even now, with no operations yet begun, it was a serious-looking, almost frightening place. Massy, bulky machines were secured to the floor by welded straps the thickness of his entire torso. The smallest of the machines was twice as big as Ftera himself, and he well knew the remarkable things they could do. Blinking his hooded eyes against the harsh glare of the lights, Ftera spotted Mahlgronig standing with a cluster of other engineers around one of the control boards. Mahlgronig's back was to Ftera, the broad, heavy tail slowly flicking back and forth over the heavy haunches.

Ftera called softly, "Mahlgronig? I have your log."

The big engineer turned and grinned, recognizing Ftera with obvious plea-sure. What pleased Mahlgronig pleased Ftera as well, and he licked his tongues welcomingly across the hard lower lip of his mouth as the engineer swung powerfully over to him. Ftera held out the calculator log; Mahlgronig took it and turned away, pausing only to look back and say, "We're just getting ready to start deploying a string. You can stay and watch if you want to."

If he wanted to! But that was what the stringship was all about, and people like Ftera were almost never allowed in the deployment room to watch. It thrilled him to think that Mahlgronig had personally invited him to stay. How jealous the other maintenance people would be!

There was so much to see—and to hear, and to touch (if Ftera had dared move away from the doorway). Even to smell, for the air in the operations room had an electrical, a scorched-chemical tang. Ftera quivered with excite-ment. Mahlgronig was displaying a readout from his log to the other engineers. They discussed it briefly; then Gadohlian, the grizzled old chief operator, hissed loudly for attention, and called, "Take your places, everybody. We're going to start the first-phase warm-up procedures."

Ftera shrank back, making himself inconspicuous, enthralled. He blinked at the string of colored light symbols that began to spin around the walls of

the room, displaying instrument readings as the engineers operated their controls. There was a distant starting-up mutter. Then the machines began to
throb. Their sound climbed slowly in pitch from the sinister subsonic that had
shaken Ftera's bones to a soft middle-range pulsing. Mahlgronig nodded to the
chief as the machines settled down in their warm-up phase. Then she came
over to Ftera to ask, grinning: "How do you like it so far?"

"It's wonderful," Ftera said sincerely. "I can't tell you how it makes me
feel." Then he added, "I'm sorry I took so long to bring your log—"

Mahlgronig laughed. "You had to make yourself pretty, of course," she
said, patting Ftera's back. "That's all right. There wasn't any hurry—and it
was worth it!"

Very few human beings would have applied the word *pretty* to Ftera. Some
human beings would have said that he looked like a cross between a rattlesnake
and a centaur. Most would simply have said that he looked nasty. The wedge-
shaped face with the fleshy little tongues licking out of the hard black mouth
was alarming; the sinuous arms with their elephant-trunk rubbery tips were
disconcerting; the four short bowed legs that carried him around were plain
ugly. That's what Ftera would have looked like to a human being, but no human
being had ever seen anything like Ftera, or ever would.

To big, good-natured Mahlgronig, what Ftera looked like was beautiful.
There were nearly forty males on the stringship, all of them in maintenance
jobs. While every one of them was young, healthy, and good-looking (some
said the Space Service chose the male crew members on long-term missions
mostly by their looks), most of the engineers, scientists, and expeditors agreed
that none of the others was quite like agile, graceful, sweet young Ftera.

"I hope I'm not in the way," Ftera said, secure in the answer because he
was quite aware of the way Mahlgronig was eyeing his supple forearms and
graceful limbs.

"Not a bit," said Mahlgronig cheerfully, resting her arm gently on Ftera's
slim back. "Nothing's going to happen for a while because we've got to move
out of range—according to the gravitometer readings, there's a shadow star
right under us. Never trust an astronomer! They promised clear space here,
just enough of a gravity well to keep the strings taut—and then this star turned
up!"

"I see," Ftera said doubtfully.

"I can see that you do." Mahlgronig grinned, shaking her head in mock
disapproval. "Ftera? Do you know anything at all about what we're doing?
Did they teach you before you shipped out?"

"Well . . . " Ftera began, and thought hard.

Of course, he knew what everyone knew. The mission of the stringship
was to study the behavior of cosmological strings, the vast "particles" that
shaped the universe.

Human scientists knew about such strings. But to any human scientist they were only theoretical probabilities, as unseen and undetected by any terrestrial agency as an unbound quark.

"I guess I don't," Ftera conceded—not really reluctantly, because everyone knew that females enjoyed explaining things to attractive young males. "I'm not sure that I know exactly what a 'shadow star' is, either."

"There's no reason anyone as pretty as you should have to," Mahlgronig said with charming gallantry.

Ftera protested, "No, please don't treat me like some empty-headed flirt! I can understand if it's explained to me. After all, there are lots of males who have earned real scientific degrees—why, my own father was a plant geneticist until he married."

"Oh," said Mahlgronig, eyeing him closely. Then she said, almost as she would to a fellow scientist of her own gender in some other discipline: "The 'shadow universe' is the name we give to a sort of mirror image of the universe we live in. The shadow universe is very much like our own, but it is completely separate in almost every way. We can't see it. We can't detect it with most instruments. It has no effect on anything in our own universe in any of the three conventional forces. Electromagnetism, the weak nuclear force, the strong nuclear force—none of those operate between the universes. There is only one interaction. The gravitational attraction of any body in either universe affects the bodies in both of them."

"And what about the strings? Are they in both universes?" Ftera asked doubtfully.

"No, no! The cosmological string in one universe isn't any more a part of the other than a star or a galaxy is. But the strings are strong gravitational sources, and our strings respond to their gravity wells as well as to our own. That means that if there's a shadow body nearby it helps keep the strings taut. That's useful; left to themselves they have a tendency to wobble around on themselves, crossing themselves and becoming loops. But if there's a nearby large shadow body, say the size of a star, the strings get hard to control. Also, the shadow sun attracts gas and dust clouds from our own universe and that interferes with our observations—if they were dense enough, they might even endanger the ship."

"Oh!"

"That won't happen." Mahlgronig grinned, stroking him reassuringly. She glanced up at the instrument readings as they spun around the walls. "The particle count's dropping fast," she said with satisfaction. "We're pretty well away from the shadow star. I think we'll be deploying our first string in a few minutes."

"Can I stay here?"

"Of course," Mahlgronig said indulgently. "As long as you don't get in the way—and unless we get a malfunction. If I yell at you to get out, please do it right away. When something goes wrong, this is no place for a male!''

In the human world that lay in the shadow of the shadow, Felicity Braun, chief scientist of the Lab's cryomagnetic applications team, was frowning in an attempt to follow the remarks of the invited speaker when she saw that the man next to her was taping the whole lecture.

Her second thought was that he shouldn't be doing that. Lab policy was clear; these extemporaneous tutorials by guest lecturers were always preliminary and speculative, and the speakers preferred not to be put on record. Her third thought was that, since the lecture was on superstring theory and she was failing to understand at least a quarter of it, it might be nice to get to know the man, so that she could borrow the tape. Felicity liked the third thought better than the second thought, because her first thought, immediately on taking her seat, had been that this was a really nice-looking man. When he gave her a half smile as he caught his eyes on her, Felicity gave him a whole one back.

Felicity Braun did not look like the conventional image of a chief scientist (though, to be sure, the cryonics applications committee of which she was chief scientist was a long way from the biggest in the Lab. It consisted only of herself and two graduate students in the Lab's internship program). Braun was twenty-seven years old. She had blond hair that hung straight to her shoulders, and eyes that were deep-ocean blue, even through her horn-rimmed glasses. She was, in fact, a very good-looking young woman.

Felicity knew perfectly well that she was good-looking. She couldn't have helped knowing, because the part-time modeling that her looks had made possible was what had supported her all the way through her doctorate in school. When she got the degree she took a week off to weigh the difference between, on the one hand, ten good years as a four-hundred-dollar-an-hour cover girl and, on the other, perhaps forty years of doing research into the bizarre things that happened to electricity and magnetism in liquid gases cooled almost to absolute zero. Cryonics won. The money didn't begin to compare, heaven knew, but Felicity Braun was just too brainy to be willing to spend her life moistening her lips and making her eyes sparkle for men with cameras. The issue had been settled for her once and for all back at MIT, when she had sat in on an address by one of the professors-emeritus. His name was Marvin Minsky, and he had outlined his moral creed in a single sentence: ''If someone has the capacity to do any kind of basic research, for him to do anything else with his life is simply a sin.''

So Felicity Braun took on scientific research as her lifework. But there was so much of science! So many things outside her own specialization to know! And even a MENSA-type IQ and a doctorate in physics didn't let you comprehend all of it. So Braun was scowling as she concentrated on what the speaker was saying. He was an elderly man from CalTech, and he was the kind of lecturer who spoke very fast and explained very little. Nor were the charts and diagrams he displayed on the ViewGraph very helpful, for to Felicity's eyes they all looked as though they had been done in the last five minutes before he got up on the platform, probably by his infant grandchild.

There were (he was saying) things called "cosmological strings." They had to do with a sort of general theory of everything, which he called "E-eight by E-eight." (What weird names these people gave things!) They were not, he said, to be confused with those other things called "superstrings"; strings came in various sizes, from very big down to itty-bitty. The big cosmological strings were big indeed, and the tiny ones were tinier than any known subatomic particle. The "superstrings"—the tiny ones—weren't themselves particles, exactly. They stood, perhaps, in the same relationship to all the familiar hadrons and leptons as a quark, say, stood in relation to an organic molecule. Superstrings *generated* particles. Superstrings were *there*. The particles that Braun's colleagues were smashing out of streams of protons in the supercollider every day, guided by the cryomagnets that were Braun's own special charge, were only the "harmonics" of the strings. The particles had to come from somewhere, the lecturer said. In order for any general theory of physics to be complete, one needed to find a theoretical source to generate them. That (if the theory was right) was the superstring. "It's like the story of the child who wanted a pony for Christmas and got only evasive talk from his parents," he said. " 'With all the manure around here, there's got to be a pony someplace.' "

Then he turned to the other variety, the "cosmological strings." Those played no part in generating nuclear particles, but they might well account for the formation of galaxies. They were almost inconceivably big. How big? "Well," said the lecturer doubtfully, "if stretched out, one might be very long. Of the order of a few light-years, even. But not thick at all. Not even the thickness of a human hair. 'String' may be the wrong kind of name for this model, because strings are three-dimensional objects. The diameter of a superstring must be just about zero." Then how could one be detected? "Mass," the speaker said promptly. "The mass of a superstring is perhaps equal to that of a small planet. If one should pass near a gravity-wave detector it would surely be recorded. If it passed at a terrestrial distance, the detector would probably be crushed—because of the inverse-square law, of course."

But that was just when Felicity Braun, looking at her watch, realized that her luncheon meeting was at hand and she would not be able to hear how the law of inverse squares applied to cosmological strings.

She sighed and got up to leave, regretful on two grounds. The first was that she wanted to hear the rest of the lecture. The second was that, as the man with the nice smile and the cassette recorder was changing tapes, she got a good look at the second finger of his left hand. It was faintly marked with the same circle of white skin as on her own, where a wedding ring had once been.

Ftera winced, holding his ears. To the hums and whines and distant rumbles of the stringship's machines a new sound had been added. It made the hard cartilage around Ftera's eyepits ache, a warbling drone that seemed to shake his whole body. The lighted symbols on the walls were racing now; they illuminated the whole operations chamber in flickering rainbow hues.

In spite of Mahlgronig's permission, Ftera tried to make himself inconspicuous. He knew quite well that if anything went wrong he would be a pure liability in the string-deployment room. He resolved to leave immediately if there was the slightest hint of anything out of the ordinary. He would not be the one to endanger the work of the stringship! The stakes were far too high for idle curiosity . . . and certainly he didn't want to get in trouble with Mahlgronig, whose picture was tacked up over at least four of the stalls in the adult males' dormitory hall.

Nevertheless, Ftera stayed where he was, fascinated. He couldn't make himself leave.

Across the chamber, yellowing old Gadohlian stamped restlessly around the controller's dais, her eyes on everything. Even on Ftera; and when Ftera reluctantly met her gaze he saw that Gadohlian—was it possible? Yes! Gadohlian was actually winking at him!

"Display exterior!" the old controller ordered, turning good-naturedly back to her work. Ftera felt warm inside. He began to relax, his fears assuaged . . . for the moment.

Then the exterior screens came on.

The image was overwhelming, for the whole center section of the room was a screen. It seemed to turn transparent, and there below them was . . . space.

To Ftera it was as though the floor had dropped away and they were standing on nothing at all, looking down on infinity.

Ftera gasped, the sound drowned by the noises of the stringship. Stars lay below his four shrinking feet—stars by the tens of thousands—stars such as Ftera had never seen through the thick air of the home planet. There were red ones and blue, yellow ones and white   yes, and ultraviolet ones, too, for Ftera's race could see a far wider optical spectrum than the eyes of human beings could detect.

"Deploy and display string," rumbled Gadohlian. A quarter of the way around the room from Ftera, Mahlgronig bent to her board. Beneath Ftera's feet a bright gold serpent sprang into light, writhing away from them. That was the string itself! Ftera's breathing was becoming difficult as he stared down at the terrible, brilliant sight.

"Deploy phase fields!"

All the lights dimmed as Verkintsunt, the phase-generator operator, applied power. In the space below them two violet arcs appeared, surrounding the near end of the string, clamping down on it to still its restless wriggling. From the dais Gadohlian rasped, "It's drifting—don't let it get away from you!" Mahlgronig nodded her head, eyes flickering from board to screen; the arcs brightened, and the near end of the string settled down.

Satisfied, Gadohlian ordered, "Give it the harmonics."

The warbling drone intensified as little Verkintsunt cut in the harmonic feed. Waves of blue light rippled out from the string. . . .

Below them, the string began to lash frenziedly about.

"Don't let it close the ring!" shouted Gadohlian, and there was a mighty yell from Mahlgronig.

"It's coiling!" she cried. "I can't hold it! Deaths! There's a shadow planet down there!"

The "luncheon" at Felicity Braun's luncheon meeting amounted to coffee in paper cups and a couple of sandwiches from the fourth-floor vending machines. Even apart from the quality of the food, it wasn't a very satisfying meeting anyway. The director of research for the Lab had been sympathetic but unpromising. "Budget," he said, as though one word explained it all. Actually, it did. "We've got to cut. If it's defense-oriented research, we might be able to squeeze something out of the special appropriations—everything else, it's belt-tightening time. No, hon," he went on as Felicity opened her mouth to venture an idea, "forget trying to convince me that cryonics is going to fit into the military program. Jesus, everybody else in the lab is trying that one! It won't work. Maybe in a few months or a year things will loosen up a little— maybe. But until then, Felicity, it's just going to have to be nothing but routine operations for your guys. No research. Just keep the magnets cold!"

And, although he said it several times in a number of different ways, they all added up to the same fact. The cryonics section would have to keep the big magnets at the liquid-helium temperature levels, but there wasn't any money for hiring even one more graduate student. So when the "luncheon" was over, Felicity Braun decided that what she most needed was a cup of real coffee and a place to sit and sulk for a while, before she went back to explain to her graduate students that all the theoretical projects were closing down.

Most of the tables in the atrium lunch area were empty now. But when she picked up her coffee and looked around, why, things began to brighten a trifle. There was her neighbor from the morning lecture, sitting by himself and reading the latest issue of *Science*.

Why not? Felicity asked herself, and answered, No reason at all.

She approached the table. "Do you mind if I join you?" she asked. It wasn't a serious question. Twenty-seven years on the Earth had given her all the assurances she needed that there were not very many men who would. When this man shook his head quite hospitably, she sat down and said, "I noticed

LEBBEUS WOODS

you were taping the lecture on strings. Any chance of borrowing a copy? I have a lot of trouble with all these different strings."

They introduced themselves to each other. The man's name was Ben Passerine, and he was from the Lawrence Livermore labs. (Oh, Braun said to herself. Lawrence Livermore. I see.) But, no, he couldn't give her a copy of the tape. "It's already been mailed off, but," he added, taking note of the blue eyes and the golden hair, "this is the third time I've sat through that lecture, so if I can help you out. . .?"

And, as a matter of fact, he not only could, he did. It wasn't his area of expertise, he said. It was as little related to his own work as to— What was it Felicity Braun did? Cryophysics? Yes, as remote as that. Nevertheless, he clarified one of the equations and two of the ViewGraph charts in about a minute each, and then went on to give Braun a quick overview of all the various other trendy "supers"—supergravity, supersymmetry and the rest—as they related to the theory of superstrings. The mysterious $E8 \times E8$? Why, said Passerine, that's only a description of—of—well, of a sort of matrix in which everything is. Not just the universe. Our universe is described by the first $E8$. The other $E8$ is another universe, perhaps just like our own, which may exist parallel to ours, but never detectable by ours. Well, gravity would affect both universes, he conceded, but nothing else would.

Felicity Braun listened attentively and approvingly. What she approved most of all was that he spoke to her as one scientist to another, without failing to note that she was a woman. And, wonderfully, he even managed to make it all make sense. It didn't become instantly clear. There were none of those wonderful flashes of insight like the ones that came when suddenly you could see how calculus worked, or why the sum of the squares of the sides of a right triangle necessarily always had to equal the square of the hypotenuse. Braun did not flatter herself that she was suddenly capable of describing superstrings to someone else; but at least she could see that the theory was knowable; she could understand it, all right, with a little more information and a lot more thought.

"But," said Felicity Braun, not trying to flatter him (but aware all the same that this guy, who was not only good-looking but apparently recently unmarried, would not mind a little honest flattery), "if you know all this stuff, why did you need to listen to the lecture?"

"I wasn't required to listen. I just had to tape everything Willem said." Passerine smiled, and explained: "So they could review it back at Lawrence Livermore."

"Review it," Braun said thoughtfully. (Oh. "Review." As in "review for security clearance." Oh again.) She thought fretfully of asking him if *his* research budgets had been cut lately, but decided against it. It wasn't his fault, after all, if national priorities went his way instead of hers. Then she made another connection. "Oh! You don't mean there's some military application for strings, do you?" she gasped.

Passerine shrugged, smiling.

"Well, I mean, I know you can't talk about weapons systems or anything— but *strings?*"

He looked around cautiously. "Actually, the problem's with some of the other things Willem's working on. Not with any kind of strings. Of course"— he grinned—"if anybody knew how to generate a cosmological string and lead it anywhere he wanted, it would make a hell of a weapon. It could just smash everything. But that's not in the cards."

"I am really grateful to hear you say that," Braun said sincerely. "Still, about the taping . . . ?"

"Well, you just never know when Willem's liable to let himself get dragged into some side area of discussion. He knows a lot about a lot of things, you know. So whenever he lectures there's one of us sitting in the audience with a tape recorder, getting it all down."

"Ah." Felicity nodded. "You mean in case he says something he shouldn't."

"Well, that for one thing, sure. Also," Passerine added unwillingly, "I guess it's also partly to get a record if somebody from the audience, you know, shows a lot of curiosity about something that's, well, sensitive. There wasn't anything like that happening today, though," he added hastily. "And, listen, I'm not with the CIA or the FBI or anything like that, if that's what you're thinking. I'm a researcher. I do—ah—photo-optics."

Oh, Felicity Braun said wisely to herself. Photo-optics. As in lasers.

"My stuff's kind of classified, too, but that's got nothing to do with my taping. The reason I'm here isn't just to keep tabs on Willem. I had a meeting at Northwestern yesterday, and then Willem and I are going to Washington tomorrow morning." He gave her a slightly embarrassed smile. "I'm sort of at loose ends for dinner, though. Listen, I'm kind of out of practice at this— I've only been divorced four months—but if you're free for dinner or a drink or something . . ."

"It's been a year since my own divorce," said Braun, smiling. "I'm free. Right here in the atrium? Say five-thirty?"

"That's fine," said Passerine, relaxing. "I think I'd like to—" He stopped in the middle of the sentence, frowning. "What's that?"

Felicity Braun never got to hear what it was that Passerine was about to say he would like. There was an interruption.

The interruption had nothing to do with cosmological or any other kind of strings. It had nothing to do with the normal life of the Lab, either; it took the form of a sudden uproar of confused shouting from the balconies over-head, high above the tables on the floor of the atrium. The bare handful of other people drinking coffee and chatting or reading papers around the tables were all looking up, as curious and as startled as Braun and Passerine.

Three or four stories up, on one of the airy, spidery balconies that surrounded the vast lobby, a man was leaning over a rail and yelling desperately down to the people on the ground floor.

Felicity vaguely recognized him. He was just one of the dozens of someones she'd seen often enough around the Lab, without actually meeting. She had never seen him like this. He was an elderly, calm, rather conservative-looking Distinguished Scientist Emeritus sort of person who never seemed to lose his temper or have run-ins with the higher authorities. Now he was not calm at all. The words he was shouting seemed to matter a great deal to him, though at that distance it was hard to make them out.

And when Felicity Braun thought she did catch a word or two, they simply made no sense. What sort of sentence could it possibly be that would contain the words *London* and *nuclear missile*?

"That was a close one," Mahlgronig hissed, staring at the bright yellow-orange ring that was fluttering away from them. "Be glad you work in the kitchen. You wouldn't want to be an astronomer today!"

Ftera glanced over at the dais, where Gadohlian was thundering at the three hangdog scientists from the astronomy section, stamping her feet and waving her huge arms as she told them what blundering incompetents they were. No, it was not a good time to be an astronomer on the stringship.

Ftera opened his mouth with a question, then hesitated. He didn't know whether Mahlgronig wanted to talk or not. Mahlgronig had addressed her remarks to him, which at least implied—didn't it?—consent to his continued presence. But that consent would vanish the minute he became a nuisance.

He took a chance. "What could have happened to us?" he asked shyly.

Mahlgronig gave him a grin. "Little man, you don't want me to tell you that."

"No, please. I really want to know."

Mahlgronig shrugged. "All right. If a coiled string passed anywhere near us, this ship would be destroyed. And that's the astronomy section's fault! We were using the gravity of the star to hold the string straight. Nobody told us that the star had planets, and one of them was right under us! We could have— Wait a minute." She raised her huge triangular head, peering at the knot of females around the controller's dais, listening. Then she nodded. "Keep your eye on the screen. They're going to display the gravity-wave interferometer readings—should've done that in the first place!" And then, as the chief of the astronomy section sulkily entered commands on Gadohlian's board and an image formed, she nodded. "Yes, there's the little devil that messed up our string! It's a shadow planet, all right."

Below them, outlined in harsh green light, a world began to appear. "Deaths!" Mahlgronig groaned, her tone more tolerant and amused than alarmed, now that the danger was over. "We were only using a short string, but it practically could have touched it! That's astronomers for you! They swore this was clean space even in the shadow domain. It's a good thing Gadohlian was on her pads; if she hadn't cut the string loose it could've swung right around and clipped us—and then, sweet Ftera, I never would have had the chance to invite you to sniff a few spores with me when I get off duty."

Ftera dimpled and shuddered at the same time. Shuddering won. He knew that he understood only part of what Mahlgronig was saying, but even the part he comprehended was scary. It was very comforting to have the big engineer close by in this strange place, and he had not failed to note the invitation to join Mahlgronig later on. But although that was exactly what he had been hoping for, his mind was on what was happening outside. He peered down at the shadow planet. The astronomers were increasing the magnification, and the planet seemed to draw nearer—no, more shocking than that: It seemed they were falling into it. Ftera took a deep breath, resolving not to turn into a whimpering *male* just when Mahlgronig was treating him almost as an equal. He said, trying to keep his voice calm, "What do we do now?"

"Oh, we just move away, that's all. About half an hour's drive and we'll be clear of it. But," she added with interest, looking at the image of the shadow planet, "I wish we could stay around awhile and get a better look at that thing."

She put an arm on Ftera's back, roughly affectionate, and pointed with the other. "See the terrain features? Mountains and valleys; you'd expect that kind of normal formation on any planet, of course. But look at those other little spiky things, especially by the big bodies of water—they're very regular, aren't they? I doubt they're natural formations. Artifacts, I'd bet my forequarters."

"Artifacts?" Ftera squealed. "You mean *people*? Do you think it might be *inhabited*?"

Mahlgronig shrugged her immense upper shoulders. "We'll never know for sure, sweetie. It's like two ships on ballistic trajectories with their lights off in space. We can't really see them, and they'll never even know we were looking at them!"

The image below them abruptly twitched. There was a startled shout from the group around Gadohlian, and abruptly the image seemed to shoot away as the field of view widened. When the planet was in full, motionless view again, Mahlgronig gasped.

The wriggling yellow ring of cosmological string had sliced right through the edge of the shadow planet. Already it was out the other side and dwindling in the distance.

"I take back what I said," Mahlgronig said hoarsely, her tongues licking out in distress. "If there's anybody there, they'll know we were around, all right."

Since the string was invisible to the photons of ordinary light, no observer in Earth's own universe could have seen it. There were six manmade observation satellites in Low Earth Orbit, however, which saw its effects quite clearly.

The six reconnaissance satellites, as it happened, came from two different sources, one in the heart of the Eurasian land mass, the other on the continent of North America. Nevertheless, their functions were the same. It was their job to watch for unusual events, specifically for anything that might suggest the launching of a nuclear strike. Their computers immediately registered the fact that this particular event certainly qualified as unusual. Yet none of the satellites' radars managed to track a missile, which was really what they were meant to detect. They couldn't, of course; there wasn't any missile to track. No satellite's optics observed the characteristic double flash of a thermonuclear blast: flash one when the initial plutonium charge detonated; flash two when it ignited the tritium-deuterium main charge. Those were the principal signals these military surveillance satellites were programmed to look for, and those signatures weren't there. There was no flash at all. There were simply two tall clouds that had appeared from nowhere, one over London, the other over a point in Byelorussia, two thousand miles away. They didn't look like the plume of a missile launch. They didn't look like the usual giant mushrooms of an H-bomb blast, either. But they looked more like that, in the velocity of their formation and their height above the ground, than they were like anything else ever seen.

If the satellites had had cognitive intelligence of their own, they would have been puzzled.

Since they did not, they simply transmitted to their ground stations what their optical systems had observed. Those same ground stations were receiving other alarming data at the same time, for all over the planet seismograph pens were bouncing off their drums as the string passed through two thousand miles of the Earth's crust, triggering fault fractures.

It was the turn of the human beings who monitored the satellite telemetry to be puzzled.

These particular human beings were extremely well trained, drilled and disciplined in their duties. That is to say, they were also programmed, and their programming dictated that when they were puzzled they should get ready for a worst-case event. They took no chances. The situation maps all went to red. Silos opened their hatches all over the United States and much of Siberia. Submarines got orders. Klaxons squawked, and air crews raced to their bombing planes.

The world had come to full alert.

The situation was touchy, but not yet terminal. No one, anywhere, had touched the button that would launch the first nuclear warhead against someone else.

In places all over the Earth, people were listening numbly to their radios.

In the Lab, Felicity Braun said to Ben Passerine: "What's happening?"

"Nothing, I hope," he said grayly. Someone had turned the Lab's public-address system on full blast, with a radio against the microphone, but the radio had fallen silent. Passerine looked at Felicity Braun in a peculiarly intimate, appraising way. She felt herself flushing, and didn't know why. When he said, "I wish we'd run into each other earlier," she didn't follow his train of thought.

Then the radio blared into life. "This is not a drill," it boomed. "Repeat, this is not a drill!"

"Oh, my God," muttered Passerine, and Braun said:

"If it isn't a drill, what is it?"

Passerine didn't answer directly. He only said, "I'm afraid we aren't going to have a chance to have that drink together after all."

The surveillance satellites, at least on one of the opposing sides, did their jobs perfectly—up to a point.

The surveillance satellites on the other side did too. It was not the fault of the satellites that their masters back on the surface of the Earth wanted more information than their deployed array could provide; but the result was that that side ordered the launch of a pop-up satellite, specifically targeted to survey the affected areas of the Earth's surface.

This was unfortunate, because the other satellites instantly reported the launch.

When the masters of the opposing side saw the launch they looked at each other. "Use 'em or lose 'em," one high officer said somberly to another.

There was really no choice that they could see. They used 'em.

"I think," boomed Mahlgronig, "that we'll have time for that sniff after all. We can't do anything with the strings for at least another hour or two, until we get out of range of this shadow planet."

"Oh, wonderful," said Ftera. But, eager as he was to get to know the big, good-looking engineer better, he couldn't help one last, regretful look at the image of the planet from the shadow universe.

Mahlgronig paused, her arm across Ftera's back. "Funny," she said, half to herself. "I wonder if by any chance there were people on that planet . . . and if the string that got away could've done them any harm. . . ." Then she shook herself. "It only messed up one little corner of the planet at worst," she boomed. "Come on, Ftera! Let's get that sniff."

And in the other E8 universe, the first launch had brought a response. A salvo of three rockets rose from the other side to counter the perceived threat; then twenty went up to respond to the three, and a hundred against the twenty. . . .

The people in the Lab never knew that it was a cosmological string that set the war off. They never knew that such theoretical strings were actually real. And now they never would.

CONTRIBUTORS

BYRON PREISS, editor, is the author of the best-selling *Dragonworld*. Considered one of the leading figures in the resurgence of illustrated books in America, he has worked with Fritz Leiber, Philip José Farmer, Arthur C. Clarke, and Leo and Diane Dillon. He also edited the 1985 best-seller *The Planets* and *The Constitution of the United States of America: The Bicentennial Keepsake Edition*.

DARREL ANDERSON has designed graphics for computer software and computer magazines. He has illustrated two children's books for Bantam and painted the cover for Time Machine #11, *Mission to World War Two*. A respected painter, he resides in Denver, Colorado.

POUL ANDERSON was one of the first science-fiction writers to move to the San Francisco area, pioneering a major settlement. Two of his seven Hugo Awards are separated by a span of more than twenty years, testimony to his enduring quality.

RUTH ASHBY, associate editor, has taught English literature at the University of Michigan and the University of Virginia. She edits nonfiction books, books for young readers, and computer games.

ISAAC ASIMOV, the most recent recipient of the Nebula Grandmaster Award, has published more than three hundred and fifty books. Among his novels are the Foundation series (winner of a special Hugo for Best Science Fiction Series of all time) and the Robot series.

WAYNE BARLOWE is the creator of the acclaimed *Barlowe's Guide to Extra-terrestrials* and the upcoming *Expedition*. He's done over a hundred cover illustrations for all the major science fiction publishers and is the designer of two lines of toys.

GREGORY BENFORD writes for the *Encyclopaedia Britannica* in the areas of relativistic plasma physics and astrophysics. His fiction, equally highly regarded, includes most notably the novel *Timescape*, which won four separate awards.

MICHAEL BISHOP's short fiction has appeared nearly everywhere, including *Best American Short Stories 1985*. He has accumulated two Nebula Awards and countless Nebula and Hugo nominations, none of them, so far, for his science-fiction and fantasy criticism, which appears regularly in *Thrust*.

BEN BOVA, besides being the author of more than seventy books of science and science fiction, has six times won the Hugo Award for best editor, for his work at *Analog* and *Omni*. He has also been a consultant to Woody Allen, Gene Roddenberry, and George Lucas on film and television projects.

RAY BRADBURY has published four hundred short stories and eighteen books. In addition, he created the basic scenario for the United States pavilion at the 1964–'65 World's Fair in New York, and for Spaceship Earth at Walt Disney's Epcot Center in Florida.

DAVID BRIN's second novel, *Startide Rising*, won both the Hugo and Nebula Awards. He is currently on sabbatical from his job as a teacher of university physics.

JIM BURNS was born in Wales. Most of his illustration appears on book covers, but he also did extensive work for the film *Blade Runner*, illustrated the Frank Herbert collection *Eye*, and has done design work for the visionary British industrialist Sir Clive Sinclair.

ERIC J. CHAISSON is a senior research physicist at M.I.T. He teaches astrophysics at Harvard University and Wellesley College. His books include *The Life Era*, the American Institute of Physics Award-winning *Cosmic Dawn*, and *The Invisible Universe*, which outlines the scientific rationale for United States space policy for the remainder of this century.

DAVID CHERRY left the practice of law to become an artist. His work can be seen in galleries on both coasts, and was included in the First Invitational Exhibition of the National Academy of Fantastic Art in 1986.

MARTIN COHEN was one of the first astronomers from the United Kingdom to be trained in infrared observational techniques. He is a research astronomer at the University of California at Berkeley and at NASA's Ames Research Center. He is the author of two books: *In Quest of Telescopes* and the just-published *In Darkness Born: The Story of Star Formation*.

JOHN COLLIER has won the Society of Illustrators' Silver and Gold medals, and is regarded as one of the most influential contemporary illustrators. His paintings are represented by major galleries and have appeared in numerous magazines.

BOB EGGLETON was first drawn to science fiction by the movies, and would rather illustrate it than any other subject. His long-term goal is to visit Mars and do some landscape painting.

ANDREW FRAKNOI is executive officer of the Astronomical Society of the Pacific, an international scientific and educational organization. He is the editor of *Mercury* magazine and the newsletter *The Universe in the Classroom*. He teaches astronomy at San Francisco State University.

DONALD GOLDSMITH is author, co-author, and editor of nine books on astronomy and physics, including the recent American Institute of Physics Award-winning *Nemesis: The Death-Star and Other Theories of Mass Extinction*. He was consultant to Carl Sagan's *Cosmos* television series, and is a visiting lecturer in astronomy at the University of California at Berkeley.

DAVID M. HARRIS, associate editor, is the author of assorted short nonfiction, three computer text adventure games, and a novel, *The Star-Riders*. Other professional activities have included editing, copy-editing, photography, and working as a literary agent.

JOHN HARRIS divides his time and effort between commercial and fine art, with signal success at both.

KIKUO HAYASHI works as a designer for a major automobile manufacturer, but his love of science fiction has led him to accept an increasing amount of work as an illustrator. Recently he has been illustrating the science fiction series *Alien Speedway*.

DAVID J. HELFAND is professor of physics and chairman of the department of astronomy at Columbia University. He spends much of his time using the Very Large Array telescope in Socorro, New Mexico, and is about to embark on a project to map the whole galactic plane at low frequencies in search of remains of supernovae past.

B. E. JOHNSON has been a member of two space shuttle ground crews and an Indianapolis 500-winning racing team, designer for the National Air and Space Museum Planetarium, and a consultant with the Voyager Imaging Team. Somehow he also finds time to paint.

WILLIAM J. KAUFMANN has held positions at UCLA, Caltech, and the Jet Propulsion Laboratory. He is currently a professor in the physics department at San Diego State University. His highly acclaimed textbooks *Universe* and *Discovering the Universe* are widely used at colleges and universities everywhere.

LESLIE MILLER, the designer, is a designer for the Metropolitan Museum of Art and director of the Grenfell Press, a highly regarded publisher of limited editions. She was the designer for the 1985 best-seller *The Planets* and *The Constitution of the United States of America: The Bicentennial Keepsake Edition*.

RON MILLER was nominated for a Hugo Award for best nonfiction for *The Grand Tour*. He has also been art director of the Albert Einstein Planetarium at the National Air and Space Museum, and is a founding member of the International Association of Astronomical Artists.

MOEBIUS is a French cartoonist and illustrator with an international reputation. His designs were an integral part of the films *Tron, Blade Runner, Alien,* and the George Lucas production *Willow*. Moebius is one of the founding artists of the influential magazine *Metal Hurlant/Heavy Metal*.

FREDERIK POHL has been just about everything it is possible to be in science fiction, including critic, book and magazine editor, agent, and award-winning author. He is the only person ever to win Hugo Awards as both author and editor. He is a founder and past president of World SF.

PAT RAWLINGS is an illustrator with Eagle Engineering, where he specializes in future technology for NASA.

RUDY RUCKER is considered the leading mathematician in the cyberpunk movement. His writing alternates between fiction and nonfiction; his latest book, *Mind Tools*, is about the mathematics of information.

ALLAN SANDAGE holds numerous honorary degrees, and his long list of awards includes the U.S. Presidential Medal of Science. He is currently visiting professor at The Johns Hopkins University and senior research scientist at the Space Telescope Institute in Baltimore. Using the Hubble Constant, he is working on calibrating the expansion rate of the universe.

ROBERT SILVERBERG has won the Nebula Award more times—five—than any other writer. His *New Dimensions* anthologies earned him accolades as one of science fiction's best editors, as well as one of its finest novelists. The latest of his novels is *Star of Gypsies*.

HARDING E. SMITH, is professor of physics at the Center for Astrophysics and Space Sciences and the department of physics at the University of California at San Diego. At present, he is involved in research on galactic evolution, active galaxies, and quasi-stellar objects.

HYRON SPINRAD is an astronomer at the University of California at Berkeley. He has been active in research for more than twenty years. In 1986 he won the American Institute of Physics Dannie Heineman Prize for Astrophysics.

E. BRUCE STEVENSON, photo editor, has written children's books and been involved in an editorial capacity with numerous science books for children.

JAMES TREFIL is Clarence Robinson Professor of Physics at George Mason University. After having spent most of his career as a high-energy theoretical physicist, he is now engaged in research on the extinction of the dinosaurs. His most recent book is *Meditations at Sunset*.

WALLACE TUCKER is a researcher in high-energy astrophysics at the Harvard-Smithsonian Center for Astrophysics and a visiting professor in the physics department at the University of California at Irvine. His latest book, co-authored with his wife, Karen, is entitled *The Cosmic Inquirers* and is a survey of modern telescopes and their makers.

CONNIE WILLIS, first published in 1978, in 1982 won two Nebula Awards and a Hugo in a single year. Her work was described by *The New York Times* as "fresh, subtle, and deeply moving." *Lincoln's Dreams*, her first novel, was published recently.

LEBBEUS WOODS is an internationally acclaimed visionary architect. He worked on the design of the noted Ford Foundation building in New York and subsequently established his own firm. *Origins*, a collection of his architectural drawings, was published in 1986.

GENE WOLFE is a former editor of *Plant Engineering Magazine*. He is also the author of the landmark short story "*The Island of Doctor Death and Other Stories*" and the winner of two Nebula Awards. His latest novel is *Soldier of the Mist*.

SELECTED READINGS
Andrew Fraknoi

GENERAL BOOKS ABOUT THE UNIVERSE

CHAISSON, Eric. *Cosmic Dawn*. New York: Berkley, 1984 (paperbound). An eloquent primer on the evolution of the universe and our place in it.

FERRIS, Timothy. *Galaxies*. New York: Stewart, Tabori & Chang, 1982. Lavishly illustrated introduction to the large-scale cosmos by a noted science writer.

JASTROW, Robert. *Red Giants and White Dwarfs*, 2nd ed. New York: Warner Books, 1980 (paperbound). Good, basic book on the evolution of the universe and humankind.

SAGAN, Carl. *Cosmos*. New York: Ballantine, 1980 (paperbound). A superbly written, highly personal tour of the universe; based on the PBS TV series.

TREFIL, James. *Space, Time, Infinity*. Washington, D.C.: Smithsonian Press, 1985. A beautiful coffee-table book introducing modern astronomy.

WAGONER, R. and Donald Goldsmith. *Cosmic Horizons*. New York: W. H. Freeman, 1983 (paperbound). A concise introduction to the universe at large.

SOME INTRODUCTORY BOOKS ON THE SUBJECTS COVERED IN *THE UNIVERSE:*

BARTUSIAK, Marcia. *Thursday's Universe*. New York: Times Books, 1986. A science journalist's introduction to some of the most exciting areas of modern astronomy.

CLARK, DAVID H. *Superstars*. New York: McGraw-Hill, 1984. Well-written introduction to exploding stars and the crucial role they play in the evolution of the universe and life.

COHEN, Martin. *In Darkness Born: The Story of Star Formation*. New York: Cambridge University Press, 1987. Introduction to the birth of stars and cosmic raw material.

FERRIS, Timothy. *The Red Limit*, rev. ed. New York: William Morrow/Quill, 1983 (paperbound). Well-written history of how large-scale properties of the universe were discovered.

GOLDSMITH, Donald, and Tobias Owen. *The Search for Life in the Universe*. Menlo Park, Cal.: Benjamin-Cummings, 1979. A basic textbook that can be read independently of a course to give you an introduction to this field.

GREENSTEIN, George. *Frozen Star*. New York: Freundlich, 1983. Eloquent book about the death of stars and what it is like being an astronomer today.

GRIBBIN, John. *In Search of the Big Bang*. New York: Bantam Books, 1986 (paperbound). Thorough, readable introduction to our quest for the universe's origin.

HARRINGTON, Sherwood, et al. "Learning About Quasars." San Francisco: Astronomical Society of the Pacific, 1984 (information packet). Collection of articles about observations of quasars and theories about what they might be.

HODGE, Paul W. *Galaxies*. Cambridge, Mass.: Harvard University Press, 1986. A thorough introduction to our modern understanding of galaxies.

KAUFMANN, William. *Black Holes and Warped Spacetime*. New York: W. H. Freeman, 1979 (paperbound). Best introduction to black holes and the theories behind them.

KIPPENHAHN, Rudolf. *100 Billion Suns: The Birth, Life, and Death of the Stars*. New York: Basic Books, 1983. Nontechnical review of stellar evolution.

McDONOUGH, Thomas R. *The Search for Extraterrestrial Intelligence.* New York: John Wiley, 1987. A good nontechnical book on the science of searching for life out there.

TREFIL, James. *The Moment of Creation.* New York: Macmillan, 1983 (paperbound). Fine introduction to our modern understanding of the Big Bang.

TUCKER, Wallace and Karen. *The Cosmic Inquirers.* Cambridge, Mass.: Harvard University Press, 1986. Well-written stories of some of the biggest telescopes on Earth and in space.

TUCKER, Wallace, and Riccardo Giacconi. *The X-Ray Universe.* Cambridge, Mass.: Harvard University Press, 1985. Fine history of how we learned about cosmic phenomena that produce X-rays.

In addition, you may be interested in reading the previous book in this series, *The Planets*, also edited by Byron Preiss and published by Bantam Books. It features a series of nontechnical essays by noted astronomers about our latest views of each planet in the solar system, followed by science fiction stories about each world. The book is illustrated with paintings by well-known space artists, and photographs obtained by spacecraft that flew by the planets.

MAGAZINES FOR KEEPING UP WITH NEW DEVELOPMENTS:

Astronomy (published by Kalmbach Publishing.)

Discover (a general science magazine published by Time-Life, New York.)

Mercury (published by the Astronomical Society of the Pacific; San Francisco, see below.)

Science News (a general science magazine published by Science Service.)

Sky and Telescope (published by Sky Publishing.)

AN ORGANIZATION FOR THOSE INTERESTED IN THE UNIVERSE:

The Astronomical Society of the Pacific (1290 24th Avenue, San Francisco, California 94122) is a nonprofit organization that brings together professional astronomers, teachers, hobbyists, and thousands of people in all walks of life who enjoy learning about the universe. Members receive *Mercury* magazine (full of nontechnical articles on new astronomy developments), a monthly sky calendar and star chart, the annual *Selectory* of interesting photographs, computer software, and other educational materials, and discounts on meetings, lectures, and attendance at some planetariums. (The society's name, by the way, merely reflects its origins on the Pacific Coast in 1889; today its members live in every state and sixty-six other countries.) You can write to the society for a free brochure about membership.

SECTION TITLE PAGE ACKNOWLEDGMENTS:

Page 33: The Eagle nebula (M16) and the star cluster NGC 6611. Photo credit: National Optical Astronomy Observatories.

Page 67: The Orion nebula, a region of active star formation. Photo credit: David Malin; © 1981, Anglo-Australian Telescope Board.

Page 97: Supernova 1987A in the Large Magellanic Cloud. Photo by Marcelo Bass, Cerro Tololo Inter-American Observatory. Photo credit: National Optical Astronomy Observatories.

Page 135: Accretion disk around a black hole. Results of a numerical simulation with a Cray I supercomputer. Photo credit: L. Smarr & J. Hawley.

Page 161: Spiral galaxy NGC 253, seen edge-on. Photo credit: David Malin; © 1980, Anglo-Australian Telescope Board.

Page 191: Centaurus A (NGC 5218), an active galaxy. Photo credit: David Malin; © 1980, Anglo-Australian Telescope Board.

Page 225: NGC 1265, a radio-emitting galaxy whose motion through the intergalactic medium has drawn its jets out into a U-shaped tail. Radiograph made with the Very Large Array radiotelescope, Socorro, New Mexico. Observers: C. P. O'Dea & F. N. Owen. Photo credit: Courtesy NRAO/AUI.

Page 247: M31, the Great Galaxy in Andromeda, as photographed with the Palomar Observatory's 48-inch Schmidt camera. Copyright © 1959 by the California Institute of Technology and the Carnegie Institution of Washington.

Page 275: Computer-enhanced photograph of the trails of subatomic particles in a bubble chamber. Color-enhancement techniques by Patrice Loiez, CERN. Photo credit: CERN.

Page 301: Illustration by Wayne Barlowe.

Half title page: View toward the galactic center of the southern Milky Way. The center itself is totally hidden by the vast amounts of dust. Photo credit: David Malin; © 1980, Anglo-Australian Telescope Board.

Frontispiece: The Horsehead nebula region in Orion. Photo credit: David Malin; © 1984, Anglo-Australian Telescope Board.